GROUP

How One Therapist
and a Circle of Strangers
Saved My Life

Christie Tate

AVID READER PRESS

New York London Toronto Sydney New Delhi

Avid Reader Press
An Imprint of Simon & Schuster, Inc.
1230 Avenue of the Americas
New York, NY 10020

First Avid Reader Press hardcover edition October 2020

AVID READER PRESS and colophon are
trademarks of Simon & Schuster, Inc.

For information about special discounts for bulk
purchases, please contact Simon & Schuster Special Sales
at 1-866-506-1949 or business@simonandschuster.com.

The Simon & Schuster Speakers Bureau can bring authors to
your live event. For more information or to book an event, contact
the Simon & Schuster Speakers Bureau at 1-866-248-3049
or visit our website at www.simonspeakers.com.

Interior design by Lewelin Polanco

Manufactured in the United States of America

1 3 5 7 9 10 8 6 4 2

Library of Congress Cataloging-in-Publication
Data has been applied for.

ISBN 978-1-9821-5461-5
ISBN 978-1-9821-5463-9 (ebook)

*For my therapist and the
group members with whom I've
been privileged to share the circle*

Part 1

1

The first time I wished for death—like, really wished its bony hand would tap me on the shoulder and say "this way"—two bags from Stanley's Fruit and Vegetables sat shotgun in my car. Cabbage, carrots, a few plums, bell peppers, onions, and two dozen red apples. It had been three days since my visit to the bursar's office, where the law school registrar handed me a notecard with my class rank, a number that had begun to haunt me. I turned the key in the ignition and waited for the engine to turn over in the ninety-degree heat. I pulled a plum out of the bag, tested it for firmness, and took a bite. The skin was thick but the flesh beneath was tender. I let the juice dribble down my chin.

It was eight thirty. Saturday morning. I had nowhere to be, nothing to do. No one was expecting to see me until Monday morning, when I'd report for duty at Laird, Griffin & Griffin, the labor law firm where I was a summer intern. At LG&G only the receptionist and the partner who hired me knew I existed. The Fourth of July was Wednesday, which meant I'd face yet another stifling, empty day in the middle of the week. I'd find a 12-step meeting and hope that people would want to go for coffee afterward. Maybe another lonely soul would want to catch a movie or grab a salad. The engine hummed to life, and I gunned the car out of the parking lot.

I wish someone would shoot me in the head.

A soothing thought with a cool obsidian surface. If I died, I wouldn't have to fill the remaining forty-eight hours of this weekend or Wednesday's holiday or the weekend after that. I wouldn't have to endure the hours of hot, heavy loneliness that stretched before me—hours that would turn into days, months, years. A lifetime of nothing but me, a bag of apples, and the flimsy hope that stragglers after a recovery meeting might want some company.

A recent news story about a fatal shooting in Cabrini Green, Chicago's infamous housing project, flashed in my mind. I steered my car south on Clybourn and turned left on Division. Maybe one of those stray bullets would hit me.

Please, someone shoot me.

I repeated it like a mantra, an incantation, a prayer that would likely go unanswered because I was a twenty-six-year-old white woman in a ten-year-old white Honda Accord on a bright summer morning. Who would shoot me? I had no enemies; I hardly existed. Anyway, that fantasy relied too heavily on luck—bad or good, depending on how you looked at it—but other fantasies came unbidden. Jumping from a high window. Throwing myself on the El tracks. As I came to a stop at Division and Larrabee, I considered more exotic ways to expire, like masturbating while I hung myself, but who was I kidding? I was too repressed for that scenario.

I fished the pit out of the plum and popped the rest in my mouth. Did I really want to die? Where were these thoughts going to lead me? Was this suicidal ideation? Depression? Was I going to act on these thoughts? Should I? I rolled down the window and threw the pit as far as I could.

In my law school application, I described my dream of advocating for women with non-normative (fat) bodies—but that was only partly true. My interest in feminist advocacy was genuine, but it wasn't the major motivator. I wasn't after the inflated paychecks or the power suits either. No, I went to law school because lawyers work sixty- and seventy-hour weeks. Lawyers schedule conference calls during Christmas break and are summoned to boardrooms on Labor Day. Lawyers eat dinner at their desks surrounded by colleagues with rolled-up sleeves and pit stains. Lawyers can be married to their work—work that is so vital that they don't mind, or notice, if their personal lives are empty as a parking lot at midnight. Legal work could be a culturally approved-of beard for my dismal personal life.

I took my first practice law school admissions test (LSAT) from the desk where I worked at a dead-end secretarial job. I had a master's degree I wasn't using and a boyfriend I wasn't fucking. Years later, I'd refer to Peter as a workaholic-alcoholic, but at the time I called him the love of my life. I would dial his office at nine thirty at night when I was ready to go to sleep and accuse him of never having time for me. "I *have* to work," he'd say, and then hang up. When I'd call back, he wouldn't answer. On the weekends, we'd walk to dive bars in Wicker Park so he could drink domestic beers and debate the merits of early R.E.M. albums, while I prayed he'd stay sober enough to have sex. He rarely did. Eventually I decided I needed something all-consuming to absorb the energy I was pouring into my miserable relationship. The woman who worked down the hall from me was headed to law school in the fall. "Can I borrow one of your test books?" I asked. I read the first problem:

> A professor must schedule seven students during a day
> in seven different consecutive time periods numbered
> one through seven.

What followed were a series of statements like: *Mary and Oliver must occupy consecutive periods* and *Sheldon must be scheduled after Uriah.* The test directions allotted thirty-five minutes to answer six multiple choice questions about this professor and her scheduling conundrum. It took me almost an hour. I got half of them wrong.

And yet. Slogging through LSAT prep and then law school seemed easier than fixing whatever made me fall in love with Peter and whatever it was that made me stay for the same fight night after night.

Law school could fill all my yearnings to belong to other people, to match my longings with theirs.

llr

At my all-girls high school in Texas, I took a pottery elective freshman year. We started with pinch pots and worked our way up to the pottery wheel. Once we molded our vessels, the teacher taught us how to add handles. If you wanted to attach two pieces of clay—say, the cup and the handle—you had to score the surface of both. Scoring—making horizontal and vertical gouges in the clay—helped the pieces meld together when fired in the kiln. I sat on my stool holding one of my crudely sculpted "cups" and a C-shaped handle as the teacher demonstrated the scoring process. I hadn't wanted to ruin the smooth surface of the "cup" I'd lovingly pinched, so I smushed the handle on it without scoring its surface. A few days later, our shiny, fired pieces were displayed on a rack in the back of the studio. My cup had survived, but the handle lay in brittle pieces beside it. "Faulty score," the teacher said when she saw my face fall.

That was how I'd always imagined the surface of my heart—smooth, slick, unattached. Nothing to grab on to. Unscored. No one could attach to me once the inevitable heat of life bore down. I suspected the metaphor went deeper still—that I was afraid of marring my heart with the scoring that arose naturally between people, the inevitable bumping against other people's desires, demands, pettiness, preferences, and all the quotidian negotiations that made up a relationship. Scoring was required for attachment, and my heart lacked the grooves.

I wasn't an orphan either, though the first part of this reads like I was. My parents, still happily married, lived in Texas in the same redbrick ranch house I grew up in. If you drove by 6644 Thackeray Avenue, you would see a weathered basketball hoop and a porch festooned with three flags: Old Glory, the Texas state flag, and a maroon flag with the Texas A&M logo on it. Texas A&M was my dad's alma mater. Mine too.

My parents called a couple times a month to check on me, usually after mass on Sundays. I always went home for Christmas. They bought me a giant green Eddie Bauer coat when I moved to Chicago. My mom sent me fifty-dollar checks so I'd have spending money; my dad diagnosed problems with my Honda's brakes over the phone. My younger sister was finishing graduate school and about to become engaged to her longtime boyfriend; my brother and his wife, college sweethearts, lived in Atlanta near dozens of their college friends. None of them knew about my unscored heart. To them, I was their oddball daughter and sister who voted Democratic, liked poetry, and settled north of the Mason-Dixon Line. They loved me, but I didn't really fit with them or Texas. When I was a kid, my mom would play the Aggie fight song on the piano and my dad would sing along at the top of his lungs. *Hullaballo-canek-canek, Hullaballoo-canek-canek.* He took me on my college tour of Texas A&M, and when I picked it—primarily because we could afford it—he was genuinely thrilled to have another Aggie in the family. He never said so, but surely he was disappointed to learn that I spent home football games in the library highlighting passages in *Walden* while twenty thousand fans sang, stomped, and cheered loud enough that when the Aggies, scored the library walls vibrated. Everyone in my family and all of Texas, it seemed, loved football.

I was a misfit. The deep secret I carried was that I didn't belong. Anywhere. I spent half my days obsessing about food and my body and the weird shit I did to control both, and the other half trying to outrun my loneliness with academic achievement. I went from the honor roll in high school to the dean's list in college for earning a 4.0 for most of my semesters there to cramming legal theories into my brain seven days a week. I dreamed of one day showing up at 6644 Thackeray Avenue at my goal weight, arm in arm with a healthy functioning man, and my spine shooting straight to the sky.

I didn't think of disclosing to my family when my troubling wishes about death cropped up. We could talk about the weather, the Honda, and the Aggies. None of my secret fears and fantasies fit into any of those categories.

I wished passively for death, but I didn't stockpile pills or join the Hemlock Society's mailing list. I didn't research how to get a gun or fashion a noose out of my belts. I didn't have a plan, a method, or a date. But I felt an unease, constant as a toothache. It didn't feel normal, passively wishing that death would snatch me up. Something about the way I was living made me want to stop living.

I don't remember what words I used when I thought about my malaise. I know I felt a longing I couldn't articulate and didn't know how to satisfy. Sometimes I told myself I just wanted a boyfriend or that I was scared I would die alone. Those statements were true. They nicked the bone of the longing, but they didn't reach the marrow of my despair.

In my journal, I used vague words of discomfort and distress: *I feel afraid and anxious about myself. I feel afraid that I'm not OK, will never be OK & I'm doomed. It's very uncomfortable to me. What's wrong with me?* I didn't know then that a word existed to perfectly define my malady: lonely.

That card from the bursar with my class rank on it, by the way, said number one. Uno. First. *Primero. Zuerst.* The one hundred seventy other students in my class had a GPA lower than mine. I'd exceeded my goal of landing in the top half of the class, which, after my less-than-mediocre score on the LSAT—I never could figure out when Uriah should have his conference—seemed like a stretch goal. I should have been thrilled. I should have been opening zero-balance credit cards. Shopping for Louboutin heels. Signing the lease on a new apartment on the Gold Coast. Instead, I was first in my class and jealous of the lead singer of INXS who died of autoerotic asphyxiation.

What the hell was wrong with me? I wore size-six pants, had D-cup breasts, and pulled in enough student loan money to cover a studio apartment in an up-and-coming neighborhood on the north side of Chicago. For eight years, I'd been a member of a 12-step program that taught me how to eat without sticking my finger down my throat thirty minutes later. My future gleamed before me like Grandma's polished silver. I had every reason to be optimistic. But self-disgust about my stuckness—I was far away from other people, aeons away from a romantic relationship—lodged in every cell of my body. There was some reason that I felt so apart and alone, a reason why my heart was so slick. I didn't know what it was, but I felt it pulsing as I fell asleep and wished to not wake up.

I was already in a 12-step program. I'd done a fourth-step inventory with my sponsor who lived in Texas and made amends to the people I'd harmed. I'd returned to Ursuline Academy, my all-girl high school, with a one-hundred-dollar check as restitution for money I stole while managing parking-lot fees junior year. Twelve-step recovery had arrested the worst of my disordered eating, and I credited it with saving my life. Why was I now wishing that life away? I confessed to my sponsor who lived in Texas that I'd been having dark thoughts.

"I wish for death every day." She told me to double up on my meetings.

I tripled them, and felt more alone than ever.

2

A few days after I learned my class rank, a woman named Marnie invited me to dinner following a 12-step meeting. Like me, she was a recovering bulimic. Unlike me, she had a super-together life: She was only a few years older, but she worked at a lab focused on cutting-edge experiments for breast cancer treatments; she and her husband had recently painted the entryway of her colonial Sherwin-Williams's Osage Orange; she was tracking her ovulation. Her life wasn't perfect—her marriage was often stormy—but she chased what she wanted. My instinct was to say no to her dinner offer so I could go home, take off my bra, and eat my four ounces of ground turkey and roasted carrots alone in front of *Scrubs*. That's what I usually did—beg off—when people after meetings invited me to join them for coffee or dinner. "Fellowship," as they called it. But before I could decline, Marnie touched my elbow. "Just come. Pat's out of town, and I don't want to eat alone."

We sat across from each other at the type of "healthy" diner that serves sprouted bread and sweet potato fries. Marnie seemed extra buoyant. Was she wearing lip gloss?

"You seem happy," I said.

"It's my new therapist." I chased a spinach leaf around my plate with my fork. Could a therapist help me? I let the hope flicker. The summer before law school, I availed myself of eight free sessions with a social worker, courtesy of an Employee Assistance Program. I'd been assigned a meek woman named June who wore prairie skirts without irony. I didn't tell her any of my secrets because I was afraid of upsetting her. Therapy, like being truly close to people, seemed like an experience I had to stand on the outside of, my face pressed to the window.

"I'm doing an all-women's group."

"Group?" My neck tensed immediately. I had a deep mistrust of groups after a bad experience in fifth grade when my parents transferred me to a local public school from my small Catholic school where class size was dwindling. At the new school, I fell in with the popular girls, led by Bianca, who gave out Jolly Ranchers every lunch period and had solid gold orbs on her add-a-bead necklace. I once spent the night at Bianca's house, and her mom took us in her silver Mercedes to see *Footloose*. But Bianca turned on me midyear. She thought her boyfriend liked me because we sat near each other in history. One day at lunch, she offered everyone at the table a Jolly Rancher except me. She slipped a note under my lunch bag: *We don't want you at our table.* All the girls had signed it. By then, I knew something was off in the connection between me and other people. I sensed in my gut that I didn't know how to stay connected, how not to be cast aside. I could tolerate 12-step groups because the membership at every meeting shifted. You could come and go as you pleased, and no one knew your last name. There was no one in charge at a 12-step meeting—no Queen Bee Bianca who could oust other members. A set of spiritual principles held a 12-step group together: anonymity, humility, integrity, unity, service. Without those, I never would have stayed. Plus, the cost of a meeting was basically free, though they suggested a two-dollar donation. For the cost of a Diet Coke I could spend sixty minutes acknowledging my eating disorder and listening to other people's pain and triumphs around food.

I speared a chunk of tomato and considered interesting topics I could raise with Marnie—the execution of Oklahoma City bomber Timothy McVeigh or whatever Colin Powell was up to. I felt the urge to impress her with my knowledge of current events and display some togetherness of my own. But I was curious about her therapy group. I feigned nonchalance as I asked what it was like.

"It's all women. Mary's going deaf, and Zenia's about to lose her medical license because of alleged Medicare fraud. Emily's father is a drug addict—he harasses her with hate mail from his one-bedroom apartment in Wichita." Marnie lifted her arm and pointed at the soft, fleshy underside of her forearm. "Our new girl is a cutter. Always wears long sleeves. We don't know her story yet, but for sure, it's dark as hell."

"Sounds intense." Not what I'd pictured. "Are you allowed to tell me all this?"

She nodded. "The therapist's theory is that keeping secrets is a toxic process, so we—the group members—can talk about whatever we want, wherever we want. The therapist is bound by doctor-patient confidentiality, but we're not."

No confidentiality? I sat back and shook my head. I twisted the napkin around my wrist under the table. No way could I do that. I once hinted to my high school social justice teacher Ms. Gray that my eating was screwed up. When Ms. Gray called my parents to suggest counseling, my mom was furious. I was polishing off a plate of biscuits and watching Oprah interview Will Smith when my mom stormed into the living room, madder than a one-winged hornet. "Why would you tell people your business? You *must* protect yourself!" My mom is a proper Southern woman raised in Baton Rouge during the 1950s. Telling other people your business was tacky and could have adverse social consequences. She was convinced I'd be ostracized if other people knew I had mental problems, and she wanted to protect me. When I started going to 12-step meetings in college, it took all the courage I had to trust that the other people would take the anonymity part of the program as seriously as I did.

"How does anyone get better?" Marnie was clearly doing better than I was. If we were a tampon commercial, I'd be the one scowling about odors and leakage; she'd be doing a jeté in white jeans on her heavy flow day.

She shrugged. "You could check it out."

I'd had other therapy. In high school, there was a short stint with a woman who looked like Paula Dean and wore pastel pantsuits. My parents sent me to Paula D. after Ms. Gray called about my eating, but I was so busy obeying the command to protect myself that I never said anything about how I felt. Instead, we chitchatted about whether I should get a mall job over the summer. Express or Gap? Once, she sent me home with a five-hundred-question psychological test. Hope coursed through my fingers as I filled in each answer bubble; these questions would finally reveal why I couldn't stop eating, why I felt like a misfit everywhere I went, and why none of the boys were interested in me when all the other girls were French-kissing and getting felt up.

Paula D. read the results in her perfectly modulated therapist voice: "'Christie is perfectionistic and afraid of snakes. An ideal occupation for Christie would be watch repairperson or surgeon.'" She smiled and cocked her head. "Snakes are pretty scary, huh?"

It never occurred to me to show her my tears and panic. To open up, I needed a therapist who could hear the echoes of pain in my silences and see the shirttail of truth under my denials. Paula D. didn't. After that session, I sat my parents down and told them that I'd graduated from therapy. All better now. My parents beamed with pride, and my mom shared her life philosophy: "You just make up your mind to be happy. Focus on the positive; don't put any energy into negative thoughts." I nodded. Great idea. On the way down the hall to my bedroom, I stopped in the bathroom and threw up my dinner, a habit I developed after reading a book about a gymnast who threw up her food. I loved the feeling of emptying myself of food and the rush of adrenaline from having a secret. At age sixteen, I thought bulimia was a genius way to control my ruthless appetite, which led me to binge on crackers, bread, and pasta. Not until I got into recovery did I understand that my bulimia was a way to control the unending swells of anxiety, loneliness, anger, and grief that I had no idea how to release.

Marnie dragged another fry through the smear of ketchup. "Dr. Rosen would see you—"

"Rosen? Jonathan Rosen?"

I *definitely* couldn't call Dr. Rosen. Blake saw Dr. Rosen. Blake was a guy I'd met at a party the summer before law school. He took a seat next to me and said, "What kind of eating disorder do you have?" He pointed at the carrot sticks on my plate and said, "Don't look at me like that. I've dated an anorexic and two bulimics who wished they were anorexic. I know your type." He was in AA, between jobs, and offered to take me sailing. We rode bikes to the lakefront to watch Fourth of July fireworks. We lay on the deck of his boat, shoulder to shoulder, staring at the Chicago skyline and talking about recovery. We sampled the vegan food at Chicago Diner and went to the movies on Saturday afternoons before his AA meeting. When I asked if he was my boyfriend, he didn't answer. Sometimes, he'd disappear for a few days to listen to Johnny Cash albums in his darkened apartment. Even if I could see the same therapist as Marnie, I could *not* see the same therapist as my ex-whatever-Blake-was. What, was I going to call up this Dr. Rosen and say, "Remember the girl who had anal sex last fall with Blake to cure his depression? Well, that was me! Do you take BlueCross-BlueShield?"

"How much does this therapy cost?" Couldn't hurt to ask, though I had no conscious intention of joining a therapy group.

"Super cheap—only seventy bucks a week."

I blew a hot breath out of my cheeks. Seventy bucks was chump change to Marnie, who ran a lab at Northwestern University and whose husband was the heir to a small family fortune. If I skimped on groceries and took the bus instead of driving, I *might* have an extra seventy bucks by the end of the month. But each week? I made fifteen dollars an hour at my summer internship, and my parents were Just Be Happy people, so I couldn't ask them. In two years, I'd have a job locked down, but on my student budget, where would the money come from?

Marnie said Dr. Rosen's phone number out loud, but I didn't write it down.

But then she said one more thing.

"He just got remarried—he smiles all the time."

Instantly, I pictured Dr. Rosen's heart: a red grammar school cutout for Valentine's Day with hash marks etched across the surface like bare tree branches in winter. I projected onto Dr. Rosen, a man I had never met, a gut-wrenching divorce, lonely nights in a sublet efficiency with freezer-burned microwaved dinners, but then a twist: a second chance at love with a new wife. In the chest of a smiling therapist beat a scored heart. My chest filled with curiosity and a slim, quivering hope that he could help me.

As I lay in bed that night, I thought about the women in Marnie's group: the presumed cutter, the felon, the daughter of the drug addict. I thought about Blake, who had formed tight bonds with the men in his group. After his sessions, he would come home brimming with stories about Ezra, who had a blow-up doll for a girlfriend, and Todd, whose wife dumped all of his possessions out on the sidewalk when she wanted a divorce. Was I really worse off than these folks? Was my malady, whatever it was, so impossible to cure? I'd never given bona fide psychiatry a chance. Psychiatrists have medical degrees—maybe whatever was wrong with me required the skills of someone who'd dissected a human heart during his training. Maybe Dr. Rosen would have some advice for me—something he could impart in a single session or two. Maybe there was a pill he could prescribe to take the edge off my despair and score my heart.

3

I found Dr. Rosen's number in the phone book and left a message on his machine two hours after my dinner with Marnie. He called me back the next day. Our conversation lasted less than three minutes. I asked for an appointment, he offered me a time, and I took it. When I hung up, I stood up in my office, my whole body shaking. Twice I sat down to resume my legal research, and both times I popped out of my seat thirty seconds later to pace. My mind insisted that making a doctor's appointment was no big deal, but the adrenaline coursing through me hinted otherwise. That night I wrote, *I got off the phone & burst into tears. I felt like I said the wrong stuff & he doesn't like me & I felt exposed and vulnerable.* I didn't care if he could help me; I cared about whether or not he liked me.

The waiting room consisted of bland doctor's office fare: an Easter lily, a gray-scale photograph of a man stretching his arms outward and turning his face toward the sun. The bookshelf held titles like *Codependent No More* and *Vandalized Love Maps* and dozens of AA newsletters. Next to the inner door, there were two buttons: one labeled "group" and one labeled "Dr. Rosen." I pressed the Dr. Rosen button to announce myself and then settled in a chair along the wall facing the door. To calm my nerves, I grabbed a *National Geographic* and flipped through pictures of the majestic Arctic sea wolf galloping across a treeless plain. On the phone Dr. Rosen had sounded serious. I heard East Coast vowels. I heard an unsmiling gravitas. I heard a stern, humorless priest. Part of me had hoped he'd be too booked to see me for a few weeks or months, but he offered an appointment forty-eight hours later.

The waiting room door swung open at exactly one thirty. A slight middle-aged man in a red Tommy Hilfiger golf shirt, khaki pants, and black leather loafers opened the door. His face wore a slight smile— friendly but professional—and what was left of his wiry grayish hair stuck up all over his head, slightly reminiscent of Einstein. If I passed him on the street, I would never look twice. From a quick glance, I could tell he was too young to be my dad and too old to want to fuck, which seemed ideal. I followed him down a hall to an office where northern windows looked out over the multistory Marshall Field's building. There were several patient seating options: a scratchy-looking upholstered couch, an upright office chair, or a black oversize armchair next to a desk. I chose the black armchair. A slew of framed Harvard diplomas drew my eye. I respected the Harvard thing. I'd had Ivy League dreams but state school finances and test scores. To me, those Ivy League certificates signified that this guy was top tier. Elite. Crème de la crème. But it also meant that if he couldn't help me, then I was truly and deeply fucked.

Once I settled in the chair, I took a good look at his face. My heartbeat accelerated as I took in his nose, eyes, and the straight line of his lips. I put them altogether and realized: I knew him. I pressed my lips together as the knowledge sunk in. I totally knew this guy.

This Dr. Rosen was the same Jonathan R. I'd met in a recovery meeting for people with eating disorders three years earlier. In 12-step meetings, people go only by their first name and last initials to preserve their anonymity. Twelve-step meetings for people with eating disorders are like AA meetings—members gather in church basements where they share stories about how food is ruining their lives. Like our more famous AA brethren whose meetings have been depicted in Meg Ryan movies and referenced in TV shows from *The West Wing* to *NYPD Blue*, food addicts collect serenity coins and get sponsors to learn how to live without bingeing, purging, starving, and maiming their flesh. Unlike AA, most of the 12-step meetings I'd attended were filled with women. In ten years, I'd seen only a handful of men in my meetings. One of them was the Harvard-educated psychiatrist sitting two feet away from me, waiting for me to open my mouth.

I knew things about Jonathan R. as a person. A man. A man with an eating disorder. I remembered things he'd shared about his mother, his chronically ill child, his feelings about his body.

A therapist is supposed to be a blank slate. There were smudges all over Dr. Rosen.

I swiveled my body so he could see me head-on. Once he recognized me, would he kick me out right away? His expression remained open, curious. Five seconds passed. He didn't seem to recognize me and was waiting for me to speak. Now the Harvard thing intimidated me. How could I come across as both witty and tortured, like Dorothy Parker or David Letterman? I wanted this Dr. Rosen to take seriously my newly developed fantasies about dying, yet still find me irrepressibly charming and maybe also a little bit fuckable. I figured he'd be more willing to help me if he found me attractive.

"I suck at relationships and am afraid I'll die alone."

"What does that mean?"

"I can't get close to people. Something stops me, like an invisible fence. I can feel myself holding back, always holding back. With guys, I always fall for the ones who drink until they puke or pass out—"

"Alcoholics." Not a question but a statement.

"Yes. My first love in high school smoked pot every day and cheated on me. In college, I fell for a beautiful Colombian fraternity boy who was alcoholic and had a girlfriend, and then I dated a pot addict. There was a nice guy after him, but I dumped him—"

"Because?"

"He walked me to class, bought me copies of his favorite books, and asked permission to kiss me. He made my skin crawl."

Dr. Rosen smiled. "You're afraid of emotionally available men. I suspect women too." More statements.

"Stable guys who express interest in me make me want to vomit. I guess that's true about women too." My mind flashed to a scene from the previous Christmas when I was in Texas visiting my family, and I'd run into a high school friend at Banana Republic. When Lia called out my name, I stood next to the blazers and oxford shirts, frozen, as she hugged me warmly. When she pulled away, a stricken look passed across her face—like *I thought we were friends*—and then she asked me about Chicago and law school. As we chitchatted among the shoppers looking for after-Christmas bargains, my mind insisted that she didn't want to be talking to me because she was now a successful physical therapist without an eating disorder or a weird affliction that made her clam up when someone from her past offered her a hug. Lia and I had been close in high school, but I pulled away senior year when my eating disorder revved up and I became consumed with getting my first boyfriend to stop cheating on me.

"Are you bulimic?"

"I'm in recovery—twelve-step," I said quickly, hoping not to trigger his memory of hearing me introduce myself as *Christie, recovering bulimic.* "The steps helped me with the bulimia, but I can't fix this relationship thing—"

"Not by yourself. Who's in your support system?"

I mentioned my sponsor Cady, a stay-at-home mom of grown kids who lived in the rural Texas town where I went to college. I was closer to her than anyone—I called her every three days but hadn't laid eyes on her in five years. There was my random assortment of women like Marnie with whom I connected during and sometimes after recovery meetings. Law school friends who didn't know I was in recovery. Friends from high school and college in Texas who tried to keep in touch with me, but I rarely returned their phone calls and never accepted their invitations to visit.

"I'm starting to have fantasies about dying." I pressed my lips together. "Ever since I found out I'm first in my class at law school—"

"Mazel tov." His smile was so genuine that I had to turn my head to his diplomas to keep from bursting into tears.

"It's not Harvard or anything." He raised his eyebrows. "And anyway, so I'll have a great career, so what? There won't be anything else—"

"That's why you picked law." His confident diagnoses were both disarming and comforting. He was no Paula D. with her questions about snakes.

"What's the story in your head about how you became you?" Dr. Rosen asked.

"Every family has a fuckup." I don't know why I said that.

"Valedictorian of your law school class, and you're a fuckup?"

"Being valedictorian doesn't mean shit if I'm going to die alone and unattached."

"What do you want?" he asked.

The word *want* echoed in my head. *Want, want, want.* I groped for a way to speak my longing in the affirmative, not just blurt out how I didn't want to die alone.

"I want—" I stalled.

"I would like—" More stopping.

"I want to be real. With other people. I want to be a real person."

He stared at me like *what else?* Other strands of desire floated through my mind: I wanted a boyfriend who smelled like clean cotton and went to work every day. I wanted to spend less than 50 percent of my waking hours thinking about the size of my body. I wanted to eat all of my meals with other people. I wanted to enjoy and seek out sex as much as the women on *Sex and the City*. I wanted to return to ballet class, a passion I dumped when I grew breasts and fleshy thighs. I wanted to have friends to travel the world with after I took the bar exam in two years. I wanted to reconnect with my college roommate who lived in Houston. I wanted to hug high school friends when I ran into them at the mall. But I didn't say any of that because it seemed too specific. Corny. I didn't yet know that therapy, like writing, relied on detail and specificity.

He said he'd put me in a group. I shouldn't have been surprised, but the word *group* landed like a punch between my ribs. A group would be filled with people, people who might not like me, who would pry into my business and violate my mother's edict not to expose my mental anguish to other people's scrutiny.

"I can't do a group."

"Why not?"

"My mother would flip. All those people knowing my business—"

"So don't tell her."

"Why can't I do individual sessions?"

"Group's the only way I know how to get you where you want to go."

"I'll give you five years."

"Five years?"

"Five years to change my life, and if it doesn't work, then I'm out of here. Maybe I'll kill myself." I wanted to wipe that smirk off his face, and I wanted him to know I wasn't going to stick around indefinitely, schlepping downtown to talk about my feelings with other broken people, if there weren't material changes in my life. In five years I'd be thirty-two. If I still had a slick, unattached heart at thirty-two, I would off myself.

He leaned forward. "You want intimate relationships in your life within five years?" I nodded, willing to bear the discomfort of eye contact. "We can do that."

I was scared of Dr. Rosen, but was I going to second-guess the Harvard-educated psychiatrist? His intensity scared me—that laughter, those statements—but it also intrigued me. Such confidence! *We can do that.*

As soon as I agreed to group, I became convinced that something catastrophic would happen to Dr. Rosen. I pictured the number twelve bus mowing him down in front of Starbucks. I pictured his lungs riddled with malignant tumors, his body succumbing to ALS.

"If you meet the Buddha on the road, kill him," Dr. Rosen said in our second session when I told him my fears.

"Aren't you Jewish?" There was the Jewish surname, the mazel tov, the needlepoint with Hebrew letters hanging across from the diplomas.

"The expression means you should pray that I die."

"Why would I do that?"

"If I die"—he clasped his hands together and smiled like a manic elf—"someone better will come along." His face burst with joy, as if he believed that anything—anything at all—could happen, and it would be glorious and better than what came before it.

"I was once in an accident on a beach in Hawaii. Someone I was with drowned." I felt a rise in my chest as I watched his eyes expand before my detonated bomb.

"Jesus. How old were you?"

"Three weeks shy of fourteen." My body buzzed with anxiety as it always did when Hawaii came up. That summer, the sweet spot between eighth grade and starting a new, all-girls Catholic high school, my friend Jenni invited me to join her family for a vacation in Hawaii. We spent three days exploring the main island—black sand beaches, waterfalls, a luau. On the fourth day, we went to a secluded beach at the edge of the island, and Jenni's father drowned in the surf. I never knew how to talk about the experience. My mom called it "the accident," other people called it "the drowning." The night it happened, Jenni's mom called family members back in Dallas, sobbing into the phone: "David's been killed." I didn't have the words for what happened or how it felt to carry the memory of dragging his limp body out of the ocean, so I didn't talk about it.

"Do you want to say more?"

"I'm not praying that you die."

If you Google "see Buddha kill," you'll find a link to a book titled *If You Meet the Buddha on the Road, Kill Him! The Pilgrimage of Psychotherapy Patients.* Apparently, psychotherapy patients, who were now my people, must learn that therapists are nothing more than struggling human beings like their patients. It was an early signal that Dr. Rosen was not going to give me answers, that he might not have them to give. I added to my fantasy reel of Dr. Rosen's grisly demise an image of me driving a wooden stake into Dr. Rosen's heart, which was unsettling, and not just because I'd confused Buddha with Dracula.

Freshman year of college, some lively, popular girls from Austin invited me to road-trip to New Orleans with them. The plan was to stay at one of the girls' cousin's place and party in the French Quarter until it was time to drive back to campus. I told them I needed to think about it, even though I knew my answer. I cited homework as an excuse, even though it was the second week of school, and my only assignment was to read the first half of *Beowulf*, which I'd read in high school.

Groups intimidated me, even all those years after Bianca and her Jolly Ranchers. Where would I sleep in New Orleans? What if I didn't understand their jokes? What if we ran out of things to say? What if they figured out I wasn't as rich or cool or happy as they were? What if they found out I wasn't a virgin? What if they knew I'd slept with only one guy? What if they learned my secrets around food?

How could I possibly do a group with the same people every week?

"I know you. From meetings." I blurted it out in the middle of my second session. I was afraid that he would one day remember me and then have to kick me out of his practice because we'd sat in meetings together. "From years ago when I lived in Hyde Park."

He cocked his head to the side and narrowed his eyes. "Ah, right. I thought you looked familiar."

"Does this mean you can't treat me?"

His shoulders shook as he burst into elfin laughter. "I hear the wish."

"What?" I stared at his jolly face.

"If you're thinking about committing to treatment with me, you're going to start coming up with excuses about why it won't work."

"It was a legitimate fear."

More laughter.

"What?"

"If you join one of my groups, I want you to tell the group every single thing you remember me sharing during meetings."

"But your anonymity—"

"I don't need you to protect me. That's not your job. Your job is to tell."

My journal entry after the second session was strangely prescient: *I feel nervous about being exposed in therapy about the way I eat . . . I've got a lot of emotion about Dr. Rosen & his role in my life. Fear about my secrets coming out. Fear is so huge.*

Dr. Rosen spoke in koans.

"The starving person isn't hungry until she takes her first bite," he said.

"I'm not anorexic." Oh, sure, I'd wished for an attack of anorexia all through high school when I couldn't stop bingeing on Pringles and Chips Ahoy, but that was never my deal.

"It's a metaphor. When you let the group in—take that first bite—only then will you feel how alone you've been."

"How do I 'let the group in'?"

"You share with them every aspect of your life that deals with relationships—friendship, family, sex, dating, romance. All of it."

"Why?"

"That's how you let them in."

ur

Before starting group, you got three individual sessions. In my last one, my shoulders relaxed as I curled into Dr. Rosen's black leather armchair. I twirled my bracelet with my index finger and slipped my foot in and out of my shoe. I was used to Dr. Rosen; he was my strange old pal. Nothing to fear here. I'd told him that I knew him from meetings, and he said it wasn't a deal breaker. The only thing left was to hammer out the particulars, like which group would he put me in? He offered a Tuesday morning coed group full of doctors and lawyers that met from seven thirty to nine. A "professionals" group. I hadn't been picturing men in my group. Or doctors. Or lawyers.

"Wait, what's going to happen to me when I start group?"

"You're going to feel lonelier than you ever have in your life."

"Hold the phone, Harvard." I bolted straight up in my chair. "I'm going to feel *worse*?" I'd just met with the dean of students at law school to take out a private health-care loan at 10 percent interest to pay for my new therapy. Now he was telling me that group would make me feel worse than the morning I drove around dribbling plum juice and praying for a bullet to my brain?

"Absolutely." He nodded like he was trying to knock something off the top of his head. "If you're serious about getting into intimate relationships—becoming a real person, as you said—you need to feel every feeling you've been stifling since you were a kid. The loneliness, the anxiety, the anger, the terror." Could I go through this? Did I want to? Curiosity about this man, his groups, and how they might score my heart inched out my resistance, but just barely.

"Can I call you to let you know?"

He shook his head. "I need your commitment today."

I gulped, stared at the door, and considered my options. The commitment scared me, but I was more afraid of walking out of his office empty-handed: no group, no other options, no hope.

"Fine. I commit." I grabbed my purse so I could slink back to work and fret over what I'd just committed to. "One last question. What's going to happen to me when I start group?"

"All of your secrets are going to come out."

4

"*Top or bottom?*" *A portly, balding guy with giant green eyes* and wire-rimmed glasses lobbed this opening salvo at me during my first group session. Later, I learned that the guy who started my hazing was Carlos, a sharp-tongued gay doctor in his late thirties who'd been seeing Dr. Rosen for a few years.

"In sex. Top or bottom?" he said.

Out of the corner of my eye, I saw Dr. Rosen shifting his gaze from one member to another, like a sprinkler on a timer. I smoothed the front of my skirt. If they wanted bawdy, sex-positive Christie, I'd serve her up.

"Definitely top."

Of course, this Christie was a fabricated version of me who welcomed intrusive questions from strangers with a smile. Underneath my skittering nerves and accelerated pulse, I felt like crying because the authentic answer to the question was that I had no idea how I liked to have sex. I didn't date guys capable of consistent sex, thanks to their depression and addiction. I said top because I had a foggy memory of pleasure with my high school boyfriend, the basketball star slash pothead who boned me regularly in the front seat of my dad's Chevy.

Dr. Rosen did a theatrical throat clear.

"What?" It was the first time I looked straight at Dr. Rosen since group started. He'd opened the waiting room door and led me, Carlos, and two other people to a corner office on the opposite end of the hallway from the room where'd I'd had my individual sessions. In the fourteen-by-fourteen group room, there were seven swivel chairs arranged in a circle. Sunlight striped the room from the slats in the mini blinds. In one corner there was a bookshelf, lined with titles on addiction, codependency, alcoholism, and group therapy. On the bottom shelf, a motley assortment of stuffed animals and a nun with boxing gloves spilled over the edge. I'd selected a chair facing the door, which was nine o'clock to Dr. Rosen's high noon position. The chair was hard on my ass and squeaked faintly when I swiveled left and right. Honestly, I'd expected spiffier accommodations from a Harvard alum.

"How about an honest answer?" Dr. Rosen said. His grin broadcast a challenge, like he knew without a doubt I'd begun my group career masquerading as a sexually healthy woman.

"Such as?"

"That you don't like having sex at all." My face flushed. That was not how I would have described myself.

"That's not true. I love having sex, I just can't find anyone to have sex with." I'd had orgasms and toe-curling sex before—in college there was that Colombian alcoholic who touched my face as he kissed me, lighting me up like a supernova. And I genuinely liked being on top those few times with my high school boyfriend, tilting my pelvis just so, charging forward into my sexuality as only a drunk-on-Zima seventeen-year-old could. I didn't know where those buried parts of me went or why I couldn't hold on to them.

A grandpa-aged guy with a military buzz cut and a Colonel Sanders goatee—a retired proctologist—piped in. "A pretty girl like you? That can't be true." Was he leering at me?

"Guys don't . . . respond to me." Tears threatened. Two minutes into the session, and I was cracking. I remembered when my all-girls Catholic high school sent us on a spiritual retreat sophomore year, and my retreat leader opened with a story about her bulimic past. I responded by bursting into tears and confessing my bulimia to a roomful of fourteen-year-olds, whom I then swore to secrecy. It was the first time I'd told anyone about my purging. Sitting across from Colonel Sanders, I felt the confusion from the retreat sidle up next to me, hovering: Would opening my mouth to spill the truth to strangers salvage my life or would it destroy me as my mother predicted?

"What do you mean, 'respond'?" Colonel Sanders was definitely leering.

"Guys *always* approach my friends, but never me. It's been like that since high school." In co-ed groups at bars or parties, I would stand slightly off to the side, never sure what to do with my hands, finding it impossible to laugh in my normal pitch or join the conversation because I was trying to imagine how to get the guys to like me. It wasn't just American guys. My college roommate Kat and I traveled all over Europe after college, and not one single guy hit on me. Not even in Italy. Meanwhile, guys from Munich, Nice, Lucerne, and Bruges fell all over Kat and ignored me.

A buzzer rang, and Dr. Rosen pressed a button on the wall behind him.

Three seconds later, a smiling woman in her late forties with chipped turquoise nail polish, overprocessed orange hair, and a raspy smoker's voice walked in. Her fringy rayon shirt was more Woodstock than downtown Chicago. I'd seen her a few times in 12-step meetings. "I'm Rory," she said to me and another older guy sitting across from me, who was apparently new to the group as well. Like a den mother, she pointed everyone out and told us their names and occupations. Colonel Sanders's given name was Ed. Carlos, a dermatologist. Patrice, a partner in an obstetrics practice. Rory was a civil rights attorney. The new guy, Marty, had Groucho Marx eyebrows and a habit of sniffing every ten seconds. He introduced himself as a psychiatrist who worked with Southeast Asian refugees.

"So you're here to have more sex?" Colonel Sanders said.

I shrugged. Literally, moments before I admitted as much, but now I was backing away because of messages embedded in my marrow: Nice girls don't want *it*. Feminists don't need *it*. Good girls don't talk about *it* at all, especially in mixed company. My mother would die if she knew I was talking about *it* with these strangers.

From there, the conversation ping-ponged to Rory, who mentioned she'd asked her father for money to pay her bills. Dr. Rosen steered Rory to her father's Holocaust survival story, which involved hiding in a trunk in Poland for several years. Abruptly, the conversation pivoted to Carlos's patient who refused to pay his bill.

As the group zigzagged from issue to issue, I shifted from butt cheek to butt cheek on that hard-ass chair. I sighed and cleared my throat in frustration. Nothing was resolved. Didn't anyone want any answers? Resolutions? Worse, as the newcomer, I had no context for any of the stories. Why did Carlos's assistant quit? Why did Rory seem so anti-Semitic when her dad survived the Holocaust in a footlocker? What was the deal with her overdue Visa bill?

At some point in the session I fingered the beads of my pearl bracelet like a rosary strand to soothe myself. Dr. Rosen watched me, his newest lab rat. Would he later write a note for my file? *CT manipulates jewelry with her digits during group discussion. CT demonstrates all the classic signs of someone with major intimacy issues, severe repression. Tough case.*

I'd left my three individual sessions feeling that, despite his cockiness and strange sense of humor, Dr. Rosen and I had a bond. I believed he understood me, but now it felt like we were total strangers. I called him an asshole in my head.

There were unwritten group rules.

"You crossed your legs," Colonel Sanders said. I stared down at my right thigh crossed over my left. Everyone turned toward me.

"So what?" I asked, defensive.

"We don't do that here." Colonel Sanders eyed my legs. I uncrossed them quickly.

"Why not?" If making me feel stupid was a way to get better, I'd be cured by Christmas.

"It means you're not open." That was Carlos.

"It means you're ashamed." That was Rory.

"You're shutting down emotionally." That was Patrice.

The group room was a fishbowl. There was nowhere to hide from the six pairs of eyes around the circle. They could read my body. Make assessments. Draw conclusions. They could *see* me. The exposure made me want to cross my legs until the end of the session. Until the end of time.

Dr. Rosen came to life and spoke. "What are you feeling?"

Instead of blurting out a bullshit answer that I thought would win me points—*I feel empowered by the group dynamics*—I took a breath and searched for the truth. I'd lost my bearings, but decided that the truth could function like a home base. It had worked in 12-step meetings—I was alive because I'd told the truth about my bulimia over and over in meetings. Nothing in my life had empowered me—not good grades, not a thin body, not dry-humping a beautiful Latin fraternity boy—like speaking the raw truth about vomiting up my meals. The first true, full-bodied sensation of power I ever felt was after my first 12-step meeting when I sat on a bench with a woman from the meeting and told her that I'd been bingeing and purging food I'd stolen all over campus. I felt the power of turning my back on my mother's proscription about telling other people my business. I released a secret, not caring who in my family might abandon me, because I finally understood that keeping the secret was an act of abandoning myself. If there was a way to health in group therapy—and I wasn't sure there was—the foundation had to be built on truth. There was no other way. And none of these people knew my mother or any of her friends. So no more fronting.

"Defensive." How was I supposed to know that *we* don't cross our legs?

Dr. Rosen shook his head. "That's not a feeling."

"But that's exactly . . ." Now I was pissed, and I was *positive* that was a feeling.

Another rule: "Feelings have two syllables or less: ashamed, angry, lonely, hurt, sad, afraid—" Dr. Rosen explained feelings like Fred Rogers talking to a preschooler. Apparently, once you veer beyond two syllables, you are intellectualizing, effectively darting away from the simple truth of your feelings.

"And happy," Rory said.

"But you won't feel that in here," Carlos said. Everyone laughed. The corners of my mouth rose in a smile.

Dr. Rosen nodded in my direction. "So what's 'defensive'?"

My first pop quiz. I wanted to give the right answer. It felt as hard as figuring out Sheldon's conference on the LSAT practice test. I ran through the roster of feelings. *Frustrated* came to mind, but that was three syllables. *Furious?* Nope, three syllables. Three blind mice. Three times the cock crowed. Three times Jesus fell. Three was holy. Three was biblical. Why couldn't I use a three-syllable word? My top choice: *adios*.

"Angry?" I said.

"I heard something else. How about shame?"

I said it aloud: "Ashamed?"

I thought of shame as something survivors of incest or ritual abuse had to work through. Shame belonged to people who had committed grave sexual sins or who did embarrassing things in public while naked. Did it belong to me? I always wore my clothes, even to bed—I often wore a bra during sex. Was *shame* the word for the feeling that everything about me was wrong and had to be buried under perfect test scores? Is shame what I felt as a little girl in ballet class when I pined for a petite body like the Jennifers and Melissas? Was that the name of the body disgust I felt in my gut growing up when I sat next to my friends and my younger sister, and compared the vast expanse of my thighs with their delicate, birdlike bones?

I wanted to be valedictorian in therapy like I was in law school. The problem with being number one, of course, was that it didn't cure my loneliness or bring me one inch closer to other people. Then there was the fact that I hadn't a clue how to be "good" at group therapy.

The cardinal rule in Rosen-land, of course, was no secret keeping among group members, which came up when Carlos discussed a woman named Lynne who was in another Rosen group. According to Carlos, Lynne planned to leave her husband because, in part, of his erectile dysfunction. I scrunched up my nose and shot a look at Dr. Rosen. How could he allow us to talk about some innocent man's broken penis? What if I knew him? When Marnie mentioned the no-secrets business, I didn't realize Dr. Rosen would actually condone gossip about other patients *in the middle of a session*.

"What about confidentiality?" I said.

"We don't do that here," Rory said. Patrice and Carlos confirmed with vigorous nodding. The memory of my mother scolding me in high school flashed in my mind. I'd bent the vow to let 12-step people in, but they were bound by the spiritual principle of anonymity, which was right there in the name of the program. What were these jokers bound by?

"How are we supposed to feel safe?"

"What makes you think confidentiality makes you safe?" Dr. Rosen looked energized, ready to school me.

"Group therapy's always confidential." My authority on group therapy was one friend from graduate school who had to sign a confidentiality agreement when she joined a group. "Maybe I don't want my secrets all over your group grapevine."

"Why not?"

"You don't get why I want privacy?" There were zero expressions of outrage on the faces staring back at me.

"You might want to look at why you're so invested in privacy."

"Isn't it standard practice?"

"It might be, but keeping secrets for other people is more toxic than other people knowing your business. Holding on to secrets is a way to hold shame that doesn't belong to you."

On one level I understood what he was saying. Food addicts in recovery meetings got well when they told their stories. But at the beginning of every 12-step meeting, there is a reminder: *What you hear here, when you leave here, stays here.* When that line is read, people in the meeting respond: *here, here!* Dr. Rosen was ethically bound to keep my secrets as my psychiatrist, but there were five other people who would hear every word I said. The walls of the group room were not a barrier to the information flowing out. What if I one day embezzled money from my future law firm? What if I developed irritable bowel syndrome and shit my pants on Michigan Avenue? What if I slept with someone who couldn't use punctuation properly? How was I going to feel knowing that some Joe Schmo in the Wednesday men's group might know details about the acrobatic sex I one day hoped to have?

"What am I going to get out of this?" I didn't know then that this question would come out of my mouth so many times that it would become part mantra, part catchphrase.

"A place to come where everything is speakable, and you are not asked to hold any secrets for anyone. Ever."

At the end of the session, Dr. Rosen pressed his palms together. "We'll stop there for today." Everyone stood up. To me, Dr. Rosen said, "We close the same way they close twelve-step meetings, holding hands in a circle saying the Serenity Prayer. If you are not comfortable with that, you don't have to participate."

I flashed him my "this ain't my first rodeo" smile. I'd just sat through ninety minutes of group therapy; if anyone needed the Serenity Prayer, it was me. The familiar prayer was meant to help addicts get in touch with a power greater than themselves without invoking any particular religious tradition: *God, grant me the serenity to accept the things I cannot change, courage to change the things I can, and the wisdom to know the difference.*

After we recited the prayer, everyone turned to the person next to them and embraced. Rory and Patrice. Marty and Ed. Carlos and Dr. Rosen. I watched them, unprepared to step forward and press my body to theirs, but when Patrice opened her arms to me, I stepped forward and let her hug me. My arms hung at my sides like empty sleeves. Dr. Rosen stood in front of his chair, and my group members stepped over to hug him, one by one.

I stepped forward and wrapped my arms around Dr. Rosen's shoulders and gave a quick squeeze—too quick to smell him or to retain memory of his arms around my body or mine around his. So quick it felt like it didn't happen. There was no imprint on my body. I hugged him because I wanted to fit in, do what everyone else was doing, and not draw any attention to myself. Years later, I'd watch new patients come in and refuse to hug anyone, especially Dr. Rosen, and my jaw would drop open, realizing it never once occurred to me *not* to hug him. I didn't have that kind of *no* anywhere in my body.

After group, I rode the Red Line train north to school, my head buzzing with the new faces, the new feelings vocabulary, the new world I'd just joined. Dr. Rosen acted like he knew all about me. His definitive statement—*you don't like having sex at all*—stung. So cocky! Just because he was a fancy psychiatrist didn't mean he knew everything. I'd once been open to pleasure, and if he ever bothered to ask me about it, I would look him and each of the group members in the eye with my legs uncrossed and tell them all about it.

The night of my first big O the spring weather in Texas was pleasant enough that I had my bedroom window open at 6644 Thackeray Avenue.

I couldn't sleep, so I flipped on the radio and heard, *"Sexually Speaking,* you're on the air." *Ooooh.* This radio program was *not* for kids. I burrowed deeper under the covers. Sister Mary Margaret told us that sex was only for married couples trying to make a baby—having sex under any other circumstances would lead to hell, far away from God, our parents, and our pets. My mom affirmed that Catholic truth over dinner one night when she explained that there were two sins that would get you a one-way ticket to eternal damnation: "Murder and premarital sex."

It was not hard to imagine myself slipping from God's favor as I scooched up the volume on the radio.

A caller confessed that she was unable to reach orgasms with her partner. What followed were Dr. Ruth Westheimer's instructions on how to get to know your body through masturbation. Helpfully, Dr. Ruth explained where the clitoris was and what it did. It was almost like she knew she was talking to a fourth grader.

I couldn't let all that sage advice go to waste. I slid my hand between my legs and touched the delicate pearl that sometimes hurt when I rode my bike for too long. Slowly, I circled it with my finger until I felt something happening—a warm wave building, making my legs go stiff. My fantasy reel: Tad Martin from *All My Children* kissed my face and told me he loved me more than all the women in Pine Valley. I rubbed myself harder. The extra pressure didn't hurt. My body climbed toward its first glorious sexual release. Then my whole body shuddered with pleasure just as Dr. Ruth promised. For the first time in my life, I thought: My body is exquisite and powerful.

There in the balmy, darkened privacy of my childhood bedroom, I tripped into my sexuality under the gentle tutelage of Dr. Ruth. I felt grown-up to have discovered the sexual secrets of adulthood. This touching myself and the warm wave of intense body pleasure must have been naughty because nobody ever talked about doing it. Masturbation was the grossest-sounding word I could imagine, and I'd never ever say it.

By fourth grade, I'd been marinating in body hatred for a few years. My stomach was too big—that was the message I received starting at age four from my beloved ballet teacher. "Christie," she'd say. "Stomach." A reminder to suck it in, make it disappear. She favored the girls whose leotards didn't bulge and whose upper thighs didn't quite touch. I wanted more than anything to be a ballerina and to be adored by my teacher, and the one thing holding me back on both fronts was the size of my body. I also suspected that my mother's sighs when I modeled new clothes in the Joske's and Dillard's dressing rooms were proof that she wished I was thin-boned. I know I did. I believed that slim, lithe girls like my sister and the Jennifers and Melissas in ballet class were happier because of their smaller bodies. They were certainly better loved. In attempts to become one of those small-bodied girls, I engaged in minor skirmishes with my appetite—trying to eat half a sandwich at lunch or skipping dessert—but my appetite always won. Every day, I'd enter the kitchen with the intention of getting a glass of water and three Club crackers, yet ended up consuming a fistful of Chips Ahoy and knocking back half a pitcher of grape Kool-Aid. Why couldn't I control my appetite? Why was my body keeping me from being who I was supposed to be?

I was a sensitive kid already gearing up for a years-long war with my body through bulimia, but in my dark room with my hand between my legs, I experienced unalloyed body pleasure. For those few minutes, I could make peace with my flesh and drift off to sleep.

Dr. Rosen didn't know about little Christie's forays into self-pleasure. That little girl had the guts to turn up the radio and explore.

5

"*Christie, why don't you tell the group what you ate yesterday,*" Dr. Rosen said.

"No!" My voice ricocheted off the walls. I jumped out of my chair and hopped around in the middle of the circle like I was trying to put out a fire. "No, no, no! Please, Dr. Rosen. Don't make me!" I begged like a child. *Not this; please not this.* I'd never acted like this before. But no one had ever asked me point-blank about my food.

"Jesus, woman. If you're going to act like that, then you have to tell us," Carlos said.

We hadn't even been talking about food. We'd been talking about the medical bills for Rory's ferret.

I was one month into treatment. In four Tuesday sessions, the group and I had gone through all the getting-to-know-you rituals. They knew I came to group because I struggled with relationships. They knew about the bulimia, and they knew about me and Dr. Ruth. But this? Telling the seven people in front of me what I'd eaten the day before? Impossible.

My eating disorder was no longer the stuff of a *Lifetime* movie—I didn't go from drive-through to drive-through eating and puking, but I ate like a weirdo. Exhibit A: Every single morning I ate a slice of mozzarella cheese rolled up in a cabbage leaf, along with a bowl of microwaved apple pieces that I poured skim milk over and ate with a spoon. "Apple Jacks," I called them. This had been my breakfast for almost three years straight. Never a Sausage McMuffin, chocolate croissant, or granola bar. If I couldn't have my secret special breakfast, alone in the privacy of my kitchen, then I skipped breakfast. This breakfast was safe. It never, ever beckoned me toward a binge.

My law school friends saw my odd lunch every day because I couldn't hide it: a can of tuna in springwater over a bed of green cabbage doused with French's Classic Yellow Mustard. They justifiably made fun of me for how disgusting and unimaginative it was. A normal person would never eat this lunch more than once; I ate it every single day. At lunchtime, the other students would saunter across campus for subs loaded with pink-and-white meats and cheeses, dripping with chunky jardinière sauce, while I sat back in the student lounge eating like a rabbit at a ballpark, prepping for the next class. They didn't know that before I got into recovery, my relationship with food led me to crouch, face-to-toilet, after most meals. The body memory of losing control of my appetite and ending up literally in the toilet haunted me. I almost met my ignominious death in college. You could say a lot about my lunch—it was flavorless, deprivational, and guaranteed to induce heartburn—but it kept me from losing control. Could those fancy subs do that?

For dinner, I ate sautéed ground turkey mixed with broccoli, carrots, or cauliflower and a tablespoon of Parmesan cheese. Every now and then I'd mix it up and use ground chicken instead of turkey. Once I tried ground lamb, but it was greasy and made my apartment smell gamy. When I got into recovery for bulimia, I picked a handful of foods that seemed "safe" because I'd never binged on them. I didn't have the courage to veer from my safe foods.

The bingeing popped up elsewhere, though. That was the secret rotting inside me. Every night, for "dessert," I'd have three or four red apples—often more. Sometimes as many as eight. When I hinted at my apple consumption to my sponsor Cady back in Texas, she assured me that as long as I didn't eat white sugar, it didn't matter if I ate a bushel of apples three times a day. White sugar was the devil's poison to many people in recovery—it would lead you to a death by doughnuts. Cady gave me permission to keep apples on the "safe food" list no matter how many bushels I went through per week.

I spent more on apples than I spent on cable, gas, and transportation combined. Apples were the reason I didn't have a roommate—I was terrified of being found out, but I also couldn't imagine eating only a single apple every night.

"Tell us," Rory said, her voice soft and gentle.

I squeezed my eyes shut and spoke fast, like an auctioneer at a cattle sale. "Cheese, cabbage, apple, milk, cabbage, tuna, mustard, an orange, chicken, carrots, and spinach." I paused, scared to go on. I couldn't imagine telling them about the apples, but keeping the secret suddenly felt unbearable. They would say I had had no recovery, that I hadn't properly worked the steps, and that I was a failure. Inwardly, I screamed hysterically. But somehow, I blurted out: "Then I ate six more apples."

Hard to say which shame burned hotter: eating half a dozen apples after dinner or that the villain of my food diary was the innocuous darling of the produce section. I'd sat in hundreds of 12-step meetings listening to people report bizarre and appalling things they did with cherry cheesecake, black licorice, scalloped potatoes. And there was me with a bag of apples on my lap.

The previous night's binge had been routine. I ate one apple right after dinner and swore I was done eating for the day. But there was a stirring in my belly: Was I still hungry? Was it a somatic signal that I needed more calories? I had no idea. A woman I knew from recovery always said that if you craved food after dinner, you should sit on your bed until it passed. I tried it—sitting cross-legged atop my comforter listening to sounds on the street below—but the craving for apples drew me off the bed and into the kitchen, where I grabbed another one from the fridge drawer. I ate another apple, fast, like maybe it wouldn't count if I ate it in under sixty seconds. Then the shame—the buzzword I'd learned in group—of speed-eating an apple alone in my apartment crested, so I ate two more. My belly was tender to the touch. What the fuck was I doing? I didn't know, but I ate two more Red Delicious. When I finally crawled under the covers to sleep, the sharp edges of the apple bits I'd failed to chew properly poked the edges of my stomach. Acid burned my throat.

How in the world could I call myself "in recovery" around food when I did this to myself every night? How would anyone love someone who ate like me? I'd been doing this for years. How would it ever stop?

Dr. Rosen asked if I wanted help. I nodded slowly, terrified he would suggest I eat bison burgers and artichoke pizza or a pint of Ben & Jerry's every night like a normal lonely person. Or worse, that I stopped eating apples.

"Call Rory every night and tell her what you ate."

Rory met my eyes with a smile so kind I had to look away or I would cry—like Dr. Rosen's mazel tov for my class rank. Head-on kindness warmed my solar plexus like a heat lamp and made me tear up.

Having my ritual revealed at last, in detail, was like having a layer of skin removed. The defining feature of my eating was secrecy. In kindergarten, I snuck cookies from the snack bin. Thanksgiving weekend of junior year in high school, I snuck-ate the top layer off a pecan pie. I stole food from every roommate I'd ever had. Even in recovery, I let go of the vomiting, but I kept the secrecy. And some version of the bingeing.

"I'm not trying to keep you from eating apples," Dr. Rosen said. "Eat as many as you want. The apples aren't killing you; the secrecy is. And the point is"—he leaned close and lowered his voice—"if you can let this group into your relationship with food, you will be closer to intimate relationships. You'll start with Rory."

I looked at Rory and imagined telling her about every morsel I put in my mouth. My whole body clenched, mostly with fear, but there was also hope. Here was a chance to be known inside the messiness of my eating, something I'd never truly let myself have before.

It wasn't a total surprise that my food stuff and relationship stuff sprouted from the same broken parts of me. What surprised me was that Dr. Rosen understood that. Paula D. hadn't seen it, and I was actively vomiting back then.

"Will calling Rory cure my apple binges?"

"You don't need a cure. You need a witness."

I wanted a cure. Apples were expensive.

⁓

Sophomore year in college I fell for the soulful Colombian with dimples deep as watering holes. He would drunk-dial me after the bars closed, and we would make out behind the Kappa Kappa Gamma house. He was the guy who taught me everything a kiss could be. Before him, I couldn't grasp the big deal about touching my lips to someone else's, but when his soft tongue met mine, I understood in an instant. A good kiss can reach every organ, every cell. It can steal your breath and make a cathedral of your mouth. Those kisses woke me up.

And then they fucked me up. The Colombian was a double whammy—an alcoholic with a serious girlfriend. The one time I slept over at his apartment, he was so drunk that he pissed in his closet because he thought it was the bathroom. Where was I when he relieved himself four feet from the bed at two A.M.? In his kitchen, shoving left-over birthday cake into my mouth. When I headed out for my walk of shame a few hours later, I ignored the amphitheater of black cake crumbs and the smear of frosting on the linoleum floor.

I was his secret side dish when his real girlfriend, the willowy Chi Omega with the straight blond hair, visited her parents in San Antonio.

The weekend of the Colombian's fraternity spring formal in Galveston, Texas, I ran by his apartment. Like a creepy stalker I watched him and the Chi Omega load up his Ford Bronco with cases of Shiner Bock. He patted her ass; she threw back her hair.

Devastated, I ran back to my dorm and consumed every calorie in our tiny cinder-block room: Teddy Grahams, pretzels, popcorn, Pop-Tarts, and leftover Halloween candy my roommate kept in her closet. Then I walked the halls, scavenging food from the common trash bins. I pulled some other kid's discarded pepperoni pizza out of the trash and popped it into the microwave for thirty seconds. While I waited for the cheese to melt, I devoured a batch of stale oatmeal raisin cookies that were still in a FedEx box from someone's mom in Beaumont.

I'd been bingeing and purging since seventh grade; I didn't need to use my finger. All I had to do was bend over the toilet. When I was done purging, I ran the shower to clean myself up before my roommate returned from a study group. My stomach felt like it would split open lengthwise. Steam billowed in the tiny bathroom, and I hugged the wall, waiting to see if more vomit was coming. Black dots swirled in my vision. I sank into the floor, half in the shower and half out. Before everything went black, I thought: This is it; this is how I die, bingeing myself into oblivion and moping over a boy.

I dialed Rory's number. Mercifully, her recorded voice greeted me, and then the beep. My turn. In a voice barely above a whisper, I recounted all the cabbage and the five postdinner apples. After I hung up, I threw my phone across the bedroom. It clattered across the hardwood floors. "Goddammit!" I yelled into my apartment, as I punched my pillows. In one moment, I thought: Why am I doing this? It hurts too much. Then: Why didn't I get to Dr. Rosen sooner?

I called Rory again the next night, and it wasn't one bit easier. My hands still shook and I threw my phone across the room when I was done telling her voice mail what I'd eaten. My arms ached with phantom pain as if I'd literally wrestled to keep hold of my precious secret. By the third night, when the voice mail beeped, I almost said "ditto from yesterday," I forced myself to enumerate each apple and cabbage leaf.

The fourth night was the worst. Seven apples. Enough for a prize-winning pie at the state fair. I wanted to hide the reality of those seven apples, but I was midway on a tightrope. If I told her, could I scurry, quick like, to the platform ahead? Either way, I wanted off the tightrope.

It's not going to work if you don't do the hard thing, I told myself. Deep breath. "Seven fucking apples."

6

Dr. Rosen was a snake charmer. He could ask a pointed question and secrets from our past would slither out. He'd coax Rory into recounting details of her father's harrowing escape from Poland, urging her to speak in her father's Old World accent. At Dr. Rosen's urging, Colonel Sanders described the dubious therapy he had with an unlicensed doctor who treated him for PTSD after his service in Vietnam. Dr. Rosen could get Carlos talking about the stepbrother who abused him after Sunday school, and Patrice misting up over her brother who hanged himself in the family orchard. Dr. Rosen sensed where our shame and grief was hidden and knew how to extract it. He prodded me to talk about Hawaii and bulimia almost every session.

Every Tuesday morning, I rode the train eleven stops from my apartment to the Washington stop on the Red Line, where I would climb to the street level around seven ten. Twenty minutes early. The day I'd committed to joining a group, I stopped sleeping through the night. I could fall asleep around ten, but then I'd bolt awake at two or three, and never get back to sleep, so it was easy to get downtown early. But I didn't want to drag my anxious, furiously beating heart to the waiting room to sit there among addiction books waiting for the door to swing open. I'd walk around the block—past Old Navy, down to Carson Pirie Scott, and then east toward the El tracks on Wabash. Sometimes I made two loops, assuring myself: *You're just a woman going to therapy; you're going to sit in a circle and talk for ninety minutes. Easy peasy.*

Sometimes sessions were as emotionally charged as a juicer demonstration at Sam's Club. One week we spent an *entire* session discussing the insurance forms that Carlos wanted Dr. Rosen to sign. Another time, when Patrice showed up with two different colored knee-high stockings (one midnight indigo, the other ebony), we debated for fifteen minutes whether it was progress for fastidious Patrice to mess up her hosiery or whether she was backsliding into self-neglect. There was no tidy conclusion, no resolution.

There were disclosures. There was feedback. There was looking, seeing, and being seen. There were no answers.

I wanted answers.

Pivots happened without warning. One second, quiet Marty, the guy who started the same day I did, would be crying as he described his disturbing cache of death mementos—namely, the cyanide tablets he kept in his bedside table in case he ever wanted to end it all—and then suddenly the group conversation pinged to the time I had pinworm in kindergarten. Pinworm, a common childhood parasite, produces agonizing nighttime anal itching. I told the group how, at five years old, alone in my room at 6644 Thackeray Avenue, I scratched my ass like a feral dog for hours into the night, long after my parents flipped off *The Tonight Show* and went to sleep.

"Did your parents know you had it?" Rory asked.

"Wait," I said, holding up my hands. "We were talking about Marty's cyanide." How had the group landed on my five-year-old butt?

"The group has a way of uncovering things you might need to let go of," Dr. Rosen said.

Dr. Rosen loved detail, so I took a deep breath and described how my parents gave me a tube of Desitin for pinworm, but it didn't relieve the itching. By morning, the stinky white paste was ground under my fingernails and smeared all over my sheets, my nightgown, my butt, and my vagina, which was not where the pinworms were, but everything got confused during the long night of scratching. My mauled vagina, the cream that smelled like fertilizer, and my itchy ass were excruciating. But worse than the physical discomfort was the horrific knowledge that there were live worms in my butt.

"Desitin is a topical solution for diaper rash, and pinworm is a parasite. You would have needed mebendazole," Dr. Rosen said, sounding super doctor-y and looking very Harvard, with his furrowed brow. I longed to dart to someone else's issues, but the group snared me with its questions. Like why I didn't tell my parents Desitin didn't work.

"I thought it was my fault the medicine wasn't working." I wasn't supposed to scratch—they told me not to, but I did. All night long. Plus, who wants to talk about butt worms? Shame, a word I didn't know at five, had clamped my mouth shut.

"You were already committed to doing things alone by age five," Dr. Rosen said like it was a big revelation, but it didn't feel like one. When I had pinworm, I was embarrassed—in Rosen-speak *ashamed*—about being a dirty girl with worms in my butt, worms that weren't crawling through my brother's or my sister's asses. Worms were proof that my body was defective and disgusting. Dr. Rosen pressed me to describe how it felt to be a little girl alone in a fight with an anal parasite.

I shuddered and squeezed my eyes shut. From a distance of two decades, I could smell the Desitin and feel the infernal itching between my legs. I'd never discussed pinworm with anyone, much less a rapt audience of six.

Without opening my eyes, I told them, unprompted, "I felt shame."

"Shame's a cover. What's underneath?" Dr. Rosen said.

I put my head in my hands and scanned my body for an answer. I lifted the corners of shame to see what lurked beneath. I saw my five-year-old face twisted in horror in my childhood bedroom as I scratched past midnight. Horror that I didn't know how to ask for help. That eventually I had to visit the pediatrician, a tall, middle-aged man with fat thumbs and a deep voice, and tell him all about my butt. That during reading circle at school I had to wedge the heel of my tennis shoe into my butt crack to ease the itching without anyone noticing. That I was dirty and lived in a body filled with food I couldn't stop eating and worms that made my butt itch. Most of all, horror that my body was a filthy problem, a problem that no one else had.

"Horror," I answered.

Dr. Rosen nodded his head in approval. "You're getting closer."

"To what?"

"Yourself and your feelings." He swept his arms around the room. "And of course us."

"How will this trip down memory lane help me?"

"Look at Patrice and ask her if she can identify." Patrice looked startled and shook her head like *don't look at me*. After a beat, she launched into a story about a medically administered enema that went wrong. Then Rory mentioned her distaste for anal sex, and Marty contributed a story about the intractable constipation he'd suffered as a kid. By the end of group, everyone had shared a butt story.

A few days after this session, I called my parents. My dad and I discussed my car's sticky brakes, the Aggies' prospects for the Cotton Bowl, and the unseasonably cool weather in Chicago. Then I pulled a Rosen: out of the blue, I asked him about my pinworm history. What did he remember? (not much) How many times did I get them? (several) Did my siblings ever have them? (no) In the background, I heard my mother's voice: "Why is Christie asking about pinworm?" I gripped the phone harder. The confession that I'd joined a therapy group gathered in my mouth, but dissolved when I imagined *her* horror upon realizing that I'd discussed my butt worm history with a group of people. Plus, if I told her about Dr. Rosen and group, I'd have to admit that I'd failed at both willing myself to be happy *and* not telling other people my business.

"Why are you asking?" my dad said.

"Just curious."

One Tuesday morning, no one said a word during the entire ninety-minute session. All of us literally sat in silence, listening to the El train lumber below, car brakes screeching, and someone shutting a door down the hall. We didn't catch each other's eyes or giggle. During the first half, I plucked lint off my sweater, jangled my leg, and picked my cuticles. I looked at the clock every thirty seconds. The silence made me feel exposed, antsy, and unproductive. *I could be reading my Constitutional Law assignment.* Gradually, I stilled and watched Lake Michigan out the window. The quiet space we were holding felt as vast as the ocean or outer space. The light streaming in the room seemed holy; the intimacy among us sacred. At nine, Dr. Rosen folded his hands and said his usual "We'll stop there for today."

As I walked down the hall with my group members, I carried the quiet calm in my body, though once we reached the street, I shook Carlos's arm: "What the fuck just happened in there?"

Whatever it was, through the rest of the day, I carried a quiet calm and sense of awe that I could sit with six other people in total silence for ninety minutes.

Dr. Rosen gave a lot of prescriptions, though rarely for drugs. He wasn't a pill guy. Carlos got a prescription to bring his guitar to group and play a song for us to help allay his fears about expanding his practice. Patrice got a prescription to rub strawberries on her husband's stomach, lick them off, and then report the results to group. And because Dr. Rosen thought that the prescription Rory's internist gave her for anxiety was suppressing her sexual feelings, he gave her his own: "Put one pill between each of your toes while your husband goes down on you."

I'd been following my prescription to call Rory every night to tell her my food for a few weeks. I no longer cried after I hung up the phone, and my apple consumption was down to a modest five per night. It was time for another prescription.

"Can I have something for my insomnia. I can't think straight." My second year of law school was under way, and when I wasn't sitting in group, I was interviewing with Chicago's biggest law firms for a summer internship, which I hoped would lead to an offer for full-time employment. Not sleeping well for weeks meant that fatigue pressed against my skull, making it hard to stay awake for classes and interviews. At Winston & Strawn, I'd pinched the inside of my arm to stay awake while a white-haired managing partner described the time he argued before the Supreme Court.

I'd already confessed that my eating was a hot steamy mess; now I admitted I couldn't sleep. I was a newborn baby stuck in a twenty-seven-year-old's body.

Dr. Rosen sat up and rubbed his hands together like a mad scientist. "Call Marty tonight before you go to sleep and ask for an affirmation."

"Before or after I call Rory to tell her what I ate?"

"Doesn't matter."

"I'm going to the opera tonight, so call me before seven," Marty said.

At six fifty that night, I stood on the train platform at Belmont, exhausted from the long day of classes and a five-hour interview at Jones, Day, where again I'd pinched in the inside of my arm to stay awake while talking to senior partners. I dialed Marty's number as wind slapped my hair into my face.

"I'm calling for my affirmation," I said into the phone as the lights of an incoming northbound train rose toward the platform.

"You have great legs, toots." Marty wasn't skeevy, like Colonel Sanders. He wept every time he opened his mouth in group and seemed genuinely astonished when we asked to know more about what made him so sad. He always said, "I just can't believe anyone is listening to me."

I laughed into the roar of the oncoming train and prayed his words would work like an extra-strength Ambien.

The next morning I hesitated before opening my eyes, afraid to see that it was only two A.M. I heard morning sounds. My neighbor's door slamming. Birdsong. A car starting. I opened my left eye and saw the clock—five fifteen. I'd gotten an unprecedented seven hours of sleep. I pumped my fist like a champion.

Maybe Dr. Rosen was brilliant.

7

As winter descended on Chicago, I practiced bringing mundane issues to group. A prickle of shame skidded down my spine when I asked my group to weigh in on matters I should know how to handle as a reasonably intelligent twenty-seven-year-old, like whether I should use some of my financial aid money to go on a ski trip organized by my college roommate Kat. The group unanimously voted yes to the trip. Dr. Rosen pressed me for a good reason *not* to go.

"It's all couples. I'll be the eleventh wheel."

"Be open," Dr. Rosen said.

I can't believe it! You never come to anything! Kat wrote when I accepted her invitation.

On the Tuesday morning between Christmas and New Year's, I dialed Rory's cell from a cabin in Crested Butte. It was my first time missing a session.

"Hi, sweetie, let me put you on speaker." I heard a rustling and then Rory's voice, slightly muffled: "Everyone say hi to Christie." A chorus of hellos in the background.

"What're y'all doing?" I asked, picturing each of them in their regular spots, the gray Chicago sky out the window.

"It's boring without you," Carlos said.

"Y'all miss me?" Weren't they grateful to have a break from me and my pitiful stories of too many apples, too many worms?

"Everyone's nodding," Rory said. "Even Dr. Rosen."

My heart soared up over the Rocky Mountains and zoomed across the plains to the fourteen-by-fourteen room where they sat, where there was an empty chair my body usually fit, where they held me in their minds.

As a kid, my siblings and I would take turns visiting our paternal grandmother, who lived in a big yellow farmhouse in Forreston, Texas. I loved those weeks—I could roam around her property, looking for treasures by the creek and picking through bones at the cow graveyard. Once, I called home halfway through my visit. I can't remember why. I think I was testing my ability to make a long-distance call. The phone at 6644 Thackeray Avenue rang and rang. *Maybe they're at the neighborhood pool or in the backyard.* I tried again that night. No answer. Where could they be?

When my dad called that weekend to arrange a time to pick me up, I grabbed the phone from my grandma. "Where were y'all? I tried to call two nights ago."

"We went to Oklahoma for a few days."

They took a vacation without me? My vision blurred as tears gathered. I'd never been to Oklahoma, and suddenly I was desperate to go—to see whatever they'd seen. Cool stuff like authentic tepees tended by women in long black braids and working oil rigs dotting a straight dusty highway. How could they travel—cross the state line!—without me? This clearly meant I wasn't an integral part of my family, and the realization made me want to curl up and bawl.

On the other end of the phone my dad explained that they'd gone to pick up an antique armoire from a family friend in Ponca City. "The Howard Johnson's a/c was broken, and your mother is still mad at me for making her eat at a Kentucky Fried Chicken, where we watched a dog eat a rat in the parking lot." He spoke as if the trip was a disaster, but all I could hear was that magical, wondrous things happened in this land called *Oklahoma.* And I heard this: *You don't matter. We vacation without you, because you don't matter.*

For years, my mother would shudder whenever the trip to Oklahoma came up. There was not a single picture, and no member of my family harbored a happy memory from their weekend jaunt to Oklahoma. And yet I too would shudder at the mention of the state due north of Texas because it was proof that I could be left behind.

ᒻᒻᒻ

Winter also brought my first date since joining group. Carlos set me up with his friend Sam, an attorney who was fresh out of a relationship. In our first phone conversation, Sam and I established an easy rapport. He admitted that he'd never seen an episode of *Survivor*, and I confessed I abandoned *Harry Potter* after the first chapter. When I got off the phone because my book club meeting was about to start, he sounded impressed that a busy law student would also take the time to read for pleasure.

I had every reason to believe that Sam and I would hit it off. We both adored Carlos and had mixed feelings about the legal profession. I watched out the window as he parked his car in front of my apartment at eight o'clock sharp. My belly stirred with excitement. In the bathroom, I applied one more coat of the lipstick Carlos picked out for me at Barneys.

When I opened the door, I thought we'd hug, but he stuck out his hand and smiled in a clinical way that didn't reach his eyes. He then turned quickly to head down the stairs, like a man who had double parked in front of a hydrant. I didn't despair, though. The whole night stretched before us full of possibility and, perhaps later, physical contact.

Sam hadn't made a reservation and offered no suggestions about where to go. An awkward silence hung between us until I suggested a Cuban place on Irving Park near my apartment. As we drove, the only sound in the car was my voice giving him directions. Had I made up the chemistry I felt on the phone?

At Café 28, Sam left his wool Burberry scarf wrapped around his neck and was curt with the waitstaff. By the time our food came, it was clear this was going nowhere. The disappointment made me want to smash my fist into the stupid potatoes and hurl my salmon across the room. I'd bought lipstick and a sweater for this. I'd been going to group, calling Rory, calling Marty, and "letting the group in" as Dr. Rosen suggested. Where were the results? Why was Sam so remote and uninterested?

We rode home in silence so complete it was nuclear. Sam did not walk me to the door; he did not cut the engine. Maybe he stuck his hand out for a closing handshake, but I'd turned my back on him after thanking him for dinner. When I walked into my apartment, the clock read eight fifty.

My date hadn't even lasted an hour.

I dialed Dr. Rosen's number; his was number one, the valedictorian of my speed dial. To his voice mail, I announced my conclusion. "Therapy isn't working. Please call me tomorrow. I'm sinking." I paced in circles around my apartment, wondering why Sam hadn't given me a chance. I shared the humiliation with Rory when I called with my food report, and Marty when I called for my affirmation.

"It's not your fault the date sucked," they promised. "Some dates just suck."

The next day I did something I'd never done in my entire educational career: Skipped class to huddle under the covers and stare into the void. I didn't watch TV, read a book, or review any notes for class. Around noon, my closest friend from law school, Clare, left a voice mail. "Hey, no one can remember the last time you didn't show up for class. Call me."

The familiar stuckness I'd felt most of my life shut out every other thought, every other sensation. It felt like it would always be there, obstructing my breath, my blood, my desire. Stuck, stuck, stuck. Therapy was supposed to change things, open me up. A cry was forming somewhere in my chest, like a hurricane gathering force way off the coast of Florida. The stuckness felt like my fault. How would this ever change? I sank into self-hate as I counted ridges on my popcorn ceiling. What was the point of those Tuesday sessions if I was going to remain this stuck?

At three fifteen, Dr. Rosen's number glowed on my phone's screen.

"Can you help me?" I said instead of hello.

"I hope so."

"Why was my date such a disaster?"

"Who says it was a disaster?

"It was fifty minutes long. I didn't even go to school today—I'm in bed."

"Congratulations."

"For what?"

"When was the last time you made this much space for your feelings?"

"Um." He knew the answer was never.

"You deserve space to feel."

"But what should I *do*?"

"What were you doing before I called?"

"Staring at the ceiling."

"Do that. And come to group tomorrow."

"That's it?"

He laughed. "*Mamaleh*, that's plenty."

It didn't feel like enough. But my body unclenched when I got off the phone. Rational thoughts filled my head: Sam was one of thousands of men in Chicago. There was nothing wrong with me. It was one lame date. Big deal. It wasn't a reason to slip into catatonia.

In group, Dr. Rosen affirmed that all I had to do was keep coming to sessions. To him, the ninety minutes I sat in the circle with him and my group mates were the be-all and end-all of emotional transformation. To him, they were potent enough to score my still-smooth heart. To him, it was enough.

Not to me. I wanted a new prescription. Something bold and hard. Something that would require all my courage. Dr. Rosen wasn't taking my distress seriously. He didn't understand how it felt in my body. I was a window painted shut, a jar lid that wouldn't budge no matter how much you banged it on the counter.

I had to show him.

ur

Andrew Barlee called me out of the blue. I remembered him from a holiday party as a quiet guy with lapis-blue eyes who laughed at my jokes.

I agreed to meet him for brunch. Over eggs and potatoes, I studied his rough hands and his haircut that was almost a mullet. Did I like him? The gut answer was no. We had nothing in common, there was zero chemistry, and I couldn't stop wondering about his unironic eighties haircut. But I pushed that no down below my ribs with a list of his positive traits: He was kind, solvent, sober, and interested in me. So what if he didn't like to read? So what if he didn't seem interested in current events that didn't involve the Bears' prospects for the Super Bowl? So what if my body convulsed with resistance when he grabbed my hand on the way to his car?

Andrew offered to make dinner for me at his place for our second date. On the drive to his new condo in Rogers Park, the Friday-afternoon traffic crawled down Western. Frustrated after sitting through two green lights without moving forward an inch, I pounded on the steering wheel and screamed at the top of my lungs. I screamed so long and so loudly that my voice sounded hoarse for the next two days. I didn't want to go to Andrew's house, but I'd made myself say yes, because saying no meant I subconsciously wanted to be alone. *Andrew was a nice guy!* I screamed at myself. *Give him a chance!* How could I claim to be desperately lonely and then decline a date with a nice, sober man?

After a tour of his bright, tasteful one-bedroom apartment, Andrew grilled two chicken breasts and emptied a bag of lettuce into a ceramic bowl after dousing it with Hidden Valley Ranch. I smiled at his earnest efforts, even though my stomach was churning with that no that longed to rise up and fly out of my mouth.

We sat on his couch, balancing our plates on our knees and making polite small talk about his work and my family in Texas. When I looked at him head-on, I couldn't tell he had a mullet, but making conversation felt like bone grinding on bone—our words didn't flow naturally. Neither of us was witty or charming. This wasn't what I wanted: Dry-ass chicken breasts with a nice-enough guy whom I could barely talk to.

When we were done eating, I panicked. There was no more small talk inside me, so I scooted toward him and put my lips on his, hoping that kissing might spark something—something that might make me want to be there with him.

Andrew's eyes widened in surprise and then excitement. He kissed me back. I turned into a mechanical doll with no heat, no heart. I wanted to go home and hated myself for it. I also hated myself for rejecting Andrew for dumb reasons like his haircut. No wonder I was alone; I was a bitch. The no pulsed in my gut, but I pushed it down. Here was a nice guy sitting right in front of me, and if I didn't like him or wasn't into him, that was my own fault.

"Do you have a condom?" I said. Maybe I could fuck my way out of this stuckness. Maybe sex would make me feel an attraction to him.

I still had on my sweater, bra, underwear, jeans, socks, and boots. Andrew's red flannel shirt was tucked tightly into his belted jeans. His shoes were still tied. Moving from a chaste ninety-second make-out session to intercourse made as much sense as robbing the 7-Eleven on the corner. But between us, we lacked the skills or desire to slow down and figure out what the hell was actually happening.

There was no music. No mood lighting. Zero ambience, unless you counted the occasional wafts of charred chicken. Andrew pulled down his pants and slipped the condom on. I shimmied my jeans over my hips.

He moved on top of me. I bit my lower lip and stared at his ceiling. Poisonous thoughts ran through my head: *This is all you get. You will never feel anything. You are broken. Faulty score.* When I blinked, tears spilled out of both eyes. I held the sob back and composed the story I would tell in group: *Look what I did. Do you get it now? This is serious.*

Andrew struggled to get inside me. More stuckness. I tilted my hips to give him a better angle and speed things up. In three or four thrusts it was over. I felt nothing outside the thrum of self-hate. My breath never changed rhythm.

His phone rang as he was finishing up. Emergency at work. Andrew yanked his pants up. "Sorry, but I have to go." I didn't even know what his job was.

Back in my car, I dialed Dr. Rosen's number. I told his answering machine about the chicken breasts, the no in my gut, the sex that I instigated. "I tried to tell you. Please hear me."

Four days later in group: My eyes locked with Dr. Rosen's. My fists were tight with rage. How many more guys did I have to fuck for him to take me seriously? What would it take to wipe that smirk off his face?

"You think I can't see you." Dr. Rosen said.

"Do you get that I'm in a lot of pain?"

"Christie, I get that you are in a lot of pain."

"Can you help me?"

"Yes."

"What do I need to do?"

"You're doing it."

"It's not enough."

"Yes, it is."

"It hurts!" I banged my fists on the arms of the chair. "I hurt."

"I know."

"I never want to fuck like that again."

"You never have to fuck like that again."

"This isn't enough."

"Christie, it is enough."

How could it possibly be enough? The night with Andrew was a disaster on every level, and it was my fault. Yet I was the one who had a high-powered therapist and five supportive group members supposedly steering my life in a better direction.

"What's the point in all of this? The brass ring is just more shitty sex and disconnection."

"You're not at the brass ring yet," Dr. Rosen said. "But you're on your way."

I swept my arm around the room. "How come they're all ready and I'm not?" Every other person in group had a significant other next to whom they fell asleep every night. "How long is this going to take?" I imagined myself growing old and feeble as I waited for the miracle of group therapy to transform my life.

"I don't know how long it's going to take. Can you celebrate the steps you've taken so far?"

No, I couldn't. I didn't want to celebrate until I knew how much was left to do. The realization that there was no shortcut to the mental health I was working toward crushed my spirit. I'd ceded to the group my isolation and my secret eating rituals. Those were my long-cherished coping mechanisms. Now, for every interaction, including every single date, I had to show up without my primary defenses, which sounded healthy in theory, but what it felt like that morning in group was a stunning, irrevocable defeat. There would be no more solace in apple binges, no retreats to my hermetically sealed life. There would be the bright light of Dr. Rosen's and my group mates' gaze illuminating all my deficits, but no secret cave to stash my feelings. So I had them right there in my chair: I wept for how lonely I felt and how deeply afraid I was that my life would never truly change or, worse, that true change would ask more of me than I could give. And had the session not ended at nine, I'm certain I could have cried my way to the lunch hour.

8

"*You should tell the group about the Smoker,*" *Carlos said.*

On the elevator ride up to group, I'd told Carlos about the Smoker— so named because he loved his cigarettes and because he was smoking hot—my newest crush at law school. He had a girlfriend, but she was never around. Her name was Winter, and she was a waitress. I'd hoped that she was ugly or dirty or mean, but when I finally saw her serving pitchers at John Barleycorn, I couldn't deny that she was a willowy, fresh-faced beauty who offered a genuine smile to all of her customers.

The Smoker and I had struck up a friendship because we both spent hours in the computer lab, typing up our notes between classes. In our first encounter, he asked me to watch his books while he stepped out to smoke. Of course I said yes. I loved his five o'clock shadow, his smoky-smelling sweater, the shy way he looked away when he laughed.

"The Smoker?" Dr. Rosen cocked his head.

"This guy at school. Has a girlfriend. Smokes like a chimney. Drinks heavily. I'm falling in love with him."

"He's unavailable," Patrice said.

Dr. Rosen paused, covered his mouth with his hand, shifted his position, and then put his hands on the arms of his chair. Finally he said, "Next time you're with him, tell him the truth."

"Which is?"

"That you're a cocktease."

I looked at Carlos. Was Dr. Rosen for real? Everyone in the circle shook their heads, like *No, Dr. Rosen, she can't say that.* Rory blushed from behind her hands.

"You want me to tell the guy I have the hots for that I'm a 'cocktease'? Then what?" Wasn't the Smoker the tease? He was the one flirting with me despite his apple-cheeked girlfriend. If you would have asked me before this session if Dr. Rosen, my middle-aged psychiatrist with the rubber-soled brown shoes who knew nothing of pop culture ("Who's Bono?" he once asked), knew the term *cocktease*, I would have sworn he didn't. Now, as part of my therapeutic treatment, he was telling me to drop it into conversation with the guy I wanted to bed.

"We'll find out."

Two nights later, I sat in a speeding yellow taxi going west on Lake Street with the Smoker and his affable sidekick, Bart, a jokey kid from our law school class. The air was sticky but the sky was clear. A sliver of moon smirked at me. We rolled the windows down to cut the stench of the tree-shaped potpourri dangling from the rearview mirror. I leaned out the window and turned my face to the inky sky and its cheerful moon. A laugh caught in my throat—I held it for a few seconds and then let it out. Over the pulsing music, I sat upright, squared my shoulders, and turned toward the Smoker, who was sitting between me and Bart.

"I'm a total cocktease." The "total" I added as a personal flourish to prove I wasn't a mindless Rosen automaton.

The Smoker stopped chewing his postcigarette gum and froze. Then a smile spread across the horizon of his beautiful face. He kept his eyes fixed straight ahead. My skin tingled as I watched him take in my words. I wanted to wrap my legs around him and rock myself against him and his perfectly frayed Levi's.

Bart craned his head around the Smoker's chest and peered over at me.

"Say what?"

"You heard me," I said, turning my head toward the window.

"No, I didn't," Bart said.

"Then why are you so determined to get me to say it again—"

"Because—"

"Because you heard me the first time."

"Damn. You crazy, girl." Bart's cackle was picked up by the wind, and it dissolved into the night, right along with my pride.

The Smoker kept smiling and drumming his fingers on his long, ropy thighs. Mortification slowly set in as I realized the Smoker wasn't going to make a move on me. He would hang out with me and Bart for another hour and then go home and slip between the covers to wait for Winter's shift to end so they could fuck until dawn. I focused on the buildings we whizzed by along Milwaukee Avenue. Furniture stores, taco joints, Myopic Books. People waiting in line to hear a band at Subterranean. None of them knew what I'd said. Below the humiliation I felt the bud of something else: pride that I'd done what Dr. Rosen said. Saying those words had been a high-dive plunge, requiring all the courage I could summon. Now that a few minutes had passed, I realized that saying those words stitched me closer to Dr. Rosen and my group. And in four days I would sit in the circle and recount this night during which I had triumphed over my nerves—and better judgment—to follow Dr. Rosen's advice.

When we got to the Bucktown bar, we found that there was no room on its outdoor patio, so the Smoker lit up a cigarette on the sidewalk. Bougainvillea spilled over the fence and smelled faintly sweet.

"Want one?" he asked, holding out his pack of Marlboros.

Oh, how I wanted to say yes so we could have a perfect moment together sucking in and puffing out like beautiful people in the movies, people with no mental health issues, no sexual hang-ups, no eating disorders, no worms. If I said yes, he would lean in close and light my cigarette. His smell—the smoke, the gum, the day's residue—would become part of my memory.

But I couldn't make myself take one. Dr. Rosen had recently explained to Rory, when she mentioned how much she missed cigarettes, that when you smoke you are inhaling toxic self-hatred.

"No thanks," I said.

The following Tuesday, I rode the Red Line train downtown before group as the sun inched over the tree line. I'd been up since four—despite calling Marty for an affirmation the night before—and decided to head downtown to sit in a coffee shop.

I nursed a cup of tea and stared out the window on Madison Street. A bright yellow backpack—like one you'd expect Curious George's handler to wear—caught my eye. The man wearing it walked a half beat slower than everyone else, as if he were touring an English garden. He looked shorter than average—barely my height—and his lips were moving slightly like he was having a conversation with himself. I took him for a tourist and fished the tea bag out of my cup. Not until he was almost out of view did it hit me: Dr. Rosen.

It definitely was him—that untamed hair, those slightly hunched shoulders. How was he so puny? In group, he seemed so huge—larger than life—as I begged him for prescriptions, solutions, and answers.

I watched until he disappeared down Madison, taking his sweet time, mumbling to himself.

Why did he walk so slowly? He was headed to work—to *my* group session—not on a pilgrimage to Medjugorje. Why the mumbling? Where'd he get that god-awful backpack?

By the time I'd finished my tea and headed to group, I faced the harder question: Was my therapist a complete freak? Why did I take his advice on what to say to the Smoker? Why did I give that strange little man so much power?

As I walked toward group, I prayed, "Please kill the Buddha."

9

Everyone else in group got a special sex assignment. Colonel Sanders got a prescription to rub his wife's back without pressuring her for sex. Patrice got a prescription involving sex toys. Carlos had been advised to get naked and hold his fiancé, Bruce, for ten minutes every night. Marty was supposed to invite his live-in lady friend, Janeen, to take a shower with him. Dr. Rosen renewed Rory's prescription to have her husband go down on her while she put her Adderall between her toes.

I listened and burned with envy. "I want a sex assignment but I don't have a partner."

Dr. Rosen rubbed his hands together as if he'd been waiting weeks for me to ask. "I suggest you bookend your masturbation with Patrice."

I rubbed my temples and squeezed my eyes shut. "Do what?"

"Call up Patrice." Dr. Rosen pretended to dial a phone and then held his hand like a receiver. "Say, 'Hi, Patrice. I'm going to masturbate now. I'm calling because I want your support with my sexuality. It's worked really well with my food and now I'd like to work on my sexuality.' Then, when you're done, call her back and say, 'Thank you for your support.'"

"No." I stood up. "Absolutely not."

Intellectually, I understood there was nothing wrong with masturbation—Dr. Ruth taught me that. Pleasure was nothing to be ashamed of. In theory. But in practice, I could manage pleasure only in secret, hidden under the covers in the dark of night. I had never—and could never—talk about self-pleasure. The ghosts of all the nuns who told me that sex was only for procreation with my Catholic husband haunted me. In sixth-grade health class Sister Callahan spent several awkward minutes explaining that masturbation was a "grave sin because each wasted sperm could have been a new life." Sister Callahan didn't mention the possibility that girls might engage in such behavior, which seemed like proof that girls didn't—and shouldn't—ever masturbate. It was unspeakable.

The technical term for my condition was *sexual anorexia*. The anorexia most people are familiar with is someone who severely restricts her food. A sexual anorexic like me starved herself of sex by chasing unavailable alcoholics, who usually had girlfriends, who did not or could not be intimate, or by forcing herself to have sex without any attraction to her partner. The label intrigued me—as a chubby kid, I'd longed for a sleek label like "anorexic." Now I wasn't sure I loved the label, but it made me feel less alone. If there was a name for me and my condition, that meant I wasn't the only one.

There was no way I could "bookend my masturbation." I stared at Dr. Rosen and shook my head.

"But you call me about your apples," Rory said.

"This is different."

"How so?" Dr. Rosen said.

"You can't see the difference between apples and masturbation?" My neck contracted into my clavicle at the thought of calling Patrice. Calling Patrice about *that* was lighting up a flare: *Guess what, world! I'm wacking off!* It violated the Catholic Church's anti-onanism rules and my mother's don't-tell-people-your-business rule. The prescription was outrageous, perverted, impossible.

"Do you want my take?" Dr. Rosen said. "Eating ten apples after dinner—"

"I'm down to four—"

"Okay, four, but eating those apples wasn't pleasurable. You wanted it to stop. Stopping a negative behavior is radically different than getting support for starting a pleasurable one. You are more resistant to pleasure. That's why I'm giving you this prescription—"

"Which I cannot do." I should quit group.

"You have other choices," Dr. Rosen said.

Rory tapped my foot with the tip of her boot and suggested I ask for something gentler. I took a deep breath. Was I going to drown in despair or was I willing to ask for what I needed?

"Can you dial it down?" I whispered.

Dr. Rosen smiled and paused. "How about this? You bookend taking a bath with Patrice."

"No requirement that I do or touch or rub anything while I'm in there?"

"Strictly utilitarian."

"Done." My whole body relaxed. I could take a goddamn bath. I was back in the game.

Dr. Rosen stared at me.

"What?" I asked.

"When was the last time you told someone that you weren't ready for what they were asking you to do?"

Senior year of high school, I dated Mike D., a basketball star who smoked pot daily. He was my first real boyfriend, and I wanted desperately to be a good girlfriend, whatever that meant. Before me, Mike dated a cheerleader who, apparently, gave amazing head. When he hinted he missed her deep throat, I felt summoned to suck his dick. But at seventeen, I'd only visited first base briefly, three years earlier. Blow jobs were third-base territory, and my ignorance about them made my throat constrict with panic. Where would my hands go? How long would I have his penis in my mouth? What would it taste like? When he pushed my head under the blankets, I shoved my fear down my throat and into my belly. When I tried to come up for air to ask for a performance review, Mike pushed my head back down. I've revisited my sweaty head under that blanket thousands of times, always wondering why I felt bereft of choices, words, and the right to lift the blanket and take a breath. Or to not suck his dick in the first place. I did it because I wanted to be a good girlfriend and good girlfriends say yes.

In college, my roommate Cherie graduated a semester ahead of me. Free-spirited Cherie's postcollege plans entailed couch surfing in Colorado until she started graduate school. When she asked me to drive her Jetta to Denver after graduation, I should have said no. I was supposed to be in Dallas visiting family and working a part-time mall job. Driving Cherie, her bike, and her duffel bag full of tie-dyed shirts to the Mile High City was inconvenient and expensive. But I said yes because the thought of saying no made my stomach clench. I wanted to be a good friend. Good friends say yes.

Before moving to Chicago for graduate school, I got a job at Express in my college town, selling skorts to sorority girls. I got promoted to assistant manager after a few months. My supervisor often showed up to work with long, bloody scratches on her forearms—either from a feral cat or a serious self-harm habit—and would ask me to cover for her several times a month. Saying yes meant I had to work ten hours without a break—assistant managers were not allowed to leave the store unattended, even to run over to Chick-Fil-A for a snack. My supervisor would be at home engaging in mysterious physical behavior, and I'd be asking a stock boy to cover the registers so I could pee. It never occurred to me to say no, though. I wanted to be a good employee, and good employees say yes.

Yes was who I thought I was supposed to be as a girlfriend, friend, employee. A girl, and then a woman, in the world. When someone asked me to jump I prepared to leap without thinking about whether I was hungry or knew the route to Denver or knew what the fuck to do with a penis in my mouth.

I told Dr. Rosen I wasn't in the habit of saying no. He asked if I knew what that cost me. I shook my head. Costs? People liked me because I was a Yes Girl. If I went around saying no, then what? They'd be mad at me. Disappointed. *Unhappy.* I couldn't tolerate that. That kind of audacity belonged to other people, like guys and hot women with no emotional baggage.

"If you can't say no in relationships, then you can't be intimate," Dr. Rosen said.

"Say that again." I held still so that each word would seep inside me, past my skin and muscle, and settle in my bones.

"If you can't say no, there can be no intimacy."

People said no to me all the time, and I still loved them. Is this what people were learning in high school when I was bingeing on Girl Scout Thin Mint cookies and making mixtapes with Lionel Richie and Whitney Houston songs?

⁓

As my old claw-footed bathtub filled with sudsy, lavender-scented water, I left Patrice a voice mail completing part one of the "bookend." I'd purposely dialed her cell phone because she turned it off at night. I held my breath as I slid into the nearly scalding water. The bubbles made tiny rustling sounds. I leaned my head against the hard porcelain edge and exhaled. My breath hitched—a hint I might cry, but I squeezed my eyes shut and shook my head. I didn't want to blubber through this—I wanted to be a normal fucking woman taking a bath to relax. After two minutes, I wanted to get out. I'd filled the prescription, swallowed the medicine. Now I had things to do, like make three phone calls to three different group members.

But then I put my palms over my heart and took a deep breath. Tears welled in my eyes, and I let them come. What I felt was relief. Intense, cascading, pure relief. *No might belong to me too.*

Everybody else said no. My college roommate Kat was blunt, sassy, and secure. In college, she told a handsy Phi Delt to "fuck off" when he asked her for a blow job. There was no fist of anxiety in her stomach telling her she had to give him head. At age five, my headstrong brother had an hour-long stand-off with my parents when they insisted he eat a bite of tuna sandwich. He won the tuna showdown while I forced myself to eat every awful, mayonnaise-filled bite, crust and all. Carlos pushed back on Dr. Rosen insisting he was never going to bring in his guitar and sing for the group.

Meanwhile, I considered quitting group so I wouldn't have to look at Dr. Rosen and say, "Nope. I can't bookend my masturbation with Patrice."

I cupped water into my hands and let it drain through my fingers. I'd always hated baths. What's so relaxing about submerging in water when there's nothing to stare at except a tiled wall or parts of my body beneath the suds? I hated looking at my body. I always ended up picking it apart—unshaven legs, unpedicured toes, unperky breasts, untoned stomach, and unsmooth thighs. All that scrutiny and shame drowned whatever pleasure I was supposed to be deriving from taking a bath, the pastime that was supposedly beloved by all womankind.

I still saw those things—the chipped red polish, the hairy legs, the lumpy flesh. And I still felt the heat of shame prickling my skin. But alongside it, a spark of something lighter and cooler chased the tail of the shame, and I had the barest sliver of a notion that I could have a different relationship with and to my body and then maybe with other people.

My fingertips pruned as the water cooled to room temperature. A shiver ran down my neck as I sat up. I wrapped myself in a pink-and-white striped beach towel and sat on the edge of the bathtub.

I dialed Patrice's cell. "I did it. Good night."

I called Rory to report my food.

I called Marty to collect my affirmation. "You've got what it takes, kiddo," he said in Groucho Marx accent.

I laughed. My neck and shoulder muscles were warm and loose from the bath. I had a woozy, half-asleep feeling. "I love you," I said, cupping the phone with my still-pruned fingers. The words just slipped out.

"Of course you do, sweetie. I love you too. Isn't this fun?" I smiled. *Fun* was not quite the word I would have used for the warm expansive feeling spreading across my chest, but I couldn't think of better one.

In bed, I had a vision: My group members' hands tucked under me like in the childhood game Light as a Feather, Stiff as a Board. They worked together to invoke whatever spirits would help lift me up, up, up. I could feel Dr. Rosen's hands cradling my head, Carlos and the Colonel at my shoulders, Patrice and Rory on each hip, and Marty at my feet. I did love them. For their presence, their effort, and their strong hands on my body. They were etching themselves into my life.

It thrilled me, made me want to bawl, and it scared me to death.

10

Fat tears rolled down Marty's face one spring Tuesday. There was a silver tin in his lap, the size and shape of a small drum or a container of Williams-Sonoma Christmas cookies. He said he was sick of all the death. He didn't want it anymore.

This was good work for Marty. He appeared congenial and functional on the outside, but we all knew about his stash of cyanide. Dr. Rosen mentioned it almost every session and urged him to bring it to group.

"It looks like you're ready to let that go," Dr. Rosen said, gesturing at the tin.

"What's in there?" the Colonel asked.

Marty held the tin up to his heart. "The remains of a child."

I dug my heel into the carpet and scooted my chair back. Babies were supposed to be fat-cheeked and loud—cooing, squalling, crying. They weren't supposed to sealed up in a tin can.

Marty explained that the baby, who died when he was less than a month old, had been the son of one of his first patients in his psychiatry practice. The patient had asked Marty to keep the remains years ago while he worked through his grief, but then the patient died. Now Marty was asking Dr. Rosen what to do with this memento mori.

Dr. Rosen loved to stir up everyone's feelings around death. If you made a pie chart of group topics, the two biggest pieces were sex and death. And if there was a trauma connected to a death experience, then Dr. Rosen would nudge you about it on at least a bimonthly basis. Rory had to talk about the Holocaust every other time she told a story, even if the decimation of European Jews in the 1940s had seemingly nothing to do with the late fees on her Citibank card. When Patrice struggled with a complex issue at work, Dr. Rosen pivoted right to her brother's suicide. Naturally, he nudged me to discuss the accident in Hawaii regularly. Usually, I backed away and reminded him to focus on my sex life, not my great misfortune of witnessing a death on a trip to the beach when I was thirteen.

Marty handed the tin to Dr. Rosen, who inspected it and said something in Hebrew. Dr. Rosen told Marty that if he was ready to let go of his preoccupation with death, he'd be able to embrace his life more fully, and he'd grow closer to his longtime partner, Janeen.

A somber silence fell over the group. A wave of feeling swelled in my chest—memory flashes from Hawaii—but I pushed it down; I was convinced it was just sadness I was manufacturing to match the group mood.

Meanwhile, I had an urge to cross my legs in defiance. Where was Dr. Rosen's magic trick for me? What had I stashed in my closet that I could bring to group and voilà! I'd be ready for intimacy and closeness? Marty and I had started on the same day, and now he was lapping me. I'd come to Dr. Rosen wishing for death because I was chronically and fundamentally alone, but Marty had *cyanide pills* in his bedside table. And somehow he was leaping forward? I let the jealousy and anger rise, but said nothing.

With only fifteen minutes left in the session, Dr. Rosen turned his attention to Marty's tin. "Pick someone to hold that for you." I gazed at the splotchy carpet as Marty scanned the room. Surely he would pick Patrice, the Mama Bear of the group.

"Christie."

Holy flaming Freud balls. I narrowed my eyes at Marty, afraid and annoyed that he picked me to hold a baby who never got to grow up, whose flesh and bones were now sealed up in a silver tin. I scowled at Dr. Rosen for orchestrating this whole morbid affair. I wanted to stand up and beat my head with my fists and scream until my throat was shredded: "I'm not here for death and bones and ashes! I'm here for life! I WANT TO LIVE!"

How did it make sense that I, a random woman from Marty's therapy group, was suddenly the custodian of this tin? Didn't the baby deserve to be in the hands of someone who loved him or his parents dearly? The randomness was unbearable.

Dr. Rosen directed Marty to look at me and ask if I would take the tin. When Marty and I locked eyes, I saw his pain but couldn't bear it. I turned to Dr. Rosen.

"How about I take Marty's cyanide pills?"

"I don't think so," said Dr. Rosen. A pause. Then, "You don't have to do that, you know."

"What?"

"Make a joke when you're scared or upset or angry. Deflect."

"How's this? Fuck you, Dr. Rosen." Dr. Rosen rubbed his heart with his palm, a gesture I'd seen before. He once explained that when someone shared their anger with him directly, it was a sign of love that he folded into his heart as a blessing.

"Better."

"Okay," I whispered, chastened. I asked Marty what the baby's name was.

"Jeremiah."

I couldn't abandon Baby Jeremiah. Some part of that beloved child was still in that tin, and I wouldn't turn my back on him. I was selfish and self-absorbed, but I was not a total monster. My outstretched arms reached for the tin.

Dr. Rosen passed the tin to Patrice, who handed it to me. I took it into my hands and held it perfectly still. I did not want to *feel* the contents inside. As I lowered the tin into my lap, I imagined it filled with tiny seashells. I tried really hard not to think about bones. An image of me rocking and sobbing, while cradling the tin, flashed through my mind, but a plume of anger at Dr. Rosen snuffed out the tender grief.

"Question," I said to Dr. Rosen. "Marty gets closer to Janeen if he lets Jeremiah go, but what happens to me if I take him?"

After uttering a few *mmm*s and *umm*s at the ceiling, he said, "For you, these ashes represent your attachment to this group. You need the group's support to lean into death, to stop running from it." He leaned forward as if he was afraid I couldn't hear him. "You want to move forward? Start feeling."

"I don't know." My shaking hands gripped the tin.

"You don't know what?"

"How to do it. Or if I can."

"*Mamaleh,* it's already happening."

Two weeks later, Marty pulled out an envelope and presented it to Dr. Rosen.

"My pills," Marty said. He poured the yellow disks into his palm and offered them to Dr. Rosen, who stood up and said, "We're going to have a funeral." We followed Dr. Rosen to the small bathroom just outside the group room. Rory held Marty's hand until he was ready to let them go. Dr. Rosen announced that he would now recite the Mourner's Kaddish.

"What are we mourning?" I asked.

"The death of Marty's suicidality."

"*L'chaim,*" Carlos said.

"That means 'to life,'" the Colonel said to me, putting a gnarled hand on my shoulder.

"I've seen *Fiddler on the Roof*," I said, moving his hand off me.

"*L'chaim* indeed," Dr. Rosen said, glowing at Marty, who dropped the pills into the toilet and watched them swirl until they disappeared.

After we flushed Marty's pills, we took our seats back in the group room. Dr. Rosen stared at me.

"You ready?" he said.

"For what?"

"You know what."

"I don't."

"I think you do."

Of course I did.

11

My luggage tag read " Christie Tate-Ramon." When Jenni's dad, David, handed it to me, he said, "I've always wanted two daughters." He hugged me, and then shooed me and Jenni into the taxi idling in the driveway. There were five of us: Jenni, her dad David, her mom Sandy, her brother Sebastian, and me. Freshman year of high school was six weeks away.

When we landed in Honolulu, everyone at the airport wore flowered shirts and greeted us with "Mahalo." On the drive to the hotel, we repeated it over and over like a blessing.

For three days, we explored the lush main island, stopping on the side of the road to marvel at waterfalls sprouting from the wall of a mountain, eating macadamia nuts, and snapping pictures of black sand beaches. The second night we attended an obligatory luau, where we all poked at the poi and wore fresh orchid leis.

On the fourth day, just after lunch, David loaded us kids into the rental sedan, along with towels and boogie boards. We were headed to a secluded black beach at the end of the highway, which we had seen during our first day of sightseeing. Sandy stayed at the condo to do laundry.

"Surf, surf, surf," David chanted as we drove along the curvy road that hugged the side of a mountain. Sebastian pushed a cassette into the tape deck and cranked the volume. The Cure sang moodily of beaches and guns. We rolled down the windows and sang at the top of our lungs, letting the breeze hit the back of our throats.

David parked the car and headed toward a shaded path where a "No Trespassing" sign hung on an iron fence, partially obscured by a flowering vine. I paused for a nanosecond, fear prickling my spine. We were breaking a rule. David continued to whistle. Above, the blue sky portended nothing but fresh air and a refreshing swim once we reached the beach. Bad things didn't happen in places with this many flowers.

We filed down in a straight line, me in the rear. My flip-flops strained to support me as I made my way down the steep mountain path.

When the trail leveled off and opened up to an expanse of wild grass, we could see the surf rolling to the shore. Black sand crystals glinted in the sunlight. David found a flat, dry spot for us to dump our stuff. There were no other people on the beach—no lifeguard chair, no laid-out beach towels, no signs of life. It felt like freedom to have this expanse of paradise all to ourselves. I peeled off my T-shirt and shorts. I adjusted the straps of my one-piece Ocean Pacific bathing suit, and Sebastian dove into the surf. Jenni and I trotted after him.

"I'll meet you down there." David hunched over his contact lens case with a travel-size bottle of saline solution.

The waves looked gentle, not unlike the swells at Padre Island on the Gulf Coast of Texas, where my family vacationed. The sky remained a harmless blue bowl. My biggest problem was that I wished my body was as lean as Jenni's.

Once I'd waded far enough that the water hit my midthighs, a wave knocked me over. My whole body sunk below the waterline, and the undertow dragged me downward. I struggled to get upright, but as soon as I cleared the surface of the water, another wave pushed me down again, and I somersaulted through the surf. Salt water stung my eyes and rushed up my nose. It felt like an invisible force below the sand was pulling me under, daring me to fight. Every time my head popped out of the water, I'd try to catch my breath, but would get knocked down before I could fill my lungs with air. Every effort to get myself upright failed.

I had to get out. Frantic, I flailed my arms and bicycled my legs, but the undertow continued to suck me back. When I finally landed in a spot where I could stand up, I gasped and coughed, almost doubled over with exhaustion. My head pounded from the effort of fighting the sea. I staggered out of the water.

Once I was onshore, my chest heaved with the effort of my escape. My arms ached from trying to claw my way through the water. Jenni emerged and walked toward me. We agreed that sunbathing would be more fun.

"Where's my dad?" she said, scanning the water.

I raised my hand to my forehead and surveyed the ocean—left, right, and left again. No sign of David. The fear prickled again, straight up my spine, nesting at the base of my neck.

"Oh my God!" Jenni pointed straight ahead and took off into the water. Ten yards in front of us, an orange object lolled in the water. David's board. Something large and white floated beside it.

David was facedown. A wave surged forward and delivered him to us in shin-deep water. We turned him over, and his eyes stared, unblinking, up at the sky. My breath came in shallow gasps. Water gushed from David's nose and mouth. So much water poured out of him. As if he contained half the ocean.

Jenni and I each grabbed an arm. We pulled him to the shore. Neither of us knew CPR, but we pumped his chest like we imagined we should. We screamed maniacally for Sebastian. With every thrust to David's chest, more water gushed out of his mouth and nose. His eyes stared unblinking at the sky, at nothing at all.

My teeth chattered uncontrollably, and my arms spasmed. I ran in place when I wasn't pumping David's chest because standing still meant that the truth of his open eyes and gushing mouth could find me and settle in. My mind spun out lies: *He'll be fine. People don't die on vacation. We'll laugh on the way home about that mean old Hawaiian surf.* I could still hear him whistling.

If we could just pump enough water out of him, he would sit up and cough.

"Oh my God!" Sebastian arrived, dripping wet and panting. He pressed on his dad's chest with his two open palms.

"I'll go get help," I said, and took off running, barefoot, still shaking— my legs desperate to be in motion. In stillness, the truth loomed, so I pumped my legs and hurled my body back up the mountain. The ghost of David whistling down the path just thirty minutes earlier haunted each step. Halfway up the trail, I tripped on a root and landed spread-eagle on the path. A long red gash opened on my knee. It looked like it should hurt, but I felt nothing. I was all heartbeat and panic. I'd flown out of my body and was already up the mountain begging someone to help us.

"No! No! Daddy, no!" Sebastian and Jenni's keening reached me from the beach. I scrambled to my feet. I had to keep running to drown out the unbearable sound of their mourning. Every time I stopped to catch my breath, I heard their cries. Picturing the two of them alone on the beach with their father's limp body drove me up the mountain.

When I made it to the top, I collapsed at the feet of four elderly golfers. I lay eye to eye with their white spiked shoes and the hems of their plaid pants. One of them bent over and stuck his face in mine. "You okay, little lady?"

"Someone's drowned—he's not dead," I insisted. To me, at that point, there was a difference between drowning and dying. "His kids are down there alone with him."

The four of them shuffled off, leaving me propped up against a boulder.

"He's not dead." A scream, a whisper, a dispatch straight from my trembling heart.

Stillness was terrifying. I scrambled to my feet and ran up the paved road for more help. Little pebbles gouged my feet but didn't pierce the skin. I ran faster. I found an abandoned cabin set back from the road. When no one answered my knocking, I burst through the unlocked door, screaming, "Phone! Phone!" In the darkened room, there was only a wooden table, a couple of chairs, and a stout bookshelf. No people, no light, no phone.

Back out on the road, I couldn't see the beach or hear Jenni and Sebastian. I stood in my bathing suit waiting for something to happen, shaking and twitching, with nowhere to run. A low guttural moan es- caped from my throat, a nonsense word, mashing up "no, no, no" and

12

After sharing all the awful details in one unbroken narrative, I felt lighter. I believed that taking up that space and letting my witnesses know what I experienced was all the healing I needed. Now my group knew about the Cure tape, David's contact lenses, the ravenous ocean, my bare feet on the trail, the root beer, the rain, the helicopter.

The next week, as I walked from the elevator to the group room, I imagined that Dr. Rosen would allude to the good work I'd done around Hawaii the week before. It was a wish: I wanted a gold star for finally letting the group witness the awful images I carried around from that traumatic summer. But as I reached the waiting room, I felt something else, something seemingly unrelated: anxiety about Dr. Rosen's upcoming vacation. He would be out for the next two weeks. Without these weekly sessions to anchor myself, I'd be pulled under by a wave of loneliness. Two weeks without group felt like two weeks without oxygen. Underneath the anxiety, I also felt angry. How could he abandon us for two whole weeks?

"Get on the floor and grab Carlos's leg," Dr. Rosen suggested fifteen minutes into the session when I shared how I felt about his upcoming absence. Grabbing Carlos's leg was supposed to soothe and ground me. It did neither.

"please, please, please." My hands held each side of my head as if it would split apart if I let go.

A family from Kansas—mom, dad, and teenage son—stopped at the lookout point. I waved my hands: "Help! Please!" Good news: the dad was a cardiologist. He and the son disappeared down the trail while the mother offered me a can of root beer and invited me to sit in her car. I sipped the sugary drink, still shaking, my body absorbing the awful truth.

A highway patrolman cruised by in a black truck, and the mother jumped out of the car to stop him. He stuck his head out of the window, and she whispered something to him. He peered at me and then promised to send help.

Thick gray clouds rolled in out of nowhere. Rain splattered the car. The rain turned to hail. I flinched as each ice pellet tapped the window. And still I shook. It felt like my molars would fall out from the chattering. I could still my body for a few seconds by holding my breath, but as soon as I gasped for air, the shaking started again.

Overhead, helicopter blades whirred in a staccato rhythm, a giant metal bird gliding toward the beach. The mother winced and grabbed my hand. She knew what it meant. The golfers appeared at the head of the footpath. I bolted from the car, hopeful still, about news from the beach, even though the two in front shook their heads. No, he didn't make it. No, he's dead. No, there is no more hope.

"The children are coming up behind us." Hope finally drained out of my body.

I could hear the hum of the blades even when there was nothing to see but the gray expanse of sky. The helicopter rose up over the mountain with a long rope hanging from its belly. At the end of the rope was a black body bag, swaying like a weighted tail. It sailed across the sky until it was only a tiny dot on the horizon.

The group energy had been frenetic and unfocused from the first moment. We zipped from Carlos's patient to Marty's wedding planning to Rory's sex life. Multiple side conversations broke out every time we switched topics, detracting from the main discussion. Dr. Rosen insisted it was our collective anxiety about not meeting for two weeks.

I wrapped my right arm around Carlos's shin and picked at the carpet with my left hand as Marty discussed life post–cyanide stash, when suddenly, the urge to scream at the top of my lungs came over me—it crept slowly upward from my stomach through my sternum and to the edge of my throat. It was too strong to hold down—like a sneeze or an orgasm. It flew out of me and stopped all movement in the room. *Aaaah-hhhhhhhhhh!* It was from my deep-down guts and it shook the walls.

"What the fuck?" Carlos said, peering down from his chair.

"I don't know what that was," I said, embarrassed by my primal wail that seemed to have no narrative, no trigger, and no explanation.

Unfazed, Dr. Rosen said, "Sure you do."

I heard the helicopter buzzing and felt my body constrict with panic. My mind zoomed to Hawaii, right above the waves and the black sand.

"Where do you think I'm going on vacation?"

"No idea."

"You have a picture in your head—"

"'Vacation' is a word, not a picture."

"Am I going skiing?"

"It's July."

"So where am I going?"

I blurted out, "Mexico. Fucking Playa del Carmen."

"What's in Mexico?"

"Pesos." Dr. Rosen didn't budge. The right answer blared in my head. "Beaches."

He slapped his hands together with an *ahhh*. "Do you have any feelings about me going to the beach?"

Pieces of the Hawaii story had trickled out during the first year of group, leading up to the gush of the previous session. Every time the subject arose, Dr. Rosen prodded me to express my feelings about it, and I resisted. I defended against the emotions by insisting it wasn't *that* big of a deal. *He wasn't my dad. It was so long ago.* It felt dramatic and somehow fake to wade into my feelings about Hawaii. I had so many excuses to scurry away from the subject. Plus, I didn't want to talk about being alone in my bathing suit, running uphill to get help, my bloody leg, David's vacant eyes, and the seawater pouring out of his face. None of the words I knew added up to the terror I felt, nor could they contain my grief.

And this: when we returned from Hawaii, Jenni and I started our freshman year at Ursuline Academy. Six weeks from that black sand beach where we watched David's limp body sway under the helicopter's belly, we put on our red-and-navy pleated uniform skirts and our penny loafers and shuffled from algebra and world history to PE and English. I sat in algebra watching Ms. Pawlowicz put complicated equations on the board and sat at lunch listening to other girls plan their outfits for the Michael Jackson concert. *Who cares? We're all going to die. None of this matters.* Those first few months, half of me was still in Hawaii, waiting for David to cough and wake up so I could resume a normal teenage life that revolved around my crush on Joe Monico or whether to get bangs. After school I slept for hours, and my parents grew concerned about my emotional state. I saw them staring at me during dinner, when I rested my heavy head on my open palm, and in the afternoon when I couldn't get off the couch. But we never talked about "the accident" in Hawaii. One evening, my parents knocked on my door and found me lying on my bed listening to the radio. They attempted small talk with me about homework and an upcoming home football game. I could tell from the way my mom gripped the doorknob and my dad leaned in against my dresser that they were working up to something substantive.

"Can you please do us a favor?" My mom stood in my doorway, her eyes, brown like mine, pleading in a way that was startling in its novelty.

"I guess. What is it?"

"Can you try to act normal? Just try it. For us. Would you try to act normal? All this moping around, it's not good for you—"

"Okay." I knew what she meant. Since Hawaii, I'd been drained of energy. There was the extra sleeping and the disinterest in all the new opportunities arising with the start of high school. All of it was passing me by. To them, my listlessness looked like childish "moping" that I could—and should—snap out of before I lost a whole year of my life. My parents firmly believed that I could make up my mind to be happy. I understand now that they were offering me the tools they relied on: willpower, optimism, and self-reliance. But those tools kept slipping out of my grasp, so I reached for the more reliable bingeing and purging to tamp down the emotions trying to surface. My parents and I wanted the same thing: for me to be normal. I longed for a "normal me" more than they did, but none of us understood that I wasn't "moping" and that the attempts to stuff my feelings might come at a high cost. I also heard an implied request that I bury Hawaii and all its terrifying images. Beneath my parents' request thrummed a subtext: *Don't think about it, or you'll get upset. Don't get upset, or you'll fall behind on the important work of being a normal teenage girl. Don't talk about it, or you'll upset yourself. Don't talk about it, or you'll upset me.* I wanted to be a dutiful daughter, so I buried it the best I could.

ur

"Not everyone gets to come home." My voice cracked. Dr. Rosen asked if I could scream some more. I didn't think I could, but then I bent over and rested my forehead on the stiff carpet and guttural moans from a previous decade rose up and spilled out of me in waves.

"What happened after the helicopter took David's body away?" Dr. Rosen asked. I'd never talked about what happened after we left the beach. In my mind, the story ended as soon as the helicopter disappeared over the mountain with David's body in the long black bag.

I started to shake as I had in the Kansas woman's car.

"Were you cold in the police station?"

"The floor was cold under my bare feet and I didn't have any of my clothes. One officer offered me a foamy yellow blanket, and a different officer led me to a private room so I could call my parents. They were at the movies with friends, so I told my brother what had happened."

"What did you do when you left the police station?" Rory asked.

"Sebastian drove us back to the condo. We were over an hour away. Then he missed a turn, and we drove miles out of our way—on and on we drove down this two-lane highway. No one said a word. I sat by my-self in the backseat and stared out the window at the stupid ocean and the brilliant Hawaiian sunset, all purples, pinks, and oranges. The Cure tape played over and over. When one side finished, there were several clicks, then the other side would start playing. It took several sides to get to the condo."

"The police let the three of you leave all alone?" Dr. Rosen asked.

"Sebastian was almost eighteen."

"His dad had just died," Rory said, her voice breaking. "You were children."

"The police should have taken care of you." Patrice reached out for my hand. I grabbed it and she squeezed it like she had that first morning during the closing prayer.

"And when you made it back to the condo?" Dr. Rosen asked.

"We had to tell Sandy. We knocked on the door because we'd lost the keys. When she looked through the peephole, she understood the terrible math. One of us was missing. She started screaming, 'No! No! No!'"

"Jesus, Christie," Carlos whispered.

I'd pushed past them in the doorway and hid in the bathtub—no water running—so I could get out of their way. Behind the shower cur-tain, I picked at the dried mud and blood caked on my legs, trying to bear their grief. They remained in the doorway, holding each other and sobbing, until the last beams of daylight faded to darkness.

"What did it sound like?" Dr. Rosen asked.

I opened my mouth to imitate their wailing. Nothing came out. When I tried again, the sound froze inside me, my aperture for grief sealed up inside my throat.

"You did it a minute ago. You can hear it in your head," Dr. Rosen said.

I could hear it, the three of them, huddled and wailing, but no sound would come out. That terror and grief were a part of me, an organ that covered everything, like skin or hair. Like a stain. I didn't know how to let it go. I managed a few guttural barks. I shook my head. "I can't."

I'd long ago accepted that I'd carry Hawaii—those screams and the terrified clenching of every muscle when I thought of the ocean—for the rest of my life. It was the price of having survived. What would it look like to heal? I couldn't conjure a version of me that wasn't haunted by the ocean gushing out of David.

Dr. Rosen suggested an experiment. "Repeat after me: 'I did not kill David.'"

I shook my head. "Jesus, Dr. Rosen, I don't think I killed him. This isn't an ABC after-school special."

"You feel responsible."

"That's ridiculous. I was thirteen—"

"The sign."

"You always mention it, hon," Rory said.

"Sign?" I said, my gaze darting around the room.

"The 'No Trespassing' sign," Rory said.

I slumped back in my chair as if I'd been hit. Did I really think it was my fault? "That's what I've been carrying all these years?"

"It's one of many stories that you carry."

We were never supposed to be on that beach. The whisper that had been echoing through me since 1987 roared in my ears: You could have stopped it. Should have. I might have been thirteen, but I could read. I understood we were breaking the law. I knew what "No Trespassing" meant.

"Ready to repeat after me?" Dr. Rosen said. I nodded. "Look at Rory and say: 'I did not kill David.'"

"I did not kill David."

"It's not my fault he died."

"It's not my fault he died."

"I don't have to blame myself."

"I don't have to blame myself."

"It's not my fault."

"It's not my fault."

"Now breathe," Dr. Rosen said. My lungs expanded underneath my ribs. When I exhaled, my breath came out jagged, its edges caught on the hooks of the resistance I'd built up over seventeen years.

"So this trauma has kept me alone all these years?"

"Your buried feelings about it has driven you away from people."

"Why?"

He leaned toward me and spoke slowly. "If you get into an intimate relationship, your intense feelings are going to come out just like they did this morning. You'll attach to someone." He pointed at himself. "He might go to the beach. He might not come back. Love will lead you to the beach a thousand times a day for the rest of your life."

"I'm never getting over this."

Dr. Rosen shook his head. "Christie, you will never get over this."

Dr. Rosen closed the session in the usual way, and Patrice and Rory both turned to me and wrapped me in their arms. Carlos stood just to the side, waiting for his turn. So did Marty and the Colonel. Each of them held me tight. Dr. Rosen also held me for a few seconds longer than usual. Just below the surface of my skin, I could still feel my body shaking with the memory of the waves hitting the black sand beach.

13

In August 2002, I celebrated my first anniversary in group by anxiously refreshing my e-mail with an index finger every three minutes in the student lounge where I was camped out with other law students. I'd finished a ten-week summer internship at Bell, Boyd & Lloyd, and the hiring coordinator said they'd e-mail us about permanent job offers by the end of the day. Over the summer, I'd written memos, researched principles of contract law, and stayed past nine several nights to prove my commitment. I also cheered at a Cubs game and sipped club soda at happy hours to prove that one future day I would be capable of socializing with blue-chip clients. But now I needed a job offer.

At four thirty, I gave the mouse one last press. My eyes seized on the e-mail from the firm: *The committee still hasn't voted.* Every other year in the firm's history, all of the interns were offered postgraduation jobs at a boozy party in the conference room overlooking downtown Chicago. This year, we'd primly sipped cranberry juice and nibbled roasted almonds as the managing partner talked about the economic downturn with a tight smile. Now this e-mail proved that the rumors that had spooked us all summer were true: they didn't have enough jobs for all of us.

My third year of law school had just started. Graduation loomed nine months ahead. The dot-com bubble had burst, and law firms typically did not hire third-year students—they hired the interns who worked for them over the summer. Some law firms were imploding; there one day and gone the next. My school, Loyola, was in the second tier, so I was competing with students who hailed from the University of Chicago and Northwestern, both of which were in the top ten. When I graduated, my debt was going to total over $120,000. If I didn't have a job, a good one, then how would I pay for rent, student loans, and therapy?

I race-walked to the career services center, where several other students were flipping through job listings in big white binders. A paltry list of firms scheduling interviews with third-year students was pinned to a bulletin board. Someone had scribbled *We're Fucked* at the bottom. Two organizations were interviewing third-year students: The Judge Advocate General (JAG) Corp. and Skadden, Arps, a top-ranked firm, famous for having the highest starting salaries in the country. The JAG Corp. was out because I didn't want to disclose my mental-health treatment or the three times I'd smoked pot to the federal government. As for Skadden, it was a powerhouse law firm stocked with thoroughbred attorneys from Ivy League schools who routinely worked sixty-hour weeks. Skadden was the Harvard of law firms. They would never hire me.

I fought the urge to vomit on the white binder.

My closest law school friend Clare pooh-poohed my fears. "You're first in our class! You have it made." Yes, as valedictorian, I would land a job, but if it only paid thirty grand, I would sink under the weight of my debt. I'd taken out a private loan, at 10 percent interest, to pay for treatment with Dr. Rosen. My law school debt was considerable. How would my life work if I had an extended job search? Would I have to move back to 6644 Thackeray?

In group, Dr. Rosen was insistent. "Interview at Skadden."

I balked. I saw myself as second tier, a middle-of-the-pack lawyer. My law school was second tier, as was Bell, Boyd & Lloyd. The Skadden partners argued before the Supreme Court and helmed complex commercial litigation covered in multipage *Wall Street Journal* articles. They wore custom-made suits with Italian leather shoes. I was a little girl with pinworms, a college student who almost died from self-induced vomiting, a young woman with an apple fetish barely in remission.

"Skadden's not for me, Dr. Harvard."

"Yes, it is."

What the hell did he know? He sat around with psychologically broken people all day. Skadden would expect me to perform at my highest level around other people who were doing the same and had been since they graduated summa cum laude from Princeton. I was a Loyola Rambler.

"You're brilliant. Skadden is going to want you."

Brilliant was a word to describe Madame Curie, Steve Jobs, or Dr. Shirley Ann Jackson, the female physicist who invented caller ID. It was not a word for me. Being first in my class made me a workhorse who desperately wanted achievements with which to wallpaper over the holes in her personal life, *not* brilliant. I had the LSAT score to prove it.

Patrice nudged me in the forearm and then exaggerated the motion of rubbing her chest like Dr. Rosen always did when someone gave him a compliment *or* an insult. I rubbed my chest halfheartedly. But some part of that *brilliant* penetrated just below my breastbone, a sliver of it nested in the soft part of me that was willing to receive it.

At home, I opened my closet door and stared at my navy Calvin Klein suit and Cole Haan flats. Of course I'd wear the lipstick Carlos picked out. At least I could get the costume right.

A week later, I sat across from a balding white guy in his sixties who stood in his stocking feet, leaning on oak bookshelves where his children smiled from chunky silver picture frames. Head of Skadden's litigation department. He winked and asked me where I saw myself in five years, chuckling as if the question was bullshit. I told him the truth: "I hope to be moving toward partnership." I didn't mean firm partnership necessarily, but he didn't know that.

The next partner who interviewed me had the most sumptuous charcoal-gray suit I'd ever seen. I studied it so I could describe it to Carlos later. During our thirty-minute conversation, he rolled up five separate pieces of Scotch Tape—sticky side up—and daubed at invisible dust specks on his desk. When he shook my hand at the end of the conversation, he said, "I promise we can give you exciting work."

The male associates had quirky artifacts in their offices: a framed vintage Cubs jersey, a Gorbachev bobblehead doll, a signed Bruce Springsteen album. None of them seemed psycho or incapable of talking about their lives outside of work. The only woman I met, Leslie, had an open smile and an easy laugh. I felt myself sink into the chair in a way I hadn't in the men's offices. When I asked her if it was possible for a woman to succeed at Skadden, she nodded her head slowly. "Yes, I think so."

For lunch, two junior associates, Jorge and Clark, hailed a cab that whisked us to Emilio's for tapas. Jorge had a regal bearing and wore a bow tie and cuff links. Clark was baby-faced, slightly disheveled, and recently married. Once we were seated, Jorge suggested we each order four plates to share. I'd never had tapas. I'd never eaten chorizo and Manchego cheese for lunch, or any other meal. I'd never shared twelve plates of food with two men while trying to land a job.

When the food arrived, I calmed my breath and took bites from each of the plates: grilled goat cheese on toast points, Spanish sausage, tricolored olives glistening with oil, sautéed escargots, and grilled potatoes. As the savory bites slid down my throat, my belly quivered with pleasure and shock. This was a long way from cabbage, tuna, and mustard. I worried the corner of a white linen napkin between dishes and thought about Rory's mind exploding when I reported my food later that night.

Even if I didn't get the job, the meal was a miracle.

They assured me they had lives outside of work: Jorge had a fiancée, Clark an abiding fondness for hours-long poker games. As I chewed my last bite, I felt desire stir in my chest. I wanted to work at Skadden too. I wanted to breathe the rarefied air of a fancy law firm just like Clark and Jorge were.

We parted ways outside Emilio's, and I walked down Ohio Street toward Michigan Avenue. My smart navy shoes clicked on the sidewalk as I turned down Michigan Avenue, past Tiffany, Cartier, and Neiman Marcus. My feet fell into a perfect staccato rhythm, and my spine was

pillar straight. My stride was that of a woman who was first in her law
school class. It might have been a second-tier school, but only one person had done it. The truth of that number—one—sizzled through my
body, finally something more than abstraction or shame. It was energy,
and it belonged to me.

By the time I slipped my key into my door, I believed I deserved an
offer from Skadden—in part, because I was first in my class, but also because down the street was a wacky doctor with an impressive pedigree
who told me I was brilliant. And even if I didn't believe I was brilliant,
I did believe that he believed I was.

I ended up with two job offers: one from Bell, Boyd & Lloyd, where
I'd done my internship, and one from Skadden. Clare said I should go
back to the smaller firm because Skadden would work me to death.
Hadn't the point of therapy been to keep me from taking a job that
would suck the life out of me? I didn't want a life consumed by work.
My favorite law school professor told me to go for Skadden because I
was young and energetic and it was too good an opportunity to pass up.

With twenty-four hours left to make the decision, I took it to group.
I'd left lunch with Jorge and Clark, high on serrano ham and convinced
I could succeed at Skadden, but doubt crept in. Would Skadden suck
me dry with billable hours? Skadden could be my nightmare come true
if work left me no time to work on my relationships.

Dr. Rosen disagreed. "It will be easier to practice law around other
brilliant people." There was that word again. "You could call now and
accept the offer."

It was one thing to tell a hot guy from school that I was a cocktease,
but it was quite another to turn a decision like this—the genesis of my
legal career—over to Dr. Rosen. I told him I needed a few minutes to
think about it. He did his "suit yourself" shrug and turned his attention
to someone else.

With fifteen minutes to go in the session, that stirring of desire and
ambition in my chest returned—quivering, translucent, fragile as a bubble. After my first year of law school, before my initial call to Dr. Rosen,
I downloaded the application for Northwestern Law School. With my
class rank, I could have transferred there and enrolled at the number

eight law school in the country. I filled out the application and put the pages into a thick manila envelope. But at the mailbox in front of the law library, my fingers wouldn't grab the small metal handle on the door. My elbows wouldn't bend, my biceps wouldn't curl. The future that beckoned on the other side of that mail chute required more of me than my body could give. I didn't belong there. I was a second-tier person. I walked ten paces back toward the library and chucked the envelope in the trash.

Skadden was prestigious, and I didn't know if I belonged, but my fear of not measuring up was suddenly not as strong as the propulsive yes in my chest. It seemed absurd to let insecurity and fear hold me back from all Skadden was offering. Plus, they would pay me enough that I could afford rent, student loans, and therapy.

As the group session ticked down, I stared at the peak of the sooty Jewelers' Building a few blocks away. I held still to keep this brand-new vision from evaporating: My business card on heavy white card stock. My five-figure bonuses. My updated wardrobe. My Tumi briefcase. My cases and clients. Could I take all of this in? Could I try?

I wanted to try.

I held up my phone like a torch. "I want Skadden."

Dr. Rosen gestured with his hands, like *go right ahead.*

I flipped open my phone and dialed, but hesitated before pushing send. Patrice scooted her chair toward me and put out her hand. I placed mine into her open palm.

The recruiting partner's voice mail picked up. When it beeped, I looked to Dr. Rosen for a boost. He nodded.

I inhaled quickly. On the exhale, I stepped into my future.

"I hope you know what you're doing," I said, when I flipped the phone shut. "This is my life."

"Maybe you'll meet your husband there." Dr. Rosen smirked. I freed my hand from Patrice's and flipped him the bird. I wasn't taking a job to find a husband. He laughed and rubbed his chest with gusto.

I had a new job to go with my new home.

A few weeks earlier, Clare, my friend from law school, called and announced: "Tater, I need a new roommate." I thought she'd ask her boyfriend, our fellow classmate Steven, to move in, but she said they weren't ready for that step yet.

Clare's Gold Coast condo had a marbled lobby, a twenty-four-hour doorman, and a pool. It was walking distance to school and three El stops from Dr. Rosen. Deep purple curtains held by gold velvet sashes hung in her living room. I'd have access to the gym and a parking spot. My whole body trilled with pleasure at the invitation. She offered to charge me the same rent I paid for my efficiency with the clanking radiator, the water-stained ceiling, and the decades-old kitchen appliances. How could I say no? Ten minutes later, I flipped through the yellow pages and hired a moving company.

⌇⌇

The night I committed to Skadden, I stretched out on my bed and took stock of my life. A new job. A new home. In the event of my death, Clare could alert the authorities. Or the doorman. I wouldn't die alone.

14

Carlos from group was my first male best friend. He would call me on the way to the gym, ranting that his fiancé, Jared, spent too much on Italian shoes or antique linens. He whisked me to restaurants in his tiny silver BMW and introduced me to foods I'd never had (pad thai, sturgeon) or heard of (cassoulet, shawarma). Without Carlos, I never would have tasted spanakopita or stepped foot in Barneys. As I headed into my second year of group, my relationship with Carlos was one of the brightest features of my steadily brightening life. When I bragged in group that Carlos and I had never had any conflict, Dr. Rosen piped up. "Pray for a fight."

"Why?"

"Because you want a truly intimate relationship."

"That means fighting?"

"If you aren't willing to fight, how can you can be intimate?"

Did wrestling with my brother at 6644 Thackeray over the remote control count? I searched my memory for a good old-fashioned throwdown—a slammed door, a fist curled, a throat raw from bellowing. I found nothing. In high school, my friend Denise snuck out of my house so she could have sex with her senior boyfriend at Caruth Park. I didn't get mad at her for potentially getting me in trouble by fleeing out my window. I swallowed my anger and let her back in when she tapped on the sill. Freshman year of college, my friend Anne invited the guy I was dating over to watch a movie with her while I was at the library. I never said a word. Instead, I moved out two months later. And when my friend Tyra confronted me for leaving her theater performance before her final curtain call, I felt hot plumes of anger shoot up from my stomach to my mouth. She ignored that I brought her flowers, stayed until she'd delivered all of her lines, and left because I had the stomach flu. Part of me wanted to get up in her wounded face and say, real vicious-like, "Could you think about someone else for one hot second?" Instead, I said, "I'm so sorry. I promise I'll be at the next one."

When it came to anger, I swallowed, pretended, ignored, withdrew. I knew nothing about fighting.

"I think you should join the Monday men's group," Dr. Rosen said to Carlos one Tuesday morning about thirteen months into my treatment. "It will help you prepare for your marriage."

I asked if I should join a second group too and Dr. Rosen shook his head and said I wasn't ready. Shame pinned me to my chair, and I remained silent for the rest of group. I didn't know whether I wanted to join a second group, but that wasn't the point. Dr. Rosen offered something to Carlos that he didn't offer me. For the rest of the session, noxious thoughts scrolled through my mind:

He likes Carlos more than me.

I'm not doing this right.

I suck at therapy.

I left group in a wordless, huffy silence. I avoided Carlos's calls— first, because I was jealous that he was the favored son, and then because I was ashamed of my petulance. We didn't speak until Sunday night, when I confessed my jealousy. "Don't be jealous of a second group, girl," he said. "It's just going to cost more money and create more hassle."

That night, I left Dr. Rosen a message asking him to call me before group so I could get his feedback on my intense reaction to Carlos's invitation to join a second group. Dr. Rosen often returned my calls between sessions. I assumed I'd hear from him.

All day Monday, I carried my phone turned up in my palm like a heart transplant patient waiting for news about a donor. By sundown, I lost hope. I called Marnie while browning a chicken breast on the fancy stove-top range in Clare's condo. She still saw Dr. Rosen, so I thought she'd understand how I was feeling

Before I could tell her anything, her other line beeped. "Hey, that's Dr. Rosen. Let me call you back."

Click. Marnie was gone.

I grabbed the skillet handle and the hot cast iron seared my fingers. "Dammit!" I cradled my burned fingers and hopped in pain, still cursing under my breath. I sat down in the middle of the kitchen and rocked back and forth. The chicken and oil hissed in the pan.

Five minutes later, Marnie called back. I took a deep breath. Maybe Dr. Rosen had called her back because she'd recently gotten pregnant after a miscarriage—maybe things weren't going well. Maybe she was cramping or had gotten bad news at the doctor.

"Everything okay?" I asked, genuinely concerned.

"It's our stupid contractor. He put in the wrong door—we ordered oak, not mahogany. Dr. Rosen coached me on how to talk to him tomorrow."

The air whooshed out of my lungs, and I doubled over. I pressed freezer-burned ice into my burned hand while glowing, newly pregnant Marnie discussed how to boss around laborers from a custom-upholstered settee in her four-story house.

Why would Dr. Rosen help her and not me?

As I dialed his number, my whole body shook. At the beep: "I can't believe you! You FUCKING ASSHOLE. You've been teaching me to ask for help. To reach out. To 'LET YOU AND THE GROUP IN.' But you don't reach back? Fuck you!" On and on, I yelled at Dr. Rosen's voice mail as my hand throbbed.

His voice mail beeped. I'd talked until the end of the message and then smashed the phone down on the floor. I wanted to smash everything: Clare's beautiful plum-colored Pottery Barn plates, the wine chiller in the corner, the vase of dried flowers, the framed Jazz Fest print above the table. Everything was throbbing: my head, my heart, my throat, my hand. I hated everything about Dr. Rosen: his smug face, his dumb elfin laughter, his arrogant prescriptions. Fuck him and that circle of chairs in that eighteenth-floor office.

ur

During the first few minutes of group, I avoided eye contact with everyone. I folded my hands in my lap, my gaze fixed on an oval-shaped stain on the carpet. Marty filled us in on his mother's hip operation, and Dr. Rosen did his routine of shifting his gaze from one person to the next.

"Did you leave me a message?" I looked up, and Dr. Rosen was staring at me. I nodded and felt light-headed.

"Do you want to tell the group about it?" He beamed at me like he did when Rory reported finishing a chapter of her dissertation. Around the room eager faces met my glance.

"I was upset and said some things that were not very nice—"

"Not very nice? Don't minimize! You were vicious!" Dr. Rosen gestured with his hands and bounced in his seat. He rubbed his heart and closed his eyes like he was savoring a great meal. "We should all go into my office and listen to it."

Everyone stood up. Field trip! It was my first time in his office since starting group and everything looked the same: the framed Harvard diplomas, the needlepoint, the uncluttered desk against the wall.

As Dr. Rosen held the receiver and punched in the passcode to his voice mail, Carlos whispered, "What the hell did you say?"

Dr. Rosen pressed the speaker button and there was my voice, shrill and clear. "You don't give two shits about me! Marnie has EVERYTHING! What about me?" My voice went on for three minutes. The group huddled around the phone.

When my voice finally shut up, he clicked the phone off. "Can you celebrate this?" He enunciated each word as if I was new to the English language.

Celebrate anger? That was rarer than fighting. I have no memory of yelling at my parents for any reason. Not even as a teenager. We weren't yellers. We were silent treatment people; we did huffy sighs and quiet seething. When my parents forbade me from attending Troy Tabucci's New Year's party sophomore year because they suspected there would be underaged drinking, I holed up in my room, making mixtapes of sad songs. When they told me that I had to go to college in Texas, I threw away the dog-eared Dartmouth brochure I'd been poring over for weeks. I used fake smiles, "I'm fines," and gigantic binges like other people used Kleenex. But now this man was treating my rant like a Chopin sonata.

"Celebrate?"

Dr. Rosen's eyes grew huge. "It's beautiful!"

"It's gross—"

"Says who?"

"The self-pity, for one thing—"

"I disagree—it's honest, authentic, and real. It's yours. And you shared it with me. Thank you." He rubbed his palm over his heart. "Welcome to your anger, *Mamaleh*. This is going to help you."

This was my first praise for the parts of me that were ugly, irrational, petty, reckless, spiteful, and spewing. I'd never heard of such a thing. If I were my therapist, I'd tell me to cut that shit out, but Dr. Rosen celebrated like it was Armistice Day with dance-in-the-streets, cancel-work jubilation.

"Don't worry," he said. "You're just getting started."

15

For the first time in over a year, I woke up after a whopping eight solid hours of sleep. I wasn't quite sure where I was, but I knew that there was a warm, buzzy feeling between my legs.

I'd had a sex dream. A graphic, steamy sex dream about R&B singer Luther Vandross. My main man Luther had caressed my face and kissed me deeply, his tongue filling my whole mouth. Then he did something with his tongue on my stomach—a circling-thrusting combo—that made me see beyond stars to other planets and galaxies. And when his soft lips circled between my legs, I mewled like a newborn kitten.

I woke up wet, hot, and satisfied.

On the train to group that morning, I hummed my favorite Luther Vandross song, "Here and Now." Oh yes, Luther, here and now indeed.

As the train lumbered past the darkened gay nightclubs and funky boutiques on Belmont, I felt buoyant—as if I could float up to the sky like an escaped balloon. I was not nearly as dead inside as I feared. The dream was also proof that whatever part of my subconscious had brought Mr. Vandross into my bed and let his tongue roam over my body was alive. And she was hungry. This sexual anorexic was working her way to the buffet table. I'd dreamed and felt sex that was hot, wild, noisy, wet, and completely focused on my pleasure. Sex with no inhibition, no nuns with their threats of hell, no disapproving parents who wanted sex linked to marriage, no worries about being pregnant or being fat or not "doing it right." There was my body, a gorgeous man, and pleasure.

Within the first ten minutes of group, I'd told them everything. "He was going down on me, and his back was smooth and muscular. I had an orgasm in my sleep."

"How long did it last?"

"Have you ever seen him in concert?"

"Is he the guy who sang that duet with Chaka Khan?"

Dr. Rosen, who had been silently taking in this conversation, finally spoke. "The dream's about me."

You could hear our necks swivel toward him.

"Come again, Freud?" I said, laughing. "No offense, but you bear zero resemblance to a smoking-hot black guy who's won a bunch of Grammys and is friends with Oprah. You're . . . well . . ." I gestured to his tufted head, his cable-knit brown sweater, and his thick-soled brown shoes. "I mean, look at you."

Dr. Rosen shook his head in that patronizing way. I scowled. If the dream was really about him, then why didn't Dustin Hoffman show up? Or maybe Adam Sandler?

"Uh-oh," Carlos said.

"What?" I asked.

Carlos and Rory exchanged a knowing glance. Then Carlos broke the news to me. "Don't you know that once you start psychotherapy all your sex dreams are about your therapist?"

Dr. Rosen nodded. "Van-de-Ross, sounds like 'Rosen.' "

"My god, they practically rhyme." I rolled my eyes. In no universe did my slim, balding, Jewish therapist resemble my new main man Luther. Dr. Rosen threw up his hands and shrugged. He wasn't going to try to convince me, which was the quickest way to get me to second-guess myself.

"Why do you have to make everything about you?" I murmured "creep" loud enough for him to hear. Then I ignored him as he rubbed his chest as if I'd said he was a stellar therapist. I refused to look at him, and the group moved on to another topic.

"Do you understand why that dream was possible?" Dr. Rosen turned to me with two minutes to go in the session. I shook my head. "Do you think it's a coincidence that you were able to express your rage directly to me two weeks ago, and then you had an orgasmic dream about me?"

I ignored the part where he connected my rage and sexual desire and bit on his insistence that the dream was about him.

"Why are you trying to ruin my dream?"

"Why would having sex with me ruin it?"

"You're my shrink." My face contorted at the thought.

"And?"

"What happened to Dr. Celebrate Everything?"

"I am celebrating. I'm not the one resisting."

"Resistant" was the one charge I couldn't ignore. It was the gravest therapeutic transgression, and I cringed when I saw it in my group mates. Dr. Rosen had been urging Rory to apply for jobs at higher-paying civil-rights organizations that would give her primo benefits, but she insisted that she could get hired only at legal clinics in Wisconsin that were run on a shoestring. With her credentials she could have worked anywhere in the Chicago area, but she continued to commute to Waupun, Wisconsin, and got pissed whenever we prodded her to reach for Something Better. Resistance—to change, to pleasure, to a shorter commute—was what held us back from what we really wanted. I would not commit that sin, even if I would rather punch Dr. Rosen in his smug little face than acknowledge my dream was about his saggy ass.

"Fine." I scooted to the edge of my seat and sat up straight. I gripped the arms of my chair and whispered in a singsong voice, "Dr. Rosen, I'd love to have your face in my crotch. I'm *dying* for you to put your tongue on me and slowly, slowly, slowly circle me until I come." I moaned a little for effect.

"Damn, girl," Carlos murmured.

The Colonel's eyes opened, cartoon-character wide. Rory blushed and cast her gaze to the window.

Dr. Rosen blinked twice. Then he said, "You're ready for another group."

Everyone waited for me to speak but I had no words, only sensations: hot Luther between my legs, annoyance at Dr. Rosen roiling in my belly, and the terror rising through my chest as I digested his words.

I mumbled the prayer at the end of group and walked out with Carlos in a haze. He put his arm around my shoulders. "I told you you'd get your chance for a second group."

Of course, now that I had it, I questioned it. Did I really want a whole other group? Coming downtown twice a week to excavate pinworm memories and pick up prescriptions to call group mates about my basic human functions? Why had I wanted this so badly? I thought it would make me feel like a favored child, like one of Rosen's Chosen, but now the invitation to a second group made me feel ashamed of how sick I must be.

The following week, I opened the session with my burning question: "Why now?" Dr. Rosen hadn't even taken his seat—he was futzing with the blinds across the room.

He took his seat and considered my question. "Your willingness to bring the dream into group, to be proud of it, and to discuss it means you're ready."

"For what?"

"For more."

"More what?"

"Heat. Intimacy. Intensity. Sex."

"Will it help me with relationships?"

"Guaranteed."

"Now group is like Best Buy?"

ᴄᴄ

Sometimes I felt like Rosen-world was a cult. I'd begun to spot Rosen-patients out in the wild. In a 12-step meeting, I heard a woman say, "My name is Ginny, and my crazy therapist told me to tell you all that I'm bingeing on off-brand Oreos." Before she said another word, I realized I'd heard about her from Carlos: she was dating Chip from the men's group, and they almost broke up because he wouldn't go down on her. In another meeting, a woman sat in the middle of the circle taking

superhuman bites of a Burger King Whopper. In the eleven years I'd
been in recovery meetings for eating disorders, I'd never seen anyone
eat so much as an oyster cracker during a meeting. Most meetings had
an explicit rule that you weren't supposed to mention any specific foods
by name because you could trigger someone's bingeing. So seeing someone devour a Whopper was shocking—like seeing the moon fall from
the sky and land in your lap. Marnie leaned over and whispered: "She's
got to be one of us." We later confirmed that Dr. Rosen had given her a
prescription to gorge on fast food during meetings instead of in secret
at home.

How would increasing my participation in Rosen-world mesh with
my daily life as a seminormal person? As a law student, it was tricky
to reconcile my public, professional trajectory with my, shall we say,
unorthodox therapy life. Keeping Baby Jeremiah in my closet. Calling
Rory and Marty every night. Telling the Smoker I'm a "cocktease." Part
of me wanted to join the second group for the same reason I joined the
first: I was curious. Curious about who would be in my group and how
my life would change if I joined. My five current group mates and Dr.
Rosen knew all the details of my eating, sleeping, and sex-dreaming.
What would I do with *more* group?

As I mulled over the possibility of joining a second group, I surveyed
the developments in my love life since starting the first. I'd been on one
official date since the debacle with fifty-minute Sam and the fiasco with
Andrew of the charred chicken breasts. Two weeks after I had sex with
Andrew, I met Greg at a house party, and he asked for my number. He'd
just gotten out of a yearlong medically induced coma. On the way out of
a sushi restaurant on our first date, he forgot where he lived. I may not
have been ready for a relationship, but he *definitely* wasn't.

Then there was Xavier, my ex-boyfriend from college—one of the
decent guys I dumped because his steady loyalty nauseated me. I hooked
up with him while visiting my family in Texas. We met in a darkened
parking lot in a sketchy neighborhood near the DFW airport. When we
started making out, I could see the faint outline of stars and galaxies. His
lips on mine woke me up. His hand on my thigh was an unlocking, and
I wanted to go further, all the way right there under the neon "Checks

Cashed" sign. Of course, I'd never felt this gut longing for him when we were together—I avoided sex with complaints about headaches and early morning shifts at my mall job.

As I hitched up my skirt, Xavier pulled away.

"Connie's flight is about to land," he said. I stared at him without blinking. "I know what you're thinking. But I'm not hooking up with you because I'm freaking out about getting serious with Connie."

My heart sunk. The word *fool* flashed in my mind. When I returned to Chicago a few days later, my group pointed out that Xavier was unavailable, which is precisely why I was attracted to him.

Now Xavier was engaged. So was my college roommate Kat, two of my law school friends, and two of my cousins. Dr. Rosen's new group felt like a rope I should probably grab.

"Okay, I'll do a second group."

"I suggest an all-women's group."

"Why?"

"It's what's next for you." My eye twitched.

He suggested the Tuesday-noon group. One hundred eighty minutes of therapy in a single day. Two round-trip train rides to Washington and Wabash on Tuesdays.

"That's insane." Plus, the noon group was Marnie's. I reminded him that we were friends. My eye twitched again.

"There are social risks for you." I squeezed my eyes shut and thought of Bianca and that table of girls in fifth grade. Since fifth grade, I'd been terrified that any group of women would eventually turn on me, and I'd end up taking my meals on the crapper. But would enduring some friendship friction be better than dying alone, unloved and untouched, heart as slick as an obsidian stone?

I said yes.

Part 2

16

I was cocky that first Tuesday. I already knew the drill. I'd tallied the minutes I'd spent doing group therapy over the past thirteen months: 5,265. My heart had a few score marks—shallow knicks, but grooves all the same—from all the work I'd done so far.

I wasn't planning to tell Clare, who wasn't a consumer of mental-health services, that I'd signed up for two groups in one day, but I'd blurted it out one afternoon on the walk home from family-law class. She paused and then smiled like she was proud of me. "Be sure to take a snack on Tuesdays because that's a long day, Tater." She loaned me her favorite Anthropologie sweater to wear on my first double-decker therapy day.

Thirty minutes before my second group session of the day, I strutted out of criminal procedure class, ready to slide like an egg into batter. I was seven minutes early, but I jabbed the group room button anyway, even though its purpose was to alert Dr. Rosen that a group member who arrived late wanted to be let in. *Guess who, Rosen? How you like me now? Two times in one day.* I took a seat and was soon joined by Emily, who was famous in Rosen-world because her father, a pill addict who lived in Kansas, was enraged when Emily started therapy, so he harassed and threatened Dr. Rosen through the mail and over the phone.

She and Marnie were close friends, and as we chitchatted before the session, I realized how weird it felt to intrude on "their" group. I dismissed the fear and greeted a tall woman wearing a straw hat. "I'm Mary," she said, taking the seat next to me. I'd heard about Mary from Marnie, but couldn't remember if she was the one Marnie loved or the one whose guts she professed to hate.

At noon, Dr. Rosen opened the door to the waiting room, offering each of us a smile. Before we were settled in our chairs in the group room, we were joined by an ample woman named Zenia, who had mulberry-colored hair and gigantic brown eyes stuck in the expression of *surprise!* She kicked us off with a story about her multi-orgasmic weekend, courtesy of an erotic online community for Dungeons & Dragons fans. She mentioned a girlfriend who lived in Croatia whom she'd never met in person.

I'd spent more than five thousand minutes in this room. Ninety of those minutes were three hours earlier. Everything looked the same: the swivel chairs, the bookshelf, the cheap mini-blinds, and the limp Easter lily hanging on for one more season. Yet it felt totally unfamiliar. Like a dream where you're in your house, but it's not really your house because the door is the wrong color and there are two stories instead of one. At the level of energy and particles, something was totally off.

Dr. Rosen looked like an unfriendly stranger: his lips were set in a stern line; his arms looked rigid and unnatural. There was nothing warm or familiar coursing between us, and my heart contracted with homesickness for Tuesday morning.

Zenia glowed as she discussed her relationship with Greta from Croatia—and the hours of sex they enjoyed online and how they were saving money to meet up for a convention in Brussels. Zenia smiled at me every few minutes, which I took as a generous welcome, and then segued seamlessly into a question for Dr. Rosen about how to treat one of her patients.

"Patients?" I said out loud.

"I'm a physician."

Dr. Rosen smirked at me. That fucker was laughing at me! Oh, look at the lonely prude sitting next to the successful doctor enjoying virtual sex with her girlfriend! I narrowed my eyes and scowled at him; his smile widened. I didn't expect him to coddle me, but I also didn't expect him to sit on his throne and laugh at me.

Mary shared that her abusive brother—the one who had threatened to kill her all through childhood—had called to ask for money. Regina, a massage therapist wrapped in what looked like two black shawls and a flowy nylon skirt, had come in during Zenia's sexalogue. She told Mary in a sympathetic, hushed tone that when her psychotic cousin pulled a knife on her, she filed a restraining order.

Dr. Rosen had misread my history. A fear-lump in my belly swelled as I realized this was the wrong group for me. I wanted to grab him by the crisp brown collar and remind him that yes, I'd suffered in the aftermath of Hawaii and battled an eating disorder, but there'd been no attempted murder. I'd turned out perfectionistic, frigid, and borderline asexual, but how could he think I belonged here? I was a lightweight, trifling thing, who was all "*boo-hoo* I wish I had a boyfriend"—I was absurd and garden-variety next to these women who were braver and more interesting and accomplished than I'd ever be.

Twenty minutes passed. Where was Marnie? She was supposed to be my swim buddy.

Marnie arrived thirty minutes into the session, dropped her orange leather bag unceremoniously on the floor, and fell heavily into her chair. I tried to catch her eye, but she wouldn't look at me. Her jaw was set tight and her brown eyes darted around the circle, looking for prey.

"I'm so fucking tired I want to die," she said. She'd given birth to a gorgeous baby girl six weeks earlier. "Pat's traveling every week, and the baby won't sleep. I can't—" Her hands were shaking as she pulled out a bottle of Voss. I'd talked to her earlier in the morning, but she hadn't expressed any of this anguish. Now she seemed to be pretending I wasn't in the room. That kind of studied avoidance could only mean one thing: she was angry at me. I could no longer hear anything because I was swept up into my own panic about how to stop Marnie's anger. I'd seen Marnie mad before. It wasn't pretty.

The door buzzed. A woman with a giant purse with leather tassels and a Styrofoam food container walked in, and all the molecules in the room shifted. It had to be Nan—Marnie had mentioned her, but had not told me she was so radiant, throwing off energy like light beams. Though I knew she was near retirement, Nan's skin glowed like a young woman's. When she smiled, two dimples appeared on either cheek. I couldn't tear my eyes away from her silver sandals, the ring of keys that jangled as she set her purse behind her chair, her sly smile at Dr. Rosen when she sat down, or her mouth as she mumbled under her breath while Marnie was talking. She acknowledged me with a quick nod of her head, and I smiled back.

"IN is having its way with me today," Nan said. "IN wants me dead."

I looked at Dr. Rosen. IN? He looked at me but offered nothing. If I wanted to know what Nan was talking about, I'd have to ask her.

Nan picked up her Styrofoam container and lifted its lid—one compartment was filled with mac and cheese, the kind with the near-orange sauce and elbow-shaped pasta. She kept talking as she took a bite. "I'm not even hungry." Her voice cracked. She looked at me and explained that the *I* stood for "inner" and the *N* stood for the racial slur that had oppressed her all her life. She made it clear that she—and only she—was allowed to say the full name of IN, and by God, I was not about to defy Nan. I nodded, grateful she had filled me in.

"Nan, I was talking," Marnie said. I knew that tone. Marnie used it with Pat right before the marital spat I'd witnessed. I curled further inward and found myself holding my breath. The air was sharp, flickering with the threat of violence. I didn't want to inhale it.

Nan pointed her fork at Marnie. "Hold. The. Fuck. Up." I sucked in a gulp of air and held it, suspended, in my lungs.

Marnie twisted the top of her water bottle. "Wait your fucking turn." It sounded like a warning, a hiss.

This was not like my other group, where Patrice snapped at Colonel Sanders or Carlos bickered with Rory about showing up on time. Between Marnie and Nan, I sensed something heavier, more corporeal and unstable. They were dragging their words from the depths of their bodies, not plucking them out of their heads. They were using their hands and arms. They were spitting. The air crackled with heat and something menacing.

"What's that?" he said, cupping his ear with his hand.

No sound came out, but I kept mouthing, "Help me." Over and over. *Help. Me.*

The attention in the room shifted from Nan and Marnie to me. I couldn't look at any of the women, and I couldn't make any sound come out.

"What's your problem?" Marnie asked, finally giving me her full attention.

I shook my head, holding Dr. Rosen's gaze.

"Seriously? What's your fucking problem? If you're going to make it here"—she glanced over at Dr. Rosen and jutted out her chin—"and for the record, no one asked me how I felt about *her* joining *my* group—you have to speak up. We do deep work here."

My only thought was *I want to go home*—to the morning group, the people who knew and loved me.

I turned to Dr. Rosen. "Why did you bring me here? I don't fit here. Everyone has been on the other end of a knife or horrific violence. I just want some people in my life, maybe a boyfriend who isn't drinking himself to death or too depressed to have sex, but I feel disgusting—"

"Disgusting isn't a—"

"Yes, it is!" My whole body shook. I wrung my hands like I was try-ing to dry them. I wanted to shake the disgust off my skin, even though it was coming from inside.

"No."

"Fine. I feel shame for intruding on Marnie's group, scared of what I'm seeing and hearing, and mad at you for putting me here. I'm never going to have a place in this group. I never should have joined a second group!"

"Good!" Dr. Rosen stuck both of his thumbs up like my distress was a movie he'd just watched and was recommending to his audience. "It's already working."

"What's working?"

"This group." Cue million-watt smile. A sweep of his arm across the circle. Elfin joy.

"*Mamaleh*, one part of intimacy is learning to express anger. You've

Nan set her food down. I thought she was going to rise and roll her sleeves, but she grabbed a napkin from her purse and wiped h mouth real slow, like a pissed-off sheriff in a Western. I let the air see out of my lungs, tiny breath by tiny breath. They kept yelling—Marni was a "skinny white bitch," and Nan was "a help-rejecting drama queen." Dr. Rosen looked alert but not alarmed. Then Nan pointed her fork at Dr. Rosen.

"You need to help me," she said quietly. Tears I hadn't noticed welling rolled down her cheeks. She bent her head low like she was addressing her leftovers. "Please help me." I wanted to cross the circle and put my arms around her. Instead, I picked the cuticle on my right thumb deep enough to draw blood and make my stomach seize.

"I'd love to," Dr. Rosen said, smiling and sitting up like an actor who'd been waiting for his big solo.

"This is all I know." She daubed her eyes with her napkin.

Nan turned to me and described a childhood filled with violence and addiction: an unstable stepfather who brandished a gun at her after gambling all night, a bipolar brother who punched the walls and broke family heirlooms. "Brute force—it's all I know."

Marnie scooted her chair toward Nan and touched her arm. "It's all I know too." Mary and Emily had tears in their eyes. Mine were stuck in my thumb, where I continued to dig at the exposed bright pink flesh. A drop of blood pooled in my nail bed.

In the five years I'd known her, Marnie had met every emotional situation with a hard-nosed defiance, a macho Italian "you talkin' to me?" bravado that I both feared and admired. I watched, mesmerized, as Nan and Marnie, two women I was sure were going to maim each other moments before, melted into a collage of mutual trauma and healing. Marnie held on to Nan's left arm.

I'd never seen two people fight—or make up—before. My thumb was throbbing, and I bit my lip to keep from bursting into tears. As the minutes ticked by, I fantasized about shrinking—losing skin, muscle, bone, cells—becoming nothing more than a heap of clothes in my frayed swivel chair.

The next time Dr. Rosen caught my eye, I mouthed, "Help me."

made huge progress in the morning group. But another part of intimacy is learning to tolerate other people's anger. This group will help you with that." He looked at Marnie, who stared him down without blinking. "It already has." In full Mister Rogers mode, he explained that my terror about other people's anger was yet another stumbling block to intimacy. Sure, I could now join my law school friends for lunch at the deli, book-end my baths, and yell at Dr. Rosen. But there was always more. Therapy was a Sisyphean trap.

"What do I do about Marnie?"

"You could celebrate her anger." I rolled my eyes. Then I asked how. "Look at Marnie," he directed. I swiveled my chair and stared into her angry eyes. "Tell her that you love her, and her anger is beautiful."

"Marnie, I love you, and your anger is beautiful."

"Now breathe." My words hovered over the circle. Every instinct pushed me to go off Dr. Rosen's script, throw myself at Marnie's feet, and promise to leave the group or stay up all night with her baby—*any*thing to stop her anger. But I kept breathing, each second pulling me away from my tired old impulses.

I broke my gaze to look at the clock, but Dr. Rosen told me to keep my eyes on Marnie. "Tell her that you welcome her anger and that you are available for more." I did. She didn't say anything.

"What are you feeling?" Dr. Rosen asked.

"Scared." My toes curled toward the floor.

"Good. If you can learn to tolerate that fear and let go of trying to fix her anger, you will be ready for an intimate relationship."

"I thought all I had to do was turn over my food to Rory. And book-end my bath. And take Baby Jeremiah. And tell the Smoker I was a cocktease."

"You definitely needed to do all of that. And this is the next thing."

The session was over. Dr. Rosen ended it in the familiar way. When the hugs began, I kept my eyes on Marnie, watching her embrace Emily, Mary, and Zenia. *Please hug me*, I wished from across the room. I heaved my backpack over my shoulder.

"Hey you," Marnie said, nudging my shoulder.

"Hey," I said, my eyes flitting to hers and then to the floor.

"You did good today." We both smiled.

"Doesn't feel good."

"I know."

She opened her arms, and I stepped forward into them. Marnie said something into my hair. "What?" I asked.

"I can be mad at you and still love you, you know."

No, actually, I didn't know that. I had no idea.

17

I slipped on one of Clare's black dresses and a new pair of black strappy sandals. Marnie was throwing a fortieth birthday party for Pat, and miraculously, I had a date. A date with someone I was attracted to. I'd met Jeremy a few years before law school at a party that was full of 12-step people. I was enchanted by his wire-rim glasses, gentle green eyes, and insightful comments. Turns out, he was also in Carlos's other Rosen group, so I heard tidbits about him from time to time. Like that he'd just broken up with his girlfriend.

The week before Pat's party I stood on the train platform at Fullerton and spotted Jeremy. He was absorbed in a thick, impressive tome—by Thucydides. His khaki pants were cuffed just so, and his blue fleece made his green eyes shine. I sidled his way. When a crush of people exited the next train, he looked up.

"Hey," he said, folding the top corner of his page and shutting his book.

"I thought that was you." I reached for the same train pole he was holding. He asked about law school, and I asked him about work and why he was reading Thucydides. "For fun," he said. His smile made me feel cozy, like we were sitting by a fire, not jammed into a rickety El train packed with short-tempered commuters.

"I've never seen you on this train," I said when I realized we lived two stops from each other.

He let out a short, unhappy laugh. "I used to stay at my girlfriend's in Bucktown. We broke up."

"I heard that." I smiled, wishing I could wink without looking stupid. He cocked his head. "I see Rosen. Tuesday morning with Carlos."

He leaned toward me, close enough that I could see specks of gold in his green eyes, and whispered, "I'd heard that."

"Touché." The whispers of the Rosen-grapevine echoed all around us.

We both laughed, and the sound of our voices rose over our heads and those of the people absorbed in their phones, books, and newspapers. Desire for this smiling, literate man flowed from my fingers twined around the steel pole, down my arm, and through my chest, belly, and between my legs.

Next thing I knew, the invitation for Pat's party flew out of my mouth, as if I was the sort of woman who routinely asked out philosophy-loving, newly single men. He agreed right away and wrote his address on a Post-it note he used as a bookmark. We touched hands when the train jerked its way to the Southport stop, and a fresh zing of desire shot through me.

He was waiting outside when I pulled up the following Friday night, dressed exactly the same as he was on the train, which put me at ease. Our first topic of conversation was Dr. Rosen. We joked about his unfortunate wardrobe choices, and his absurd optimism that group would cure absolutely any emotional impairment.

"He sure loves group," Jeremy said, laughing.

"He sure loves brown sweaters."

My limbs felt loose and relaxed as we ran through the common ground of our mutual therapy experiences. I had none of my usual first-date stiffness, no impulse to hold any part of myself back. I didn't have to: he saw Dr. Rosen.

By the time I pulled up to Marnie's house, I'd decided that the only thing Jeremy was missing in his life was the love of an emotionally available woman. By the time I'd found a sparkling water and a stuffed mushroom cap, I'd decided that would be me.

"Come here, I want to show you something." I led Jeremy upstairs to the nursery, where Marnie had hand-stenciled ducks on her daughter's buttery-yellow walls. Without any shame, I opened each drawer to fawn over Landyn's tiny diapers, impossibly minuscule socks, and a powder-pink sleep sack, soft as a snow owl.

"Cute," he said, when I held up a little bathrobe with an attached hood and bunny ears. Jeremy kept looking back toward the door like we were committing a crime. I offered him a baby cap to snuggle, and he stepped back. "Is this a prescription—to show me these clothes?" I shook my head and ran a cashmere sweater across my cheek. "Maybe we should head back to the party." Jeremy stepped into the hall and waited for me to put Landyn's clothes away.

Downstairs, he made conversation with Pat, Marnie, and their suburban friends. My limbs remained loose as I drove him home after eleven.

Whenever our conversation veered from Dr. Rosen, I noticed a few flags—not red exactly, but pinkish.

"I'm a bit of a loner," he said when I asked if he hung out with his group mates outside of sessions. I wondered if that might one day backfire on me. When I thought of the type of man I wanted to date, *loner* was nowhere on the list.

He also mentioned that his car wasn't working, and he couldn't afford the spare part. Money trouble gave me a touch of heartburn—Carlos had told me that Jeremy's breakup with his girlfriend had something to do with money he borrowed from her. I gripped the steering wheel and tried to stay loose. Would he resent my impending financial security? Was he anticapitalism? Was he, at the ripe age of thirty-six, still lost, professionally and financially? If so, how much did that matter to me?

A little, but he was so cute in those glasses.

"I don't think I know much about your work," I said, hoping a job description would ease the nub of tension at my neck.

"I run the front office for an industrial janitorial company. A small operation on the west side." The nub didn't budge. I'd had the impression he was an IT manager for a big company downtown. I adjusted my grip on the steering wheel again.

So we were different. Big deal. Lots of couples were famously different: Arnold Schwarzenegger and Maria Shriver. James Carville and Mary Matalin. Homer and Marge. Maybe we wouldn't make it to a silver anniversary celebration, but surely we could go on a second date.

When I pulled up to his building at the end of the night, I took my right hand off the steering wheel and let it fall to my side.

"There's a Polish movie playing Monday night that's getting rave reviews. Want to go?" I nodded, eager as a Yorkie. He gave me a not-entirely-chaste squeeze on my arm as he got out of the car.

A second date! I pumped my fist in the air. As I turned my car around to head home, I banked the curb with a jolt that snapped my neck and knocked my water bottle out of the drink holder, but I barely felt it. My joy hugged the border of hysteria.

✐

"Tell me more about this Jeremy," Clare said the next night over dinner. She dropped her head into her open palm when I told her I gave him a tour of Landyn's nursery. "Tater! You don't show a man a nursery on your first date!"

But I felt no shame. "Don't worry. He sees Rosen. I don't have to play games with him. I can be myself." She cocked her head, skeptical.

"This sounds really promising, Tater. This is your reward for joining that second group!"

That night, I drew a line down the center of a piece of paper. No more haphazard romantic follies for me. I was in therapy now. I started with the "pro" column. He was undeniably intelligent. Who reads Thucydides for pleasure? He was sober, so he wouldn't piss on me in the middle of the night. He had a cat, so he knew how to take care of something. The glasses, the smile, the rapt listening. I wrote it all down. Then I wrote the biggest pro of all: *Sees Dr. Rosen.*

Dating a man who saw a therapist—any therapist—was ideal. Therapy made you more sensitive and self-aware. It gave you tools to navigate a relationship. Seeing a man who saw *my* therapist was a way to build a bulletproof relationship. After all, I trusted Dr. Rosen. Mostly. I knew his work. I *was* his work. Jeremy and I would have acres of common ground. We would never run out of things to say. Bonus: we'd have free couples counseling—we'd just see the therapist at different times and with other people.

On our second date, we sat on lumpy seats in the crowded Music Box Theatre reading the subtitles of a Polish film about two sad people walking through a city park. Jeremy elbowed me when I crossed my legs. "The great group no-no," he whispered, and we both laughed. He put his hand on top of mine and left it there until the end of the movie. Its warmth and heft felt like solid pleasure.

On the walk back to his place, we huddled together as the wind whipped all around us. We told each other our hardest prescriptions. I trotted out my cocktease prescription—not a story I ever pictured telling on a second date. He told me he hadn't done his hardest one yet. When I asked what it was, he looked away.

After a few steps, he said, "Rosen says I should ask my ex-girlfriend to forgive the loan she made me." He grimaced and looked down at his feet.

His living room featured a brown couch and matching coffee table. He'd positioned his desk and computer by the window in his kitchen, and his bathroom, while not exactly reeking of bleach and free of stray hairs, struck me as reasonably clean. I was impressed by his silver kettle and an array of teas.

A plump tabby with orange-and-white coloring purred at his feet. "This is Mr. Bourgeois."

"That's his name?"

He nodded and smiled.

"Looking at your bookshelf, I shouldn't be surprised." Machiavelli, Sartre, Plato, Socrates, Heidegger, Kant. The lightest read was Saint Augustine.

I slipped off my shoes and told him I hated my new group.

"Why?" he asked, sitting next to me on the couch. His knee touched mine.

"It's so raw and intense in there. Everyone screaming and eating, then crying and hugging. And Marnie isn't thrilled I'm there—"

"Why do you think Rosen put you in there?"

"Well."

"What?"

"He thinks it will help me open up to a relationship." I upended my teacup to hide how embarrassing it sounded.

He took my hand. "I hated my second group too. Every second of it."

"Why'd you stay?"

"I wanted to see what those feelings meant, where they came from." He shrugged his shoulders. "Now here I am." My heart lurched to the edge of my rib cage.

He leaned toward me.

"Is it okay if I kiss you?" he asked.

I felt a welling in my chest, the novel sensation of safety inching toward desire. I nodded, and our lips met. I tasted chamomile tea, and when he put his hand on my neck, I leaned into him and the chance he offered. I hadn't really tasted a man's lips in almost two years—with Andrew I was too busy dissociating to feel anything, and in the parking lot with Xavier all I could taste was my own neediness. Now, with Jeremy pressing his lips and tongue against mine, his goatee tickling my upper lip, I felt my libido flicker a few times and then ignite. The pressure between my legs was a mix of pleasure and pain, desire and ache, satisfaction and hunger. I was coming to life.

This is what I'd been waiting for.

18

"*No secrets,*" *Dr. Rosen advised when I showed up in group with* the epic news that I'd been on two dates with Jeremy. "Anything that happens between you and Jeremy—emotionally, romantically, sexually— bring it to both of your groups."

"Also financially," Carlos said, aware as he was of Jeremy's past issues.

Quick math: my two groups plus Jeremy's two equaled approximately twenty people who would know when we went dutch on dinner, gave each other house keys, or had sex during my period. I balked and held up my hands. "Whoa. Hold up. Won't weekly play-by-plays to every-goddamn-person take the *zing* out of the relationship."

"My suggestion is no secrets," Dr. Rosen repeated.

"Your suggestion sucks."

"How well has it worked to do it your way?"

On our third date, Jeremy and I babysat Marnie's daughter, Landyn, for a few hours so she and Pat could go out for an anniversary dinner. As the baby slept in my arms, Jeremy peeked in the cabinets, stared at Clare's dishes, and stood on the balcony admiring the view.

After Marnie and Pat retrieved Landyn, I suggested to Jeremy that we join Clare and Steven at a bar on Belmont for some live music. When he agreed, I was dumbstruck. Could it really be this easy? All I had to do was ask?

"Do you want to pack a bag so you can stay over?" he asked.

I couldn't hide my giddiness. I raced around the room stuffing contact lens solution and a fresh sweater into a bag.

The bar was not exactly Jeremy's scene—a cavern full of fraternity boys and aging Cubs fans sloshing drinks out of plastic cups. After the first set, Jeremy whispered that he was ready to go. My whole body trilled. I drove through red lights and rolled through stop signs. I couldn't wait to press my body against his.

I sat on his bed in the dark while he fed Mr. Bourgeois. When he sat next to me, I leaned into him. He pressed his lips against mine. "Is that okay?" he whispered. I nodded and pulled him toward me. I pressed my body against his, and he held me tight as he kissed me, harder and deeper.

He pushed me off gently and rolled onto his back. "I'm not ready for sex," he said. A simple admission—five words I'd never heard anyone, including myself, say. Was it a prescription?

"It's okay." And it was. What I wanted was a chance to be close to someone. It didn't have to be sex, not tonight.

As soon as he said sex was off the table, my body relaxed further into him, the bed, the moment. For tonight, kissing would be where it began and ended. He rolled toward me and held me close—chest to chest, belly to belly, thigh to thigh.

"Maybe we could just sleep," he said.

"Of course."

We settled into each other, our breathing deepened.

"Do you always sleep with this many clothes on?" he whispered into my neck.

I still had on my jeans and T-shirt. The only article I'd removed was a light wool sweater.

"Yes." I actually always slept in my bra. I had since ninth grade when my breasts exploded from buds to D's. I liked sleeping with my breasts bound, tucked into the underwire and lace. With past boyfriends, I would slip out of my bra when we were having sex, but when it was time to sleep, I put it back on. I'd never been with a man who noticed, or who was willing to ask me about it.

The next morning, shards of light sliced through the edge of Jeremy's blackout curtains, and Mr. Bourgeois sat on the edge of the bed considering me. I padded into the living room and found Jeremy at the little table in his darkened kitchen, typing on his computer.

"Hey." I stepped into the foot of space between the fridge and the metal shelves he used as a pantry. I crossed my arms and hugged myself.

An awkward silence gathered between us. I cleared my throat. "What are your plans for the day?" Would we brunch and walk down the street swaddled in the gauzy intimacy of the night before? Would we go back to bed?

He turned most of his body back to the computer. I crossed my right leg over my left.

"Catching up on stuff. AA meeting tonight. What about you?"

"Some reading for my cyber law class. Clare and I might see an early movie." I paused. Was I supposed to invite him? He looked at the computer screen, where a grid of pound signs, dots, and percentage symbols lit up a black background. "What's that?"

"It's an ASCII video game called NetHack." He blushed and looked at his feet. "It's a bit of a preoccupation."

Video game? Preoccupation?

"No judgment here." I smiled at him. But a frisson of warning shot through me. A grown-ass man sitting in a darkened room playing a video game? The claustrophobic image made my throat constrict.

"You say that now. But I literally might play this all day—" His green eyes were not filled with levity, but something shadowy I recognized. Shame.

"If it brings you joy, what's the harm?" My voice was shrill with false cheer. His face relaxed, but then I hugged myself tighter, aware of an urge to flee. "I think I'll get going soon."

When I pulled into my parking spot at home, I dialed Rory's number. "I'm not sure about him," I said.

"Honey, he just got out of a relationship. Bring it all to group."

On Tuesday morning, Patrice, Rory, Marty, Ed, and Dr. Rosen

cheered Jeremy for being explicit about his sexual boundaries. When I was with Jeremy, I'd felt comforted by his admission that he wasn't ready for sex, but now their cheers felt infantilizing—they were adults entitled to regular hot sex, and we were children who were stuck with kissing and cuddling. I hated their gaiety, and I hated myself for agreeing to disclose everything to my groups.

There were no pep rallies in the afternoon group. Marnie thought his sexual reticence signaled that he wasn't ready for a relationship. "I don't like it," she said, shaking her head. Nan and Emily wondered why he didn't offer me breakfast. Mary wondered why he didn't have a proper pantry. I shrugged my shoulders and swallowed lump after lump of shame.

"Dr. Rosen, morning group loves everything about this guy. Afternoon group sees nothing but red flags. Which is it?" The sharpness of the afternoon group's critique scared me.

"The two groups reflect your own internal conflict. The split's in you—you don't know if Jeremy's pacing is a gift or if you are going to starve in this relationship. If he's a videogame addict or an introvert who likes computers."

"How do I find out which is true?"

"Keep showing up."

"Where?"

"Everywhere."

Dutifully, I reported to both groups with updates every session. All ten of my group members knew I paid for most of our meals with money I saved over the summer. That I drove us everywhere because his truck was still out of commission. That we mostly hung out at his place. They learned that the first time he touched my breasts, I shuddered with a pleasure that bordered on nausea—a cake too rich, a sunset too vibrant. "Is this okay?" Jeremy asked whenever he touched my body in a new way—a kiss on my belly, a hand on my upper thigh. My morning group loved his commitment to consent, but my afternoon group pronounced it "kinda lame."

As it happened, our slow sexual progress was indeed Dr. Rosen's doing. One night, while we were making out on his bed, Jeremy admitted that Dr. Rosen warned him not to rush. "He said I should take it slow or I would end up hating you like I hated my ex." Apparently, their relationship combusted not only because of unresolved financial conflicts, but also because the sexual progress of the relationship outpaced his emotional readiness.

I wrapped a blanket around my body. I felt exposed—I was the one who wanted more physically. It felt like rejection and made me want to hide my face from him, from Dr. Rosen, and from the twenty-odd people who knew I wanted to have sex with him.

A poll on the radio revealed that most couples go "all the way" by the third date. When I complained in my morning group about falling way behind the national norm, Dr. Rosen insisted that *we* weren't ready. I sensed a conflict of interest—because, really, it was Jeremy who wasn't ready. Dr. Rosen held his ground.

"What's your rush?" he asked.

"I've endured a lifetime of failed relationships and sexual repression."

"Then what's a little more time?"

Arguing with Dr. Rosen wouldn't work. I had to adjust my strategy if I wanted him to cosign intercourse. A few minutes later, I leaned toward Dr. Rosen and said in my most rational voice, "Can we talk about Jeremy? He's hiding out in video games. You should consider giving him a prescription to spend some time with his emotionally and sexually available girlfriend."

Cough. Cough. Cough. Dr. Rosen's theatrical throat-clear. Translation: *You're full of shit.* I ignored it.

"He exhibits classic signs of avoidance. He's afraid of intimacy—"

More coughing. Then a question: "And what about you, *Mamaleh*?"

"Me? I'm totally available." I stretched my arms out wide. Nothing to hide here. The whole room laughed.

"What's so funny?"

"Serious question?" Dr. Rosen said. I nodded. "How many bras are you wearing?"

"*Busted,*" Carlos said under his breath.

Confused, I looked at my shoulder, where three bra straps crisscrossed under my tank top. I'd run before group, and my chest was a double D. A single sports bra didn't keep my girls in place, so I wore two, sometimes three.

"Do you hate your breasts?" Dr. Rosen asked.

Of course I hated my breasts—they were bags of fat hanging on my clavicle. I associated them with being ungainly, not being sexual. And there was something scary about them—how important they were to other people (men) and how unwieldy they were. All my life I'd coveted a flat chest. Flat like the earth after a glacier scrapes by. Flat like a ballerina's, a model's, a little girl's.

"I don't love them."

"You're trying to make them small—"

"I was exercising, not trying to win a Playboy bunny contest."

"Do you think that hating your breasts might interfere with your sexual relationship?"

The correct answer was yes, but I couldn't bring myself to say it. I'd never discussed how I felt about my breasts with anyone before. I sat there shaking my head, trying not to cry. It had never struck me as sad that I hated my breasts.

"How does Jeremy feel about them?"

"I'm sure he thinks it's weird that I sleep in a bra."

Dr. Rosen's eyebrows disappeared into his scalp. Everyone else gasped as if I'd just confessed to murdering baby gorillas. The Colonel looked more animated than he'd been since the time Carlos mentioned lesbian porn.

"Are you curious about why you sleep in a bra?" Dr. Rosen asked.

A fist of anger filled my mouth. "I know what you're doing! This is where I'm supposed to remember something my dad or uncle or the skeevy gym teacher did or said. I don't have one of those things. Everything that's happened to me has been run-of-the-mill—"

"Nothing about Hawaii sounded run-of-the-mill," Rory said.

"That's insane! David's drowning isn't the reason that I'm wearing all these bras."

"Are you curious why you are?" Dr. Rosen repeated the question, steady and calm.

"There's no story. I was a young girl who wanted to be thin because everybody loves thin girl bodies. Because I was into ballet, an art form built on anorexia, and breasts are not thin. They are filled with fat. They make it hard to shop for tops at J.Crew and Anthropologie. They make me feel fat." I adjusted my tank top so all the bra straps were hidden. "Welcome to the female body in America, buddy."

"Do you want some help?" Dr. Rosen sat still as a bird of prey.

Why hadn't I picked a female therapist? I didn't believe that my male therapist could fathom my relationship to my breasts. Sure he was in recovery for an eating disorder, but he'd never been shopping with his grandmother in Waxahachie, Texas, and overheard the saleslady say that his breasts made him look much "fuller" than he was. He'd never had a ballet teacher advise him to go on an egg diet—three eggs for breakfast, lunch, and dinner and nothing else—when his breast buds appeared. He'd never walked by Hooters in downtown Houston and endured drunk men leering at his chest. Even if he had perfect scores in every subject at Harvard and a genius-like understanding of group dynamics, a man simply cannot know how it feels to walk the planet as a woman. But I nodded—*yes, I want some help*— because getting inadequate help from my male therapist was better than nothing.

"Get a henna tattoo on your belly that says 'I hate my breasts.'"

"Hate? I thought we were aiming for love and acceptance."

Dr. Rosen shook his head. "First accept the hate. Stop trying to outrun it." He gestured to my shoulders and the bras. "Take Jeremy with you."

19

Jeremy and I pulled up to a crumbly industrial warehouse build-ing on the corner of Racine and Grand. I pressed the buzzer that read Big Ernie. Big Ernie advertised himself in the *Chicago Reader* as a magician, dog walker, and henna tattoo artist. He buzzed us up, and we took the stairs to the second floor, where a man with a long black ponytail dressed in black genie pants greeted us from the doorway of his apartment. He could have been thirty or fifty years old—it was impossible to pinpoint. His warm smile soothed me, and the fifteen-foot ceilings in his loft made me feel like a prop in a dollhouse. The brick walls had been painted a lacquer white. He told us to take a seat in his living room while he prepared the henna. I took the couch and Jeremy crouched by the fireplace, where one hundred Pez dispensers were arranged in perfect order, like colorful, cartoon versions of white crosses in a military cemetery.

I'd called Big Ernie right after my second group the morning I made the mistake of wearing two bras to group. I'd told the ladies all about my prescription. They all nodded when I described my lifelong hatred of my breasts and shared their own stories. A man had recently grabbed Nan's breast while she shopped for lipstick at Marshall Field's. Zenia's dad had commented on her breasts all her life. Mary was ashamed her breasts were so small. Emily described a fight she'd had with her husband after he'd grabbed her breast playfully while they were watching *The Daily Show*. That was when I covered my mouth with my hands and started to cry.

I was sixteen. Junior prom. I wore a size-ten Laura Ashley strapless black dress that had a sweetheart neckline and a spray of giant pink gardenias across the front. I'd been going to the tanning salon every other day for four weeks, so my skin was an unnatural shade of brown-orange and tingled with almost-pain from staying too long in the coffin-shaped booth. My date, Matt, and I barely knew each other; we'd been thrown together after everyone else had coupled up. He was a few years from announcing he was gay. After the corsage-boutonniere exchange and dinner, a caravan of us stopped at a park to pound beers and wine coolers pilfered from parents' bars. The sweet fizziness of berry wine cooler sloshed in my stomach and made my head go fuzzy. The ground under my feet felt pleasantly unsteady, like trying to walk on a water bed. I remembered standing next to Jared Meechum's black Cherokee, surrounded by ten guys.

We were all laughing. Slurry clouds drifted by, hiding the moon every few minutes.

Jared approached me with a dare in his eye. My hands were at my sides—one clutched an empty Bartles & Jaymes bottle, one had gathered a handful of dress to keep me steady. I smelled the beer on his lips and saw the mound of dip bulging in his lower lip. I was midlaugh when he reached two fingers down the front of my dress between my breasts. I finished my laugh as if nothing happened, because I wasn't sure it had.

Had it? He'd stepped away quickly so it was easy to blame my sloshy stomach, my fuzzy brain. My breasts were so smushed into the dress that the sensation was muffled, and the memory easily dissolved.

I upended the bottle in my hand and licked the last drop from the rim.

Spencer was next. He did it quick-like and avoided my eyes. He had the decency to blush. But shame didn't stop him from whispering to P.J.

and Tad, both of whom seemed to tower over me as they slid their two fingers between my breasts. I watched the tops of the trees, swaying just so in the breeze even though the night was still and thick with late-spring humidity. My hands gripped harder at the dress and the bottle. There was nothing else to reach for.

The clouds continued to skate past the moon.

Where were the other girls? Where was my date? Why was I still laughing, acting like I was having the time of my life with these good Catholic boys I'd known all my life? I'd been longing for any of them to ask me on a date, to invite me to dance, to call me, kiss me, want me. Each of them was dating one of my friends. This was the first time any of them had ever touched me.

Jared appeared for a second time. On this pass, he stuck his whole hand between my breasts. Only then did I step back. Only then did I feel the crush of shame slamming through the buzz, the dress, the laughter. Only then did I let myself understand that they were laughing at me.

I continued to laugh.

Laughing, laughing, laughing. The sound of it covered so much—it covered the whole Texas sky with its false notes that disguised my terror.

My group sat quietly as I said the names of those tall Catholic boys and how their clammy hands felt down my dress.

ur

Now Big Ernie's soft wet brush on my exposed belly tickled, but I wasn't laughing. I stared at the ceiling and squeezed Jeremy's hand. An expectant feeling tickled my throat. It was a cry or a scream—I couldn't tell which—but I wasn't letting whatever it was out in front of the Yogi Bear and Flintstones candy dispensers. I kept my eyes on the ceiling and never looked down.

Back at Jeremy's place, I stood in the bathroom and surveyed my tattoo, the top layer of which was a crust I peeled off. Smooth burnt-orange swirls and curlicues danced over my belly button and adorned the script: *I hate my breasts*. Honestly, it looked and felt hokey as hell. Still, I held my hand over it as I called Rory to report my food, and Marty for my affirmation.

I slipped off my bra before putting on Jeremy's soft black T-shirt with the words *Ars Technica* printed across the chest. He found me curled in his bed under the covers and asked if he could join me.

I scooted over to make room for him and unfurled my body. He shook off his jeans and got into bed with his boxers and T-shirt on. I rolled into his body with my arms still curled into my chest in a protective X. I took a deep breath. Then another. I relaxed my arms and let them rest at my side. Tears welled from the tender part of my chest where all that breast hatred had lived for so long.

"What is it?" he asked.

"I've been very afraid." He smoothed the back of my head with his palm.

"Me too."

"I don't know what I'm doing."

"Me either." He held me closer.

I kept crying, imagining the dye on my belly seeping through my skin and joining my bloodstream.

20

Jeremy waited for me in the lobby of the law library, head buried in a battered Nietzsche book. I slipped my hand into his. "Let's head up Michigan Avenue." I'd been dreaming of the two of us, hand in hand, walking down the strip of Michigan Avenue famously nicknamed "the Magnificent Mile" for its dazzling array of shops and restaurants. This time of year Christmas lights hung from every lamppost, and Salvation Army volunteers dressed as Santa rang bells in front of Neiman Marcus.

My fantasy was a nice dinner followed by sex at my place. I'd been holed up in the library all Saturday studying criminal procedure. It was early December. Finals time. My job at Skadden was locked down and everyone said that your third-year grades didn't matter, but I wanted to keep my class rank. My back ached from hunching over the textbook as I mastered the laws governing arrest and detention. I'd decided it was time to master my relationship. I was sick of Dr. Rosen controlling my love life. My relationship needed some leadership, and I was ready to step up. The kissing and light petting were gratifying, but I was hungry for more. Starving, really.

The wind off the lake hit my chest. I burrowed deeper into my coat and closer to Jeremy. The sidewalk was jammed with tourists carrying huge holiday bags from the Disney Store and Ralph Lauren. Jeremy got whacked in the thigh with an oversize Crate & Barrel bag. He scowled and pressed the pace. I lengthened my stride to keep up.

"Where are we going?"

"I can't take the crowds." He turned off Michigan Avenue.

I swallowed my disappointment in two gulps. My fantasy reel didn't include side streets—we were supposed to be on Michigan Avenue under the holiday lights and in the fray, where life was pulsing with energy and cheer.

Half a block up, he ducked into a California Pizza Kitchen. More gulps. My fantasy reel definitely didn't include a chain pizzeria packed with suburban teenagers.

"Want to share a pizza and a salad?" I said.

"Nah, I'm going to get a sausage calzone. I can polish it off on my own." I nodded hard. I ordered a California veggie personal pizza and a side salad with Italian vinaigrette.

He'd spent the day playing video games. I pushed down the bubble of contempt that my boyfriend, a grown-ass man within spitting distance of his fortieth birthday, spent his day trying to win the Amulet of Yendor. I'd run four miles, gone to a 12-step meeting, and studied for a criminal procedure exam for four hours.

Conversation stalled. When the food came, I wanted to mouth "help" to the waitress.

Telepathically, I informed her that I was drowning in the dead space between me and my boyfriend, who still wasn't ready for sex after almost two months.

Jeremy punctured his calzone and a puff of steam escaped. I moved the tomato slice from the high-noon spot on my plate to six thirty, and thought of things to say that would make him want to take me to bed.

"Want a bite of my salad?"

When we got back to my place, Clare and Steven were on their way to Lincoln Park to listen to live music. "Come with, you guys," Clare said, throwing her coat over her shoulders.

Before I could open my mouth to ask where, Jeremy said, "I'm going to hit the hay." He saluted Clare and Steven and beelined to my bedroom.

Clare whispered, "Get you some, Tater," and wiggled her eyebrows suggestively.

I played along. "Don't wake me in the morning!"

By the time I'd turned off the living room lights and walked into my bedroom, Jeremy was a snoring mound. I sat on the bed roughly, hoping to jostle him awake. I propped myself on a pillow and stared at a shadow on the wall. What exactly, I wondered, made me so different from Clare, whose boyfriend wanted to touch her and talk to her all night? Was it my years of bulimia? Was I subconsciously pushing Jeremy away? I knew I was attached to Dr. Rosen and my group mates. Why couldn't I do that with a man? I wasn't afraid of sex like Dr. Rosen insisted—I wanted to have it with Jeremy right then.

The clock glowed eight forty-five. Five minutes earlier than the end point of my abortive date with Sam. Disappointment and anger—at Jeremy, myself, Dr. Rosen, my groups, and this whole stupid night—rushed through me, making my fingers twitch. I sighed loudly. Jeremy didn't budge, so I climbed out of bed. In the cabinet under the kitchen sink, I found the box of mismatched plates and glass tumblers I'd brought from my old apartment. Clare and I kept an Ace Hardware hammer in the junk drawer for various home improvement projects that we never actually did. I took the box and the hammer and nudged open the balcony door with my elbow.

Hammer raised, chest heaving. *Smash.* Shattered bits of glass flew across the balcony. My bare knees scraped the concrete. *Smash. Smash. Smash.* My cheeks burned from effort, from the cold.

⟡

Rory and Carlos gasped.

"Did you protect your face?" Patrice asked.

I'd felt driven to smash. My body simply couldn't hold the impulses to bring the hammer down. I was brimming with rage. All I knew was that if I didn't destroy those dishes, I was going to turn that hammer on myself.

"Were you hoping to wake him up?" Patrice asked.

"I guess. But the breaking was purely physical, like sneezing or—"

"Vomiting," Dr. Rosen said.

"Yes! It was like having something in my body that felt—" What was the word?

"Toxic?"

"Exactly! Something that my body had to eject."

"Vomiting is your body preventing you from dying of food poisoning," Dr. Rosen said. "This anger is old. It's the anger you used to puke up, but it's still in there. By avoiding an intimate relationship, you've been able to avoid feeling this."

"I've been enraged with you. Remember when you marched us to your office to listen to my voice mail?"

"We're not sexually involved."

"Fair point." I understood the difference. To Jeremy I offered my body and I wanted his in return. But it wasn't working. "So what do I *do* now?"

The answer I would have accepted: break up with Jeremy. But Dr. Rosen suggested that I keep expressing my rage and invite Jeremy to join me. As if Jeremy would budge for me and my hammer.

"The question is whether you're willing to ask." What good would it do? I slumped down. Dr. Rosen seemed willfully blind to the obstacles.

"You honestly think I should stay in this relationship?"

"It's just getting good—"

"But it's totally dysfunctional."

"Not totally."

"Did you hear that story? I was on my twenty-eighth-floor balcony whacking at discounted stemware with a hammer in the middle of the night!"

"You said it was nine o'clock." The Colonel smirked across the circle.

My spittle flew in all directions when I told him to fuck off. I banged on the arms of the chair. "Help me!"

"I fully support your anger," Dr. Rosen said, smooth as a chalkboard.

"I want more from you. Give me something more."

"Buy safety goggles."

Three hours later, I stormed into the noon group and told Dr. Rosen
to fuck off. The group leaned in as I told them about the dishes, and
about Dr. Rosen and his safety goggles. Marnie side-eyed Dr. Rosen
and accused him of not helping me. Emily suggested that Jeremy and I
"take a break."

"I need more from you, Dr. Rosen." I was banging the same chair
arms I'd abused that morning.

Dr. Rosen said nothing. He shifted his gaze around the room just
like normal, letting me yell at him.

I slithered to the floor. I screamed into the carpet. Over and over,
nonsense words of rage. Guttural sounds of exertion poured into the
floor, shimmering over to the other women's feet. The more I yelled and
beat the carpet with my coiled fists, the deeper I fell into a black hole of
despair. Sweat rolled down my neck and my hair stuck to my forehead.

When I was in third or fourth grade, my parents planned a family beach
vacation to Padre Island. My dad steered our cloud-blue station wagon,
brimming with rafts, sunscreen, and beach towels, south toward the
coast. Halfway through the eight-hour drive, the weather reports turned
ominous: a hurricane had changed course and was zooming toward the
curled tip of Texas, just miles from where we were headed. My parents
said we wouldn't make it. Too dangerous. A new plan developed. We'd
check in at a Holiday Inn in Houston and hang out with my mom's
friend from high school. Maybe visit NASA. The next morning, in the
hotel pool, my brother and sister splashed and frolicked while I moped
in the shallow end. Come on, Christie. Get in the pool. Have some pea-
nuts. Check out the ice machine down the hall. I wouldn't. Or couldn't.
I'd had a picture in my mind of the moat I wanted to dig around my sand
castle, and this stupid hotel pool in the middle of this humid, concrete
city didn't fit in my imagination. Whatever skills my siblings had that
allowed them to pivot, readjust, and find joy in the detour, I lacked. I
could only seethe in silence, swallowed up by my internal gale-force fury
and disappointment. My family, unsure of how to reach me, eventually
let me be. No one had any tools to offer me then, or later when I didn't

get ballet solos, or boyfriends broke up with me, or I didn't get into the graduate program I wanted. All I'd ever done with anger was swallow it or throw it up. Now it was pouring out, messy and loud.

~

Here, in this room in the middle of downtown Chicago, the side of my fists bearing streaks of bright pink carpet burn, I sat slumped on the floor and tried to calm my breath. Every single set of eyes on me was filled with compassion. Except Dr. Rosen's. His looked exactly the same: intense but impervious. Almost annoyed at his histrionic patient who was sinking, sinking, sinking.

"YOU! YOU! YOU!" I grabbed fistfuls of my hair with both hands and pulled as hard as I could. My scalp rang with pain, but I pulled again. And again.

Someone said something I couldn't hear. I sat up, still holding my hair as if for ransom.

"The poor baby," Nan said. Her voice wobbled. "Poor, poor baby." My body went slack in the lullaby of her voice. She scooted closer so she could pat my back. I let go of my hair and clambered to my seat. My scalp and hands throbbed with my heartbeat. Stray hairs twined between my fingers. I could not even look at Dr. Rosen. The women beamed me with love, but it stung like pity.

I had a boyfriend, ten group mates, and almost two years of Dr. Rosen under my belt. I felt as stuck as ever.

21

After the Night of the Broken Dishes, Dr. Rosen coached me on how to ask for what I wanted from Jeremy. Pretending to be me, Dr. Rosen would say, "Jeremy, my love, I want you to take me out to dinner tonight," or "I want us to take off our clothes and hold each other in bed." As me, Dr. Rosen sat up tall and smiled broadly. He made it look so easy, this asking for what I wanted.

When it was my turn to ask in real life, I sputtered like an old lawn mower. "I want—do you think we could—would you be open to, maybe—I don't know—leaving your apartment with me sometime?"

Jeremy smiled sweetly. "Where do you want to go?"

"The sushi place down the block?"

He hesitated and then said, "Sure."

One Tuesday morning I got a prescription: invite Jeremy over for the sole purpose of kissing me for five minutes straight. I was skeptical that Jeremy would make the effort for a five-minute kiss, but the point was whether I was willing to ask.

We giggled as I led him to my bedroom, where we stood on the strip of carpet between my closet and my bed. In the living room down the hall, the TV blared *Wheel of Fortune* while Steven and Clare cooked dinner. The night sky was a dark blanket over the window. Jeremy futzed with his watch. He stepped toward me with his finger over the button for the timer.

"Ready?"

I took a deep breath, and let out a shudder and a tiny squeal. Part of me wanted to break role, call this exercise stupid, and pick a fight. I pulled myself together, squeezed my eyes shut, and tapped into the other part of me: the one willing to have this kiss.

"Ready."

Beep.

He slid one arm around my waist and one behind my head and kissed me softly. I was stuck in my head—worried about the timer, whether to slip in some tongue, whether I was getting the most out of this prescription. Then I sent my mind to my lips. I inched closer to Jeremy. The tips of my toes touched his shoes and I pressed my body into his, testing. Could he bear my weight? He smelled like sweat, coffee, and mints. I pulled him closer to me for the final few seconds, knowing time was almost up.

Beep.

"That was cool," he said, fiddling with the button on his watch. He threaded his arm through his backpack, getting ready to go. I felt settled and calm, almost like a baby swaddled tightly and held close. When Jeremy hugged me good-bye, he held me for an extra beat. His body felt solid against mine, like he could hold me up for a long time. I stood at the front door until the elevator dinged and then watched him disappear behind the silver doors. The kiss had filled me up. I wanted it to be enough.

I stayed with Jeremy. I stayed with Dr. Rosen. I stayed with my two groups. I stayed because I believed the agony of staying was necessary to score my heart. I thought that leaving—wanting to leave *and* actually leaving—was proof I wasn't cut out for true intimacy. I had to prove to myself that I could endure whatever pain came up in my relationships. I could survive the heat without letting go. I could attach.

On Christmas morning, I left Jeremy sleeping to meet my friend Jill for coffee. As carols blared through a packed Starbucks, Jill cried about being single with no plans except to visit her abusive father, and

I teared up about the sexless state of my relationship. When I returned to Jeremy's apartment, he called me back to bed. "Take off your jeans," he said.

Merry Christmas!

I liked his initiative.

There was a condom on the pillow next to him, and my starving body heaved into him. An exhilarating openness overtook my body. He thrust once, and an orgasm seized my whole body in a split second.

I promptly burst into tears.

"What is it?" he said.

Underneath all the frustration and anger was an ocean of hurt and sadness. Waves of loneliness, just as Dr. Rosen had long ago predicted.

"Why is it so hard?" I said it over and over. Why, why, why? Was it that hard to love me and my body? Why couldn't we have this physical intimacy all the time? All those weeks I'd chased Jeremy's love and attention reinforced my fear that something wrong with the way that I loved and how I wanted to be loved. The neglect I experienced confirmed my defective capacity for attachment. I'd picked a boyfriend who doled out unsustaining portions of love and attention. And I'd picked him because he was all I could tolerate, even though I wanted so much more. I was like an anorexic who continued to eat rice cakes and celery even though she dreamed of filet mignon and a buttered baked potato.

As 2003 dawned, I sailed into my final semester of law school. Jeremy still needed more time apart than I did. He would occasionally shut down and roll over without any explanation, and his passion for his ASCII video games made me roll my eyes. But instead of breaking household items, I sent texts to Rory, Marty, and Carlos: *I'm so lonely. He's playing video games.* Between those blackout times when he drew the curtain between us, we inched forward, like Dr. Rosen promised we would.

But Dr. Rosen's conflict of interest was no small thing. Was he working for my welfare or Jeremy's?

One Thursday night, Jeremy returned from his men's group and asked if I would buy him a subscription to the *Financial Times* and a pair of running shoes. I could tell from the way he was asking—and because he'd just come from his group—that it was a prescription from Dr. Rosen.

"How dare you set me up to be his sugar mama!" I screamed at Dr. Rosen during my next group session. "You're supposed to be helping me, not using me to bankroll his hobbies."

"I *am* helping you."

"Bullshit."

"What are your two biggest complaints about Jeremy?"

I'd mentioned that Jeremy seemed stuck professionally. He was a member of Mensa and read Greek philosophers with names I could hardly pronounce, yet his job had no future and didn't cover his bills. He hated his boss and felt like he was wasting his potential. He once mentioned going to law school. I'd also expressed concern about his sedentary lifestyle, which I was afraid would negatively impact our nascent sex life.

"If he reads the *Financial Times*, might it help him focus his ambition? If he gets running shoes, he'll be more active. Maybe you can run together and then have sex."

Dr. Rosen, the great puppeteer, yanked the strings. He'd gotten Jeremy to ask, and he would get me to pay. He knew I had the money because the week before I'd brought the seven-thousand-dollar salary advance check that Skadden sent me. Dr. Rosen suggested I pass it around the circle. When it got to him, he held it above his head: *Baruch atah Adonai something-something.*

The rage that had brought me to my knees in group before Christmas surged—rage that Dr. Rosen couldn't truly help me, so he settled for using me to help Jeremy—but I stayed in my chair, pursed my lips, and let it fester. I didn't have words, just the sensation of anger heating my body.

The following weekend, Jeremy started receiving a daily copy of the pink-paged *Financial Times*, and we shopped for a pair of retro black New Balances. When I asked him if he wanted to run with me, he said, "Nah, you go ahead."

After he went after my money, it got worse. Dr. Rosen took aim at my vagina.

One late-winter evening, Jeremy swiveled away from his computer game and declared that March would be "going down on Christie" month.

"Where did this come from?" I said.

"I just decided."

We'd been dating for months, and there'd been little oral action on either of our parts. Now I was looking forward to the gifts that March would bring my way. But on the last Thursday in February, Jeremy returned home from his group with an announcement: "Dr. Rosen thinks it's a bad idea."

I dropped the law book I was holding. "Excuse me?"

"He thinks I'm trying to blow up the relationship."

So now my therapist, who had promised to get me into healthy relationships, including *sexual* relationships, was actively working *against* my pleasure. I excused myself and took the phone into the bathroom. I dialed Dr. Rosen's number, but got his voice mail. I hung up. No voice mails. I would gift him the full force of my anger in person.

"I hear your anger." Dr. Rosen answered with calm confidence when I confronted him in my morning group. I pounded fists on the arms of my chair. I called him a misogynist and a control freak.

"I hear you experience me exerting control."

"You told my boyfriend not to go down on me! What the fuck?" He smiled like *ooh, goody, she's really mad!* "Stop pulling the strings."

Dr. Rosen held up his hands and shook his head. "There're no strings. I don't control anyone's tongue."

"You make suggestions to people who pay you to tell them what to do."

"What do you want?"

"I want you to fuck right off." The anger was stuck halfway between my throat and my chest.

More stuckness. In my chair, in my body, in my relationship with my boyfriend and my therapist.

When Dr. Rosen put his hands together, it signaled the end of the session. I stood up with everyone else, but I didn't recite the Serenity Prayer, and when everyone split off in twos to hug, I took turns

22

That seven-thousand-dollar salary advance from Skadden made me bold. All my law school friends were planning post–bar exam trips with their beloveds. I dreamed of international travel with my boyfriend. I dreamed of us in Italy, holding hands on medieval bridges and feeding each other bites of pizza margherita, surrounded by languid rivers and soaring cathedrals. I dreamed of us laughing, touching, exploring, and loving. The man holding my hand in my daydreams bore little resemblance to Jeremy. But I set my sights on the trip and wouldn't back down. I'd worked hard in law school to earn a place at Skadden, which earned me seven thousand dollars in advance salary, and I worked hard in therapy to have a relationship. How hard could this be?

Negotiations were tense from the start. I would suggest Tuscany or the Cinque Terre, and Jeremy would shrug his shoulders and sigh heavily.

"We could do Greece, the birthplace of philosophy."

More shrugging.

"Can't we discuss this?"

"You get to control this because you have the money."

"So you pick." I threw up my hands. Honestly, I didn't care where we went so long as it was *together*.

embracing Patrice, Rory, Marty, Carlos, and the Colonel. But I turned my back on Dr. Rosen. I wouldn't pretend everything was okay just because ninety minutes were up. I felt betrayed. His loyalty clearly belonged to Jeremy, and he brought all his Harvard expertise to bear in treating *his* sexual hangups. Dr. Rosen didn't have my interests or sexual pleasure in mind at all.

In the afternoon group, I refused to look at Dr. Rosen but explained to all the women how Dr. Rosen was interfering in my relationship by advising Jeremy not to pleasure me. Marnie narrowed her eyes and yelled at Dr. Rosen for using me to help Jeremy. Then she swiveled her chair toward me and scolded me for being so willing to starve in my relationship. "This isn't all Dr. Rosen," she said, pointing at me. "You're going along with all of this." I wasn't upset that she was yelling at me—I could hear that she loved me and wanted more for me. I did too.

After a long pause, he said, "Italy's fine."

Both of my groups and Dr. Rosen advised me to focus on myself and plan the trip I wanted to take. "He'll either come with you or he won't," Dr. Rosen said. So comforting. I pushed aside my brewing dread. I barreled ahead in the face of Jeremy's resistance because being a young woman alone in Italy was not a story I was willing to inhabit. Solo travel was not one of my heart's deep callings.

The temperature in Florence soared into the nineties, and BBC Radio reported seven heat-related deaths. Jeremy and I ate a breakfast of soft scrambled eggs, fresh strawberries, and toast with homemade orange marmalade on the sun-flooded second-floor terrace of the Hotel Silla. We moved our chairs to take cover under the shade of a fig tree. I could have stayed there all day, looking over the Arno River and listening to the pigeons coo, but I'd scheduled a bike tour that started at ten. The day before I'd taken a bus to Siena. By myself. Jeremy hadn't wanted to face the heat.

"Are you up for the bike tour?" I asked in my upbeat vacation voice, the voice of my heart holding on to hope.

"You go ahead. I'm going to study." He pulled out an LSAT workbook and his special black pen. He'd recently decided to apply to law school, which was an undeniably positive development given how much he hated his job. But his ironclad study schedule was not to be interrupted by the Florentine countryside, even though the LSAT was months away.

"Is there something else you would rather do? I can cancel the bike thing—"

"No, you go. I need to do a practice test."

Leading up to the trip, Dr. Rosen had encouraged me to accept Jeremy's introversion. Stop trying to change him. I understood the importance of acceptance, but when Jeremy said he wouldn't be joining me for the second day in a row, I wanted to flip the table and send his precious LSAT book flying into the cobblestone street. How small could I fold my desire so that Jeremy's rebuffs no longer stung? How could I make myself want less from this man who said he loved me, but who seemed to have so little desire to spend time with me?

He flicked his pen and started sketching out his answer to one of the questions.

I kissed him on the top of his head and set out for the bike tour, fuming. Who pays for her boyfriend to come to Italy and ignore her? My heart thrummed its familiar rhythm: alone, alone, alone.

A lanky expat named Sherry with a yoga teacher's posture showed me my bike. "Where's your partner?"

"Oh, he's—" Like the wife covering for an alcoholic husband who couldn't get out of bed, I lied. "Sick." I blamed the heat and jet lag.

The twelve other people in our group arrived in pairs. Honeymooners, fathers and daughters, college roommates, a couple celebrating thirty years of marriage. Our first stop was an old stone farmhouse, where a sunburned groundskeeper served us a morning snack. I sat on an ancient stone bench eating the salty cheese and buttery quail egg surrounded by strangers who were snapping pictures of each other.

"Want a picture?" a father from San Diego asked me. I wiped the sweat from my brow and stood by a fig tree, trying to look natural, even though I didn't know what to do with my hands. Clasp them in front of me? Put them on my hips? Steady myself on the stone wall?

The father whispered to his daughter, "It's so brave to travel alone in a foreign country." Believe me, buddy, I'm a lot of things, but brave comes well after desperate, foolish, lonely, depressed, sad, lost, humiliated, and starving.

When the other bicyclists headed back to Florence at the end of the tour, I broke away, pedaling so fast my quads burned. After I returned my bike, I followed the narrow streets back to the hotel but then stopped halfway there. Why rush? Jeremy wasn't pining for me. Would he even be happy to see me? I veered away from the hotel and toward the tourist strip by the Ponte Vecchio instead, where leather belts hung from stalls like slabs of meat. On a side street, I spotted a pay phone. I chucked coin after coin into the slot until I reached Chicago.

Dr. Rosen's voice mail picked up after three rings. At the beep, I let it out. "I just went on a bike tour, *alone*. Yesterday, I went to Siena, *alone*. I thought you said you could fix this—that you could fix me." I sobbed into the grimy Italian pay phone until a computerized voice cut me off.

After all the therapy sessions I'd sat through. The prescriptions I'd willingly done. The *feeling* of my feelings. Here I was, still so terribly alone. The loneliness was supposed to recede. I thought my progress in therapy would be a graph line that trended up and only up, but sitting alone in Florence, I felt that same desperate stirring I'd felt in Chicago before starting group. If I hadn't changed yet, when would I? Maybe it wasn't possible for me. I loved my group mates—and even Dr. Rosen—but they couldn't come to Italy with me. Dr. Rosen was right: I'd tasted the company and fellowship of sitting in group week after week, and now the loneliness was darker and more devastating than it had ever been.

When I returned to the room, Jeremy was asleep on the bed, his study guide tented on his stomach. He smiled when he opened his eyes. I lay down next to him, our bodies barely touching. In silence we watched the light fade from the window as the sun sank behind the Duomo.

That night after dinner, he clicked off the light and lay down on his back. Would we have sex? I breathed deep and commanded my body not to want. I folded my desire like a tiny origami crane and tucked it away.

"I'm going to masturbate before bed. You're welcome to join me." Jeremy slipped off his boxer shorts, and his busy elbow tapped my forearm with every stroke.

"Want me to do that?" I whispered, a strand of my desire shaking loose.

"I've got it."

I rested my hand on his shoulder, grateful he let me keep it there.

After Italy, I started working the long hours of a first-year associate at a big law firm, never leaving the office at night before seven. Suddenly I had a secretary, an expense account, and an office with a window overlooking the Chicago River. During my sixth week of work, I pulled my first all-nighter. My main task as a young lawyer was to review financial documents ten hours a day for a client whose beverages I grew up drinking. Skadden also sent me to the client's headquarters to interview the bigwigs who set up their sales strategy so we could defend them to the SEC. After a long day of back-to-back meetings with the all-male-except-me team and a long dinner, I would collapse on a hotel bed and call Jeremy, who was home playing his NetHack.

"You're doing great. I'm so proud of you," Jeremy would say.

While I was off learning how to be a Skadden lawyer, Jeremy slipped into a depression. He gained weight, stopped shaving, skipped AA meetings, and sat at his computer playing his game most of the hours he wasn't at work. Mr. Bourgeois puked up a hairball that languished in the middle of his living room for a week. The bathtub grew furry with hair and scum. When I spent the night over there, I held my pee as long as I could. I could almost make it eighteen hours. And we were *always* at his place these days. I understood he was unable to expend the energy to come all the way to my house.

In my spare time, I tried to pull him out of it by buying him groceries and suggesting he hit a meeting or call his sponsor. In group, I begged Dr. Rosen to help him. "Can't you see he's depressed?" Dr. Rosen's answer was always the same: "What are *you* feeling?"

The feedback from both of my groups was unanimous: "Concentrate on your new career."

"Focus on your new Skadden life. Maybe your tastes will change," Dr. Rosen said. It sounded like an offhand comment. My tastes?

I craved action. My boyfriend was not going to mentally deteriorate, or God forbid, relapse on alcohol, on my watch. I bought him a new comforter—a masculine plaid—took a bottle of bleach to the bathroom, and pulled globs of God knows what out of the drain. I scrapped cat puke out of the rug. I stocked his fridge with fresh fruit and lean proteins, his pantry with low-sugar cereals.

In my frenzy, I remained deaf to the one need he had expressed—to be left alone. Today, I have compassion for him and the illness that robbed him of joy and energy. I also have compassion for myself as his ex-girlfriend who thought she could cure his malaise with new linens and fresh pineapple. At the time, all I could manage was scrambling harder to "fix" him by fashioning him into the man I wanted him to be.

One night during this dark period, under the stiffness of Jeremy's new plaid comforter, I shimmied down to give him a blow job. I'd been working as a lawyer for six months. My standard of living had shifted from law student to Big Firm attorney. I occasionally let myself shop at Whole Foods. I bought a full-price skirt at J.Crew. My savings account swelled to two grand. During the daylight hours, I squared my shoulders and stood like a woman worthy of the thick white business cards Skadden printed with my name on them.

At night, I slumped and ached.

The blow job was my idea. An attempt to bridge the wide gulf between me and Jeremy. As my head bobbed between his sweaty thighs, I had a single thought: *I don't want to be doing this.* I violated myself by forcing the blow job and violated him by feigning desire and using oral sex to get him to pay attention to me and arrest his clinical depression. Jeremy hadn't showered in days—his body smelled sour with neglect and so many days' residue. I breathed out of my mouth, trying to ignore the stench of his body and the swells of my own disgust.

The following Tuesday morning I didn't mention the blow job because I was ashamed. Jeremy's unwashed body felt like something I should protect, even though Dr. Rosen advised me all along to bring *everything* to group. I was also ashamed that I forced a blow job I hadn't enjoyed. My relationship was a farce, and I continued to act dishonestly and against my own interest and pleasure. By the afternoon, everything I wasn't saying about my relationship was a loaded gun pointed at my throat. During a lull in the conversation, I spoke up.

"I don't want to suck dirty dick."

Everyone turned toward me.

"What did you just say?" Marnie said.

Nan's eyes grew wide as I described the blow job. "Hell no," she whispered.

When I finally looked at Dr. Rosen, I saw compassion in his eyes. "You don't have to suck dirty dick," he said.

My eyes teared up. He said it again very slowly. *You. Don't. Have. To. Suck. Dirty. Dick.* Then added: *ever again.* I nodded.

"I'm done," I said. My spine straightened in the truth of those two words.

Dr. Rosen held his arms out straight in front of him, palms turned up. Then he slowly turned his palms over. "This is how you let go."

I wasn't following. It looked like tai chi. My group mates put words to the gesture.

"Stop calling him."

"Stop trekking to that shithole apartment after work."

"Stop paying for everything."

If I just stopped—the chasing, planning, schlepping, conniving, cajoling, cleaning, shopping, pining, buying, and sucking—it would all be over. On his own, Jeremy wasn't going to pop over to my house. He wasn't going to make a dinner reservation or get tickets to see Wilco at the Riviera. If I let go, there would be nothing. I would be truly alone, but I would be free.

"So if I let go—" I said, grabbing Dr. Rosen's hairy forearm with both hands. I leaned toward him until our faces were less than a foot apart. I wanted him to finish the sentence. Whatever he said, I was going to hold him to it.

"You're going to find out what a real relationship feels like."

23

"Can you let yourself have an orgasm with him?"

Dr. Rosen and the morning group were waiting for an answer from me. I was three months out of my relationship with Jeremy and two weeks into a flirtatious fling with a Skadden intern who was in pursuit of a full-time job offer.

"Aren't there laws against this?" I asked. "I'm not supposed to bed the job aspirants."

"You're the lawyer," Nan said.

"I don't do sexual harassment."

"Apparently you do."

I'd met "the Intern" at a dinner the firm hosted at Japonais. Over a steady stream of raw tuna and unagi, I let him compliment my eyes and insinuate that his sexual prowess would blow my fucking mind. He was such a boy—cocky, loose-limbed, and unabashedly sexual in his designer jeans and hipster Adidas tennis shoes. He was six years younger than I was, but it felt like more. He grew up driving his dad's brand-new Lexus SUV and taking SAT prep classes. He'd never worked a full-time job. I accepted his offer to walk me home from the restaurant, thinking that a wiry thing like him would never be able to batter through the invisible fence that kept sexually alive men away from me. But he sailed over the fence, and in one smooth moment when he pressed his lips to mine under a busted streetlamp on Clark Street, I opened my mouth and received him. As his lips moved softly against mine, there was a zing between my legs, and my appetite for anything in the world other than his lips on mine vaporized in an instant.

The next day he tracked down my personal e-mail address. *That was some kiss*, he wrote. I didn't tell him I'd stayed awake all night thinking about it. I didn't tell him that every one of my limbs was thrumming with activity—still, after fifteen hours. I didn't tell him that I'd skipped breakfast and didn't have lunch until almost three because I was feasting on the memory of that kiss. What I told him was: *I've had better*. A delicious lie that drove him to promise me that he would be the best I ever had. *Prove it*, I demanded.

Dr. Rosen was impervious to sexual harassment laws. "So? Will you let yourself have an orgasm with him?"

Yes, I desperately wanted to bed the Intern and let him make good on all his promises. I wanted him to lick my honey until the sun rose over Chicago. But I also wanted a real relationship, a go-to-Costco-on-Sunday type of thing. And this boy-child didn't seem the type to appreciate a woman in her sweats, face dotted with zit cream after a sixteen-hour workday. In his third e-mail, he confessed to being both bi-curious and recently snorting cocaine in Miami.

"Nothing on his résumé screams 'suitable lifetime partner for a woman in recovery.'"

"You could fuck him and find out," Dr. Rosen said.

Toto, we are not in Catholic school anymore.

Our first date was on a Monday night, a few days after he accepted his offer from Skadden, so I was no longer in violation of harassment laws. He had classes all day Monday, so he pulled up to my office in his shiny black Lexus after his constitutional law seminar. He opened my door like a valet. The car was spotless—shiny black leather, clean cup holders, and a sound system that lit up the dashboard.

"My usual move is to take girls to Jane's in Bucktown and then to a neighborhood bar, but you're getting the deluxe treatment." His smile was sly. He'd already put more thought into this date than any man had ever put into planning time with me.

He drove to a bistro on Grand Street. I'd written him off as a smart-ass player, which he most definitely was, but underneath his relentless sexual swagger, he displayed a fascination with legal ethics and the contours of civil liberties. His face softened with genuine tenderness when he talked about holding his baby niece for the first time. He lost points for having voted for George Bush, but earned a few back when he mentioned his therapist.

"It's not Dr. Jonathan Rosen, is it?" He shook his head. Thank God.

By the end of the pumpkin soup course, I was ready to go full Luther Vandross with him. He brushed my calf with his foot, and I felt that heat between my legs again. As I sliced through my sea bass with the edge of my fork, I had only one thought: *Oh my God, I'm having sex tonight.*

When the check came, he pulled out his wallet and slipped a black American Express in the pocket of the leather folder. He scribbled a figure for a tip, signed his name with an illegible flourish, and stood up. "Let's get out of here." He held out his hand and I grabbed it. His suggestive smile told me that he had no intention of playing video games all night.

On the way back to his place, he asked me questions about Texas, as if it was an exotic region in outer space.

"It's flat, hot, and conservative."

"Any Jews there?"

"A few. My ballet teacher was a French Jew. Why?"

"We Jews are always thinking about our relative numbers." This was the first I'd heard of the Intern's religion. I could picture you-know-who's self-satisfied smile when he realized he'd instructed me to have an orgasm with a Jewish man. *Mamaleh, I'm so proud of you.*

As the elevator doors in his lobby closed on us, the Intern hooked his fingers into my belt loops and pulled me close. He smelled like clean laundry and something spicy, like cinnamon. He kissed me like he was starving for me, and I matched his intensity when I kissed him back.

When his hands cupped my breasts, I groaned with pleasure through my *one* bra.

I felt so free—like I could feel the air molecules dancing between us, celebrating my liberation. I slipped my hand under his shirt, and he moved closer to me. It felt like magic—a man moving closer to me, a man staying awake for me, a man hungry for me.

"You like that?" he whispered. Each time he touched me another layer melted away. He bit my lip playfully, and it was good-bye to the nuns who said French kissing was a sin because it mirrored the sex act. He touched the small of my back, and the grip of my mother's edict to save sex for marriage released its hold on my body. He held my face as he kissed me and washed away the stain of my relationship with Jeremy—the hairballs in the drain, the bad blow job, and the constant grinding of my flesh against the stone of his isolation.

When the doors opened with a ping, I tried to pull away, but he held me close. "Don't we need to get off?" I said. He flicked his tongue in my ear and whispered, "Oh, we're definitely going to do that."

We raced down the hall, him ahead of me, reaching back for my hand. Who was this guy who wanted to freebase pleasure and take me with him?

We barely made it to his apartment door before he had unhooked my bra. I'd never been kissed that deeply. Parts of me that had never stirred in the presence of someone else sprung to life. This, this, this, my body sang with pleasure. *More, more, more.*

He led me to his small, neat bedroom. The light was off, but I could make out a plain gray comforter on the bed, and some law books on the shelf next to a small clock with glowing red numbers. I opened my arms wide and belly-flopped onto his soft, clean bed.

There was nothing between us—no video games, no mental illness, no therapists. He reached for a condom and pulled off his pants. His forehead rested on mine, and I looked into his open, unafraid eyes. I pressed against him and shuddered into my prescription.

When I opened my eyes, his smirk offered a single message: *I told you I was good at this.* The waves of pleasure rose from between my legs and crested through my entire body. And then, I burst into tears.

"I don't know why I'm crying. I'm not sad." I tried to stuff the sobs back into my treacherous heart. The Intern kissed the tears as they slid down my cheeks. He asked what was wrong.

"You're just so—"

He raised his eyebrows and leaned closer, kissing my neck, chasing the tears that escaped. "What?"

"Clean." Tears continued to stream down my hot cheeks. "Oh my God," I whispered, covering my face with both hands.

"It's kind of hot, actually." He lifted my chin and kissed me on the lips. "What's your therapist going to say?"

"I did it, and then I cried." My afternoon group was rapt. I'd slept through my morning group for the first time in my therapeutic history. Finally. I'd waited three years to be too busy having sex to attend group.

Nan was incredulous. "What did that little white boy do to you?"

Dr. Rosen shook his head, his hands at his temples. "You let him pleasure you, and then you showed him all the feelings you had about it. Do you understand how intimate that was?" He gazed at me with amazement.

"I want to do it again."

"When's your next date?"

"Next week." Thumbs-up from the Good Doctor. "He's Jewish, by the way." Exactly as I suspected, Dr. Rosen gasped and held his hands to his heart. "I knew you'd do that."

"Why do you think I'm reacting like this?"

"So you can insist this is all about you. Like Luther." Dr. Rosen's head was bobbing maniacally, and he stuck up his thumbs like I'd gotten the right answer.

"You're so annoying," Marnie said to Dr. Rosen with a dismissive wave of her hand.

Dr. Rosen kept his gaze on me. "Do you understand?"

All I understood was that my therapist had a Freudian bug up his ass. Dr. Rosen accurately read my blank look as ignorance.

"If you attach to me—here, in treatment"—he pointed toward his

dorky brown shoes—"then you will be able to attach to men out there."
He gestured out the window. "Assuming we have a healthy attachment,
you can use it as a foundation for your romantic relationships."

"Is it working?" I held my palms to my chest.

"Does a bear shit in the woods?"

Once a week, the Intern picked me up in his shiny black car and whisked
me away to a trendy bistro where we would pass innuendo back and
forth like a basket of tortilla chips. It was hypercharged flirting—him
bragging about how he could please me; me hinting I was far hungrier
than he imagined. "I've been deprived a long time," I would say. "Nothing I can't handle," he would insist. Back at his place, he would hunch
over his stereo, laboring over the perfect mood music. He favored Al
Green and hip-hop. Watching him work so hard to set the mood was a
huge turn-on.

The third night we were together, he pulled me into his bedroom
with a puckish glint in his eye. "I have a surprise for you. Wait right
here," he said, backing out of the room. When he returned, he handed
me something blue and white that was folded like a flag.

"What the?" I giggled as I unfolded the heavy fabric and held up a
giant football jersey with a number eighteen on it.

"It's Peyton Manning's jersey. I want you to wear it."

"Just because I'm from Texas doesn't mean football makes me hot."

"It'll be hot to sleep next to you if you are wearing that."

My body surrendered to the force of his easy freedom. I wanted to
crawl into the jersey, into his body, into his world, where desire was
naked and blatant and having sex was always on the table.

Both my groups loved the Intern. Both unanimously predicted that
he was falling in love with me. Both pronounced me cured of whatever emotional injury or character defect led me to stay so long with
Jeremy. Dr. Rosen beamed at me, session after session, praising my
detailed disclosures of our intimate encounters, my joy, my surrender
to pleasure.

I floated through my workdays. The glow of hot sex and a real, budding relationship softened the daily humiliations of being a junior female associate at a law firm. One Tuesday, when the partner asked me, the only female in the room, to take notes during a team meeting like I was a secretary, I bit my lip, but let it go when I saw an e-mail from the Intern pop up on my BlackBerry.

Two hours later, I handed Dr. Rosen a hard copy of the e-mail. "Read it," I said. "Start with the second paragraph."

"'It's imperative that I marry a Jewish woman.'" Dr. Rosen looked up.

"Why's he talking marriage? Y'all fucked, what, six times?" Nan said.

"Five."

"He's just scared," Marnie said. Emily and Regina agreed.

"White people are so weird." Nan laughed to herself, her golden hoop earrings catching the sunlight.

Panic coursed through me, making it hard to sit in my chair and hear what everyone was saying. How could they be so calm? The Intern was going to pack up all the pleasure and freedom and drive it away in his fancy black car.

"You don't know that," Dr. Rosen said.

"A lot of good dating Jewish men has done me! Thanks a lot, Dr. Rosen."

"It has done you a world of good. And you don't know what's going to happen next."

I knew the next time I walked into this stupid fourteen-by-fourteen room, I'd be sitting in a heap of my own heartache, kicking the tissue box away as tears streamed down my face.

When the Intern rolled up to my office for the last time a few days later, his smile looked fake and betrayed no hint of his trademark sass. His hug was the swift A-frame embrace you'd give your great-aunt Beatrice. Heat and the promise of sex no longer warmed the air between us.

He drove us to Sai Café in Lincoln Park, where we ordered separate sashimi rolls. I avoided the shrimp to prove what a good Jewess I could be. I called Rory from the bathroom where water softly trickled through a miniature rock garden. "I can feel a 'good-bye forever' coming." My stomach was at the top of a hill about to plunge into free fall. Rory told me to breathe and stay open to all possibilities. "Maybe he'll ask you to convert," she said.

"It's not going to work," he said as he pulled in front of my building at the end of the night.

I asked why we couldn't just keep hanging out. He shook his head, insisting it would be wrong to lead me on. I told him I'd consider conversion.

"You're Catholic."

"I haven't been to mass in years, and I'd be a wonderful Jew. I hate ham. I'll send my kids to shul. I'll blow the shofar." His lips turned up, but it wasn't a true smile. It was a pity smirk.

"I'm serious. I'm not talking about an Internet conversion course. I'll go to Anshe Emet or KAM Isaiah. I'll have a mikvah and a bar mitzvah—"

"Bat."

"I'll keep kosher, bake challah, circumcise—"

"I'm sorry."

I shut my mouth and stared straight ahead at the spot where he first kissed me, where my appetite shriveled, where this thing I called a "love affair" but would later downgrade to a "fling" had started.

"Can't you come up for one more night?"

"Let's not turn into caricatures of ourselves."

From my office the next morning, I begged Dr. Rosen to call me back. I couldn't wait until the next session. I needed him now. When he called, I cried into the phone, asking him to tell me why. Why didn't the Intern want to be with me? Why was I on the phone with him crying again? Why did I have to be raised Catholic? Why did my parents have to name me after Christ? I twisted the phone cord around my finger and listened for the hope in Dr. Rosen's answers. Nothing he said soothed me. He asked me if my life was getting better than it was before I started treatment. Yes, my life was better than it was before—I felt close to him and my group mates. Clare knew about my groups and my recovery. I was learning how to be who I really was in front of other people. But a relationship with a man felt as impossible as ever.

"I need more help. Something more. There must be something more. Maybe I've gone as far as I can with you, Dr. Rosen." I had no idea what I was asking him for. My thoughts were not coherent—I was babbling into the phone trying to beat back my sadness. My index finger turned white under the black phone cord.

"I have something in mind. We can talk about it in your groups tomorrow."

I took a ragged breath. "What're you thinking?" My heart lifted at the thought of a shortcut through the heartsickness.

"We can discuss it tomorrow." What was he planning? Individual sessions? Match.com for sexually anorexic women?

"Give me a hint."

"I'll see you tomorrow."

24

I showed up in the waiting room ten minutes early, my face tight and splotchy from crying. I slumped into a chair across from the particle board bookshelf and closed my eyes. When someone walked through the waiting room door, I opened one eye, expecting to see Carlos or Patrice, but it was a tall man in a gray business suit holding a brown leather briefcase. Total lawyer or finance type. Ten years or so older than me.

I'd forgotten that Dr. Rosen had announced we were getting a new member.

"I'm Reed," he said, sticking out his hand like he was at a cocktail party. I didn't stand up, but I offered my hand and felt something flicker in the air between us when our palms met. His salt-and-pepper hair was short on the sides and longer on the top, and his shoes were polished to such a high shine that I could see my sad, puffy face in them. Of course, I noted the gold band on his left hand and a dimple on his left cheek when he smiled. Seconds later, Dr. Rosen opened the door, and we filed into the group room. Carlos and Patrice arrived before we sat down.

"What's that?" Reed pointed to a purple terry-cloth hand towel in my lap. I'd been carrying it around with me since the Intern dropped me on the curb.

"This is my mourning rag. I just got dumped." I grabbed a thread between the fingernails of my index finger and thumb and yanked. I pulled another and then another. Soon individual purple threads criss-crossed my lap. A few drifted to the floor. As I yanked, hot tears rolled down my cheeks. Having something to do with my hands soothed me, and yanking threads out of the cloth helped me parcel out my anger in microdoses. Patrice scooted the box of tissues on the floor over to my chair. I kicked them away. "I don't do tissues."

Patrice ignored my outburst, rubbed my arm, and reminded me that the Intern was not marriage material.

Carlos took the lead on the interrogation of Reed and elicited the pertinent information: hotshot investment banker, married, twin girls, sober a few years, and then the jackpot:

"Why are you really here?" Carlos asked.

Reed's face reddened, and he looked at Dr. Rosen, who nodded encouragingly, like *tell them*.

"Out with it," Carlos said. When Reed hung his head, Carlos caught my eye and mouthed *he's so hot*. I nodded and yanked out another purple thread.

"I'm struggling in my marriage." Ah, intimacy issues.

"Go on." Carlos raised his eyebrows.

"Oh, brother." Patrice sighed. She sensed what was coming—a tale of unfaithfulness, a long-suffering wife, a mistress who made him feel vital. Dr. Rosen's face wore his widest grin.

"I was at cocktail party for one of our funds a few weeks ago. There was a woman—" Reed looked around the room, unsure. Could he trust us? "She and I went back to her office, and she gave—"

"Oh my God, she sucked your cock!" Carlos clapped his hands.

Patrice asked if he'd told his wife. He hadn't; he hoped to save his marriage. Patrice and Rory praised Reed for his bravery in telling us.

I spread my towel out on my lap. I'd plucked a four-inch bald spot in the middle of it. I ran my hand over the sheared fabric. What would it be like to run my hand over Reed's lapel? His leg? This was the longest I'd gone without thinking about the Intern in a week. I felt something like hope bore its way into my rubble heap of a heart. I wished group was longer than ninety minutes.

Before group closed, I gathered my purple threads and lobbed a burning question. "Do y'all think I'll ever have sex again?" Reed's mouth curled into a half smile.

"If you want to," Dr. Rosen said.

"I do. Really soon." My body hurt from missing the Intern and the pleasure he offered.

"You're open to suggestions?"

"I'll do *anything*." Our fidelity-challenged, hot new group member had made me forget that Dr. Rosen was going to suggest something to me. "What'd you have in mind?" I dropped the towel into my lap and opened my palms.

"I suggest you join the Monday/Thursday group."

I sucked in a sharp breath and grabbed the towel with both fists.

"You cannot be serious. Another group? *Twice* a week?" Did he know I had a full-time job? Did he know that lawyers have to bill forty hours a week? I shook my head and pursed my lips. I picked up the towel and yanked hard at a thread on the border of the bald spot.

"This group is different. It's the same members twice a week, which creates additional intensity. Every member is a long-term patient—"

"I need to come here four times a week to get into a real relationship? How fucked up am I?"

"You're very fucked up." Dr. Rosen smiled.

"Nice sales pitch."

Dr. Rosen suggested I stay in the Tuesday-morning group, but drop the afternoon one to make room for this Monday/Thursday group. Where was this offer a year ago when I would have rather shaved my head than return to the group where Nan and Marnie almost came to blows? Now I felt a pang of sadness. Those women carried me through my Jeremy days and all through my fling with the Intern. Nan had held me that day I tried to pull my hair out. Zenia had taught me about fan fiction and long-distance lesbian sex. Was I ready to leave them behind?

"I'll think about it."

When we stood up for the closing, I let my sheared towel and all the plucked threads fall to the floor.

Here I was again, debating whether to join *another* Rosen-group. I'd said yes twice and now my life was filled with people who knew me well. Intimately. Rory knew about every drop of food I put into my mouth. Marty offered my nightly affirmations. My groups knew about the dirty dick I'd sucked, my pinworms, my temper tantrums. Wasn't that what I'd always wanted? People to fully know me and all my stories while also sharing theirs with me. That was definitely part of it and now I wanted more. I wanted a family of my own, one like Marnie's, Patrice's, Rory's, and Nan's. I was grateful for what I had but new desires bloomed: To have a family of my own with a partner. To become a mother. To settle romantically. To find my power at Skadden. I believed Dr. Rosen could get me there, though it stung that it would take three sessions, as in two hundred seventy minutes, of group each week.

I'd heard of the Monday/Thursday group. It was the only Rosen-group that met more than once a week. It was known as the "advanced" group. There was some pride at being invited. And there was also suspicion that Dr. Rosen just wanted my money—I was vulnerable and making six figures. He could be offering me a way to get where I wanted to go or using me as a cash cow to finance a sailboat. How could I know which it was?

And yet, of course I said yes. With three days a week of group, surely I would have everything I wanted in a less than a year.

Part 3

25

The temperature was well below freezing the third Monday in January, but I was too nervous to feel the burn of the wind on my face. When my feet went out from under me, I skidded on the fresh layer of ice blanketing the sidewalk, ass on concrete, two blocks from Dr. Rosen's office. Was joining this new group a horrible idea? My throbbing hip-bone suggested yes.

"What have you heard about us?" Max asked. He had tousled blond hair and perfect posture, and wore a blue blazer with the gold buttons. Midforties. Very country club. I'd heard of Max. The word on the Rosen-grapevine was that he had come to Dr. Rosen years earlier strung out on drugs and living in his car. I'd heard something about felony charges. But he'd cleaned up and risen through the ranks of a pharmaceutical company. Now he was a hotshot exec, served on the board of his daughters' fancy private school, and summered in Snowmass. Something in his raised eyebrows and smirk told me he knew I'd heard the rumors.

"Nothing much." My skin felt too tight.

"You're lying." Max stared at me. My eyes darted away from his. I glimpsed Dr. Rosen, who offered nothing but his goofball smile.

"Well." I took a deep breath. "I heard you're a recovering addict."

"And?" My too-tight skin turning red.

"You used to party pretty hard."

Max didn't look away. He knew exactly what I wasn't saying. It was a test, and I'd failed.

Here, there was no plum-headed Zenia describing her fan-fiction sex. No one was eating or screaming or bawling. Everyone had a brief-case or a dignified leather purse tucked beside their chair. "We're the advanced group." Max was clearly the spokesperson for this highly composed and civilized group of people.

Patrice from Tuesday morning was there. She'd graduated to this "advanced" group a year earlier, but hadn't said much about it, other than that Max could be a handful. This morning, she smiled warmly but did not offer any tips on how to survive the next eighty-five minutes. The bruise on my hip pulsed with my heartbeat, but if I winced or rubbed it, I would draw attention to myself. No thank you.

Lorne was another familiar face. He was midforties and slightly disheveled—wrinkled khaki pants and frayed maroon sweater—but had an open smile that felt like a welcome. I'd met Lorne at his wedding, which I had attended as Jeremy's date. Jeremy and Lorne were in the men's group together. My left foot jangled as I considered what that meant.

"We've heard about you," Brad said, as if he had read my mind. Brad was slightly older than Lorne, tall and thin like Ichabod Crane with salt-and-pepper hair. The only thing I'd heard about him was that he was obsessed with money.

"What'd you hear?"

He and Max exchanged a look. Both smiled.

"That you had anal sex with Blake," Brad said with only a hint of sheepishness. Not what I was expecting, a memory from a relationship before I started group. My mouth twisted into a scowl. Whatever, Brad. I could own my sexual history.

"With Jeremy too, actually," I said.

"I'd heard that too," Brad said.

My stomach heaved with anxiety. Was I going to throw up? What was I doing, letting men I didn't know quiz me about my sex life? This was the first moment in my three and a half years with Dr. Rosen that

I wished desperately for confidentiality. All these years, I admired Dr. Rosen's insistence that secrets were toxic. Now I saw the murky downside: I'd just joined a group full of people who knew everything there was to know about my anal sex résumé.

The group let me stew in my discomfort and went on to discuss Lorne's unhinged ex-wife and Brad's upcoming job interview for a position that would increase his base salary by 20 percent. When there was a lull in the conversation, I caught Dr. Rosen's eye. "What makes this the advanced group?" I asked. Before he could answer, a woman with shoulder-length silver hair wearing a navy polyester pantsuit jumped in.

"Max and I are charter members of this group. Going back to the late eighties. I'm Maggie, by the way." She was sitting right next to Dr. Rosen. "We knew Dr. Rosen back when—" She paused.

"When what?" I said.

Maggie rolled her eyes. "Let's just say Dr. Rosen used to have very different boundaries."

"What does that mean?" I asked.

"Max once had lunch at his house—"

"He served me a ham sandwich," Max said. Ham? Dr. *Baruch Attah Adonai* served *tref* to a patient? "He used to be less Jewish. His über-Jew thing started when he married his second wife."

Maggie leaned over and told me she was once "very close" with Dr. Rosen's ex-wife, who was anorexic and cheated on Dr. Rosen with a man she met at the Checkerboard Lounge. "I think it was a Black man."

"Guess that explains your reaction to my Luther Vandross dream," I said to Dr. Rosen. He clutched his belly and laughed.

Max mentioned that Dr. Rosen took an extended leave of absence in the early nineties for an undisclosed reason. Brad and Lorne debated whether it was treatment for sex addiction or codependence.

With each revelation, my stomach clenched tighter. The shiny Dr. Rosen who lived in my imagination, to whom I gave the power over my deepest desires, was splattered with mud with each new divulgence. I curled my lips over my teeth and pressed down hard.

Max turned to Dr. Rosen and slapped his forearm. "Remember when you had diarrhea for months? When was that? Eighty-nine?

Ninety-one?" The rest of the group called out different years. Why did they know about Dr. Rosen's bowels?

I wanted to vaporize and float out of the room and out of treatment. Max and Maggie were fire hydrants gushing story after story about Dr. Rosen dating back to the first Reagan administration—when I was still in junior high. *That time his dog ran away. That summer he wore seersucker. That time he had to physically restrain Maggie from attacking Max and broke one of her ribs.* In fifteen minutes I learned more about my therapist than I had in the past three-plus years. The blank slate was slathered in muck.

Dr. Rosen smiled in his usual unguarded way. He wasn't embarrassed by these disclosures. I looked around the room—no one else was alarmed. Their bodies were loose in their chairs. These stories were like family lore shared around the Thanksgiving table year after year. If Max stopped in the middle of a story, then Maggie or Brad would keep going. So many stories. So much history. So many layers of shit slathered on my Dr. Rosen.

Until this moment, I'd admired what an iconoclast Dr. Rosen was, even when my friends who saw other therapists raised their eyebrows when I told them about Baby Jeremiah, the cocktease prescription, my nightly calls to Rory and Marty. I believed Dr. Rosen was courageous, smart, and gifted at treating addicts like me. But now I worried that he was something else: deeply flawed and possibly negligent. Maybe even dangerous.

The longer I sat and listened to my new group mates laugh about the past, the more nauseated I felt. They all had marriages, children, and careers. Maggie was a grandmother. None of them were desperate for something like I was, though Brad definitely fixated on increasing his net worth. None of them needed Dr. Rosen to be the powerful Oz and not an ordinary con man as much as I did.

Dr. Rosen cocked his head toward me and smirked. "Yes?"

"I have nothing to add to this trip down memory lane."

"Did you want to share something? You were mumbling under your breath?" Maggie said through her innocent-as-Grandma smile.

Everyone stared at me. My hands were shaking as if I'd stepped up to a podium to address hundreds of people, not a circle of six. "Look, I'm here to get into healthy relationships and start a family of my own. I don't want to know about Dr. Rosen's fecal history." I turned to Dr. Rosen and asked my favorite question: "How is this going to help me?"

Before he could answer, Max did. "How do you know it's not helping you?"

"Listening to stories about his history as a shrink with bad boundaries is helping me?"

"Why not?"

Max knew nothing about me. I glanced at the clock again. Why couldn't I make my feet move to the door? Why was I putting myself through this? This group—all of this therapy—might never lead to any of the things I wanted. I might come here faithfully twice a week, pay my seventy bucks a session, and still die alone.

Grandma Maggie held up her left hand and pointed at her wedding band. "Dr. Rosen is really good at getting women like you married. You'll see. I got married two years ago." Maggie was easily in her midsixties and had been with Dr. Rosen since George H. W. Bush was vice-president. It was hardly consoling to think I had decades to go before settling down and starting a family.

"Six months," I said. "If my life isn't better by July, then I'm leaving." Never mind the five-year timeline I started with at my first appointment. I'd been in treatment with Dr. Rosen for three and a half years, had now signed up to come three sessions a week and spend eight hundred dollars a month on therapy. The stakes had risen. I wanted results.

"Threatening to leave is an interesting way to build trust and intimacy." Max smirked.

"I come here three times a week—"

"So do I," Lorne said.

"Me too," said Patrice.

"This really is a cult." Everyone laughed. "Six months."

"Would you leave Tuesday-morning group too?" Dr. Rosen asked.

"Yes. All or nothing. Six months."

That evening, I sat in my office as the sun slunk below the horizon. I typed a search into Google: "Therapists in Chicago." A list of links appeared. A psychologist named Linda, an analyst named Francis, who was in the same building as Dr. Rosen. I imagined calling Linda or Francis, but it felt impossible. It took too much energy to fill someone new in. The apples. The worms. Jeremy. The Intern. Dr. Rosen and my first two groups had taught me to eat, sleep, and have sex. I'd miss Dr. Rosen and his goofy-ass laugh. I'd miss my Tuesday-morning crew. The first session in the "advanced" group was not exactly life-altering, but I owed it to myself to give it some time. Just in case, I bookmarked the website with Linda's and Francis's contact information.

My new life with three group sessions per week: I went to group before work on Monday and Tuesday; on Thursdays I went in the middle of the day. "Long lunch," I called it. I worked from nine thirty in the morning until seven at night, unless there was a project that required me to stay late. At night, I'd log off and walk home to my new apartment across the street from Clare, who'd recently gotten engaged to Steven. Instead of entrenching myself as their third-wheel roommate, I'd rented a one-bedroom in a high-rise on Clark and Maple from Kathryn, a Rosen-patient in the Friday women's group. While I missed Clare's company, it felt good to spread out into all corners of my new space and to watch the sunset from my western windows. Dr. Rosen viewed this move to a place of my own as evidence that I was making space for a romantic relationship. I narrowed my eyes when he said that, afraid to abandon my skepticism, solid as shale, for flimsy, see-through hope. On the weekends, I'd go to 12-step meetings and spend at least half a day at the office, reviewing documents and proving (to myself) that I deserved to be at Skadden. Behind the regular hum of my life, I waited for Something Big to happen. I waited for the "advanced" group, which I imagined as a blowtorch aimed straight at my heart, to work its magic on me. But there was no magic, no sparks flying from a naked flame, no fast-tracking my ability to attach to other people. There was sitting in the circle and talking, listening, feeling—the same things I'd been doing since I started with Rosen.

The six-month clock ticked on.

There were a few changes. The first thing was that I contracted severe constipation. My bowels would release only every eight days, so I walked around for seven days with a dull throbbing in my lower belly. It hurt to bend down. It hurt to run. It hurt to sneeze. I felt fatter than my fattest PMS day. My digestive system had turned off as soon as I started the new group. Nothing was moving through me. If this was the only gift of the new group, then I didn't want it. To console myself, I would flip the calendar to July like a kid counting the days until Christmas, except instead of anticipating a jolly man in a red suit with presents, I imagined how I would terminate my relationship with my elfin therapist who promised I wouldn't die alone. When I complained in Monday group about my constipation, it spurred Max to remind Dr. Rosen of his legendary diarrhea in the late eighties. When I asked what I should do about the constipation, Max would bark, "Maybe if you didn't have a six-month deadline, you wouldn't be so full of shit."

On Tuesday mornings, I told my original group that I had no idea what to do in the new group. I tried to describe how it felt to have no idea what to do with my hands or my voice for ninety minutes straight. Patrice shook her head. "She's doing just fine in there."

"It doesn't feel like group therapy. No one except Lorne comes in with any issues. They chitchat like old friends. No one knows about my pinworm or my eating disorder or how I debased myself with Jeremy. They don't seem to care about anything but what's right in front of them."

"And the problem is . . . ?" Dr. Rosen asked.

The problem was that I sat through two hundred seventy minutes of therapy per week and didn't feel any better.

During Monday/Thursday sessions, I felt like a stranger who wandered into someone else's family reunion. Pulsing through each conversation were layers of history, memory, story, and relationships that I couldn't access. When Max or Lorne asked me how I was doing, I voiced my heart's most immediate desire.

"Seriously, how can I get rid of this constipation?"

"Lots of water," Dr. Rosen said. "You could also try psyllium husk. That's the active ingredient in Metamucil." Apparently, I was now paying eight hundred forty dollars per month to learn about the active ingredient in a laxative.

In Monday/Thursday group, Dr. Rosen didn't give prescriptions. Nobody called anyone else to get to sleep or to discuss their after-dinner fruit binges. For ninety minutes twice a week, we sat in the circle and pinged off each other. Brad would talk about getting cheated out of a commission at work, and Max would call him out for being pathologically obsessed with money. Patrice would complain about the partners in her practice, and Dr. Rosen would confront her on not owning her authority as the most senior member of her practice. If I was quiet for too long, Max would turn to me and ask how many months until I quit. I'd ignore him and ask Dr. Rosen how this was helping.

"Of course it's helping you." Max sighed with annoyance.

"But nothing's changed except my bowels."

"That's bullshit. And you know what?" Max said, his voice raised. "Stop trying to convince us you're pathetic. Just stop. It's annoying."

No one could shame like Max. When he shook his head and sighed with disgust, I felt chastened. When I looked to Dr. Rosen for guidance or comfort, I saw only his inscrutable smile, so I shifted my gaze to a blotch in the carpet shaped like Australia.

A few minutes later, Dr. Rosen turned to me. "Why don't you ask Max to tell you all the reasons you aren't pathetic?"

My chest constricted. In the split second before I took Dr. Rosen's suggestion, I imagined Max repeating the same messages that thundered through my head: *It's your own fault you're alone. You're untreatable. You* are *pathetic!* Planting my feet on the ground, I looked directly at Max.

"So, how come I'm not pathetic?"

Max looked at Dr. Rosen and said, "I have to do all the work around here." Then he sighed and turned to me. "You're this brilliant attorney who's working at one of the most high-powered firms in the city. You've graduated to this advanced group. You're working hard to figure out how you're fucked up and what you should do about it. You're not pathetic—you're pissed that you haven't gotten all the things you're working hard for, which is better than this 'poor me' thing you do." He paused for a beat, and I held my breath, thinking he'd saved a zinger for his closing salvo. "Don't fucking do that."

I knew I was supposed to keep looking at Max and breathe, but I couldn't. Who would I be if I saw myself the way that Max did?

One March afternoon, I sat at my desk eating a box of raisins—still working on that constipation—when my work e-mail dinged. *Would you like to go for drinks?* It was from Alex, who lived four floors above me. I'd chatted with him in the elevator a few mornings earlier when we were both on the way to the gym and learned that, like me, he was a junior associate at a huge law firm. He'd chosen a treadmill close to mine. In the mirror, I watched his lean legs turn round and round. Zero body fat, perfect form, easy breathing despite his six-minute-mile pace. His physical beauty was so distracting I had to move to the bikes.

I covered my mouth with my hands to conceal my joy at this invitation, this potentially Big Thing.

26

We met at an Irish pub on Clark Street the following Monday after work. And even better: I was no longer constipated. Less than an hour after receiving Alex's e-mail, my bowels cranked back to life.

Alex and I compared notes on our budding legal careers—"so much document review"—and split the shepherd's pie for dinner. I hesitated for only a millisecond when the dish arrived covered in a layer of browned mashed potatoes with mystery brown lumps floating underneath. I could do this: I could eat stew from another country with this beautiful man.

From the bathroom, I called Rory to tell her I was on a date with a neighbor who looked like Brad Pitt, only cleaner and taller.

"Gay?" she asked.

"Possibly." He was raised by a single mom and had two sisters, so it made some sense he was not bursting with machismo. What hidden thing in this physically beautiful man's heart could hurt me later?

Alex and I e-mailed throughout the week, and I put my best Christie forward. Witty responses. Jokes about law firm life and pop culture. I waited a few hours before responding to his e-mails, even though I prepared my responses within seconds. I curated a Christie I imagined would appeal to him. My best guess about what a man as beautiful and put together as Alex might like: Lighthearted humor. Intelligence and ambition. Independence. And based on his BMI, a commitment to physical fitness. I had all of those things, and I shined them up for Alex and served them in balanced doses in each missive. As for all my emotional ups and downs, I sequestered those in group.

Two days after our first date, he asked me out for a second: Italian food and then live jazz.

The darkened club was packed with couples who looked at least a decade older than we were. Alex and I sat against a far wall beneath a picture of a young Billie Holiday. A round-top table big enough for only our two drinks separated us from the aisle, where harried waiters brought mixed drinks to the tables crammed all around us. As a trio played a set, Alex held my hand, his thumb tapping to the beat against my palm.

When the band took a break between sets, he asked follow-up questions to the getting-to-know-you ones he'd asked at our first dinner.

"You think you'd ever move back to Texas?"

"No way." When he asked why, I paused. There were multiple answers. I could tell him that I didn't like the heat or the conservative politics. Or that I felt like I had to make it on my own in the city I'd adopted and that moving back home would smack of defeat. Or that I'd failed to secure any attachments to any of my friends who still lived in Texas, so I wasn't itching to return. Those were true, but when I looked at the curve of his lips and his perfect jawline, I felt emboldened to give him the real reason. "I'm pretty attached to my therapist." And once I trotted out Dr. Rosen, I decided to go all the way. "And I do group therapy, so I'm attached to all of my group mates too." No need to tell him it was two groups and three sessions a week. I stared at the image of Billie Holiday singing into an old-fashioned silver microphone. Oh God, what have I done? Was I subconsciously trying to scare Alex away by hinting I was crazy?

"That's cool," Alex said. He smiled in a curious way. Like he was surprised that I'd revealed something so vulnerable. He inched closer. "Would you like me to join you out on that limb?"

I smiled. "Sure."

"I told you my parents got divorced, right?" I nodded. "What I didn't mention is that after their divorce, they remarried. Each other. And then divorced again." He shifted his gaze to the vacant stage. Then he turned back to me. "So, that's complicated."

"Sounds like it."

What I wanted to say was "thank you." Thank you for understanding vulnerability. For meeting me on the limb. For showing me it wasn't disastrous to mention therapy on our second date.

As the band shuffled back on the stage, Alex scooted his chair closer to mine. In the darkened club, we sat hand in hand, knees touching, letting the music seep into our bones. I recognized the familiar feeling of warmth and safety that settled after the rush of emotional risk. This was how I felt in group after sharing something difficult and then hearing my group members say "same here" or "I relate to that." Like the time I told the women's group about my breast hatred and each one of them offered me a story about her own tortured relationship to her breasts.

My turn, your turn. Back and forth.

So this was how it happened. This was how you built an intimate relationship. Word by word. Story by story. Revelation by revelation.

Just like group.

He invited me up to his apartment after the jazz club. "I want to show you the view from my southern balcony." He put one arm around me as he pointed out the Big Dipper. With the stars as our witness, we shared our first kiss. When he pressed his perfect lips against mine, I swallowed starlight, and my heart began to glow. He walked me up to my place. "There will be more," he said, kissing me again.

If this was the gift of the advanced group, I'd stay forever.

Alex was wonderful. Our dates were the stuff of my deepest longing. I could hardly believe how much I enjoyed being with him. The only downside was the low-grade anxiety I felt all the time about how to make it last. I agonized about how and when the relationship would sour or fizzle or implode.

I brought my anxiety to group. "This can't last," I insisted. "Tell me what to do to keep this thing going."

"Can you let go of your need to control it?" Dr. Rosen said.

"No." Dr. Rosen didn't understand. Alex's body was near perfect, he smelled like fresh sport deodorant, and I could see my sexual prime on the horizon. If I gave in to this relationship and let myself believe it was something real, then what if it failed? Would that destroy me?

"Can you let go of your expectation of failure?"

"I'll try."

Life with Alex, who had signed up for two triathlons for later in the summer and a marathon in the fall, meant early morning runs and bike rides before work, followed by swims at the gym or in Lake Michigan after work. Within a month of dating, he began inviting me to join him most mornings and evenings. One Saturday, he knocked on my door at six in the morning. He had a race bib pinned to his fleece jacket and his hands stuffed into thin black gloves. He fastened my bib to my shirt and handed me a water bottle. At the starting line of the ten-mile race he signed us up for, he rubbed my shoulders when he noticed I was shaking from the cold. Patches of snow still clung to the ground by the running path, and only several hundred runners had showed up for the lakefront race, where the wind promised to slap our exposed faces. I'd never run a ten-mile race, but my body had taken on a new buoyancy since dating Alex, which was part anxiety, part joy. A loopy willingness to try anything, including this freezing-cold road race, made me say yes to whatever he was offering.

Each time we walked to dinner after work or ran on the lake, a featherweight optimism knocked on my heart, inviting me to let go of projecting the failure of the relationship. Maybe every relationship wouldn't end with me huddled in the group room crying into a rag. Maybe every relationship wouldn't end at all. Maybe it would last.

After the race, my hamstrings ached and my shoulder stung where my sports bra strap dug into it. But with Alex, the pain gave way to pure joy.

Dr. Rosen held up a picture for everyone to see one Monday morning. Patrice slipped on her reading glasses and Max leaned forward. "This is what it means to get unblocked," Dr. Rosen said. It was a picture of me and Alex: I wore a pink cocktail dress, and Alex wore a tux. We'd gone to a gala for the Joffrey Ballet. In the darkened theater, the dancers twirled in brilliant tulle and Alex held my hand in both of his. I inched closer to him in my red velvet seat, until our legs were touching. During dinner in the giant, gilded Hilton ballroom, he rubbed my back and played with the clasp of my necklace. On the dance floor, he held me close as the band covered Otis Redding. Later, he kissed me again on his balcony. "It feels like you're my girlfriend," he said. I leaned into him and exhaled.

Grandma Maggie pointed at the picture and then tapped her wedding ring. "You're next, kiddo."

Alex, who was so comfortable in his skin, made me feel like I could be too. With complete ease, he talked about all the things we would do in the future. A boat trip on the Chicago River with his firm in June. A sprint distance triathlon in July. A trip to visit his sister in Iowa at some point over the summer. A comedy show, a concert, a trip to the zoo. He acted as if we had a future, and I slowly let myself imagine us being a couple for more than a few months.

"Seriously, what's the catch?" I asked my group mates and Dr. Rosen.

"You tell us," Max said.

I shook my head. The situation with his parents sounded tricky, but he didn't come across as secretly hobbled by trauma or afraid of a relationship. His workout schedule bordered on obsessive, but it never depleted him to the point he was too exhausted to hang out or have sex with me. His taste in books struck me as a tad immature, but plenty of people loved Harry Potter—that wasn't a valid reason to discount someone as wonderful as Alex. I was just afraid.

One morning, Alex and I stopped at Corner Bakery for breakfast before work. We sat in a booth by the window feeding each other bites of muffin and acting like the kind of couple I would have scorned when I was single or struggling with Jeremy. At one point, I got up to get some napkins, and Alex called my cell phone, buried in my purse right next to him. The voice mail I heard later melted my anxious, defended heart: "Hello, pretty lady in the café. This is your boyfriend calling. He thinks you are quite lovely." I played it again and again, thinking, It's going to suck when this falls apart.

Dr. Rosen became a broken record. "Trust it, *Mamaleh*. Trust."

As the weeks went on, traces of anxiety remained, but my constipation eased, my joy soared. Both groups cheered my weekly check-ins.

"Stability suits you," Dr. Rosen said.

"I hope you're giving us credit for this relationship," Max said. "In those other groups, you sucked dirty dick and got dumped for being a shiksa. You're welcome."

Lorne gave me a thumbs-up, and Brad calculated mine and Alex's combined net worth given our high-paying legal jobs. Grandma Maggie patted my hand, whispering, "I knew it."

I beamed and floated. On the July morning that marked my six-month anniversary in the Monday/Thursday group, I announced I was staying. Forever.

"Oh, goody," Max said in mock annoyance.

"You can stay," Lorne said, "but I'm not dressing up for your wedding. If I can't come in jeans, I'm not coming." He winked from across the circle.

I beamed at them all, my advanced group members. Alex and I had a solid, healthy, sexual relationship, and I gave them most of the credit for that.

⌇⌇

"Mom," I said during a Sunday-afternoon check-in call. "I've met someone. He's great. Really great. We ran a 10K together this weekend." I danced around my apartment as I told her the news. I'd stepped into the new reality of Christie as a woman who enjoyed her highly hygienic, functional, attentive boyfriend. Christie as a woman worth spending time with and paying attention to. I could leave my dysfunctional past where it belonged: behind me.

"How wonderful, honey. You sound so happy."

ссл

"Come up for some chili," Alex said one night. He browned ground beef and emptied canned tomatoes into a small Dutch oven. The smell of cumin wafted through the air. I wrapped my arms around him from behind. He kept stirring.

"Do you know what the secret ingredient is?" he asked. I shook my head.

"You really don't know?" His shoulders slumped, and his face registered confusion bordering on hurt.

Had I forgotten an inside joke about chili? Did Harry Potter love chili? I didn't want to let him down, but the only thing coming to mind was a tasteless fart joke.

"Tell me."

"Love," he said. "The secret ingredient is love."

I ate two bowls.

ссл

"Oh my God," Lorne said when I bragged in group about the love in Alex's chili. "He's so cheesy."

I swiveled my chair toward Lorne and kicked the air between us. "Don't ruin it! It was so sweet."

"Cheesy."

"You're just jealous."

"Of Alex's stupid chili?"

"You had to buy Renee a giant ring from Cartier, and all Alex had to do was serve me chili."

"Can you hear yourself?"

ссл

One Sunday, Alex and I woke up at five, before the sun glinted across the lake, to ride thirty miles up and down Lake Shore Drive. We wore bike shorts and pounded Gatorade. When we slipped off our bikes for a late breakfast of eggs and English muffins, our backs were stiff, and our gaits were unsteady.

"Come upstairs," he said.

We kissed on his brass bed, our tired bodies heavy from the early morning and the hours of pedaling. He pulled off my shorts. The noonday sun streamed brazenly across his clean white sheets. His skin tasted like salt, and I wanted to gulp. He filled me up. I came and came again.

This sweet boy-man who cried through *Les Mis*. Who showed me how brilliant the sunrise over Lake Michigan could be from a bicycle. Who filled his food with love and offered it to me. This man-boy with no sharp edges that could hurt me. My heart and body leaned into him. In my mind, Alex and my new group formed a double helix that wove around my grooved heart.

"This guy is 'The One,'" Marnie said after she met me and Alex one night for sushi. Clare said the same thing. So did Patrice and Dr. Rosen.

"I really like him," I told my groups and my friends. I said it over and over; I shined my teeth with it. I slept deeply.

In mid-July we attended the wedding of my friend Kathryn, the Rosen-patient who rented me her apartment in Alex's building. Kathryn married Jacob, a man she'd met in a Rosen-group. Across the room at table four, Dr. Rosen and his wife ate their steak and smiled as patients streamed by to say a shy hello. By the chocolate fountain, I introduced Alex to Dr. Rosen. As they shook hands, I watched Dr. Rosen's face fill with warmth and welcome. A swell of wholeness flooded my chest. I'd never been so full. *Christie*, they said. I heard love and claimed it as mine. An insistent joy spun inside me like cotton candy.

That night, in my darkened bedroom, Alex slipped my white cotton nightgown over my head. It felt like falling and being caught over and over. He leaned back.

"You're so beautiful," he said.

"I'm so happy," he said.

"I love you," I said, holding his beautiful head in my hands.

I sat tall in my Monday-morning group, letting the summer sun bathe my arms from the western window. I wore the million-watt smile. "I told him I loved him."

"Did he say it back?" Lorne asked.

"Not in so many words." Brad and Max shared a quick look across the circle. Grandma Maggie gazed down at her hands. I chased away the fleeting worry by sinking into my body. I remembered our skin against skin. Of course that was love.

In late July, I traveled to St. Petersburg with Patrice and her family for a vacation planned before I started dating Alex. Our apartment off Nevsky Prospekt was infested with mosquitoes that left angry red marks up and down my legs and arms. I ached for Alex at night as I stared at the moon and scratched the welts. During the day, I stole into cyber cafés to check my e-mail. My stomach twisted when there was nothing from Alex after two days, three days, four days. By then, I could hardly eat a full meal I was so distressed. Why wouldn't he write? Weren't we attached? Wasn't it love?

"He's gone," I cried to Patrice outside the Hermitage. She wrapped her arm around my shoulders and told me to enjoy the view: a street performer with a boom box coaxing a chained black bear to dance to Cyndi Lauper's "Girls Just Want to Have Fun."

"I can't. My stomach hurts." I bent low to scratch at a cluster of bites on my ankle. "I hate Russia, its dumb domes, its mosquitoes, its dancing bears." In Russia, I was cold, nauseated, and so far away. Lonely and forgotten. I scratched until my ankles bled. My blood and skin mingled under my fingernails. Patrice rubbed my back in a circle and offered me a piece of dark chocolate. I closed my eyes and missed group, where I could cry, gnash, and let all the feeling pour of me.

"I had some time to think while you were in Russia." Alex and I were walking down Dearborn after a 5K race for the Legal Aid Society. My body was spinning in space, somewhere between Russia and Chicago, throbbing through the jet lag that made me feel drunk.

"The thing is, I know you're not the one." He marched down Dearborn without breaking his stride or looking at me.

No, no, no. I breathed through my nose to smooth out my voice. "What are you talking about?"

"I just know. You're not the person I'm supposed to be with."

My arms shook in the humid August air. I tasted the postrace banana I'd swallowed four blocks back. Sweat on my neck turned icy cold.

In the lobby he stopped to check his mail, while I shivered like a stray cat by the elevators. Did he really need to get his Visa bill and the grocery store circular at this moment?

When the elevator opened, I shuffled in, but he stepped back to wait for the next one.

I brought the shards of all the dishes I broke that night to my Monday-morning group and dumped them in the center of the circle. Pieces of a ceramic Thanksgiving platter I bought at Walgreens, the IKEA glasses, the pale blue fruit bowl from the Tag outlet that I bought with Carlos. I'd shoveled them into a double-ply Macy's shopping bag, which I hooked on my arm as I walked the mile from my apartment to group. The jagged edge of a dinner plate pierced the bag and tore the skin on my calf as I crossed Chicago Avenue. A stream of blood ran down my leg and into my black ballet flats.

"He's gone," I said to this group that brought Alex into my life. Now I needed them to catch me because I was really falling. "I'm not 'the one.'" Tears fell, soft and incessant. Patrice got out of her chair and pulled me to my feet. She wrapped her arms around me. "I'm so sorry."

Dr. Rosen leaned toward me as if he was telling me a secret. "*Mamaleh*, he just got scared when you left for Russia."

No, he was gone for good. That bomb I'd once imagined beneath his smooth skin and beautiful ribs had detonated. I was in pieces.

"Aren't y'all disappointed in me? Y'all thought Alex was my person." I looked at the faces around the circle. Max's concerned stare. Lorne's and Brad's attentive gazes. Grandma Maggie, who was always flashing me her wedding ring and calling me "kiddo," now shaking her head with pity. Patrice, who was yet again spending her group time consoling me. And of course Dr. Rosen, who still believed in his little

Mamaleh, even though she'd broken all of her dishes (again) and carved up her leg on the walk to group.

"We don't know that he's not."

Dr. Rosen, eternal optimist or raving lunatic?

As I walked out of group after the prayer and the hugs, Lorne, Brad, and Max invited me to breakfast with them. "But you can't bring that insane bag of broken dishes," Max said, so I left them in the group room. I ate eggs while they drank coffee. We talked shit about Dr. Rosen's wardrobe, speculated about his marriage to the stylish Mrs. Rosen, who we sometimes saw walking down the hall after our Thursday group. When I stared off into the middle distance, thinking about Alex, his chili, and his brass bed, Lorne snapped his fingers in front of my face. "Come back, Christie! Eat your eggs. Tell us what you think of Dr. Rosen's wife!"

At ten o'clock, I rose from the table. "I have a conference call in thirty minutes," I said, grabbing a napkin in case I cried on the walk to work. All three of them stood up to hug me. Lorne reminded me that Alex was "cheesy as hell." Max told me to order new dishes for express delivery. Brad, who'd paid for my eggs, offered to walk me to my office across the Loop. He carried my work bag all six blocks and assured me at every stoplight that I would find love again. He stayed by my side even when I openly wept on LaSalle Street.

At work, there were no group members to distract or comfort me, so I cried without bothering to shut my door. My coworker Raj stopped by several times to see if I was still blubbering. If I was, he shut the door and speculated about the partners' sex lives until I let a smile break through. I had a small CD player under my desk that played *Riverdance* on a constant loop. Billable hours passed as I sat listening to the haunting Celtic songs that matched my mood. I pressed the brass tip of a letter opener into the pad of my left index finger. The skin didn't break, but the prick of pain soothed me. I *could* break the skin if I needed to.

I cried through Tuesday group, barely uttering a coherent sentence. On Thursday, I sat directly to the right of Dr. Rosen with my purse in my lap so I could secretly press the top of the letter opener into the pads of my index finger. Of course, hiding was impossible in that fourteen-by-fourteen room. The entire point of group was to be witnessed, to come out of hiding.

Dr. Rosen extended his right hand to me, palm flat and open. "I want your weapon." I shook my head. "I want you to give it to me."

I surrendered the blade because I didn't really want to hurt myself. Dr. Rosen took the letter opener and continued to hold my hand. I let him because I wanted him to save me from myself, from my attraction to sharp objects that made me bleed, from men who didn't love me, from my mental illness, whatever it was. I wanted him to save my heart, which would never be scored deep enough for lasting attachment. I would die like this: paying someone to hold my hand while my life slipped away. The thing that had always been wrong with me felt worse than ever. I couldn't meet anyone's eyes, only their shoes. Max's expensive broughams, Lorne's scuffed brown Eccos, Grandma Maggie's thick-soled white shoes, Brad's gray New Balance tennis shoes, Patrice's navy flats. It was the only view I could take in.

"Do not cry alone. Be with your group members, as much as you can," Dr. Rosen said. My gaze lingered on their shoes.

"Renee is being induced this weekend. Come to the hospital," Lorne said.

"Come over for dinner on Saturday night," Patrice said. "You can spend the night."

"I've got tickets to the opera, and William doesn't want to go," Grandma Maggie said.

I cried in the grocery store. I cried at work. On the train. In group. At home. On Marnie's couch. On Patrice's couch. On the phone with Marnie, Marty, Patrice, and Rory. I went to the hospital to meet Lorne's baby boy and cried up and down the maternity ward, frightening the nurses on call. I went to the gynecologist for a checkup and cried when she asked me if I needed contraception. Concerned, Dr. Spring put down her pen and offered a referral to a therapist.

Every morning I startled awake with a violent stomach cramp. Diarrhea. One morning I didn't make it to the bathroom and shit in my favorite cornflower-blue cotton pajamas in the middle of the living room.

Dr. Rosen promised it wouldn't last forever—the crying, the shitting. I believed him one second, but not the next. Shame consumed me. Shame that I was coming undone over a five-month relationship. Shame that I was literally losing my shit over a beautiful man I'd slept with twenty-seven times. Shame that after nearly 380 therapy sessions—more than 34,000 minutes of therapy with an Ivy League–educated therapist—my heart was still defective, could not attach.

27

"*Is your passport up-to-date?*" Jack, a middle-aged partner with thick glasses and a friendly chortle, stuck his head in my office, where I was drafting a memo on my beverage-company case. I paused *Riverdance* and sat up straight. It was August 2005, and my two-year anniversary with Skadden was two days away.

"Good until 2014."

"Do you speak German?"

"*Nyet?*"

"That's Russian."

"Then, no."

"Doesn't matter. We've got a new matter. The Department of Justice is involved, so we have to move fast. Can you leave Sunday?"

"For Germany? Absolutely." This was the best news I'd ever heard. I'd let my career simmer for months while I biked, ran, and ate chili. Jack was a rainmaker—his star protégée was about to make partner. If I impressed him, I could end up on the partner track. A glow in my chest: I'd been chosen. Never mind that years ago I'd called Dr. Rosen with the express purpose of building a life filled with relationships, not billable work.

"At the partner meeting, we discussed which associates had no commitments—no spouses or children—and your name popped up first."

"Excellent." My face froze in a smile.

I showed up at Thursday group two days later, smiling for the first time in days.

"I don't recognize you without all the tears and sharp objects," Max said.

"My firm is sending me to Germany. I'll be flying there every other week for the next few months. Maybe longer."

Everyone nodded, impressed. No doubt they were picturing me scaling stone steps to a stately German high court building during the day and raising a stein in the Hofbräuhaus at night.

"You're getting an opportunity to work on your professional life." Dr. Rosen nodded approvingly. "Now you can stop pretending you're not interested in making partner and admit that you want success in both work—"

I covered my ears. "I *hate* it when you do that." Professionally, I was successful and would always be successful because I knew how to work my ass off and get shit done. I'd risen to first in my class before I ever stepped foot in Rosen-world. I'd learned to kiss partners' asses and knew how to treat the support staff like human beings who deserved my respect. I knew how to laugh with colleagues at happy hour and how to hold clients' hands when the SEC threatened legal action. Personal relationships housed my stack of failures. "Focus on my personal life, buddy. Eyes on the ball."

That night, I called my mom out of the blue. We usually spoke once or twice a month, usually on Sunday after she and Dad returned from mass. I wanted to tell her about Germany, but the first thing out of my mouth was that I was terrified there was something seriously wrong with me, something that would keep me from having a family of my own.

"I'm so alone," I said, bursting into tears with my mom for the first time in my adult life. We'd never discussed my isolation from the family or my fears about ending up alone. My plan had been to have Dr. Rosen fix me so I could present myself as the daughter who wasn't fucked up after all. But we'd both be dead at the rate I was going.

"Honey, I felt the same way."

I sat up on the couch and wiped my nose on my sleeve. As far as I knew, my parents met at a volleyball party and the rest—three kids and a redbrick ranch house on 6644 Thackeray—was history. It was impossible to picture my mother—with her late-1960s bob and postcollege job as a bank teller in Dallas—curled under a blanket, worried she would die alone.

"I was just like you. All my friends were married and had babies on the way, and I never thought it would happen for me. I was still single at twenty-six, which in 1970 was pretty ancient. It felt like nobody wanted me."

This was genetic? I felt strangely exhilarated—maybe this wasn't all my fault. Maybe it wasn't a failure of imagination or feminism or will. This state of believing that something was wrong with me around relationships was something I shared with my mother like brown eyes and a mortal fear of dental procedures. Maybe I could stop trying to outrun it. Maybe I didn't have to hide my grief and confusion from her anymore. I wasn't ready to tell her I was back in therapy to the tune of *three* group sessions a week, but it was a relief to share some emotional truth.

"Do you want me to come to Chicago?"

Her offer made me cry harder. I needed her mothering, but I couldn't stomach her flying all the way Chicago. It was enough that she asked and that I no longer had to hide my greatest fears from her.

I never saw the Autobahn. Or a German courtroom. What I saw day after day in Germany was a giant, un-air-conditioned room in a nondescript four-story office building in the middle of a field outside Augsburg. The low sound of cows' mooing greeted me in moments of unexpected silence. The sharp smell of dung also made its way into the second-story work space, where lawyers and paralegals from Germany, Chicago, and Atlanta worked elbow to elbow on long tables. The office was stingy with toilet paper, so you had to go before three in the afternoon if you wanted to wipe.

The high point of the day was lunch in the staff cafeteria, where the main food group was brown gravy. It appeared on absolutely everything: main dishes, side dishes, salads. Brown, viscous, fatty, and flavorless.

I hated Germany. I hated my work. I hated my life.

I was grateful to be busy, but in the downtime between tasks, I'd stare at the clock and compute the time back in Chicago. One Tuesday afternoon, I used the office phone to call Rory's cell while she was in group. She didn't pick up.

That night, alone in my German hotel, I collapsed on the bed. I'd been expecting fancy four-star digs, but instead, we stayed at the German version of a La Quinta, minus the friendly staff and Denny's next door. In the shower, the temperature hovered at lukewarm. I missed home, where at least the water was scalding hot.

The only thing on TV was the brewing destruction of Hurricane Katrina—startling images of surging brown water and displaced people crammed into the Superdome in New Orleans—and violent German porn. Room service was my last hope. The "pizza" I ordered arrived as a hunk of semimelted white cheese on a plain pita swimming atop a smear of ketchup. I crawled under the covers, still shivering from my tepid shower. Sleep mercifully delivered me from consciousness.

The clinking of glasses and muffled laughter woke me less than an hour later. I lifted the window shade and saw that directly below me was the pool, an open bar, and a dozen people eating appetizers and having drinks, buck naked. My room was just above the *Schwaben Quellen*, which apparently means "eating schnitzels and drinking Heineken in your birthday suit."

I dialed the international operator and gave her Dr. Rosen's number. Across the Atlantic, Dr. Rosen sat in his final group of the day and would check his office voice mail soon.

Beep.

"There are naked people cocktailing outside my room. I can't do this. Please call me. Please." I left the number where he could reach me.

At two in the morning German time—seven back home in Chicago—I accepted the truth: Dr. Rosen wasn't going to call me. I rolled myself up in the scratchy comforter and closed my eyes. *How dare he abandon me.* I unrolled myself and asked the international operator to connect me again.

Beep.

"Show me the goddamned *JAMA* article that says doctors can't help patients across international lines! How could you possibly withhold five minutes of your time to assure me that you're still there? I would have paid you back for the charges, you know. Asshole!" I slammed the phone down. Fuck him. After all the money, time, and trust I'd willingly given him—he had nothing for me?

On Friday, in the Augsburg conference room, Jack asked for a show of hands: Who wants to go home? Those who flew home would brief the team back in Chicago and return the following week. Most associates wanted to stay for weekend jaunts to beer gardens and the Black Forest. Oktoberfest was days away. My hand shot up, high and tall. *Send me home.*

I arrived at the airport three hours early, but the Augsburg-to-Frankfurt leg of my flight was canceled. An officious woman at the United counter offered me a flight the following day. I shook my head. No. I bought a train ticket to Frankfurt; I booked a later flight to Chicago. If I had to crawl across Germany, I was going home.

An hour later, I handed the train conductor my ticket without looking up. I'd made a decision: when I returned to group, I would break up with Dr. Rosen. My hurt and anger wasn't hot and fiery. It was cold and sharp. A decision made. A contract signed. A door locked. If I was sinking all the way down, then let my feet hit the bottom. Dr. Rosen proved he couldn't tend to me when I needed him most, so I didn't want to be in his care. I'd look up Linda or Francis. Get myself a real therapist. One who gave a shit about me.

I curled toward the window, not seeing the German countryside zooming by. I was supposed to be better by now. No one else had made so little progress after so many years of treatment. Other group members came in and got better. Their careers shot off in promising new directions. They paid off debts. Their kids graduated and went to liberal arts colleges. They moved in with their boyfriends. They got married. They had babies.

And then there was me. Relationships kept slipping through my hands no matter how many groups I joined. What a damn fool. Maybe Dr. Rosen was mad at me because I ruined his track record. I was the quarter horse who was expected to win but couldn't make a clean lap around the course. Someone should shoot me. I was back to where I was before I ever called Dr. Rosen, except this was worse because I'd learned to *feel* so much more. All those one- and two-syllable words: Angry. Hurt. Lonely. Ashamed.

I pulled out my BlackBerry so I could let someone know I would be arriving in Chicago six hours later than expected. But who? I could tell my parents that I was now on a train instead of a plane, but that made me feel like a thirty-three-year-old loser. Who cared where I was at this very minute? No one. Absolutely no one.

I typed a message to Dr. Rosen: *I'm so sorry. I really tried. I swear I did.*

On Monday morning in group, I did not say a single word for the first hour and twenty-five minutes of the ninety-minute session. Everyone seemed to sense I needed space. I felt Max and Grandma Maggie staring at me, but they said nothing. I lacked the energy to break up with Dr. Rosen. It would take too many words, spawn too much discussion. For now, I would float until my head went under.

"I won't be here next week," Patrice said at five minutes to nine. "Conference in San Francisco." Dr. Rosen pulled out the blue appointment book he kept in his pocket—his customary practice for when someone announced they would be gone from group. I once asked why he always wrote our absences down in his little book, and he'd said it was because he cared where we were. I remembered when I believed that.

He looked at me, his pen poised, waiting for me to announce when I'd be back in Germany—so he could write my initials in the Monday, Tuesday, Thursday squares. I said nothing. My head slipped below the waterline.

Dr. Rosen clipped his pen to his book and cleared his throat. "I need to turn something over to the group." His lips were a straight line, his eyes blazed serious. I felt him looking at me, but my gaze bored into Brad's New Balances.

"When I got your last e-mail, Christie, for the first time ever"—he paused and looked around the room—"I feared for your safety."

I'd scared the impervious Dr. Rosen? The guy who thought every-thing was hilarious, useful fodder for emotional growth?

"Normally, you're full of passion and fury." He waved his hands spastically and bobbed his head back and forth, imitating me. "You're screaming and frothing and outraged. This was different. Scary."

It couldn't be good to scare your therapist.

A memory flashed into my head: two summers earlier, I hunkered down with bar exam study guides seven days a week, and in my off-hours, dug my claws into my dwindling relationship with Jeremy.

"Can I borrow one of those?" I pointed at the motley stash of stuffed animals that Dr. Rosen kept in the group room. "I could sleep with it at Jeremy's house when he's too busy playing video games to sleep with me." Dr. Rosen opened his palms like *go ahead*, and Carlos tossed me a careworn brown teddy bear. I tucked it under my chin and pretended to snooze. "Perfect."

One Sunday night that summer, my youngest cousin—the one whose diapers I'd changed growing up—called to tell me that she and her fiancé had signed a contract on a house in Houston. When I got off the phone, I burned with shame. I hadn't even known my cousin was engaged. I also burned with envy at her forward momentum, while my boyfriend couldn't be bothered to swivel away from his computer screen. Now, couples composed my entire family tree. It was only I who still dangled alone on a branch by myself.

When Jeremy fell asleep that night, I sat in his darkened living room, mentally decorating my cousin's new house: a Mission-style din-ing room table, a sleigh bed in the master. As I dreamed up her perfect life, a streetlight glared through the window, emitting just enough but-tery light to see a pair of orange-handled scissors on Jeremy's desk. I grabbed them and hacked at the teddy bear's right arm with the scissors. The following Tuesday, I tossed the dismembered bear and the Ziploc bag full of its arm stuffing onto the floor in the middle of group.

Dr. Rosen stared hard.

"My baby cousin's buying a house. It's two stories." The group was used to my outbursts by then, but Dr. Rosen sat still as poured concrete.

"He looks mad." Rory sounded anxious.

"Why is his jaw twitching?" Carlos said.

The Colonel grabbed the one-armed bear carcass. Pieces of white fluffy stuffing rained to the floor.

"Why are you acting so weird?" I asked Dr. Rosen. He was definitely not beaming with pride. He sighed, started to speak, and then shifted in his seat again. I imagined him opening his mouth and hissing: *You're in trouble, trouble, trouble.*

"You destroyed something that belongs to me. What does that mean to you?"

"It means I'm an isolated loser next to my entire family tree! Every last one of them is on the way to joint tenancy—"

"And the bear?" I searched my body for the feeling Dr. Rosen insisted should be there. I knew I was in trouble. Shame churned in my belly.

"I grabbed the first thing I saw."

Dr. Rosen didn't blink or soften. "The bear represents me and the group." He gestured around the circle. "Are you willing to look at what it means to take scissors to that?"

"But I hammered all those dishes on my balcony—" My hands began to shake.

"Those didn't belong to me."

Why wasn't he smiling? Why were my eyes filling with tears? I picked up the bear and placed it in my lap. I ran my finger along the hole where the arm had been attached, trying to feel something. What I found under the shame of being in trouble was a cold lump of fear. It scared me that I didn't understand my subconscious mind. Why, since starting group, did my response to jealousy and disappointment involve sharp objects?

"How can I fix this?"

Dr. Rosen's jaw softened slightly. "Ask the group for help."

Marty met my gaze. "Come to my office this afternoon. I'll suture the arm." Before settling on psychiatry, Marty had dreamed of being a surgeon. He looked excited about the prospect of getting out his needle and thread.

In Marty's tiny Uptown office, I stuffed as much of the polyester filling back into the bear as possible, and then gathered the edges of the wound for Marty to stitch. "Like this," he said, pulling the thick thread through the bear's fur. I sewed the last few stiches, and then held it up for him to inspect. With the arm sewn up, the white stuffing had no way to escape.

⁓

When I'd hacked up his teddy bear, Dr. Rosen seemed angry. Now, in the wake of my e-mail from Germany, he seemed afraid and sad. I knew better than to ask for a quick fix. Those didn't exist in Rosen-world. It was nine o'clock. Group was over. We all stood up, and I offered my open hands to Lorne and Patrice, but it was only muscle memory, not a genuine gesture of connection. Their warm palms against mine did nothing to thaw the chill. When each of them hugged me, I went through the motions of hugging them back. More muscle memory. None of it reached the frozen center of my being. And I didn't join Brad, Max, and Lorne for breakfast. I didn't let Brad walk me to my office. I rejected their concerned joviality and refused to watch them take turns keeping me afloat with jokes and affirmations. I wanted to be alone. I wanted them to let me sink all the way down. I walked back to my office, shut the door, turned on *Riverdance*, and drafted memos all day until the sky darkened at eight fifteen, and I went home.

28

I had to get off the German case.

I'd returned for my second stint in Augsburg and found myself in a room overlooking the naked schnitzel nibblers. Again I'd fantasized, briefly, about swallowing a bottle of Aleve. When I got back to Chicago that second time, Dr. Rosen suggested that I tell Jack that personal matters would prevent me from traveling to Germany for the near future. I e-mailed Jack saying I needed to discuss a personal matter. He responded right away. *Let's have lunch!*

He was an important partner and a decent person. He'd invited me to lunch; he'd used exclamation points. Maybe I could do a few more weeks in Germany? I thought of the hotel, the naked happy hour, and those long lonely nights. My whole body howled *No.* If I was ruining my legal career by turning down this plum assignment, so be it.

Jack and I walked to One North and sat at a table on the terrace, surrounded mostly by other people in power suits eating power lunches. I took a few deep breaths while Jack ordered a chopped salad, feeling the seconds drag me closer to my confession.

"So what's up?" Jack's face was so open that I almost lost my nerve. I flexed my fingers under the table and leaned forward.

"I can't travel to Germany—there's a personal matter—"

Jack held up his hand. "Say no more. There's plenty for you to do here. I'll let the partners know." He picked up his BlackBerry and typed a new message. I stared out at Wacker Drive, praying I had not completely derailed my career.

Twice, I ran into Alex in the elevator, and both times he was with a blond woman wearing Duke University spirit-wear and running shoes. Both times we ignored each other. Both times I held my breath and stared straight ahead, but as soon as they disappeared down the street, I dialed Rory to cry about Alex's new no-fat girlfriend.

"You should buy a place in another building," Max said.

"With your income, you could afford a three-bedroom," Brad said.

"A woman in your position should definitely own property," Grandma Maggie said.

When Dr. Rosen asked about my resistance to buying a condo, I told the truth: "I don't want to do it by myself." Buying a condo alone would cement my status as a successful but single, alone-in-the-world woman. How depressing to visit empty homes and dream of the future with only a real estate agent at my side. How lonely to embark on a massive financial transaction by myself. Buying the condo might be a win for feminism, but it felt like the exact future I had hoped Dr. Rosen would help me avoid.

"It couldn't hurt to look," Max said on the way out of group.

On a Thursday in late January, I sat on the tenth floor of a title company in a navy-blue suit signing a stack of documents. I wasn't totally alone: a lawyer I hired sat on my right and Lorne's wife, Renee, sat on my left. I signed my name dozens of times under the line that read: *Christie O. Tate, Unmarried Woman, Spinster.* "Wow," I whispered.

"Some of the standard real estate documents have retained rather antiquated language," my lawyer said with a chuckle.

"Ha-ha," Renee said sarcastically. "Maybe someone should update them." She rubbed my back in a circular motion as I signed page after page.

When I got to group, a few minutes late, I pressed the group room button with my right index finger, and with my left, I twirled the keys to my condo, amazed that I now owned, along with the bank, a fifth-floor loft in River North. Two bedrooms. I felt high on progress and my ability to put 10 percent down on a piece of real estate. What good fortune, what a blessing. Everyone congratulated me as I took my seat, but as the session wore on, the high drained away, leaving me with one thought: Christie Tate, Spinster.

I interrupted Max. I can't remember what he was saying, but I sliced into his story with my panic. "Y'all, I'm not sure about this condo." All those papers. All that official evidence of my spinsterhood under the Illinois state seal. I had to fill those empty, echoing rooms all by myself.

Annoyed at my intrusion, Max huffed. "It's fine. You'll be fine. You did the right thing." Then, he returned to his story. I sat quietly as long as I could, but the anger at Max and panic about the condo were too intense to stifle for long. My hands clenched, and I pitched forward, about to scream.

"Oh, here we go," Max said. I wasn't looking at him, but I heard the eye roll in his tone.

Fuck him. I slipped my feet out of my shoes—pink Uggs for the snowy streets—and threw one of them in Max's direction. I swear I aimed for the wall above him, not his face. And I didn't hit him, but I got close. As my shearling-lined shoe sailed across the circle, my "FUCK YOU" traveled with it. I stared directly at smug-ass Max. "I'm sick of being intimidated by you. Sick of your sighs. Your telling me what is and is not fine. You never had to buy—"

Max grabbed the shoe I threw and strode right over to my chair, pointing it at me like a gun. He stopped in front of me, and I rose to meet him.

"Fuck you too!" he yelled in my face.

"No, fuck you!"

We stood so close I could feel the brass buttons on his coat brush against my abs. My fury unfurled into his mouth, and his rage blew straight into mine. In his eyes, I saw flecks of gold and pure hatred. For me. And I hoped he saw my ferocity and hatred for him and every other person in the circle—in the world—who never had to buy a condo alone or date in their thirties or swim through thousands of hours of therapy to end up at the exact place she'd hoped to avoid. *Christie Tate, Spinster.*

"You don't fucking know me, Max!"

"Yes I do! Of course I do! Why do you say such stupid things?"

"I'm not stupid!"

"Then stop acting like it!"

All I knew is that I would scream into his face as long as he would scream into mine. I would not crumple into my chair, breaking the spell with pitiful tears. I would stand my ground and scream as long and loudly as he did. I would hold my power in my own body. He couldn't have it.

Then we were silent. Still inches from each other. Fury still pulsing between us. He backed away and sat down. Only then did I take my seat.

Dr. Rosen didn't make a grand pronouncement after the fight. There was no *This means you're willing to be intimate.* No leading questions like *Have you ever had a fight like that with a man? With anyone? Do you understand what this means,* Mamaleh? I wouldn't have heard it anyway with my heartbeat galloping in my ears. And for the first time in all my hours of group therapy, I wasn't secretly hoping that Dr. Rosen would turn his attention to me and praise me for all the deep work I was doing. For the first time, I didn't need his affirmation to prove I was moving forward and doing the hard things to become the person I wanted to be. I had keys to a new condo in River North in my purse. I'd thrown my shoe at Max and stood my ground in a highly charged confrontation. It was undeniably life altering to buy real estate, but I'd sat through enough group therapy sessions to recognize that my willingness to fight full out with Max might be an even bigger indication of transformation than a new address on Ontario Street. My body buzzed with adrenaline that was sure to wear off, but in those dizzy moments after the shouting match, there was a solid, still part of me that knew: I was moving forward in my own messy, noisy, frightened way.

At the end of the session, I stood up, unsure if my shaky legs would hold me up. I wasn't ashamed exactly, but I wasn't sure how to deal with Max during the hugs or on the walk to the elevators. It was he who approached me after he hugged Dr. Rosen. For the second time in thirty minutes, he stood a few inches in front of me. This time, he opened his arms wide. I opened mine too. Neither of us said a word, but we held on to each other tightly.

29

I hung my red trench coat on the back of my office door, took a seat at my desk, and pressed the start button on my computer. It was still booting up when the phone rang. I checked the number on the curled business card clutched in my damp hand. Yes, it was him, just as he promised.

"Christie Tate speaking," I said to sound official, to steady my nerves, to prop up the sham that this was a business call. Reed, the new man in my Tuesday group, had been running deals—or whatever hedge fund managers do—for two decades. I'd been a lawyer for two years. He didn't need my legal advice. When he laughed on the other end of the line, I could picture his dimples because I'd just seen them in group when we'd laughed at something Rory said about her dad.

"You sound like a real lawyer," he said.

"That's because I am a real lawyer." My body temperature rose. I fanned myself with the card he'd pressed into my hand.

"Did you think I would call?"

Would truth function here—in the untamed, unsupervised space outside of group—like it did in there? Would it rescue me from the cliché I saw myself diving into like a shimmering pool in a 1970s night-time drama like *Dynasty* or *Dallas*? What did I think would happen between me and this married older man with the ropy forearms and lean neck with a hairline like the seashore? The married man who joined my therapy group because he couldn't stop getting blow jobs from other women?

"I wasn't sure." But I hoped he would, was glad he did. "How can I help you?"

"Do you know anyone who does M&A work?"

My turn to laugh. Skadden was internationally famous for mergers and acquisitions work. I sat one floor away from thirty M&A lawyers. "I can give you the name of the head of the department."

"I'll take a name and a number."

I gave him the name and number of the partner with the snow-white hair who wore custom-made pinstriped suits and closed deals that ended up on the front page of the *Wall Street Journal.*

There was a pause. I flicked the corner of Reed's business card, and then pinned it to the bulletin board behind my phone, even though I'd already memorized his number.

There was another pause. Then another.

"So," he said, and I could hear his smirk and picture the glint in his eye. "If I keep you on the phone, are we going to need a chaperone?"

"What for?" I wanted to make him say it.

"For all the things we are going to say and do to each other."

When I hung up the phone, still smiling, still warmed and thrumming from my thighs to my scalp, I stood up and wrung my hands, trying to break the spell, the heat, the throbbing, the pleasure of having Reed's attention. I relived each beat of our conversation, thrilled that he'd punctured the pretense that our conversation was work related.

I cracked my neck and arched my back, but my body begged for release, so I pressed in the metal lock on my door. Pushed back my chair and lay on the floor. I slid my hands between my legs. My jaw tightened as I touched myself, thinking of Reed's dimples, his strong hands, and his crisp collars. His voice on the phone. Those delicious pauses. I came with such force that I bumped my head on the edge of my computer tower. My whole body pulsed—fingertips, triceps, lips, belly, Achilles' heel, toes.

I was still breathing hard when I sat in my chair, straightened my sweater, and began to answer e-mails from Jack and the team in Germany.

From group, I knew that Reed viewed his marriage as a stalemate. He was the guilty, straying husband; his wife Miranda's rage simmered just below boiling. Their communication was limited to terse exchanges about the logistics of getting their girls to gymnastics and tutoring. They slept with their backs to each other.

I also knew it was cliché for me to run headfirst into a relationship with him while I was still reeling from Alex. And yet I sprinted.

The following Thursday and Monday sessions, I didn't mention Reed, an omission I justified because he was in my Tuesday group, so I should talk about him then. On Tuesday, I set my alarm fifteen minutes early so I could take extra time getting dressed. My stomach somersaulted when the train pulled into the Washington stop. *I get to be with him for ninety minutes.*

Reed arrived a few minutes late. He put his briefcase next to my chair, and as he sat down, he scooted several inches closer to me. Could they all feel the heat rising between us? My heart was pounding. Surely Dr. Rosen and everyone else could hear it.

During the session, I stared at the dark indigo of Reed's slacks, the fine hair on his wrists. When he talked, I watched his lips move; when he brushed his hand through his hair in frustration, I couldn't make myself look away. But I also watched the clock obsessively, because at nine o'clock, group would end, and Reed would head north to his office and I would head west to mine, where my gray life of document review and *Riverdance* awaited me. But in group, less than a foot away from Reed, my life shimmered with color and promise because I could watch him challenge the Colonel, brush his foot with mine, listen to his laugh.

And this: my feelings for Reed were undeniably of a sexual nature, which meant I should share them with the group. The pressure to disclose pressed against my lips, but Reed beat me to it.

"I think about Christie all the time. When I get in bed with Miranda,

I wish she was Christie. At the girls' soccer games, I wish Christie was with me. We talked on the phone the other day, and it was really—" Reed looked at me as if for permission. I nodded. "It was really nice."

Everyone looked at me, waiting for my half of the confession. I admitted that I enjoyed talking to him. I didn't mention how I shut my door and touched myself in my office after our first conversation. What words matched the sensations in my body? The constant thrumming, the woozy feeling like I'd pounded shots or snorted laughing gas. The only words I could imagine were ridiculous. I couldn't tell them I was falling in love.

At the same time, I wasn't a woman who stole another woman's husband. I'd taken women's studies classes. I'd read MacKinnon, Chodorow, and Cixous. Plus, I knew better than to believe that married Reed would leave his colonial in the suburbs. I hadn't sat through hundreds of therapy sessions to dive into the cliché of the lonely girl who falls for the unhappily married man *from her therapy group*. I'd already tried dating a man who saw Dr. Rosen, and it hadn't worked. I remembered Monica Lewinsky—the public scorn and the rescinding of her Revlon job offer when the blow-job scandal broke. Given the loose boundaries of Rosen-world, I too could end up publicly shamed, not to mention I was jeopardizing my therapeutic home base.

"What do you want?" Dr. Rosen asked me.

"I don't know how to answer that."

"Why not?"

"I don't know what I'm allowed to have." I stared back at Dr. Rosen and believed he knew the answer: I wanted Reed.

Each morning my cell rattled on my bedside table. Reed on his way to work before dawn. Stock market hours. He always called my office midmorning to say hello, and then again when the market closed. At night he called on his walk from his office to the train. I could hear his shoes clicking on the sidewalk. Sometimes we talked from the moment he left his office, all through his train ride and walk to his front door when he'd put his key in the lock and whispered that he had to go. He showed me how to send PIN messages on my BlackBerry—messages that bypassed our firms' servers and allegedly left no record. When my BlackBerry light glowed with a blinking red light, I knew it was a PIN from Reed and my body responded with a jolt.

He told me I could ask him anything, so I asked about Miranda. Maybe then she would be real to me, and I would back off. What did she smell like? (Clean) How thin was she? (Size four) What was his favorite thing about her? (Her devotion to the children) When was the last time they slept together? (Couldn't recall) Why did he marry her? (It felt like I was supposed to) Why hadn't he left her? (The girls) I drew a picture of her in my head: a woman my height in a plum-colored dress with silver sandals with perfect sun-kissed highlights in her mostly blond hair and a coldness that I associated with super-thin wealthy women who didn't have to work. I imagined she had a signature lipstick shade and nibbled at her food. I dreamed her as flawless but cold; self-possessed but starving; perfectly manicured but brittle. My body had more flesh, more warmth, more vitality, more youth, more power.

I felt guilty. I was a fake feminist after all. A husband stealer. A cliché.

And yet: I'd never felt so alive.

⸻

"I have to go to my noon AA meeting. Meet me there," Reed said one morning.

Jack was expecting me for a meeting in ten minutes. After he'd supported my German travel ban, I was loath to cause any trouble. How much would I risk for Reed?

I e-mailed Jack: *Something has come up. Can we meet at 1:30?*

The AA meeting was four blocks from my office, and I raced over in my heels with no coat, even though it was thirty degrees. I had no wallet, no money, no fucking sense in my head. All I had was the force of Reed's voice inviting me to be with him and my reckless yes. Across the Chicago Loop, I bobbed and weaved between pedestrians and stepped into traffic so I could get to Reed sooner, so I could flee my gray, loveless life that turned vivid in his presence. Yes, I sprinted to an AA meeting:

Even though I wasn't technically an alcoholic.

Even though I had to push back a meeting with the largest rain-maker in my department.

Even though Reed was a married man with well-documented fidel-ity issues.

I sat next to him in the back at the end of a row. He pressed his shiny black lace-up shoe against my black wedge heel. My breath hitched. I leaned back in my chair and snuck my hand into the space between his elbow and his rib cage. The throbbing in my fingertips was my own pulse, but it felt like his. The chairperson of the meeting passed around a flyer for a 12-step retreat, and when I passed it to Reed, I let my fin-gers rest on his palm. Skin to skin. Everything disappeared. The white-walled room packed with sober lawyers, secretaries, traders, and a massage therapist. The serenity coins. The stackable chairs. The woman in a security officer uniform eating her Chipotle burrito in the far corner. It was all gone and with it, the Loop, the El train, the traffic on Wacker.

There was only my fingertips and Reed's palm.

And that throbbing through my body.

He walked me back to my office. I matched his long stride so that every few steps our hands would brush. Each time, we pulled our hands away quickly as if shocked. Or busted. We wore goofy smiles.

Oldest fucking story in the book. Older successful guy and his younger mistress. The end of this story would find me huddled some-where bawling, leaving messages for Dr. Rosen, shaking my fist at my stupid-ass decisions. But this moment on corner of Wacker and Ran-dolph with Reed's hand centimeters from mine and my body bursting with unexpressed longing was all that mattered. It was enough.

"I want you to know everything about me," he said as we stood before the great glass revolving door that would churn me back into my office.

"Like what?" Thanks to group, I already knew his dad was a pre-scription pill addict who pressured Reed into an MBA program even though he wanted to be an architect. I'd heard the story about the track coach who got him drunk and molested him at an out-of-town meet during middle school. I'd been privy to the sessions where he described who he was when he drank every day, and of course that blow job that brought him to group. And the other extramarital shenanigans that fissured his marriage. I knew things. Knowledge was power that felt like love.

"Everything. How I open a bottle of water. How I hold the steering wheel or swim laps in the pool. Stuff I can't show you in group or on the street." He leaned over and whispered in my ear: "I want you to know what I look like when I tell you that I love you."

"I did something yesterday," I announced in Monday-morning group, where it was easier to disclose because Reed wasn't in that group. For weeks, I'd come right up to the line of committing a sin with Reed. I rationalized each near transgression as harmless because nothing overtly sexual happened. Grazing his palm at an AA meeting wasn't an affair. Neither was meeting him for lunch in a dark bar hidden under the El tracks or talking to him late at night after his family had gone to bed. We hadn't even kissed. I lied to myself that I was blameless, though deep down I suspected what I was doing with Reed was like secretly eating a dozen apples but professing to have recovered from an eating disorder.

"What happened?" Lorne said. He'd predicted for weeks that my "friendship" with Reed might get too friendly. His wife, Renee, had been in group with Reed years earlier, and they'd come close to having an affair, which should have given me pause. It didn't.

"We were talking on the phone yesterday—and things got—out of hand."

"What does that mean?" Patrice's brow furrowed with motherly concern. Grandma Maggie clucked as if she knew what was coming.

"He called from the grocery store." On the weekends, Reed and I patched together a series of guerrilla phone calls whenever he was able to sneak away from his family. I was glued to my phone at all times. "He said things—he was in the frozen foods aisle—"

"Jesus, we don't care about frozen peas!" Lorne sniped.

"Fine. We had phone sex."

"While he was buying food for his wife and kids," Patrice mentioned helpfully.

"He did this with Renee, you know," Lorne said. "Did he tell you how special you are? That he loved you?"

I told myself the same things every woman in my position tells herself: I was different. But a braided knot in my stomach—one strand for Reed's wife and each of the girls—tightened. I pressed my lips together and looked at Dr. Rosen, who prompted me to say more, so I described how I'd touched myself on the floor of my closet while Reed told me to imagine him inside me. He'd told me that he loved me, that he'd do anything for me. When I'd heard the cashier ask if he wanted paper or plastic, I tried to hang up, but he wanted me to stay on the line until he got into his car.

"Why the closet?" Max always with the relevant questions.

When the conversation with Reed had turned racy, I'd been standing in my closet looking for a sweater. Next thing I knew, I was on the floor, fingers between my legs, phone cradled to my ear, staring up at the hems of my pants and skirts.

Dr. Rosen spoke up. "Where better to hide sexuality than the closet? It's an obvious choice." Unable to meet his eyes, I stared at the outline of Dr. Rosen's chin. He asked what I was feeling. There was only one answer: Shame. Shame. Shame. All the throbbing excitement turned to liquid shame, sloshing through my body.

"I'm a fucking cliché. I should be better than this. I'm moving backward." A married recovering alcoholic with teenage children was a trapdoor in the space I'd previously labeled "the bottom." There was no way Dr. Rosen could convince me that moving from single-but-not-in-love-with-me Alex to married Reed was progress in the right direction. Dr. Rosen insisted I was moving forward. "I want my *own* husband and my *own* children, not someone else's! I want more than phone sex on my ballet flats."

"What if this is exactly what you need to do to get where you want to go?"

"You can't mean that."

"When was the last time you let yourself be adored by a man who wanted to fuck you?"

"The Intern—"

Dr. Rosen shook his head.

"You should be warning me, raising a red fucking flag right under my nose." It would never happen. Dr. Rosen was die-hard about letting us find our way without judging us. If I, as a so-called sexual anorexic, needed to have an affair with a married man to finally hit bottom with unavailable men, then so be it. To me, Reed was a category-six hurricane about to make landfall, and I wanted Dr. Rosen to pick me up and carry me to higher ground. But that wasn't what Dr. Rosen did. He was a witness, not the National Guard.

Patrice balked at Dr. Rosen's laissez-faire approach. "Maybe you shouldn't talk to him outside of group, Christie."

I nodded, knowing I should heed her advice, but positive I would stay the course, following the immortal words of Martin Luther: *Be a sinner and sin boldly*—though Luther wasn't referring to getting off in the closet to the murmurs of a married group mate.

"How is this going to get me where I want to go?" I asked.

"We'll find out." Dr. Rosen shrugged—not an inspiring gesture as I headed toward inevitable devastation.

"Max, help," I said.

Ever since our showdown, I sensed that I could trust Max more than anyone else in the circle. When you scream into someone's face, you learn something about how solid they are. Max was a goddamn redwood whose roots ran deeper and wider than anyone else's in the circle. If he told me to run from Reed, I'd consider lacing up my shoes.

"I think you have to play this out." Though the serious look on Max's face scared me, I also heard his blessing for my folly.

But Dr. Rosen was the authority figure, the doctor, the Harvard alum. He should make a decree or recommendation. "Isn't it malpractice for you to bless this affair?"

"You think driving this underground and making it *more secretive* would be helpful for you? Come on."

30

When my group mates considered Reed's potential as a mate for me, they stopped at the solid-gold band on his left ring finger. I wasn't ignoring that detail—even when he hinted that I'd be a great stepmother and that he could move into my new condo. Instead, I focused on how much better he was than the other men I'd dated. He told me he loved me every time I talked to him, so he was the anti-Alex. He didn't care about religion, so he was the anti-intern. He answered my e-mails within thirty seconds and asked me to lunch every other day, so he was the anti-Jeremy. I rationalized that it was good practice to bask in Reed's love and attention. Eventually, I would transfer my attention to a man who was just like him, except without that gold band.

As soon as Reed sat down in group on Tuesdays, he would extend his hand toward me. I'd held a lot of hands in group: Patrice, Marty, Nan, Emily, Mary, Marnie, Max, Grandma Maggie, Lorne, and Dr. Rosen. Sometimes those hands supported me, and sometimes my palm served as someone else's ballast. But this was different. Holding Reed's hand didn't feel like a gesture of therapeutic support. It felt like foreplay.

The first time we held hands in group, Rory and Marty both gasped. Patrice sighed in frustration. Carlos whispered, "Girl, please." Dr. Rosen made a show of seeing our hands together, fingers like a lattice to each other's body, but said nothing. When I caught Dr. Rosen's eye, the seed of fear and frustration would blossom into protest.

"What's your plan, Dr. Rosen?" I held up my hand still knitted to Reed's.

"Plan? I'm not God."

"What about Reed's wife? Don't you care about her?"

"She's not my patient. You are."

He asked me what I was feeling. My answer was always the same: shame and hunger. Dr. Rosen asked me what I wanted. "Reed. I want Reed. Are you helping me? I came here for help with relationships—"

"I *am* helping you."

"The sum total of your therapeutic advice for me is come here, feel feelings, and disclose everything?" As I confronted Dr. Rosen, Reed held my hand, his thumb tracing a circle across my palm.

"Yes."

Did Dr. Rosen think that Reed and I should be together? *Together* together? I stared hard at Dr. Rosen—his unblinking eyes and straight neck, the slight hunch of his shoulders, his shoes planted on the floor. When he peered into the future, what did he see for me? A life with Reed and his girls? A life with someone like Reed, but whom I could have all to myself?

Patrice and Grandma Maggie begged me to cut it off. Lorne trotted out Renee's history with Reed as a cautionary tale. Max continued to say I had to play this out and that the mysterious alchemy of the advanced group would somehow immunize me from total destruction. Rory, Marty, Carlos, and the Colonel looked to Dr. Rosen, who smiled inscrutably and held his palms open. In the elevator one Tuesday morning, Rory, in a quiet voice, said, "I don't know what Dr. Rosen is doing with you." Her eyes darted from my gaze in fear.

In late February, Steven threw a party for Clare's birthday and invited all of our law school friends. When I stepped into the dark restaurant, I spotted Clare decked out in a silk top and skinny jeans. I felt like I'd just returned from a long trip to a faraway country. My relationship with Reed had so consumed me that I'd forgotten there was a big wide world beyond my three-inch BlackBerry screen, where I read and re-read Reed's messages while waiting for him to break from his family and call me.

All through dinner, my BlackBerry buzzed. Each time it vibrated, I pretended to search my purse for lip gloss or gum or a pen so I could read the message from Reed: *I miss you.* Two minutes later: *When are you going to be home?* Ten minutes later: *I have a second to talk. Can you pick up? Where are you?* Five minutes after that: *We are driving home soon. I won't be online for about an hour.*

"Tater, what on earth are you expecting on that BlackBerry?" Clare cornered me in the line to the bathroom.

I told her I was involved with someone, and she wanted to know why he wasn't with me. My mouth froze in a smile as I realized with perfect clarity: Clare would never meet Reed. I was a secret, a *mistress*. Having to look Clare in the eye and tell her I was with a man who was currently at his niece's ballet recital with his wife of nineteen years was a sickening jolt of reality. I mentioned that he was "sort of attached," and she understood instantly.

"Are you in love with each other?"

I pulled out the Valentine's Day card Reed gave me that I kept in my purse. She opened it and read aloud. " '*I love you, Reed.*' "

"How'd you meet him?" Clare knew all about group therapy, but the truth stuck in my throat. The words vibrated with sheer insanity as I said, "Group therapy."

"Well, he clearly loves you!" She waved the card in the air and hugged me again. I absorbed her genuine good cheer for my counterfeit relationship.

Hours later when I climbed into bed, my BlackBerry glowed red with a new PIN message. I typed in my passcode, but stopped myself from clicking on his message. The look on Clare's face when I told her Reed was married made me want to curl my legs into my body and groan out loud. Reed was never going to leave Miranda and his girls. And if he did, would we even be attracted to each other anymore? How could I ever trust him given his history? And what if the real draw to the relationship was the illicitness, the secrecy, the current of shame

that animated our connection? Wasn't this covered in the most basic of
Lifetime movies?

I hurled my BlackBerry into the closet. The pain of not connecting
with Reed before falling asleep was physical—a stomach cramp that felt
like something scrambled in my guts. Reed might love me, but he wasn't
available. Didn't I want something real? How did screwing around with
a married man make me a real person if the whole thing was a secret? I
rocked back and forth. I stuffed a corner of my pillow in my mouth and
bit down hard. The red blinking light on my BlackBerry flickered like a
heartbeat.

31

I ducked into a Starbucks in Logan Square on a Friday night at six thirty. Commuters were rushing home, and darkness had chased the weak winter sun well below the horizon. Reed's call was ten minutes late. My resolution from the night of Clare's party had dissolved the next day, and we resumed our daily phone calls. There was also a week-night trip to a suburban mall where I helped him shop for a winter coat—when the mall closed, we groped in his minivan by the light of the Cheesecake Factory. Ours was a very classy romance.

When my phone finally buzzed, I moved to a quiet stool away from the espresso machine. Reed's breath swallowed his voice. It sounded like he was running down the street. I pictured him sprinting down Madison so he could get home. To his family. *I want him to run to me.* Something cold and sharp in his voice made me sit up taller. He always swore he had no secrets from me, that I could ask him anything. Now it took all my courage ask: "Where're you going?"

"I'm taking the girls out for pizza." *Girls* undoubtedly included his wife. The lump in my throat held the shape of her in that plum dress and those Hollywood highlights. "It'll be an early night. We're headed back to Iowa tomorrow." Miranda's father had recently been diagnosed with terminal liver cancer. I was sure the diagnosis would bring Reed and his wife closer together, but so far, he reported she was shutting him out more than ever.

"Are you okay?" I rocked back and forth on the stool, one hand on the phone, one on my chest.

"Nervous about the trip." That cold thing in his voice was sharper still.

"I'm here if you need me—" The espresso machine grinded and whirred, drowning out all other sounds.

"I've got to go."

For the first time ever, he hung up without saying *I love you*. The noisy Starbucks counter spun in my vision as genuine panic set it. I'd felt this before. Reed was loosening his grip on me. Now he would slide under the water and disappear, just like all the others, just as I always knew he would.

Reed's PIN message popped up just after eleven that night. *Sorry,* he wrote.

I wasn't about to interrogate him. I was the anti-Miranda—never suspicious, never prying, never difficult. I wrote back: *No need to apologize! I love you! Let's talk tomorrow.* I certainly didn't ask why it took four hours to eat pizza "with the girls."

"I lied to you." It was six the next morning. I'd been up since four, wandering around my apartment and swigging skim milk from the carton, trying to calm my stomach.

"Dude, I already know about the wife and kids." I forced a laugh; he was silent.

"Last night, Miranda and I went out for our"—I sucked in my breath, mouthing the word before he said it—"anniversary."

I pressed my back against my bedroom wall and slid down.

Anniversary. Such a beautiful word, now turned bitter in my mouth. The truth of his lie settled in my belly. My body craved expulsion: vomit, tears, screaming. But I sat against the wall, my body perpendicular to my legs.

He hadn't said a word about his anniversary in group. In all the therapy sessions we sat through together—holding hands—I got the impression that there was insufficient civility between Reed and Miranda to sustain them through a meal without the girls. Now I couldn't get the picture of them sitting down to fillets and flourless chocolate cake out of my head. I saw candlelight, apologetic caresses, and a softening of all the hard hurt between them.

I shook and shook and shook.

"I love you. Please don't doubt I love you," Reed pleaded. "Say something. Please."

"This is boring." I'd been smart enough to know we'd never last but dumb enough to hope for a different ending.

Still gripping the phone, I crawled to the bathroom and peered over the toilet seat, a comforting view I'd known so well as a teenager. Nothing came out because I hadn't been able to eat any dinner, unlike Reed, who'd had a lovely anniversary meal *with his wife of twenty years.*

"I'm hanging up now." I flipped my phone shut and threw it as hard I could against the bathroom mirror. It clattered to a stop by the bathtub. I turned off my BlackBerry and locked it in the trunk of my car.

No more PIN messages.

No more phone sex.

No more secret thrills.

The fury in my body—at myself, at Reed, at Dr. Rosen for calling this "progress"—made it impossible to stand still. I was also mad at Max for encouraging me to "play this out." At Rory, Patrice, and Grandma Maggie for being right all along. I laced up my running shoes and ran ten miles on the Lake. I pounded past groups of runners and clumps of tourists taking pictures of Navy Pier. I pulled my hat low over my brow and didn't make eye contact with a soul. My music was set to the highest volume, and I let it drown every thought about Reed and what a fool I was. When I was done, I still felt pumped and jittery. I could have run ten more miles. I could have run until I shredded every muscle in my legs, scorched my lungs, and made bloody stumps of my toes.

But what I really needed was to cry.

I sat through a 12-step meeting without hearing or saying a single word. Several people approached me afterward asking if I was okay, and I shook my head no. I leaned into the white of my knuckles. No, I'm not okay.

I sat in my car after the meeting, unsure where to drive. Sunlight streamed in on all sides, and laughing DePaul students and clusters of suburban tourists wandered down the street. The world beyond my car was too noisy and scary.

I called Patrice. "I've shut off my BlackBerry. I'm done."

"I've been so worried about you. You shouldn't be alone right now."

I drove to Lorne's house and cried into his throw pillows and fought the urge to unlock my trunk and grab my BlackBerry to check in with Reed. Lorne's wife, Renee, patted my head, telling of the nights she too cried over Reed once she realized he would never leave his wife. Lorne and Renee's son, Roman, toddled on the floor at my feet, making sweet baby sounds.

The crush of grief worked me over, and I kept landing on the absurd notion that I was unfairly abandoning him. "His father-in-law is dying. Maybe I should break up with him this summer."

Lorne and Renee shook their heads.

"Dr. Rosen is going to be so proud of you," Lorne said. Tears sprung to my eyes. What must Dr. Rosen have thought as he watched me holding hands with Reed, describing our silly trip to the mall, our closeted sex life? He'd kept a poker face all these weeks in group, but surely he shook his head back in his office, wondering when his fool of a patient would come to her senses.

"I have an idea. Follow me." Renee led me to her desk and sat me before her computer. She pressed a few keys, and the screen filled with the smiling faces of a young couple. In the background, blurry images of people holding sparklers surrounded the couple. The words on the screen read, *Discover where Jewish relationships begin. Start browsing now.*

"JDate?"

"These guys are single—"

"And looking for *Jewish* women. I'm literally named after Christ."

"Trust me. They're going to love you. We'll call you 'Texas Girl.' Once they meet you, they won't care if you're a nun."

I hesitated, but she gave me a look: *Are you willing or not?* She'd built a happy life with Lorne, a nice Jewish boy, shortly after she broke off her relationship with Reed. Now she had a beautiful son, throw pillows, and farm-fresh eggs in her fridge. She seemed so sure this could work for me. On day one of treatment, Dr. Rosen suggested I could get well if I let him and the group into my decisions. Surely, this counted as not "going it alone."

Renee coached me through the questions on the profile form. No, I was not Ashkenazi. No, I didn't attend shul every week. Renee insisted I check the box indicating I kept kosher because I hated ham. I had sparse hope that the men on JDate would embrace me, but Renee had me laughing. She sent me home with leftover challah from their Shabbat dinner. "Shalom," I said as I shut the door behind me.

Lakeshore Drive heading downtown from the north side on a clear, late-winter night is one of the most gorgeous scenes imaginable—the stony Drake Hotel looms like a castle and the Hancock building grazes the stars. As messed up as I was about Reed, I couldn't look at the city and feel anything other than awe. It was my third night as an aspiring Jewess on JDate, and I was driving home from a recovery meeting. I knew my apartment would be cold and empty, but I preferred the harsh punch of loneliness to the electric, buzzy instability of trying to build a life around Reed. So far I hadn't broken any dishes or palmed a letter opener.

I dialed Dr. Rosen, who'd been out of town for a conference and didn't know about the lie and the anniversary dinner. "I let go of Reed. I won't have any contact with him outside of group," I told his voice mail.

I took a deep breath. There was so much more to say. For weeks, I'd wondered how Dr. Rosen could live with himself as he stood watch over my affair with Reed. Group members had repeatedly confronted Dr. Rosen on my behalf: *Why aren't you doing something about this? Christie's going to get hurt. This is totally unethical.* Dr. Rosen met each confrontation with a neutral expression, asking what, exactly, he should do to stop me.

During my tenure in Rosen-land, various group members had referred to Dr. Rosen as *brilliant*. I'd seen him speak fluent German to the Colonel and Max; I'd watched Hebrew blessings roll off his tongue. He made deep connections between seemingly disparate events in group members' lives. Pet ferrets and the Holocaust. Guitar lessons and cyanide pills. Pinworm and credit card debt. He was sharp, but was that brilliance? Maybe.

What I valued most in Dr. Rosen were his balls of steel. He trusted himself enough to allow two group members to have an affair literally on his watch. He watched me make one questionable choice after another, patiently waiting for me to come to my God-given senses. If I would have killed myself over this, surely he would have found himself before a licensing board. But he trusted himself—and he trusted me. Waiting for me to wise up must have felt like having teeth removed without Novocain. I could never stand to watch someone I cared about make such questionable decisions.

I was grateful that he could.

32

I was naked, shivering, holding my arms across my chest like a V, which was inadequate to the task of hiding my breasts. Sort of silly given that I'd just had sex with him. My clothes were across the room on the radiator. The only light was the glowing isosceles triangle from the closet. Sade crooned in her timeless voice.

I stood there for several minutes watching Brandon, who had already buttoned himself into his matching pajama set. He made hospital corners with the bedsheets and folded the comforter just so after pulling it tight. He didn't acknowledge me, standing there shivering; he was in another world, a fugue state composed of sheets, blankets, comforters, flat lines, and surfaces with no ripples. My arms shivered against my breasts and goose bumps rose on my belly as my mind tried and failed to return to the moments before Brandon's vision tunneled to his linens.

Brandon stepped back, hands on his hips, and surveyed the bed. He nodded and mumbled something to himself. He strode to his side of the bed and peeled back the covers gingerly. He shimmied his body down carefully so as to not disturb that hard-won smoothness. With his head on his pillow, he turned to me with a wide, unguarded smile.

"Coming to bed?"

After Renee set up my JDate profile, a series of men who were seeking Jewish partners rejected me upon discovering that "Texas Girl" was actually a shiksa named after the savior of the New Testament. Aaron and Oren seemed offended that my profile had been designed to dupe them, while Daniel, Eric, and Marc were amused at my claims to a kosher diet. Jerry, who must have been sixty-two years old, offered to take me to Manny's deli and then show me his Jewish sausage. I let my JDate membership lapse and moved on to eharmony.com.

Brandon's first e-mail charmed me immediately. He asked if I liked to eat breakfast cereal for dinner, which launched a lively debate about the merits of Frosted Flakes versus granola. From his missives, I gathered that he was experienced at dating because he knew how to flirt over e-mail. I also assumed he was well educated, because he knew when to employ a semicolon.

Brandon met my sole criterion for a date: he wasn't a married man in my therapy group. He had the settled air of a man in his late thirties who now wanted a steady plus-one. On our first date we met for lunch at the East Bank Club, Chicago's version of a country club that boasted the membership of Oprah and the Obamas. He wore a blue blazer and smiled with kind eyes. He stood an inch taller than I was, and his hair was longer than it was in his profile picture. He looked boyish and approachable, like a Beatle preparing for his first gig on *The Ed Sullivan Show*. For our second date we saw a play called *Love Song* at the Steppenwolf, followed by dinner at Boku on Halsted. Brandon was the type of guy who ordered off the specials menu and wore pressed khaki pants on weekend nights. He always paid, always held the door open, always insisted on sharing dessert. His college, the same place he went to medical school, was famous for educating dozens of presidents and Supreme Court justices. When he laughed, he held his hand over his mouth shyly. He'd recently taken up rock climbing to force himself to learn something that didn't come naturally to him. His hygiene was impeccable—he brushed his teeth before and after we made out, and showered twice a day. He never cursed, didn't drink, and never lost his cool. I was 90 percent sure he was Republican, but he had yet to demonstrate any misogyny, racism, or classism, so I let myself be wooed by his blue-blooded manners and kind demeanor.

With Brandon, there were no spontaneous jolts of desire that propelled me to the floor of my office in search of orgasmic relief. During our first kiss on my couch after the play at Steppenwolf, I felt pleasant, if not particularly turned on. And that was mostly fine by me. The loss of appetite around the Intern and the illicit charge from my relationship with Reed had left me wrung out. With Brandon, my body was a calm lake on a quiet June morning.

Sometimes, in group, I whispered that I was almost bored.

"Good," Max said. "The hallmark of a healthy relationship is boredom."

"It's true, kiddo," Grandma Maggie said, beaming her smile my direction. "It's part of every marriage."

Dr. Rosen agreed: If I was bored, I was doing something right. But when I listened to other people talk about their early days with their beloveds—Clare or Marnie or Renee—they mentioned not sleeping, not eating, not being able to concentrate. No one described a rippleless lake. Part of me missed the excitement that crashed through me with my previous lovers, even as I recognized that it hadn't served me. Now, when I pictured my heart, I saw that it was grooved from Reed, gouged a few times by Alex and the Intern, nicked by Jeremy. Of course each group member and Dr. Rosen had left their marks. I tried to imagine attaching to Brandon. Once, at dinner, I stared at his starched white shirt, imagining the surface of his heart. Did his grooves match mine?

And now I'd watched Brandon straighten his sheets like someone in a sketch routine about OCD. What, I wondered, did his obsessive bed-making ritual portend? I could only imagine that some unspeakable childhood trauma led him to demand such order from his bedsheets. I wanted to ask, but his eyes were already heavy with sleep. He looked so youthful with the sheets tucked around his shoulders—I felt like I should offer him a glass of milk and a graham cracker.

The sex was weird. We'd walked home from his favorite Thai restaurant, hand in hand. Back at his place, Brandon put on Sade. He led me to his darkened bedroom, where we kissed on his bed for the first time. The calm lake of my belly rippled slightly as he pulled off his shirt and then mine. When all of our clothes were removed, he sat up on the edge of the bed and rolled the condom on. He crawled over to me and straddled my hips with his legs. It was less foreplay than I'd imagined or wanted, but he hadn't had a girlfriend since medical school fifteen years earlier. I didn't fault him for being rusty, and I hadn't been willing to speak up.

Instead of the standard missionary-style sex I'd expected, Brandon put his right palm under my left shoulder and flipped me over in one swift motion. Everything went black as I face-planted into the pillow. Before I could lift my head or say anything, Brandon hoisted my hips up and entered me. Brandon's thrusts were swift and clinical, though not unpleasant. I was stuck in my head: surprised and mildly titillated that someone who seemed so straitlaced, so possibly Republican, was into sex from behind.

But I didn't want my face jammed into a pillow. I wanted to see him, to hear the music, to breathe freely. The words to get myself flipped back over—*Wait. Hold up. Stop. Flip me back. This isn't what I'm into*—wouldn't come out of my mouth. As I lay there trying to sort out how I would tell my group about this flip, Brandon's fingers reached between my legs and my mind went blank as the pleasure rose through me, quick and hot. My back arched, and then my face hit the pillow with a muddled thud. When I rolled over to look at him, he was putting his arms through his pajamas.

Thoughts swallowed every bodily sensation as if my body rolled up into my brain like a window shade: *What's with the pajamas? Did I enjoy that? Where had Sade gone?*

And this: *What happened to my voice?*

From the moment we entered his bedroom, we'd been totally silent. There was no moaning, no panting, no oohing, and no aahing. There was no conversation—no "What do you like?" or "How does that feel?" It was neat and tidy, just like the stack of old-fashioned pajamas lined up in his impeccable linen closet.

As Brandon slept, I replayed the whole scene, from the flip sex to the hospital corners. None of it turned me off, exactly. He wasn't mean or inattentive or checked out. I diagnosed him as phobic about face-to-face sex and psychotic about sheets. But we all had our baggage. I could bring all my judgments, insecurities, fears, delusions, and feelings about everything that just happened to group. They would help me sort through it.

⁓

"You're dating Dr. Flipper," Lorne joked, "but he's better than Reed."

Max said it wasn't clear if the sheets thing was endearing or a sign that he was rigid and unyielding. "You'll probably have to get him into therapy," Max suggested.

I told them we hadn't discussed therapy yet, and Max raised his eyebrows at me. "I'm not hiding it, it just hasn't come up."

"You're waiting for him to ask you if you come to group three times a week?" Max smirked.

The rule was to tell Dr. Rosen and my groups everything, not to tell my potential love interests everything about my therapy. "I'm not sure if I like him. My body doesn't really respond to him."

"Did you have an orgasm?" Lorne asked.

"Yes."

Dr. Rosen beamed like a full moon hanging in a cloudless sky.

⁓

On my thirty-fourth birthday, Brandon stood in my kitchen while I packed my overnight bag. We always spent the night at his penthouse overlooking Navy Pier because it had imported furniture, a surround-sound stereo, and, of course, his pajamas.

"Who's this?" Brandon pointed at a picture stuck to my fridge, every surface of which was plastered with pictures, 10K-race bibs, and ticket stubs. Of the dozens of faces he could have pointed to, he zeroed in on the one I didn't want to discuss. Were we really going to do this on my birthday?

"That's my—" I paused.

He cocked his head like *well?* and kept his finger pinned to the picture.

"My mentor."

Brandon leaned in close and studied the picture. "Really?" It was a close-up picture of Dr. Rosen's face from Kathryn's wedding right before I'd introduced him and Alex. "What kind of mentor?"

I didn't want to tell Brandon about Dr. Rosen because I had no idea what he thought about mental-health treatment. When, a few weeks earlier, I'd told him I was in a 12-step program for an eating disorder, he scrunched his face and said, "I don't get why you need all those people or why anyone can't stop eating when they're full."

"Well, actually"—fuck it—"he's my therapist."

He leaned toward the picture and gave it a good hard look. "Therapist? How'd you get this picture of him?"

"From a wedding. Two of his patients married each other—I'm friends with the bride."

A flicker of alarm in Brandon's eyes. "Two patients married *each other*? What, they passed each other in the waiting room and then fell in love?" I explained about group and how Dr. Rosen didn't forbid out-of-session consortium. Brandon's lips settled into a tense line. He paced the floor and asked a dozen questions about how group worked, where my group mates came from, how it all worked. I assured him it was like regular therapy just more crowded. He wanted to know if I ever talked about him, and when I nodded, he stuffed his hands in his pockets. The temperature in the room seemed to drop several degrees.

Back at his place, the sex was even quicker and more perfunctory than usual: he flipped me, and we were tucked in within twenty minutes. Afterward, I laid my head on his chest, but I could feel him staring at the ceiling. I sat up.

"What's going on?" I asked.

Brandon's gaze didn't waver from the crown molding. "Please don't talk about me in your group."

"What?" Did he know how therapy worked?

"Don't mention my name." I'd yet to tell him that my "group" was actually *two groups* and that I went three times a week.

"They already know I'm dating you." They knew *everything*. One Monday after group, Max and Brad googled Brandon and discovered that his apartment was worth more than a million dollars and that his mother was a major donor to Catholic Charities.

"Do they know my name?"

I nodded, and I felt my face burn red. I wasn't supposed to say his name?

"Please"—he turned to face me—"just leave me out of it."

I nodded—not because I agreed, but because I understood what he was asking. He took my silent nodding as assent, leaned over to kiss me on the cheek, and settled back on his pillow.

33

"How was the birthday?" Max said.

I praised the salmon and the black truffle panna cotta at Custom House.

"Did he give you a present, like looking at your face while he fucked you?" Lorne asked. I gifted Lorne my middle fingers.

"Can we move on?" I asked.

Max narrowed his eyes. "You're usually such a blabbermouth—what he said, how he kissed you, whether he was in denial about his OCD—"

"How he flipped you—" Lorne said, and I gave him two more middle fingers.

"Now you're acting like it's none of our business." Max said.

I looked at Dr. Rosen. "Can you help me?"

Dr. Rosen and I had spoken on the phone the morning after my birthday. He said he would not force me to talk about Brandon in group, but he strongly suggested that I let the group know what Brandon had asked of me. Now he gestured for me to go ahead. I took a deep breath and explained Brandon's request and my tacit agreement not to discuss him in group.

Everyone asked the same question: Why would he jeopardize my treatment? I pursed my lips. They were so dramatic. Brandon simply

wanted privacy. Just because I was comfortable telling my groups what I
ate and how I fucked didn't mean he was. What was the harm in trying
it Brandon's way? If I returned to suicidal ideation and apple binges, I
could always change course.

The group lobbed more questions at me. Grandma Maggie wanted to
know how I would get help with the relationship. Lorne wanted to know
if Brandon knew his nickname was "Flipper." Max's question landed
hardest: Was this relationship worth the sacrifice I'd agreed to make?

Dr. Rosen sat silently as I fielded questions. I looked over at him several times. In one moment, I would see approval for my decision to be
open to Brandon's request. When I looked again, I'd see the straight line of
his lips and detect a wariness that made my spine stiffen. I wanted to press
my palms to my ears and scream. Why did every one of my relationships
have to be such a goddamned production? When would this get easier?

By the end of the session, I'd struck a bargain with the group: I
would not bring in stories about Brandon, but when I needed help with
the relationship, I would leave a message for Dr. Rosen, who would
counsel me outside of group. Then I would disclose to the group, not
the substance of the conversation with Dr. Rosen, but simply the fact he
gave me feedback outside of group.

"This is never going to work," Lorne said. I saluted him with my
middle fingers once again. But even as I acted confident about the bargain I'd struck, worry tugged at me. I'd spent five years learning to bare
myself to Dr. Rosen and my groups, learning to "let them in." What
would be the cost now of shutting them out?

"Christie," Max said in his most serious voice. "Seriously. What's
this about? Why can't you talk about him in your therapy?"

I figured there was some ancient family secret he was protecting out
of allegiance to his bloodline. My best guess was a family history of something he was ashamed of, like addiction, mental illness, or a pregnancy
out of wedlock. I knew that his dad died when Brandon was young, and
I sensed both pain and shame woven through that story, which Brandon
had alluded to only once. In time, Brandon would learn from me that secrets were toxic and that disclosure was the route to freedom and intimacy.

That night over sushi, I told Brandon that I was willing to sequester him from my group as long as I could tell Dr. Rosen anything I wanted. He said he could live with that. I rose from my chair and walked around to his side of the table so I could give him a hug. He blushed at the public display. We ordered a lemon tart with two forks. The mood was celebratory.

The next few weeks in group were awkward. Before Brandon's edict, I had a place in the hot center of the action every session, talking about who I was sleeping with, who just dumped me. I tore up rags, tore out my hair, and demanded to know how group would help me. They had taught me to laugh at myself and look at my relationships from multiple angles. Now I curled into myself when sex or relationships came up, pressing my lips together to remind myself and all of them that I would not be sharing anything.

After every date with Brandon, I left data-filled messages on Dr. Rosen's voice mail ("we had dinner with his college roommate" or "I slept at his house Friday, Saturday, and Sunday!"). I wasn't committing the cardinal sin of *going it alone*. I still called Rory every night to tell her what I ate.

Un

Brandon and I sat side by side at his custom-made oak table, eating steel-cut oatmeal on a Thursday morning. He was in his monogrammed robe, and I was dressed for work. We'd been dating over three months and had a comfortable rapport on weekday mornings. The *New York Times* was filleted on the table, and we each had a section: Business for him, front page for me.

"I have to get going," I said, folding up the paper. "Conference call with a client in an hour."

"What time is it?" he asked.

"Eight thirty."

He turned back to his paper. "My appointment's not until ten."

I assumed he was referring to a patient. When I leaned down to kiss him good-bye, he said, "I'm meeting with Dietrich—" He waited a beat, then: "my shrink."

"Your *what*?"

He laughed, grabbing his stomach right where his robe was tied around his waist.

"My shrink."

He continued to laugh. I suddenly saw Brandon not as eccentric or inexperienced and brainy, but calculating and cruel. I took a deep breath and shifted my bag from the right shoulder to the left.

"How long have you been seeing him?" He pretended to count on his fingers, still chuckling to himself. "Brandon. How long?"

"He's an analyst, actually."

"How long?"

"It's not group. I don't know how you do that—sitting around, listening to other people's problems—" He was chuckling and folding the paper with studied precision. "The group thing would never work for me." He followed me to the door. "Why are you so mad?" He talked to my back as I fumed toward the elevator.

"You're making fun of me." I stabbed the down button. Brandon followed me with a contrite look on his face.

The elevator dinged.

I stepped inside.

As the doors shut, I heard, "Nine years."

I'd thought Brandon was a good person—quirky and a little repressed, but fundamentally good. The mixture of his smile, soft-spokenness, and impeccable manners left me with the impression that he was a gentle soul who, like me, was finding his way. Despite his wealth and privilege, he treated everyone with a quiet respect. He tipped well. When I told him I loved *King Lear*, he got tickets to see a production at the Goodman. Even when I learned about his weirdo bedroom habits, they didn't seem like latent sociopathy. He was just socially awkward, like Justice Souter or Bill Gates. Or me.

But this was too much. He'd asked too much of me—to stop discussing him in therapy—without even telling me that he had a therapist. Not okay. If I could survive the other guys, the ones who made my body zing to life, I would survive him too. I fantasized about calling him later to say, "Have a nice life. Enjoy your penthouse and your money."

But I didn't think I was allowed to let go. That was literally the word in my head: *allowed*. I'd been bellowing about relationships for years. I'd invested thousands of dollars in therapy. I'd joined J-fucking-Date even though I was named after Jesus Christ. I'd recently been involved with a married man. Therefore, I wasn't *allowed* to walk away from Brandon. He was single, solvent, and mostly kind. As the cab roared down Wacker and made a whiplash-inducing turn right in front of my office, I knew I wouldn't break up with him. The urge to flee was overpowered by my need to prove I was willing to do the hard work I was sure intimate relationships required. I'd learned to hold anger, to face it head-on. I'd had too much therapy to simply cut and run. But now I faced a true dilemma: Should I tell my group what just happened?

I had four and a half hours to decide.

cer

"Nine years?" Max said. Technically, I didn't break my promise to Brandon because I'd said, "The man I slept with last night told me he's been seeing a therapist for nine years."

"Yes, almost a decade. Asshole."

Dr. Rosen held up his hand. "Can we slow down?"

I pointed at Dr. Rosen. "He's known about you for months. You should have seen him laughing at me. And his secrets—"

"It's not a secret. He told you about it." Dr. Rosen spoke in his calming voice, which only made me angrier.

"Don't you want *more* for me?"

Dr. Rosen raised his eyebrows. "What do you mean, more?"

"He cut me off from the group and didn't tell me about his own therapy. This relationship is another dead end. My specialty."

Dr. Rosen wore his thinking face and stared at me. He rubbed his chin and started to speak a few times. Finally he offered his sage wisdom: "I don't know."

But I didn't pay him eight hundred forty dollars every month to *not* know. I paid him to use his fancy degrees to transform my life by teaching me relationship skills so I could use them in healthy relationships. I asked if it was time to break up.

"Why would you break up with him?" Dr. Rosen looked as if I'd announced a plan to steal Brandon's silver.

"He lied by omission for weeks. I'm going to end up right back where I started. For all I know, he has a wife and kids in Peoria."

"That's impossible," Dr. Rosen said.

"Why?"

"Because Peoria sucks," Lorne said.

Dr. Rosen leaned toward me theatrically as if he was going to tell me a secret. "Pssst. Confidential to Christie. This is the best relationship you've ever had."

I wanted to knock his half-bald noggin off his scrawny neck. *This was my best?* "Fuck you, Dr. Rosen."

"It's true," Patrice said. Grandma Maggie nodded along.

"Reed would never have kept his therapy a secret from me."

"He lied to you plenty," Brad said.

"Fine. But Alex—we did sunrise bike rides and had sex twenty—"

Max let out an exasperated sigh. "He didn't love you, remember? Remember the letter opener and that sack of broken dishes." Everyone jumped in with reasons Brandon was my best so far. Dr. Rosen broke into a self-satisfied grin. I quit arguing. I'd sacrificed the jolt in my belly I had with Reed and Alex so I could have a so-called real relationship with an available man. But that available man had some deep-seated issues that scared me.

"You're sexually attracted to the prospect of being abandoned," Dr. Rosen said.

I wanted to argue with him, but how could I? In every previous relationship, at least half of the attraction was the inherent dare to overcome the obstacles—the Intern's religion, Reed's wife, Alex's ambivalence about me.

"Brandon's not going anywhere," Dr. Rosen said. In the silence that followed, I swear I heard him say, "Neither are you."

Brandon showed up at my office with a *please forgive me* smile that night. "It's hard for me to get close to people," he said. All my breakup bravado slipped away. Instead of saying, "This isn't working for me," I said, "What should we do for dinner?" Later that night, when he flipped me, I detected urgency in his thrusts, and I imagined that he'd been afraid of losing me. It bothered me that we never talked about our sex life—the flipping, the weird silence we slipped into once we were being intimate. I drifted off with a single question in my mind: Could I honestly make a family with this man? Was this better than being alone?

34

I tested Brandon. Would I have done it if I'd been free to talk about him in group? Probably not. I wanted to know if he thought he could love me. If he saw a future with me. If he cared about me as much as he cared about those hospital corners on his bed. It felt easier to test him than to come right out and ask him directly.

The first test: when John, a tall, introverted corporate attorney from work, asked me out to dinner, I said yes. All I knew about John was that he liked golf, didn't own a TV, and had a long-winded way of telling a story. I said yes to John because a date with another guy was just the thing to force a *so where's this going?* conversation with Brandon.

When I told Brandon about dinner with John, he didn't even look up from the newspaper. "Sounds fun," he said. The next day, I canceled on John.

One night, Brandon and I ate prosciutto sandwiches and black olives on a ledge overlooking North Avenue Beach after the sun went down. He put his arm around me as we stared at Lake Michigan quietly lapping the sand. He kissed me in the shadow of the trees by the chess pavilion, and I imagined something deep stirring in me. Not the zing or thrill of lust. Something more substantial. Was this how functional adults fell in love? When he pulled away, he stared at me. "You may not know this, but I usually spend the winters in London," he said. He reached for my hand. "This year, I want to stay here. To see where this goes."

Later, when we had sex, he didn't flip me.

On a Monday night a few weeks later, Brandon called from the sidewalk in front of my condo. Did I want to go for a walk? Outside, Brandon was typing something on his phone with a distressed look on his face. He started walking without saying a word, and I followed and waited for him to speak. He stopped abruptly at LaSalle Street. A bus whisked by.

"I want to tell you something, but you can't tell anyone. Including Dr. Rosen. This is just between us."

I stared at the red letters that spelled out *Sports Authority*. Now *I* was being tested. Why was he asking this of me? Worse, why would I agree?

In five years, I'd never shifted my allegiance from Dr. Rosen to one of my boyfriends. Would cutting my dependence on Dr. Rosen help me move forward? Maybe it was necessary to draw a circle around something and keep Dr. Rosen out. But should I really put my mental health in the hands of a guy who gazed more lovingly at his thousand-thread-count sheets than at me? Would saying yes score my heart? Or would saying no?

Yes. In the time it took for a light to turn green, I officially jettisoned my treatment so I could sequester Brandon's deepest secret inside me and let it wedge me apart from Dr. Rosen, who was legally obligated to keep any secret I told him.

Brandon admitted: "I don't have a libido."

I burst out laughing. A real Rosen laugh where I grabbed my belly and folded forward. One, because I already knew that. Two, because who cared if Dr. Rosen knew about his libido? No one expected Brandon to fuck like Mick Jagger circa 1975. Relief coursed through me, and I felt warm and powerful. We could work through this.

He shook his head. "It might not ever change."

"What does Dietrich say?"

"That I have intimacy issues." Huh.

"Anything else?"

"Not really."

Lights from the two-story McDonald's lit the sidewalk ahead of us. The traffic on Clark Street jammed up by Portillo's drive-thru. Libido was not a deal breaker. If we stayed together and worked on this—him with Dietrich and me with, well, I had just promised to do it alone— then who knew where we could end up? I wasn't giving up over his big "revelation."

"I should want to tear your clothes off, but I don't." He touched my arm and said he'd never felt like that about anyone, ever. His eyes told the story of his self-torture. I knew that story. My whole life I lived in a story that there was something deeply broken in me. I'd searched for years to find solutions to my own troubles. I'd battled who I was sup- posed to be as a girl, a dancer, a Texan, a student, and a girlfriend, and that battle led me to the toilet for years. Like me, Brandon had always exceled at academics and then rose through the ranks in medicine. But his personal life—how he felt about himself, how he coped with the early loss of his father, and how he interacted with other people, espe- cially women—had been neglected for years. How could I turn my back on Brandon when he was finding his way through the same thicket I was? He requested emotional safety, and I loved him enough to try it his way. At least for a while.

When I showed up for group the next day, I was skittish as a squir- rel. I felt an urge to cross my legs every ten minutes. Fragments of my conversation with Brandon swam in my head, but I said nothing. In ninety minutes, I barely said a word.

Two days later, the same thing happened in Thursday group. Lorne asked what was going on with Dr. Flipper, and Patrice asked if I was okay. When I refused to give any meaningful answers, everyone left me alone until right before group ended, when Max asked if I thought the secret-keeping thing was working. Patrice said she was wondering the same thing.

Dr. Rosen started to say something and then stopped. "What?" I asked. I'd left him a message explaining that I'd agreed to keep a secret for Brandon, but I gave no details.

"Can I say something about the message you left?" Dr. Rosen said.

"Go ahead."

"I won't tell your secret, but—"

"Secret?" Lorne asked.

"Christie," Max said, drawing out both syllables in a low voice. "What are you up to?"

Dr. Rosen assured me that I didn't have to tell Brandon's secret, but he wanted to be sure I understood how secrets work. "When you agree to keep someone's secret, you hold their shame." I already knew this was Dr. Rosen's philosophy. What I didn't understand was why it was such a bad thing to help my boyfriend work through his shame? Would it kill me to hold it for him while we sorted out our relationship? Weren't relationships all about making compromises so you didn't die alone next to a tin full of baby ashes?

The group's appetite for revelation surged. They tried to guess the secret: Embezzling? Bankruptcy? Secret wife? Gambling? Check-kiting? Pedophilic impulses? The very group of strangers Brandon entrusted me to protect his secret from now suspected him of possible money laundering and child molestation. I looked at Dr. Rosen and begged him to make them shut up, but he shook his head and insisted they were helping me carry the shame.

"They're showing you the price you're paying."

I looked at the faces in the circle. The levity from moments before had vanished. How I longed to tell them what Brandon had told me. I could tell his secret, and Max would laugh and say something about the myth of the sexually insatiable male. Lorne would say something snarky about the flipping. Patrice would rub my arm and coo soothingly, and Grandma Maggie would point at her wedding band. Brad would work in a question about Brandon's financial portfolio. I loved my group more than I loved Brandon, but I couldn't take them all home with me at night. They couldn't be my date for the next law school reunion. They couldn't hold my hand at night or start a family with me. They couldn't keep me from dying alone.

Dr. Rosen asked me what I was feeling. My voice broke as I said it.

"Lonely."

35

The Monday before Thanksgiving, I sat through group quietly while everyone discussed the complications of their Thanksgiving plans: Max was in trouble with his wife for not ordering the right kind of bread crumbs for the stuffing. Patrice's daughters were in town, but spending too much time with their father. Grandma Maggie's stepson from Arizona violated her house rules by smoking pot in the basement. Dr. Rosen listened and offered feedback to each of them. Several times he looked at me, but I kept my face impassive.

Max tapped my toe with his brougham. "You're quiet."

I nodded and shrugged.

"So? What're you allowed to tell us? Can you say what your Thanksgiving plans are?"

I swiveled in my chair to check the clock on the wall behind me. Five minutes left. Could I ignore his question for the next three hundred seconds? The truth was, I didn't have plans. And while there were plenty of people—Clare, Rory, Marnie, Patrice, Lorne and Renee—who would gladly take me in, I was ashamed to have to scrounge for a seat at someone's table. I'd told my family I was staying in town with the guy I was dating because I assumed Brandon and I would be together. But Brandon had announced on Friday night that he was leaving the next day for a week-long trip with his family. There'd been no time to process all of my feelings—the shame, loneliness, hurt, and anger. They sat bundled like a homemade explosive under my rib cage.

"Where's Brandon?" Max asked.

I looked at Dr. Rosen, hoping he knew I was about to blow from the shame of facing another holiday with nowhere to go even though I had a boyfriend. It was Italy with Jeremy all over again.

"Go ahead," Dr. Rosen said. He knew.

I shook my head, resisting.

"You want to keep it all to yourself?" Dr. Rosen said as he glanced at the clock. Two hundred seconds left.

"No!" I screamed. NO! NO! NO! NO!

"No, what?" Dr. Rosen kept his eyes on mine.

No to all of this—to gagging myself for a guy who didn't want to spend the holidays with me after months of dating. No to Brandon telling me about his trip forty-eight hours before his flight. No to this loneliness. No to flipping and having no voice and sitting through group, isolated, lonely, and stuffed with secrets. Dr. Rosen was looking at me the same way he looked at me after I got back from the trip to Germany. He was still worried about me, his little failure. He should hate me. I hated myself.

"What do you want?" he asked.

"Stop being nice to me!"

"I won't stop loving you and neither will this group."

I squeezed my eyes shut. I hated all of them for what they had: in-laws they loathed, forgetful spouses, drug-addicted stepkids. Stuffing recipes. Family. Places to be, people to be with. If I opened my eyes, I would see their faces as I admitted I had nowhere to go. I collapsed onto my legs, grabbed my hair with my fists, and pulled. Hard. The sharp, physical pain brought relief. My fists were full of hair I'd pulled out of my head.

I wanted therapy to be linear. I wanted to point to measurable improvements with every year I put in. By this point, after five years and two months, I should be immune from the fury that made me pull hair out of my head with my own fists.

Patrice put her hand on my back. "Please don't hurt yourself. Come to my house."

"I don't want pity! I want my own! I want my own family! I thought you would help me, Dr. Rosen!" The windows vibrated with my screams. I was the sobbing woman with fists full of hair in group therapy again. Would I ever be anything else?

"Can you stay with the hurt?" Dr. Rosen asked.

"No!" There were zero seconds left in the session. My head pounded. "Stay with the hurt."

I stood up and grabbed a ceramic flowerpot from the windowsill. I hoisted it over my head with both hands and brought it down on my head—right where my forehead met my hairline. White-hot silence stunned me before the rush of pain to my head. I let the pot slip through my hands. The dirt, dotted with tiny white balls, rained on the carpet along with a hunk of eucalyptus. Dr. Rosen grabbed my wrists and guided me back to my chair. I didn't struggle. I fingered the welt already forming on my head. The room fell silent, except for my ragged breathing. "Say it, Dr. Rosen: 'We'll stop there for today.' It's over."

It was two minutes after nine. Nobody moved. Without looking up, I asked, "What do I do?" I was asking all of them. We weren't meeting again for a week. A sob lodged in my chest broke through. "I thought I was getting better."

"Don't hurt yourself anymore," Patrice said. "Please."

"Christie—" Max hesitated. "Keeping Brandon's secrets isn't working."

I nodded and opened my palms, hoping that the gesture might save me from myself. Dr. Rosen suggested, as usual, that I be around other people as much as possible over the holiday weekend. Go to meetings. Sleep on Lorne and Renee's couch. Like a preschooler, I should make playdates with people from group or recovery meetings.

At five after nine, Dr. Rosen took a deep breath and clasped his hands together. We all stood up for the regular closing. I held out my right hand, now streaked with my own blood, to Patrice. Dr. Rosen grasped the other. Tears trickled down my cheeks, and my head thrummed with my pulse. After we let go, everyone moved in slow motion. I bent to pick up my bag, keeping my back to the group. I was embarrassed about my tantrum, the bloody wound on my head, my nonlinear movement in therapy.

"Can you all stick around for a few minutes?" Dr. Rosen said. Max, Brad, Patrice, Maggie, and Lorne stood silently in front of their chairs. "I want to get Christie some medicine for that cut." Dr. Rosen pulled a small first-aid kit out of his file cabinet. He squeezed some ointment onto his finger and rubbed it on my forehead. He patted my head tenderly. "You're going to be okay." He repeated it twice. "It's fortunate you have a very hard head."

I slid open the curtains to let the bright December sun fill the room. The Pacific Ocean rolled toward the shore like a frothy tongue. The sand shimmered in the midmorning light, and the Ferris wheel on the dock sparkled against a perfectly cloudless sky.

It was Christmas Day, and Brandon and I were in Santa Monica.

After the flowerpot incident, I summoned the courage to be more direct. As soon as he returned from his Thanksgiving trip, I told Brandon straight up: I'd like us to be together for the next holiday. It wasn't a test or a demand—it was simply what I needed. He suggested we go to LA for a few days. "I know a great hotel on the beach," he said. He never asked about the bruise on my forehead.

Dr. Rosen appeared agnostic about my relationship with Brandon—he never hinted that I should let go of the secrets—but all of my group mates were skeptical. They would speculate among themselves during sessions. About the secret, whether he was still flipping me during sex, how long we would last. *Is she even enjoying this relationship?*

On vacation, Brandon and I were loose and loving. He joked more and hummed while he shaved. We had more sex and sang along to songs on the radio and ate dishes with fresh avocado. We saw *The Pursuit of Happyness*, the movie where Will Smith played a destitute salesman who ends up with an unpaid internship at a prestigious brokerage firm and eventually becomes a wealthy businessman. Brandon held my hand the whole time. The movie proved that seemingly impossible transformations could happen. Under the bright California sky, the ocean as my witness, I let happiness seep in.

≈

"I'm meeting my mom for brunch at the Peninsula on Sunday." Brandon paced around my living room one January night as I scrolled through work e-mails on my BlackBerry. "Do you want to join us?"

My head jerked up. I dropped my BlackBerry on the counter. Brunch. The Peninsula. His mother. "Yes. Yes, I do want to brunch with you and your mother at the Peninsula."

It was the first week of January, and everything in Chicago was still and frozen: ice-laden trees, slick roads clogged with old snow, the frigid metal rail leading to the El train. But underneath my wool sweater, my down coat, and my fleece hat, I was humming with life. I'd never met a Mother at a five-star hotel brunch before. My heart warmed my body. I hinted to my group that things were going well. "Maybe I'm having a fancy brunch on Sunday with a friend and his mother." Subtle.

The morning of breakfast, Materfamilias's driver picked us up in her long black Mercedes. Her fur coat was so thick that it was hard to see her head underneath all the mink. She shook my hand and offered a slight smile. After we ordered, we talked about Barbara Kingsolver novels and ordered the same entrée: egg-white frittata with farm vegetables and goat cheese. She kept the mink draped on her shoulders, but her smile widened, and she laughed at my jokes.

Later, Brandon reported that his mother enjoyed my "lively company." I assumed that the next step would be meeting his younger brother, who lived in London full-time, and then he could meet my parents when they visited in the spring. In every vision of my future, I Photoshopped Brandon into the frame. Just out of the frame, I could feel my group members and Dr. Rosen cheering me on, even though no one could see them but me.

36

Brandon stopped kissing me on the lips. When I asked him about it, he said that my breath turned him off, even after I brushed, flossed, and rinsed with mouthwash. Hurt, I brushed harder, swilled more mouthwash. Still no kisses.

Then he started working longer hours. He booked meetings out of town and declined my offer to drive him to O'Hare. We still had sex about once a week, and my face always met the pillow. One hundred percent flipping. And every single time, my voice failed—it sat quivering and useless on the pillow next to my head. At work, I'd imagine rearing up and saying something—anything—the next time he flipped me. Or bringing it up in the car, over dinner, in a text. I'd promise myself I wouldn't sleep with him if I couldn't discuss how we were having sex. But in his bedroom, on his fancy white sheets, I couldn't utter a single syllable.

In group, I stayed silent too. I wanted so badly to spill my guts and ask for feedback. It had been so long since I'd filled them in that I could no longer imagine what advice they'd give me. Would they tell me to ask for kisses on the mouth? To discuss how the flipping made me feel? To accept him exactly as he was? To let go altogether? It terrified me that my connection to my group members and their voices was dissolving into memory.

Sunday mornings with Brandon still felt normal. We still slept in, read the *New York Times*, and went to the gym. For those few hours, passing the paper or high-fiving after a run on the track, I trusted that the relationship was stronger than whatever was going on with Brandon's work. Real relationships had ups and downs. I'd heard that from everyone. Our hearts might not perfectly match, but surely there were enough grooves to attach.

On a Sunday in early February, we ran into Brandon's college friend Bill in front of the gym. The three of us stood in the parking lot, bouncing to keep warm as fat chunks of snow fell from a cashmere-gray sky. I listened as Brandon and Bill talked about mutual friends, orthopedics, and the Dow Jones.

"How's Marcie doing?" Bill asked Brandon. I'd met Marcie—one of their mutual college friends—in the fall when she was in Chicago to meet buyers of her exclusive line of high-end eyeglass frames. I'd been envious of her long curly hair, her killer leather jacket, and her funky-framed glasses. Next to her New York chic, I felt like a midwestern lump of dough.

"I'll see her in two weeks," Brandon said. News to me.

"In New York?" Bill asked.

"Actually, Cancún."

If my life was a movie, I would have spit out my food or spewed a mouthful of soda all over someone's face. My boyfriend of ten months had just casually announced his upcoming vacation with another woman in another country. I must have misheard. Brandon didn't notice my shock. A few minutes later, Bill touched my shoulder, said good-bye, and walked away. Brandon walked toward the gym. I didn't move. After a few steps, he turned to ask me what was wrong.

"Are you serious?" My voice sounded low and powerful. I spoke from my deepest place.

"About what?"

"You're joking, right?" I turned and walked toward my car. I was done.

By the time I opened the driver's-side door, he'd caught up to me. In the car, I looked straight ahead as I put the key in the ignition and turned on the heat full blast. I cupped my hands over my mouth and breathed warm air into them. A random CD was in the player, and I cranked the volume all the way up. He slid into the passenger's seat and turned down the volume.

"Christie."

I turned the volume back up. He punched the power off and held my hand away.

"Why are you so upset?"

"Please get out." He didn't move. For once I wasn't hysterical, even though I knew by sundown I would be single. "Don't play dumb. It's a bad look. Also, Cancún is where Texas high schoolers go to puke for spring break—"

"She has a meeting and asked me to come—"

"Tell me what's going on or get out of my car." He sighed heavily, which made me want to punch his face. It was all such a burden for poor Brandon.

Then he said things like "You should be with someone who wants to be with you," and "You deserve better."

"If you want to break up, do it like an adult."

"I'm telling you that you deserve someone who wants to be with you."

"You're saying that's not you."

He didn't answer.

⁓

"You don't look so hot," Max said.

I still had on the same clothes from the day before—a sweater, now wrinkled, and shirt, now untucked. "Brandon and I broke up last night."

Gasps. All eyes wide.

"Are you hiding any sharp objects?" Lorne asked.

I held my hands up in the surrender pose. No weapons. I had no urge to hurt myself or smash my stuff. This breakup, unlike the others, carried something novel: a strong whiff of relief. Now I could stop pretending that Brandon was my soul mate and get on with my life. When I told them about Marcie and Cancún, no one seemed shocked.

"Dr. Flipper has major issues," Lorne said.

"Money can't fix crazy," Max said, shooting a look at Brad, who remained steadfastly convinced it could.

Dr. Rosen stared at me long and hard.

"I know what you're going to say," I said to Dr. Rosen. My palms were open, all fight drained out of me. Dr. Rosen opened his palms. A mirror image of mine.

"I'm listening."

"You're going to say that this group loves me. My other group loves me. That you love me. That I'm going to be okay." Of course he would insist that this—sitting in this circle in my rumpled clothes turning my thoughts and feeling over to him and the group—was enough.

"Wait—" Lorne's face lit up like a jack-o'-lantern. "Can you tell us his secret now?"

I looked at Dr. Rosen, whose face was wholly inscrutable. I wanted to tell them everything—to go back to the way it was before I picked Brandon over them, but not like this. Not to satiate Lorne's curiosity, and not while I was still so raw. I shook my head—I'd tell them later. I started to shiver uncontrollably. My teeth chattered like pennies falling on marble. My knees jolted up and down. I hugged my arms into my body and tried to sit still. It was impossible.

"What's going on?" Dr. Rosen asked.

I shook my head. No amount of effort could stop the shaking that was growing more violent.

"Give her a blanket," Patrice said. I glanced in the corner at Dr. Rosen's sad collection of 1970s fringed pillows and a ratty old brown blanket that screamed *smallpox*.

"No thanks," I said through clattering teeth.

Dr. Rosen stood up and moved his chair back. He sat on the floor with his legs hips width apart and opened his arms wide.

"Oh boy," Max murmured under his breath.

"What're you doing?" I asked.

Dr. Rosen smiled broadly. "I have an idea." He opened his arms wider. "My sense is you need to be held. You're on the edge of a new identity and a new way of thinking about yourself." He stretched his arms wider.

"He's offering to hold you," Max said.

"How?"

Max tossed me a pillow. I walked over to where Dr. Rosen was sitting and handed him the pillow, which he positioned like fig leaf. I knelt and then eased myself onto my butt. I stuck my feet out so they were perpendicular to his body. He bent his left knee so it was supporting my back and his right knee formed a bridge over my outstretched legs. I was still shivering, hands and legs jerking.

"Breathe," he said.

I inhaled until it felt like my chest would explode. I slowly let the air out, molecule by molecule. The shivering continued but with less force. A wave of shame about being in this room with another failure on my docket washed over me. I let it. I didn't try to outrun it in my mind or spook myself with thoughts about dying alone. Dr. Rosen held me. I let him.

After a few minutes, I put my head on Dr. Rosen's shoulder. He put his arm on my back and held me closer. I buried my face into his shirt like a child and began to rock back and forth. He patted my back gently. On and on I rocked. I went to some other place—some preverbal time when I was rocked to sleep as a little girl before I had language and knew the words *failure* and *loser*.

The group continued as usual: Lorne told a story about his ex-wife, and Max said something about his daughter's college application. They were all right there, but I was far away—I was a child, a toddler, a baby. When Dr. Rosen spoke, his neck vibrated against my scalp. I kept my eyes closed, but when they flickered open now and then, I saw Dr. Rosen's watch, Max's shoes, the mottled carpet. Twenty minutes went by. Then twenty more.

At some point, Dr. Rosen said, "We'll stop there for today." We were still on the ground, and now group was over. I opened my eyes and sat up. My hip flexors ached, and I wasn't sure I could get to my feet by myself. Max grabbed one hand, Brad the other. I stood up and joined the circle.

37

*To help me move past Brandon, Dr. Rosen gave me two prescrip-*tions: to feel my feelings anywhere, anytime, and to commit no acts that required safety goggles. I agreed and decided I would be single differently this time. I would embrace and explore it. I would let go of the story that being single was a death sentence or a fatal disease. At night, I'd sit on my couch and stare at the Chicago skyline. When my fingers itched to throw something that would shatter, I would call Rory, Lorne, or Patrice. I'd crawl through the loneliness to their familiar voices that promised comfort.

One night, the stillness felt like a curse, and no one was around. I paced from my kitchen to my bedroom, where I stood in the doorway staring at my bed and imagined the ghosts of Jeremy, the Intern, Alex, and Brandon hovering just above my comforter. *Good-bye*, I whispered, and then turned to my laptop, where I scrolled through furniture stores looking for a new bed. I liked the symbolism of a new bed for this new chapter of my life, whatever it held. Even if it only held me.

Click. Click. Click.

Now I was the new owner of a giant sleigh bed, a heavy, curved monstrosity in light oak set to be delivered in two weeks. A warm gust of triumph made me raise my fist. I'd dreamed this bed for my betrothed young cousin the night I cut up Dr. Rosen's teddy bear, but now I'd claimed it for myself.

A week later, I gave myself a challenge to say yes to any social invitation. Period. No qualifications. In some cosmic way, word must have spread about my new resolution because invitations rolled in. Did I want to see a country band I'd never heard of with a friend from work? Did I want to accompany Nan to the store to replace her dildo? How about catching a Preston Sturges black-and-white movie at an old bank that had been turned into a movie theater ten miles west of Chicago? Yes, yes, yes. *I'm in. I'm alive. I exist.*

On Presidents' Day—a below-freezing morning in February—I woke up in a fog of shame and anger. My fists curled and my head throbbed.

This is it. Here's where I skid off the ledge. Brandon and I were supposed to be in New Hampshire for a wedding—had we stayed together we'd be there now. Brandon had probably taken Marcie and they were doing whatever you do in New Hampshire in mid-February: Tapping trees for maple syrup? Ice fishing? Fucking by a fire? Before me stretched an empty day: the office was closed, and I had no plans other than group. Looming holidays had always been my undoing. I could hardly breathe. To beat back the despair, I laced up my running shoes and headed outside.

The sky was still inky gray and the temperature hovered around ten degrees. A coat of ice slicked the sidewalks, so I ran in the street. The air was so cold and thin that breathing took extra effort. By the time I reached the lakefront path, the sun was rising over the half-frozen water. With every step, my breath huffed out in a puff of white air. This run teetered on self-abuse—the world was frozen all around me—but I decided: If I saw another runner in the next two minutes, I would keep going. If not, I would get in a cab and sit in a coffee shop around the corner from Dr. Rosen's office until group started.

A half mile ahead, I spotted a lone runner in a green jacket, and I followed her like the North Star.

Left foot, right foot, breath.

Left foot, right foot, breath.

Follow the green jacket. The green lights. Go, go, go.

When the sun made its full appearance on the horizon, I stopped to stare at the blazing, defiant fist rising out of Lake Michigan. I shook my fist back at it. As I rounded the turn where Wacker meets Lake Shore Drive, I stopped, hands on my knees, and tried to slow my breath. Something was happening. My whole body felt inexplicably warm—from the inside.

Then, staring at that fist of light, I heard a voice. "You are okay." I looked over my shoulder. There was no one. Whose voice was that? Never once in my life did I think such a seditious thought: that I was okay just as I was, even without a plus-one, a lover, a prospect, a beloved, a partner, a family of my own, a gleaming future filled with people who truly knew me.

Frost was forming on my nose, so I had to keep running. My pace doubled. The speed of a quiet surrender. *I'm okay, I'm okay, I'm okay*— with each thump of my pumping heart. It was a revelation. And they kept coming. Brandon didn't own my okay-ness; neither did anyone else. Even Dr. Rosen. He couldn't make me okay. All he could do was show up for the sessions and bear witness to all the shenanigans that composed my personal life, offering to hold me when the pain threatened to break me. I was okay, or okay enough, for the first time in my entire life. Because I said so.

I wasn't going to mention these thoughts in group because I thought they were fleeting. But then it happened in the middle of group. Lorne was reading the latest court order related to his custody fight and that feeling came over me again—the sensation of okay-ness right here, right now.

"Y'all, something's happening to me."

Patrice touched my cheek with the back of her hand. "You're freezing."

"I had a revelation, but it's hard to describe. It was like someone was talking to me, but it was me. I told myself I'm okay. Like right now, this very second, I'm okay." Dr. Rosen's face curved into a bemused smile. "Even if the Big Relationship never shows up, even if I have to adopt a child as a single woman, and even if I fail at every romance from this day forward—I'm okay. I get to live and go to work. And I get to come here."

Dr. Rosen leaned toward me. "We've all loved you like that—just as you are—for a long time."

They had always loved me. So did my Tuesday group. They stuck by me even when I raged, detonated self-pity bombs, keened, snotted, fought, and monopolized the sessions with my tribulations. I wouldn't die alone. These people would surround me. They would help my family plan a proper burial. They would say nice things about me and explain Baby Jeremiah to my confused, grieving mother.

I visualized my heart and saw slashes from each group session I showed up for, from each man I dated, from each squabble with Dr. Rosen or with a group mate. Each "fuck you" to Dr. Rosen was a nick. Each screechy voice mail, each temper tantrum during a session, each dramatic hair pull and broken dish. Nicks, gashes, hash marks, chips, gouges, striations. My heart, a messy, pulpy thing, was scored from each attempt, each near miss, each lunge toward other people, those who loved me back and those who didn't.

In addition to my policy of saying yes, I started expressing exactly what I wanted from other people as a way of making amends to myself for having been voiceless with Brandon. Never again would I abandon myself in a sexual situation. But to keep that vow, I had to start speaking up in nonsexual situations. *I want to hang out this weekend*, I e-mailed my friends, instead of the safer *we should hang out*. When a coworker, Anna, responded with a plan to see a Rusted Root concert at House of Blues, I filled in the blank calendar square. My voice, expanding into the void, began to shape my life.

Then I sent another e-mail. *There's a group of us going to a concert, and I want you to come.* I hit send, and then laughed. Did I really just send an e-mail to John out of the blue? John was the guy from Skadden, the one I'd used to test Brandon. The e-mail was a voice lesson. Right before I'd hit send, I'd smiled at the line: *I want you to come.* I'd never said that to any man before.

I had no hidden marriage agenda, no secret hope that John and I might hit it off. He just popped into my head. After hitting send, I got back to work without compulsively checking my e-mail for a response. Honestly, I didn't care if he joined us or not.

After I'd canceled dinner with John back in the fall, I thought I'd never hear from him again. But six weeks before Brandon and I broke up, John offered me an extra ticket to see Puccini's *Turandot* at the Lyric Opera. When I told Brandon about it, he of course was unperturbed. At that point, I wasn't testing him—we'd already brunched at the Peninsula. But then, three days before I was supposed to go out with John, Brandon called me at work to ask if I had plans for the evening. It was a Wednesday night in the snowy dead zone of early January—my plan was to swaddle myself in flannel and curse Chicago weather patterns. He asked if I wanted to see *Turandot* that night. His parents' season tickets. Fourth row center. In our typical dysfunctional way, neither of us mentioned that I was seeing the same opera on Saturday night with John. I smiled through the conversation because Brandon was showing me that he cared about me. About us. Maybe he felt a little bit threatened by John.

Three nights later, I watched the same opera from the second balcony with John and his two friends. After the opera, John's friend Michael drove us all home, the CD player blaring "Nessun dorma." From the backseat, I listened to Michael and John discuss the best dessert places in Chicago. All night I'd been thinking John was more attractive than I remembered, but then it crossed my mind that he might be gay.

Asking a potentially gay guy to join an outing to a concert: low stakes.

I'd love to see the concert. Let me know what time.

Six hours before the concert, I went to group in a foul mood. Embracing my new life, the way I was doing it, was exhausting and expensive. Concert tickets, a new sleigh bed, sushi dinners for one—none of it was cheap. I was so tired of all of it, I was so frustrated. I yelled at Dr. Rosen. Lots of *fuck you*'s and *this doesn't work* and *why can't you admit you can't help me?* Nothing Dr. Rosen or the group members said got through to me. A single thought pounded through my mind: *I hate how fucked up I am.*

After group, I stormed back to my office, dreading the concert where I'd have to paste on a smile and be social. Six o'clock came and went. I remained at my desk. Then it was almost seven. I was supposed to meet everyone, including John, in twenty minutes. I called Rory from my office and cried as the sun melted behind the Chicago River, leaving my office dark save for the glow of my computer. No one was around other than the cleaning crew. "I'm sick of saying yes."

"Can you go for an hour? Just one." Rory stayed on the phone until I agreed.

Before leaving work, I went into the bathroom to check the damage from an hour of crying. All of my makeup had washed off. I didn't have a brush, lipstick, or anything resembling a beauty product in my possession. I finger-combed my hair into a bun that I hoped looked sexy and devil-may-care, not like proof of my ongoing existential crisis. On the walk to the bar, I found an old Burt's Bees lip gloss in my coat pocket, which felt like the universe throwing me a sparkly mauve bone. There were lingering patches of snow on the ground, but you could smell spring preparing her entrance. The closer I got to the bar where we were meeting, the better I felt. I remembered that I was okay. And I could go home to my sleigh bed after one hour.

Anna and the others were huddled around the corner of the bar. Someone slid an oversize square plate of cheese and dried fruit toward me. I stuffed creamy Roquefort and smoked Gouda into my mouth. John walked in ten minutes later. A flicker of worry: Would I have to babysit him? As he made his way to the bar, I took in his confident stride, his calm smile. He greeted the coworkers he barely knew and side-hugged me. He smelled like fresh air and clean clothes. This guy could take care of himself; I could leave whenever I wanted.

"Sorry, I'm late." He leaned toward me so I could hear over the din at the crowded bar. "I just bought a new bed and had to wait for the delivery." I told him about my new sleigh bed. There was something suggestive about the bed talk and it stirred something in me. Maybe he wasn't gay.

More friends arrived, and our group reshuffled around the bar. I kept ending up next to John.

I watched him. He didn't say much, but his eyes sparked with life as he followed the conversation. When it was time to walk over to the House of Blues for the concert, again, John and I fell into step. His style was simple: blue sweater, jeans, lace-up black dress shoes with a rounded toe. His jacket was warm, but neither trendy nor businessman serious. I didn't sense any dark secret stash of shame in him—no well of loneliness or hint of a dark side that would be tempting and maddening to try to fix.

In my purse, my phone buzzed with a text from Rory checking to see if I'd made it home. From the bathroom, I texted her back: *Still out and almost having fun!*

The House of Blues was jammed with sweaty drunk people in sweaters and boots. John bought me a bottle of water. I found myself actively hoping he wasn't gay. He reminded me of someone, but I couldn't place who. A vague connection tickled at my consciousness. I didn't mean to grill him. It was just a question. A harmless question to a guy I was enjoying talking to.

"Do you have a religion?" I have no idea why I asked that question in those words.

He raised his brows in amusement. "I didn't see that question coming." He took a swig of his water before answering. "I was raised Jewish."

Everything went still and silent: The dance floor. The bar area. The people setting up the stage. In an instant that stretched into the next day, I froze too. This guy, whom I had blown off months before, then wrote off as gay, but now wanted to kiss, reminded me of Dr. Rosen. It was the Jewish thing that pushed me into revelation. Suddenly it was so obvious. They were both introverts with sharp senses of humor and a gentle but solid masculinity they didn't have to flaunt. Simple style that didn't flash their status or the current trends. Both had an air of confidence that, at times, bled into cocksureness. And their directness—they were not men who would ignore an elephant in the room. Good God—standing before me was a young, single, age-appropriate, gainfully employed man who reminded me of my therapist.

The rest of the concert was a blur of sweating, dancing, and losing myself in the music. John stood off to the side taking in the whole scene. At two o'clock in the morning, he walked me home. The city streets, dotted with snow flurries, were empty except for a nocturnal dog walker. I felt something I'd never felt with a man before: calm, quiet, happy, and excited. I wanted to be close to him. I wanted to fall asleep listening to his voice. I wanted to hear what he thought about all the people we knew in common and where he'd traveled. I liked him, and it felt like a secret power collecting under my skin. We laughed again that we'd both bought new beds in the past forty-eight hours. It meant something—the two of us with our new beds. A good omen.

The next day John left a voice mail: "I don't know if you're single, but if you are, then we should hang out."

The excitement I felt about John was a steady pillar of hope, one that could guide me, not distract me and obliterate everything else in my life. It was quieter than the gale-force winds of the Intern and Reed. It was brighter and rose higher than the flat line of my desire for Brandon. But it wasn't overwhelming. I still had an appetite. I slept normally. I wrote briefs at work and went to 12-step meetings.

"He's Jewish, single, handsome, gainfully employed, liberal, kind, and just bought a new bed." I ticked off all John's positive traits to the group. "We're going out tomorrow night."

"And he took you to the opera," Max said. "I'm calling it now: John's the one."

"Don't do that." Too much pressure. "It's just dinner."

I sat back in my chair and matched Dr. Rosen's smile, beam for beam. "He reminds me of you."

Dr. Rosen rubbed his chest.

La Scarola looked like a dive from Grand Street, but inside it was bright, smelled of garlic frying in butter, and bustled with waiters running trays of lasagna and fried calamari through its haphazard aisles. Dozens of people loitered by the front door, but John spoke to the host, who showed us right away to a quiet table in the corner. We split the angel hair pasta with shrimp and the pasta arrabiata. The conversation drifted from the stuff we did in college, how we felt about the partners we worked for, how often we went home to visit our families. My gaze never once drifted beyond the world of our table for the next three hours. I was genuinely surprised when the houselights came on and the music stopped. "I'm sorry," our attentive waiter said, "but we must sleep." I'd just spent almost three and a half hours with John and hadn't called any of my group members from the bathroom. My heart still held the steady joy I first felt when he walked me home the other night.

At the end of the date, John squeezed my hand, which sent a jolt straight through my whole body. Back at home, I didn't send a long e-mail debriefing to my groups or call Rory about my food. I climbed into my sleigh bed and drifted off to sleep with a smile on my face.

The next day at work I focused on the brief I was working on and ended the day with a 12-step meeting. I'd had the best date of my life and was still able to function. Before going to bed, I checked my e-mail and saw one from John.

I think I just went on my last first date.

I read the line again and again and then tiptoed over to my bed, as if a sudden move might make the expansive feeling in my chest disappear. I put my head on my pillow. I'd waited all these years for a chance to build a relationship with someone without drama, doubt, alcoholism, or protective eyewear. Now that opportunity was sitting in my in-box.

I put my hands over my heart—my beautiful, scored heart.

38

I waited for John to get drunk and urinate on me, but he didn't like alcohol. He didn't play video games, have a wife, or follow strict religious rules. When he told stories about growing up in LA, I listened for signs he was enmeshed with his mother or subconsciously enraged with his father, but he didn't appear to be anything other than emotionally steady and hardworking. There seemed to be no extreme elements in his personality. He worked out, but moderately; he had a corporate law job that required long hours, but he worked only as hard as the task required; he watched his finances, but wasn't cheap. I braced to be bored by his stability, for my body to curl into itself like a winter leaf. But being with John was like eating a perfectly seared piece of Arctic char, rosemary roasted potatoes, and grilled asparagus. Filling, tasty, nourishing. My tastes had changed, and John was delicious. He made me feel like I could stretch out like a starfish, bursting with life.

"There has to be a catch," I said to Dr. Rosen and my groups. "How did I go from Brandon to this in just a few weeks?" I thought you had to wait months after a breakup to find a healthy relationship. "Is he my rebound guy?"

"Ask him about his past relationships—whether he had them and how they ended," Dr. Rosen said. "You might see evidence that he's afraid of commitment."

Lorne groaned. "Don't do that. Guys don't want to discuss 'fear of commitment.'"

"Don't worry, I'll be super casual when I bring it up."

That night, John started a fire after dinner while I huddled under a white wool blanket. He settled next to me on the couch and closed his eyes—he'd worked past midnight the night before.

I threw off the blanket and faced him. "Have you had any long-term girlfriends?"

He opened one eye and looked at me. "We're going there right now?"

"I'm wondering if you've ever . . ."

"Been serious with anyone?"

"Right. Like committed, and if so, what happened?"

"Is this a test?"

I nodded. He laughed in his good-natured way and then described his two serious girlfriends. One from right after college, and one from a few years later. He described both women as good people whom he would probably still be friends with if they weren't ex-girlfriends. The first relationship fizzled because she cheated on him, and there was too much drama. In the second, they broke up because they were too much alike.

"It wasn't exciting to be with someone who thought and acted just like I did."

While I might bring him more drama than he had a taste for, we didn't have to worry that we were too much alike. I wasn't moderate about anything, and I spun through more emotions in an hour than he did in a month.

During the second week of dating, John and I were parked in front of my building, kissing—neither of us wanting to say good-bye for the night. I was seized by the impulse to confess.

"I go to twelve-step recovery meetings for an eating disorder. I also go to group therapy three times a week. If you don't like the sound of that, then we should part ways right now. And I don't keep secrets from my group, so don't even ask. They're going to know the size of your penis and whether you flip me during sex." I braced for a tense negotiation.

"The flip thing sounds like a good story." No signs of angst on John's part.

"I'm serious about the group thing."

He shrugged. "Talk about whatever you need to in therapy."

"And I don't suck dirty dick, like ever."

"Duly noted." He smiled like *what else you got?*

I put my hand on his cheek. Where did he come from?

We kissed again, but then John pulled away and looked down at his hands. His expression was serious.

"What is it?" I asked.

"I already knew about your therapy and your twelve-step meetings."

"What? How?"

"I read some of your essays. The ones you saved on the Skadden system."

Oh my God, I'd forgotten about those. Sometimes, while waiting—occasionally for hours—for partners to get back to me with edits on a brief, I'd write essays, scraps of stories. Stuff about growing up in Texas, going to Catholic school, and anecdotes about group therapy. I saved the writing under my name on the firm system with deceiving titles like "Tate Billing Information" or "Tate Litigation File." I thought they were well-hidden Easter eggs.

"You found those?"

He blushed. "I wanted to know more about you."

"By reading 'Tate Billing Info'?"

"It worked."

We went back to kissing. But then I stopped us again. My conscience ached like a sore muscle.

"I saw *Turandot* with my ex three nights before I saw it with you."

Surprise spread across his face. "But you acted like you didn't know anything about it." Before the opera, John invited me over to his house to present a PowerPoint he'd prepared about Puccini's life and the plot of *Turandot*. He'd added a cartoon video of Puccini's car accident right before he completed *Madama Butterfly*. I'd been utterly enchanted by the work he'd put into educating me on the opera so I could enjoy it as much as he did. I wasn't about to raise my hand and tell him I'd just seen it from the fourth row.

"I didn't want to hurt your feelings."

"It takes a lot to rattle me."

"Have I?"

"Almost."

⟶

After three weeks of dating, I got up to leave John's place one night well past midnight. He told me I was welcome to stay, but I wasn't quite ready. It had only been six weeks since I had slept in Brandon's bed.

"We don't have to have sex," he said.

"I'm just not ready."

He walked me out to my car and held me underneath the navy sky.

"I'm not up for having sex with someone who isn't in love with me. I'm not interested in that." My beautiful clear voice.

"I do love you, you know," he whispered in my ear.

"What?"

He looked me in the eye and said it again.

"How do you know?"

"I can feel it."

"We've only been dating three weeks."

"So I've known for three-ish weeks."

We eventually progressed to spending the night at each other's house and stayed up talking and doing "everything but" until morning's first light bled through the curtains. Whenever we got to the part of the night where either we were or weren't going to have sex, I pulled away. "I'm still not ready," I would say, unable to explain why. He was infinitely more suitable for me than any of the men I'd ever slept with or groped in a suburban mall parking lot, but I couldn't move forward sexually.

"Why are you torturing him and yourself?" Max said. "I feel so sorry for him."

"What are you afraid of?" Everyone wanted to know, including me.

Dr. Rosen pointed out this was the healthy relationship I'd been waiting to find myself in. I was using my voice, setting boundaries, and staying in my body when I was with him. He thought I was scared of sex because it would bring me and John even closer. For once, I fully agreed with him, but I still wanted to know: "Why can't I just have sex with him already?"

"*Mamaleh*, you will when you're ready."

And then one spring night, I no longer needed to keep John at a distance. Our bodies fit together. The physical part of our relationship was an extension of all the things we were already doing—talking, eating, laughing, kissing, touching, and sleeping. For the first time, I understood that sex was a big deal for me not because it involved private parts or because the nuns told me it was one of God's major preoccupations or because my mother told me I'd wind up in hell if I did it before marriage. It was a big deal because with sex, I gave John my body in a singular way, and he gave me his. Together, we shared the pleasure of that exchange. And even though he was kind, committed, and loving, it was super hot.

39

When my thirty-fourth birthday rolled around, John and I had been dating for only four months. I hoped for a dinner that required a reservation and some heartfelt words on card stock, signed *Love, John.* Dr. Rosen hinted I might get an engagement ring, but I cut him off. The last thing I needed was the weight of expectations on my four-month-old relationship. The joke was on Dr. Rosen when John gave me a Sonicare electric toothbrush and a homemade wooden picture frame. Lovely, but not gemstones that announced "lifetime commitment."

Several months after my birthday John and I took a two-week trip to India with his high school friends. Nothing like a trip to a third-world country where you can't always control your bowels to solidify a relationship. John held my hand during Diwali fireworks, helped me find tampons in a Goa supermarket, and carried the souvenirs for all my group members in his carry-on, including a brass Hindu symbol that represented luck and fortune, which happened to look like a backward swastika. That was for Dr. Rosen.

In December, John and I spent our first Christmas-Hanukkah in Los Angeles with his family. During his family's epic thirty-person Hanukkah gift exchange, his mother gave me a Victoria's Secret gift certificate, and his grandmother gifted me a white marble box with intricate tile from her long-ago trip to India. John's cousins taught me how to make latkes, and his brother showed me old family pictures of their Russian forebears—stern men with long beards and black hats and women in black dresses with high collars. When John set the camera on the tripod for a group photo, I stood next to him, and he put his arm around me. I folded into the welcoming arms of his family.

We stole away from the official celebration one afternoon for a quiet walk on the beach in Orange County. The brilliant California sunshine on the hot white sand almost hurt my eyes—it was the same ocean that Brandon and I had walked along just a year before, the same water that stole David's life. It was comforting to see it still churning toward the shore. I rolled up my jeans and slipped off my boots so I could feel the sand, warm and gritty between my toes. We stopped at a rocky ledge to watch the ocean. There, underneath a surreal blue sky, I scanned the beach for celebrities and their dogs. John was quiet, until we headed back to the car.

"I want to move forward. With you." He said words I'd never heard a man say to me: *engaged* and *certain* and *together* and *future*. I held my hand over my galloping heart.

ller

On a Monday morning in March, I walked into group a few minutes late and sat in the empty seat to the right of Dr. Rosen. I sat quietly, not overly gesticulating or calling attention to my left hand.

"I'm sorry, I'm almost blinded by the ring on Christie's finger," Dr. Rosen said when he'd waited long enough for me to speak up. Laughing, I jumped out of my chair and spun around the room sticking my hand in everyone's face.

"Not too big, not too small," Max said approvingly.

Patrice held my hand up to the window to see it in the sunlight.

Grandma Maggie beamed. "I knew it, kiddo."

I'd never cared about jewels, but this ring was so much more than its stones. John and I designed it together. There was a larger stone in the middle, flanked by three smaller ones on each side. The big stone represented me and John; the three smaller stones on either side were

Dr. Rosen and my groups. Those three smaller stones were the foundation of my life. They'd introduced me to myself, my appetites, my rage,
my terror, my pleasure, my voice. They made me a real person. There
was no "John and me" without them. Every single day of my marriage
would be a tribute to the work I'd done in group, and I could not separate my romantic relationship from the hours and hours I'd spent in
group, growing up and growing into my life.

"I *cannot* believe that John puts up with you," Lorne said, winking
at me. "Good job finding a man who doesn't have to flip you every
night."

Dr. Rosen had oohed and aahed over my ring and offered a genuine
mazel tov that landed on my heart like a blessing. I could tolerate this
mazel tov in a way I could not take in the mazel tov he offered for my
class rank seven years earlier during my first appointment. Now I knew
that Dr. Rosen loved me and that I deserved his praise and whatever
"mazel" was. But I longed for more. An explicit blessing. Not permission, but consecration. I looked at him and said, "I want something
more from you."

"What did you have in mind?"

"Not exactly sure."

"Talk about it in your groups and see if you can get clarity."

Dr. Rosen answered the door to his tidy white town home in jeans
and brown sandals that exposed his toes. Were you supposed to see
your therapist's bare feet? I thought not, so I directed my attention to
his bright kitchen. But then I felt my head practically crack open with
pain—a ferocious stress headache from having dinner with my fiancé at
my therapist's house. I'd felt vaguely nauseated as John drove us out to
Dr. Rosen's quiet suburban neighborhood, but now all I wanted was a
cold compress and extra-strength Motrin. I squeezed John's hand and
tried to steady my nerves. *It's perfectly natural to have dinner at your
therapist's house.* I handed Dr. Rosen's wife a bouquet of light pink pe-
onies that she smelled and said were her favorite.

"Can I use your bathroom?" I asked, not because I had to go, but because I wasn't ready to make small talk over apps with the man I planned to marry and the man who'd witnessed multiple temper tantrums and pinworm-inspired monologues. I sat on the toilet and massaged my temples, willing the pain around my skull to dissolve. I counted the number of toilet paper squares I used (six) and the pumps of liquid soap (three). The temptation to swing open the medicine cabinet made my fingers itch, but the prospect of confessing my snooping next week in group held me back.

As I cruised through the living room on the way back to the kitchen, I wanted to look at the books on the shelves, the pictures in frames, the tchotchkes on the coffee table, but I was too scared. You're not supposed to surveil your therapist's personal possessions. Plus, what if I saw embarrassing things, like Nicholas Sparks novels or pictures of Dr. Rosen and his wife posed with Goofy on a Disney cruise?

Mercifully, his wife invited us to sit down. She spoke with a thick Russian accent and smiled warmly. Between John's and my plates was a wrapped present. "Open it," Dr. Rosen said, smiling. John pulled off the paper and held up a white tile with colorful painted flowers and script that read *Shalom Y'all*. They'd found it on their recent trip to Israel and loved that it celebrated both of our heritages: Texan and Jewish. I couldn't even summon words—all I could do was stare at the script, absorbing the fact that when Dr. Rosen traveled across the globe, he still continued to hold me in his mind. Me and John.

Dr. Rosen lit two candles and said a prayer in Hebrew. Then, as we'd discussed in group, he put his hands on my head and recited the Hebrew blessing over a child. The press of his hand on my head stopped the pulse from my headache, but when he moved on to John, the pain roared back. As Dr. Rosen said the prayer over John's head, tears sprung to John's eyes, making me tear up as well.

Dr. Rosen's wife apologized that parsnips were not in season. I looked at Dr. Rosen, who smiled at me. A week before, Dr. Rosen had asked me in group what my favorite foods were and I answered by starting to cry. Foods were coming to mind, but the words were stuck as pictures in my head.

I remembered when I first got into recovery for bulimia and latched on to dozens of rules so I wouldn't fall back into bingeing and purging. I didn't eat sugar, flour, wheat, corn, bananas, honey, or potatoes. I didn't eat between meals or after nine at night. I never went back for seconds of anything and never ate standing up. Shortly after I got into recovery, my parents and I drove from Dallas to Baton Rouge for my brother's college graduation, and my dad stopped for lunch at Lea's Lunchroom in Lecompte, Louisiana—my parents' favorite pie shop. The only thing on the menu was honey-cured ham sandwiches and four kinds of pie. I asked the waitress if they could take the shredded iceberg lettuce from the ham sandwiches and make me a salad. Not possible, she said. Starving, I ordered two ham sandwiches, ate the lettuce with salt and pepper, leaving the ham and bread behind. My plate looked like a crime scene. I watched as my parents ate their ham sandwiches and split two pieces of pie, one chocolate and one lemon. I didn't know how to ask them to take me somewhere to get food I could eat. I didn't know how to tell them my belief that adhering to my food rules kept me alive. All I knew how to do was sit in my chair and smile stupidly as my empty stomach growled and begged me to take up a fork and load it with pie.

In group, Dr. Rosen employed eating metaphors with me from day one. But this dinner at his house wasn't a metaphor: it was Dr. Rosen and his wife feeding and blessing me and John. He wanted to feed me exactly what I wanted. My favorites. In group, Rory had told me to close my eyes and shout out my favorite foods. I squeezed my eyes shut and ground my fists into my eye sockets as I whispered, "Parsnips. Mango. Salmon. Potatoes."

Dr. Rosen's wife served a brilliant-orange carrot soup with a dollop of melting cream in the center. I swirled my spoon around, and the cream dissolved. It tasted rich and earthy. Dr. Rosen listed all the ingredients in each dish, even though I had let go of most of my food rules by then. The salmon was perfectly pink, and the potatoes had a touch of rosemary and salt. As they carried empty plates to the kitchen after we ate, Dr. Rosen and his wife spoke softly in another language that sounded half Russian and half Hebrew.

I don't remember uttering a single word the whole night, though I must have spoken. I was all sensation: My throbbing headache. The flavors on my tongue. John's hand on my leg. The feeling of wanting to cry for no reason other than that the night was so lovely, the food so delicious, the occasion so improbable. I remember that it seemed like Dr. Rosen's wife was in charge as she told him where to find the silver spoons for the tea and the knife for the cheese. What a thrill to watch someone boss Dr. Rosen around! I couldn't wait to tell Max.

For dessert, Dr. Rosen placed a wooden cutting board with several hard cheeses, grapes, and dried cherries in the middle of the table. I popped a grape into my mouth. Its slick sweetness beat my headache back by an inch. The last bars of daylight streamed through the window making shadows on the table. Dr. Rosen said sometimes they saw deer in their wooded backyard. My body ached with fullness. I'd taken in so much; I was ready to go home.

On the way back to Chicago from the suburbs, I reclined the seat and cranked up the a/c, aiming the vents at my face. I cried all twenty-one miles back to the city. John held my hand.

"Is this happening?" I cried. John held my hand tighter.

"Where did you come from?" I cried some more.

Mile after mile, I cried. Feeling pouring out of me. "I can't believe any of this is happening. How did I get here?"

John held my hand as the city skyline sparkled beyond the windshield.

"I feel afraid," I said as we pulled up to my place.

"Of what?" John asked.

"You." He raised his eyebrows and smiled. "We're stuck with each other now. I feel a strange loneliness. I'm not sure where I am." John squeezed my hand as if he understood.

I thought once you got engaged, you were filled with certainty and bliss about the person you were marrying and the life you were building. I thought that finding the man I would marry would cure my deep loneliness. But I didn't feel pure bliss. I felt whispers of fear and loneliness. I was still me.

"All these years, I've been the single-est person everywhere I went— group, law school, Texas friends, family. Christie—unattached, single, no-plus-one Christie. I hated that role, but now that it's no longer mine,

I feel like I'm free falling. Like I'm losing something. It feels like I'm not special anymore, now that I'm not crying in all corners of Chicago about my shitty love life and unpopulated weekends. Now I'm just like everybody else. Does that make any sense?" Where did the apples go? The worms? The purple towel that I'd ripped the threads out of? Who was I now and where did the old me go?

John brushed my cheek. "You still cry more than most people. That probably won't ever change."

40

Barack Obama was hours from winning the title of Forty-Fourth President of the United States. All of Chicago went bonkers—jubilant people were streaming from their offices downtown to Grant Park, waiting for Obama to take the podium as the president-elect. Raj popped his head into my office around four and offered me an extra ticket to the rally. I turned him down, even though John and I campaigned for Obama in Wisconsin and were dizzy with joy at his victory. Physically, I didn't feel like myself and hadn't for a few days. That afternoon, I'd had to mute a conference call because I was about to go off on an opposing attorney who insisted our client was liable for fraud. I'd punched my desk so hard that my stapler clattered to the edge. An hour after the call I was so walloped by fatigue that I put my head down on my desk and slept for twenty minutes. I suspected flu and was convinced if I went down to Grant Park in the cold November air, I'd end up hospitalized with mono.

That night, John and I ordered takeout and waited for Obama's speech. The TV cameras panned to the crowd assembled five miles from our house, and I regretted not being there. John saw friends he knew from law school standing five feet from Oprah. "That could be us!" What was wrong with me? It was the most historic night of my lifetime, and I'd opted to sit on the couch, braless, shoveling a Cobb salad in my mouth with my feet propped up on two Crate & Barrel boxes—early wedding presents from John's aunt.

McCain's face filled the screen to concede the election. He was flanked by a perfectly coifed Cindy McCain in a yellow suit and flawless red lipstick. McCain wasn't my candidate, but when he put his hand over his heart and bid his supporters farewell, sobs from way down deep pressed forward, racking my whole body. Into our new red chenille blanket, I cried for poor John McCain as if he were my most beloved friend. I could not stop crying, no matter how much I tried to convince myself that McCain would one day know happiness again.

The next thing I remember is John shaking my shoulder. "You're going to want to see this," he said, turning up the volume. I lifted my head—where the hell was I? "You were crying about McCain, and then you fell asleep." We stared in awe as Obama spoke. Again, tears streamed down my face. This time: pure joy.

The next night, I fell asleep right after dinner again, only to find myself staring at the bedroom ceiling at two in the morning. John stirred and opened his eyes. I told him I had to pee. "While I'm there, I'm taking a pregnancy test." He laughed and wished me luck as if I was joking.

I squatted down and rifled under the sink for the purple box with the generic drugstore pregnancy test. We'd had unprotected sex on the fourteenth day of my cycle, so it was possible. But so many women I knew were struggling to conceive while on Clomid that I didn't think there was any chance I was harboring a fetus. My ob-gyn warned it might take a while because I was over thirty-five. I peed on the stick and then crawled back in bed.

"So there's a bun in the oven?" John asked in a good-natured but mocking tone.

"Probably twins. We'll need a bigger place."

After three minutes, I elbowed him. "Go check." I wasn't getting out of the warm cocoon of sheets and comforter to confirm a negative pregnancy test. I flipped my pillow and laid my cheek on the cool side. I heard John pee, and then: silence. He stepped into the doorway, his head backlit by the bathroom light, his face obscured by the shadow.

"I think there may be two lines."

"Ha-ha." I wasn't even positive my period was late—I'd lost track because October had been busy with out-of-town settlement negotiations on a new case with Jack. I snuggled deeper under the covers and waited for John to join me, but he stood in the doorway, staring at the pee stick. He was serious. I threw off the covers and lunged at the stick.

Two lines, bright as peppermint stripes, showed through the little circle.

I screamed and danced with joy. A baby! A baby! A baby!

Lucky peppermint stripes. Lucky us.

41

You've been to a wedding. You've seen pearl-colored dresses, black ties, bridesmaids in jewel tones. You've heard string quartets and heartfelt vows. You know the drill: a procession with music, readings, vows, and a pronouncement on behalf of the state.

Here's what I want you to see from our wedding:

See me and my six bridesmaids, four of whom were Rosen-patients, running through Chicago's Millennium Park so the photographer could snap pictures of us in front of "The Bean" before the sun faded across the western sky. See us dashing across the lobby of an office building with cool hexagonal mirrors on the ceiling, laughing still, and filling in the bewildered photographer: "We are going to see my therapist!" See me, six weeks pregnant in white strappy heels and a dress tight across the bodice from all the first-trimester carb loading I'd been doing.

See Dr. Rosen in his smart gray suit and shiny black shoes opening the door to a chorus of seven screaming women treating him like a rock star we'd been escorted backstage to meet. See Dr. Rosen smile and usher us back to the room I knew better than any other space on the planet with its fritzy light in the back corner, the coffee stain by the window, the askew mini-blinds. See that he'd arranged the chairs in a circle—just like for a session—except it was a Saturday night, ninety minutes before my wedding. See him take a seat in his usual chair and ask us where we'd been. See him ask me if I was ready. *Yes, I'm ready.* See me close my eyes and take in a deep breath as first-trimester nausea roils through my body. Hear me exclaim with a twinge of panic: *I forgot my crackers!* See Dr. Rosen disappear through the door and return with a red plastic cup full of milk and cereal. Muesli. Hear me say, *Is this what you eat before morning sessions? You seem more like a toast guy.*

See me and John standing together in a side room before the ceremony. See us embrace and hold the moment between us. See how much love my scored heart holds within its swollen boundaries. See me and John walk together down the aisle—there is no giving away, only choosing, accepting, showing up. Hear us promise to build a home and life together with the support of the people who love us. Hear us speak our family into being.

See us vowing before our witnesses. See me resting my palm against my belly, where our baby's heartbeat clocked in at one hundred and seventy-five beats per minute.

You've also been to wedding receptions. You know all about centerpieces, chair covers, and calligraphied place cards. You've tasted appetizers with mushrooms and Brie, dry champagne, and buttercream frosting. You've heard toasts to the new couple and the opening bars of "Brown Eyed Girl."

Here's what I want you to see at our wedding reception:

See table five, where Dr. Rosen and his wife sit flanked by Max, Lorne, Patrice, and their spouses. See table six ringed with the women from my Tuesday-afternoon group. See table seven, where Rory, Marty, and Carlos pass pasta and fish to one another. See each of them embrace me throughout the night, wishing me well, and holding me tight—just as they always have.

From the miracle department, please see Reed and his wife, Miranda, weaving through the crowd toward me after the second course. *Congratulations,* they say. See me hug them both, dumbfounded at what the human heart can do, how it can surprise and delight, how it can rejoin, regenerate, forgive, and connect across oceans of hurt, canyons of loneliness. *Thank you for coming. It means so much to me.*

Most weddings are a blending of families like my Texas Catholic clan and John's Jewish family from the West Coast. Every dance floor at every wedding is a blur of bodies, some that belong to one side and some that belong to the other. As John's family members scooped me into a chair and lifted me above their heads for the hora, I saw our reception from above. My parents and siblings gamely clapping along on one side, absorbing a custom that didn't belong to them. Dr. Rosen and his wife amid a throng of his patients, linked arm in arm as they circled us, singing the words they knew by heart. Jeff's brother, parents, and cousins waving their napkins in the air. As "Hava Nagila" played on, the chaotic, joyous scene below me became a collage of loving faces and arms holding me and John up.

In the weeks leading up to my wedding, I asked Dr. Rosen if we could share a dance during the wedding. I wanted to honor the work I'd done with him in group that made my life with John and our baby possible.

"I don't want to step on your father's toes."

"Don't worry, of course my father will get his own dance. Ours can be later. A traditional, mid-reception, therapist-patient waltz."

"Talk about it in your groups."

The more I discussed it, the more I wanted to dance with Dr. Rosen. I wanted to commemorate that I'd showed up for hundreds of therapy sessions and was no longer the isolated young woman with nothing but billable hours in her future. After all the crying, gnashing, rending, and screaming, it was now time to dance.

I wanted to dance.

Right after John and I got engaged, Clare asked me if I would have eventually ended up with John even if I hadn't gone to group all these years. I said, *I doubt it,* but what I really mean to say was *No fucking way.*

Hear the opening bars of the iconic song from *Fiddler on the Roof*— the one the father sings about the swift passage of time and the blossoming of seedlings to sunflowers. See me leading Dr. Rosen to the dance floor from his seat next to his wife. See him twirl me left and then right, and then no more twirling because of the surging, first-trimester nausea.

See the dance floor ringed with my group mates, past and present, who knew exactly what this meant to me and perhaps to Dr. Rosen. When the music ends, hear him give me one more mazel tov. Hear me say, *Thank you for everything. I'll see you Monday.*

Because this story doesn't end with a wedding.

The next day, John and I hugged our families good-bye and sent them to the airport. Snow flurries swirled all afternoon, and the late-November sun didn't even pretend to shine. At home, John and I sank into bed, surrounded by presents and leftover cake. John's heavy eyes succumbed to sleep, but I couldn't settle. I picked buttercream roses off the cake and popped them into my mouth. I called Rory and then Patrice.

"Now what?" I asked them. "I feel weird, and yes, I know weird's not a feeling." I loved John and was happy to be married, but I also felt lonely and exhausted and anxious. Weird. Kind of like I wanted to bawl into my leftover wedding cake.

They both told me what I knew they would. "Bring it to group."

*

Everyone was in their usual seats. My body still trembled with excess adrenaline from the weekend filled with family, friends, joy, and cake. I was still in shock that I was pregnant and dizzy in love with our little fetus.

Max opened the session by asking why the DJ made such a production out of my dance with Dr. Rosen. Patrice asked if my sister enjoyed the jaunt to Dr. Rosen's office before the ceremony. Brad and Lorne teased Dr. Rosen about the cut of his suit, and Grandma Maggie praised Dr. Rosen's wife's merlot-colored gown.

And then, just like that, we moved on. Lorne reported on the latest with his ex-wife and the kids, and we debated whether Max should follow up on a lead for a new job. Dr. Rosen transferred his gaze from member to member around the circle while the rest of us did our best to offer our whole selves to one another. I felt my heart beating—its scored surface protecting the chambers, the ventricles, the atria, the valves, the aorta. I held my hands close to my chest and listened to the music of my group.

POSTSCRIPT

Ten Years Later

Before I sneak downstairs, I kiss my daughter's head. She stirs and whispers, "Bye, Mama," without opening her eyes. "See you tonight." Her little brother in the room next door continues to sleep deeply even as I tussle his hair and kiss his cheek. They don't expect to see me on Monday mornings. They know I have an early appointment with Dr. Rosen. They're old enough to be curious. "Why do you go there?" "What do you do?" "Do you ever wish you could have Dr. Rosen all to yourself?" I don't know what they picture when I tell them I sit in a circle with Dr. Rosen and my group mates—people they've known all their lives—and we talk and listen, and sometimes cry and yell. And no, I would never trade individual sessions for my group. Sometimes, on Monday nights at dinner, my kids will ask about Patrice or Max. I laugh to think of my children holding the images of my group mates in their heads just like I do.

In the kitchen, I throw my lunch in a bag and then race out the door to catch the six fifty-five train. As the train lumbers downtown, I think about what issues I'll discuss in group. I should probably tell them about the spat John and I have had the past two times he'd returned home from a business trip. As he wheels his suitcase into the foyer, the kids besiege him with hugs and requests to show him their art projects, their spelling tests, their new dance moves. He slips out of his coat and gives them his full attention. Oohing and aahing. Beaming the full bright light of his love on them. From the kitchen, where I'm washing dinner dishes or prepping lunches for the next day, I love hearing them reconnect. I know those hearts; they belong to me and to each other. The fight comes later, after John has read to them and checked their math homework, and they are fast asleep. It happens when we collapse into bed, and I launch into a story about a grievance at work or a perceived slight from a friend. John strains to keep his eyes open, but he's been up since five, attended various meetings, traveled across the country, and then parented through the bedtime gauntlet. His drawn face tells the story of the miles he's traveled. Intellectually, I understand how weary his bones must feel, how sleep drags him by the ankles into sweet respite. But I also want him to listen to me. I want him to save some of his bright-light energy for me. Dr. Rosen will ask me how this makes me feel, and I'll say, "Lonely for John and ashamed that I'm jealous of my kids." Max will smirk and say, "This is the life you wanted, remember?" Then the group will offer suggestions on how John and I can reconnect when he comes home without ignoring his physical limitations or the kids' needs. Someone will probably suggest that John and I schedule a sex date for the day after he returns.

I can also let the group know about the conversation I had with my supervisor at work on Friday. I surprised myself by saying, "I work really hard and do a good job. I don't need more money or a corner office, but I would like a thank-you." I'd filed a record number of briefs in the past thirty days and wanted acknowledgment. Brad will give me a thumbs-up, and then push me to ask for that corner office. And the raise. Patrice will high-five me for asking for what I want. At work, I struggle to set boundaries and say no when asked to take on thankless tasks with no discernible upside, but at least I spoke up to ask for acknowledgment.

The group will also get a kick out of the meltdown that happened at my house over the weekend. My kids had a piano recital, an activity they ranked behind teeth cleaning and flu shots. When it was time to head to the recital hall, the kids protested by putting on raggedy shorts and pajama tops. John and I explained that the event called for slightly more formal clothing, emphasizing that we should respect the other students, the teacher, and all the work they'd done to prepare. "Think of dozens of times you practiced 'When the Saints Go Marching In.'" They reacted by stomping and slamming doors. They refused to walk down the street next to us. I was sure I'd get a handwritten letter, like the one I got when I wouldn't let them buy Skittles in bulk: *Dear Mom, Thank you for ruining our lives*, but there was no time to take pen to paper. I'll report to group that I managed to celebrate my kids' intense emotions, instead of insisting they stuff them back into their little bodies. I'd actually channeled Dr. Rosen for a good twenty minutes before I lost my composure and hissed at them to get it together through gritted teeth. We arrived at the recital late, each of us fuming.

It still scares me, other people's anger, but I know it's part of intimacy. I know it's okay to let it be. I breathe through it the best I can.

All my basest impulses still live inside me, lying in wait. Impulses to keep my ever-wacky relationship to food a secret. Impulses to demonize John for making the reasonable decision to put his energy into parenting after a few days away. Impulses to dive into unremitting despair instead of taking a breath and feeling whatever emotion is trying to surface. Impulses to suck up frustration and invisibility at work instead of having a measured conversation about what I'm thinking and feeling, what I want and need. Impulses to do anything to keep other people from feeling angry at me. I still need help overriding those impulses. I need help figuring out what two-syllable word best describes my feelings. Telling the truth of my desire, even when I'm ashamed of it. Tolerating other people's intense feelings. Tolerating my own.

Sometimes I run into former Rosen-patients. "You're *still* with Dr. R?" they ask. "Yep, I'm one of the lifers," I say with an impulse to explain that it's not that I'm hopelessly fucked up or stuck in crisis mode. I have the attachments I craved when I first crawled into Dr. Rosen's office; now I need help deepening them. And I've dreamed new dreams. A more creative life. An intimate relationship with my two children as they pass through middle school, high school, and beyond. A graceful path through the impending corporeal chaos of menopause and the stress of caring for aging parents who live three states away. Dr. R and the group guided me through my early adulthood issues. Why not the middle-aged stuff? Don't I still deserve support, witnesses, and a place to bring my confusion and inner turmoil, even if I no longer pull out my own hair or drive around hoping for a bullet to the brain? And what about my love and attachment to Dr. R and my group mates? Why would I cut that off just because our pull-yourself-up-by-your-bootstraps culture says therapy should get you up and out in thirty sessions or less? Dr. R offers us tenure if we want it. I do.

When the train pulls into the station, I walk two blocks west to Dr. Rosen's office. Up ahead, I see the new guy who joined our group a year ago. He's in his midthirties, a brilliant physician who speaks six languages, and is sick and tired of being alone. He has no close friends in Chicago to hang out with on the weekends, and his specialty is falling for women who ghost him after the second date. In group, he despairs that nothing will change his lifelong patterns. He fears he will never have a family of his own, that it's too late for him. I borrow the moves of my group mates, who consoled me for so many years. I pat his arm when he shares the pain about yet another woman who won't return his texts. I say soothing things when he reports doing something he didn't want to do to win the affection of a woman who isn't available. *I've been there. I did that too. Have you heard about the dirty dick I sucked?* I answer his calls on Sunday afternoons or Tuesday nights when he buckles under the weight of his loneliness. I tell him I have no doubt he is in the process of transforming his life. In group, when Dr. Rosen assures him that coming to group and sharing himself is enough, he looks at me, and I nod my head.

"I promise. It's enough."

ACKNOWLEDGMENTS

When I was writing this book (and the four others that live in my computer), I thought of "the publishing industry" as a group of terribly fancy New Yorkers with Anna Wintour bangs and clothes from Barneys or boutiques I'd never heard of and could not pronounce. I never pictured the faces or bodies or hearts of the people I hoped would one day open the gates for me. Now I will never picture publishing without thinking of the hearts and minds that have touched this book and changed my life forever. Their minds are sharp, their hearts generous. And they poured them both into this book during a harrowing, uncertain time for the entire planet. They also have names. Thank you to Lauren Wein for the thoughtful editing and all the ways you saved me from some very poor choices, particularly in the sex scenes. Thank you to Amy Guay, Meredith Vilarello, Jordan Rodman, Felice Javit, Morgan Hoit, and Marty Karlow for bringing your hard work and expertise to the book.

Thank you to Amy Williams, who always makes me laugh while also wearing so many hats: agent, big sister, mother, friend, fellow traveler. I'm so blessed to have you on my team.

This book would not exist without the oceans of love and support from Lidia Yuknavitch and her Corporeal Writing program. The writers whose understanding of story and body changed the course of this book and my life include these midwives: Mary Mandeville, Tanya Friedman, Lois Melina Ruskai, Anne Gudger, Jane Gregorie, Anne Falkowski, Emily Falkowski, Kristin Costello, Helena Rho, and Amanda Niehaus. Special heart shout-out to Zinn Adeline, who gently contributed her careful reads and incisive comments, especially the one about how my jokes were distracting from the real story.

Thank you to Tin House for pairing me with the generous and talented Jeannie Vanasco in Winter 2019. And special thanks to my workshop mates: Wayne Scott, Sasha Watson, Melissa Duclos, and Kristine Langley Mahler.

To my favorite soul sister who inspires me every single day as a writer, mother, daughter, wife, podcast creator, lawyer, and all-around baller: Carinn Jade.

Way back in the day, I started writing online with a group of madcapped writers who taught me about voice, hooks, arcs, and aspects of the craft that I felt in my bones but had been too scared to practice. Thanks to the Yeah Write crew: Erica Hoskins Mullinex, William Dameron, Mary Laura Philpot, and Flood. Thanks to my early writing groups who had to slog through some pretty tortured drafts: Sara Lind, Samantha Hoffman, and Mary Nelligan.

Gratitude is not a debt, but I can't help but feel like I owe so much to the writers and friends who read drafts of this book, some of them more than once: Krista Booth, Amy Liszt, Andrew Neltner. You're saints, you really are. Joyce Polance read multiple drafts and was always game for a conversation about the pain and ecstasy of trying to get a story right. This book wouldn't exist without her generosity, support, and wisdom. Frank Polance is pretty swell too.

I'm grateful to all the babysitters we had through the years whose labor made it possible for me to write this book. Thank you to Sabrina, Tiffani, Christian, Brittney, Molly, Hailey, Mattie, Kathi, Dayane, and Gesa.

Thank you to Irvin Yalom, whose life work make it possible for a woman like me to get help in group therapy and then tell the world about it.

Special thanks to Marcia Nickow, Psy.D., who read an early draft and urged me to keep going. Sara Connell's commitment to and belief in the power of writing brought immense pleasure and joy to the final stages of this project. Eternal gratitude to Dr. Dana Edelson for taking time off from saving people's lives to help me proofread this book.

I'm pretty sure my therapist knows I'm grateful, but I'll say it again: I gave you enough money over the years to buy a deluxe yacht, but you gave me an entire life, so I guess we're even.

My group mates have put up with so much shit from me all these years. I love them with my whole heart. Special shout outs to my favorites: R.S., T.L., C.C., D.E., J.T., S.M., K.S., M.N., J.S., K.B.B., J.P., C.G., A.R., B.A., S.M., S.N., and S.K. And to M.C., who is no longer with us but whose loving wisdom continues to guide and comfort me.

I'm grateful to every person who shares their recovery stories both inside and outside meetings. They mean everything to me. I'm forever grateful to Dax Shepard for his commitment to honesty and truth-telling about addiction and alcoholism several times a week on his podcast *Armchair Expert*.

When my parents heard about this book, they said the words that every writer hopes their parents will say: "It's your story. You have the right to tell it however you want." I'm grateful for their years of support and all the gifts they've given to me.

To Doug and Alex Tate for their support and enthusiasm, which I hope never to take for granted. I'm glad you are my family.

Thank you to Leslie Darling, Michael Lach, Keme and Jamail Carter, Thea Goodman, Marc Dubin, Caroline Chambers, Betty Seid, Maria Tamari, Davey Baby, Carol Ellis, Karen Yates, Steve and Celia Ellis, and The Writing by Writers Program.

My kids are going to be mortified if they ever read this book. No one wants to read about their mother's sex life. The good news is that I've given them ample material for their own therapy sessions. I thank them for making me a mother. To be present and to love and be loved by them are the reasons why I stay in recovery and continue in therapy.

Lastly, to my main man who has more patience and know-how than anyone I know. Thank you for loving me and for championing my story-telling and my voice. I feel so lucky every single day. Everyone who goes into therapy in hopes of finding a relationship is dreaming of someone as bighearted and steady as you are. Thank you for being part of the ending of this book and the center of my happiest days.

ABOUT THE AUTHOR

Christie Tate is a Chicago-based writer and essayist. She has been published in the *New York Times* (Modern Love), the *Rumpus*, the *Washington Post*, the *Chicago Tribune, McSweeney's Internet Tendency, Eastern Iowa Review*, and elsewhere. Kiese Laymon selected her essay "Promised Lands" as the winner of the *New Ohio Review*'s nonfiction contest, which was published in fall 2019.

When I Was a Young Man

BOB KERREY

When I Was a
Young Man

A MEMOIR

B KERREY

A James H. Silberman Book
HARCOURT, INC.
New York   *San Diego*   *London*

Requests for permission to make copies of any part of the work
should be mailed to the following address: Permissions Department,
Harcourt, Inc., 6277 Sea Harbor Drive, Orlando, Florida 32887-6777.

www.HarcourtBooks.com

"And the Band Played Waltzing Matilda." Words and music by Eric Bogle.
Copyright © 1976 by PLD Music Ltd. All rights reserved in the USA and
Canada. Administered by Music Sales Corporation (ASCAP). International
copyright secured. All rights reserved. Reprinted by permission.

"These Boots Are Made for Walkin'" written by Lee Hazlewood. Copyright ©
1965–66 Criterion Music Corporation. © renewed and assigned 1993
Criterion Music Corporation. All rights reserved. Used by permission.
International copyright secured.

Library of Congress Cataloging-in-Publication Data
Kerrey, Robert, 1943–
When I was a young man: a memoir/by Bob Kerrey.—1st ed.
p.   cm.
ISBN 0-15-100474-9
1. Kerrey, Robert, 1943—Childhood and youth.   2. Kerrey, Robert, 1943—
Family.   3. Vietnamese Conflict, 1961–1975—Personal narratives, American.
4. Soldiers—United States—Biography.   5. Lincoln (Neb.)—Biography.
I. Title.
E840.8.K43 A3 2002
959.704'3'092—dc21   2002000764

Text set in Electra
Designed by Linda Lockowitz

Printed in the United States of America

First edition
K J I H G F E D C B A

AND THE BAND PLAYED WALTZING MATILDA

When I was a young man I carried my pack
and lived the free life of the rover
from the murray's green basin to the dusty outback
I waltzed my Matilda all over;

Then in 1915 my country said: son,
it's time to stop rambling there's work to be done
and they gave me a tin hat and they gave me a gun
and they sent me away to the war;

And the band played Waltzing Matilda
As our ship pulled away from the quay
Amidst all the cheers, flag waving and tears
We sailed off to Gallipoli.

How well I remember that terrible day
the blood stained the sands and the water
and how in that hell that they called Suvla Bay
we were butchered like lambs to the slaughter;

Johnny Turk he was ready he'd primed himself well
he rained us with bullets and chased us with shells
and if ten minutes death he'd kicked us all to hell
nearly chased us clear back to Australia;

And the band played Waltzing Matilda
As we stopped to bury our slain
The Turks buried theirs and we buried ours
And we started all over again.

Then a big Turkish shell knocked me ass over head
And when I awoke in my hospital bed
I saw what it had done and wished I were dead
Never knew there were worse things than dying;

They collected the crippled, the wounded, the lame
And they shipped us all back to Australia
The legless, the armless, the blind, the insane
The poor wounded heroes of Suvla;

And as our ship pulled into Salika quay
I look down at where my legs used to be
And thanked Christ there was no one there waiting
    for me
To mourn and to grieve and to pity;

And the band played Waltzing Matilda
As they carried us down the gang way
But no body cheered, they just stood and stared
And turned all their faces away.

And now every April I sit on my porch
And watch the parade pass before me
I watch my old comrades how proud they do look
The tired old heroes of Suvla;

The old men march proudly all bent stiff and sore
The tired old men from a forgotten war
The young children ask what are they marching for
And I ask myself the same question.

Waltzing Matilda, Waltzing Matilda
Who'll come a waltzing Matilda with me
And their ghosts can be heard as they pass by the
    Billy bong
Who'll come a waltzing Matilda with me?

To Ben, Lindsey, and Henry

PREFACE

THIS IS NOT THE STORY I intended to tell. I wanted this book to be about my father and his brother. That is how it began. After my father's dying request to find out what happened to his only brother, John, during a tour of duty to the Philippines with the United States Army Signal Corps in 1941, I began to examine their past. Their lives began on the other side of the Bolshevik revolution and the First World War, two events that altered their fate and mine.

The story has become more about me than I expected. In part, my plan changed because I never found out enough about John to write the whole story. In part, because I still cannot judge my parents and their generation in an objective way. Mostly, though, the story changed because this is the one I wanted to tell my own children. I wanted to tell it because of the powerful needs that oppose remembering the bad along with the good when we Americans rev up our patriotic engines. The forces of modernity encourage forgetfulness. Terrible stories do not inspire sacrifice the way the noble ones do.

At the 1992 Democratic National Convention in New York City one of our party's leaders — planting a rhetorical flag in the decision by President Harry Truman to confront and contain the expansionist desires of the Soviet Union — repeated a statement I had heard many times since the Soviet Union collapsed in 1991: "We won the Cold War without firing a shot." The audience cheered. Although I knew the speaker meant to say that the United States and the Soviet Union avoided the Third World War that so many had predicted was just around the corner during my lifetime, his words still caused me to wince in pain. We had fired real shots during Korea and Vietnam, and more in Central America, South America, and Africa fighting Cold War battles using proxy soldiers.

As will become clear to anyone who reads this book, I am not a historian. I am a man who has discovered that none of us can isolate ourselves completely from the force of decisions made by men in power. And by living, I am a man who has acquired sympathy — that magic ingredient that turns the bland stew of facts and dates into the rich and flavorful soup of history.

In the first half of my life, history was one of two things: sterile and meaningless information to be memorized for school tests or myths told to generate good feelings and memories. The patriotic and heroic stories I heard in my youth caused me to believe that my nation was never wrong and that my leaders would never lie to me. When the sand of this foundation blew away, I lost my patriotism. In the second half of my life, I rebuilt this foundation on something sturdier: the observation that Americans at their best can be unimaginably generous and willing to put their lives on the line for the freedom and well-being of others.

The story that follows fulfills the promise I made to my father as he lay dying. And it fulfills a promise I made to myself not to forget that wars are not what our slogans, propaganda, and childhood fantasies have taught us to believe.

When I Was a Young Man

1

ONE SATURDAY AFTERNOON in the spring of 1954 when I was ten years old, I discovered my father had a brother. My parents, brothers, and sisters were out. I was home alone, a rare and exciting moment, made more exciting by my mission to find a storage room where my mother kept items too important to throw away. My goal was to find a wooden chest that a year earlier I had helped carry into the basement.

I had followed the box's movements from smaller house to larger house during the eight years our family grew from the four small children who arrived in Lincoln, Nebraska, in 1946 following my father's discharge from the U.S. Army, to the seven children who lived there now.

My father's entire name — James Henry Kerrey — was stenciled in black on the top of the faded olive green box. It had leather handles on either end, a brass-hinged clasp that held the lid closed, and, fortunately for me, it was not padlocked.

Our new house was built on three levels. Upstairs were my parents' master bedroom and two other bedrooms for my sisters. In the basement were four smaller bedrooms, a large bathroom, and a recreation room for my brothers and me. In between was the entry level with spaces used by us all: dining room, music room, living room, laundry room, and an office.

Under the stairs going to my sisters' and parents' rooms was a crawl space where the green wooden chest was stored. That day I carried a chair down to the basement and placed it below the wooden doors that hid my treasure. As I opened the doors, my heart beat fast from the fear I might be caught and the excitement of discovering the secrets inside the box. I pulled a string that switched on a single incandescent bulb and climbed into the closet, moving things around so I could reach what I presumed was a war chest full of bloody memorabilia.

As I opened the lid the smell of camphor filled my lungs. On top were brown wool army jackets, trousers, and shirts. I pushed the uniforms aside, hoping to find souvenirs from some great battle. There was nothing of the sort. No pistols or muddied boots or a jacket with a bullet hole surrounded by the bloodstain of a fallen comrade. No battered helmet marked by too many days on the head of a weary soldier.

Underneath the uniforms I found a bayonet, but the blade looked as new and unused as any hardware knife in my father's store. I found hats, which were too large for my head, and four envelopes of pictures marked Iowa, Florida, Chicago, and Japan. I went straight for the one that said Japan. Inside were three-by-three-inch black-and-white images like the ones we took on our summer vacations. Men in uniforms stood in front of a metal building with a rounded roof. I recognized my father's smiling face, looking young and happy. I saw odd-shaped houses and strange, misshapen plants, and in one, a twisted, melted glass bottle. But nothing in the box lived up to the delights I had imagined.

Just as I was beginning to lose interest, I opened a large folder that held an eight-by-ten-inch black-and-white photograph of the head and shoulders of a man in a white uniform. He looked just like my older brother John, tan and handsome, with dark thinning hair combed straight back. The resemblance was so strong that I decided to take the picture with me when I left the basement.

After dinner that night I waited for my father to go into his office, where he and my mother shared a desk and a set of filing cabinets. The room was always cluttered with broken chairs, torn clothing, and discarded toys. My father often made phone calls from this room after supper. My mother used it late at night when we had gone to bed to pay bills or make entries in a black book that held the income and expenses of their lumber, coal, and hardware business.

I stood in the doorway until he finished making a call. Then he turned and asked in a kind voice what I wanted. With the photograph in my outstretched hand, I said, "I found a picture of a man this afternoon. It looks like John." My father looked at the man's face and his expression grew sad and worried. "It isn't *your* brother John. This is *my* brother John. He was killed in the war." Before I could ask any questions, he said, "Where did you get it?"

When I answered truthfully his face reflected something I had never seen — a mixture of anger and pain. In that instant I thought he might either cry or shout at me. He chose anger. He rose and walked quickly past me and out the door, yelling, "You kids leave my things alone. Leave them alone." And he was gone. I stood as if I had been turned to salt like Lot's wife. I could not move; I could only stand there and cry. My mother came into the office and asked me what had happened. When I told her, she said gently, "Your father had an older brother named John. He was killed ten years ago. Your father doesn't like to talk about it. Please leave his things alone." Which is exactly what I did.

2

LEAVING HIS THINGS ALONE was easy. Leaving his life alone proved impossible for me, even though my father was one of those men who spent little time discussing his past and even less contemplating past events. He could not have cared less about his mysterious genealogy and would turn away questions about his mother or father or grandmothers or grandfathers with a simple "I don't know." His children were left to guess or to ask someone else in the family who might have answers.

Knowing the answers matters. Understanding the lives of our parents helps us understand who we are. Names, dates, and places accumulate slowly and acquire focus. Suddenly we know what it might have been like to have been them. And with that knowledge we are more likely to know ourselves.

Though our memories are different, my father's life and mine were a lot more closely connected than I had assumed was the case. Nebraska-born anthropologist and naturalist Loren Eiseley told of a way to get at these early memories. His friend, the poet W. H. Auden, once asked him a simple question: "What was your first memory of a public event?" Auden believed you could learn a lot about a person by his answer. My first memory of a public event was the 1949 World Series when Casey Stengel's New York Yankees defeated the Brooklyn Dodgers. And I remember China becoming Red China that same fall.

If my father's first memories occurred at the same age as mine, they would probably have been of Jack Dempsey's surprise defeat of Jess Willard for the heavyweight boxing championship on July 4, 1919, and of Cincinnati beating the Chicago White Sox in the World Series. And he must have remembered American troops returning from World War I.

My father's cousin told me of her uncle's homecoming in 1919: "I was standing in the kitchen with my mother and I heard her let out a scream. 'He's home,' she said. 'He's walking up the road.' I went to the porch and saw this strange man in a brown army uniform looking very dirty and very hot. It was my mother's brother but he wasn't the same. He would not sleep in the house. My mom made a bed of straw for him in the barn. He wouldn't remove his leggings or help with the farm. In the fall he moved to Ann Arbor, where he worked for a casket maker and lived alone the rest of his life."

In my life the important public events in 1949 centered on the early days of the Cold War. In my father's life the important event in 1919 was the negotiations taking place in Versailles, France. Versailles made both of our lives radically different. The First World War, which began unnecessarily, ended prematurely in November 1918 without a decisive military victory. Instead of destroying the German military and providing the stability needed for the creation of a new order, the great powers were exhausted by the unprecedented destruction inflicted by new weapons against old strategies and driven by the desire for vengeance. The result was isolationism and reparations, a deadly and tragic combination especially since the world was rapidly moving away from the old order of monarchies and colonial power to a new order of nationalism and self-determination.

The Versailles peace agreement and the passionate desire to return to normalcy led America and the other great powers to set the stage for a second world war worse than the first. Rather than preparing for a new age of prosperity and peace, they enabled the rise to power of two of the world's most evil leaders: Adolf Hitler and Joseph Stalin. They also set the stage for the bloody wars of liberation from colonial rule, including the war in Vietnam.

The point of all this is clearer to me today than it was

in 1954 when I learned my father had an older brother. That was the year after Joseph Stalin died and the Korean conflict ended. It was the first year in six that my New York Yankees did not win the World Series. It was the year my youngest sister was born. She was the last of seven and part of the great postwar baby boom.

And 1954 was the second year of President's Eisenhower's first term. Dwight David Eisenhower was the first politician I heard my parents praise, and they even wore I LIKE IKE buttons. Perhaps they liked him because he was from Abilene, Kansas, and his wife, Mamie, from Boone, Iowa. Perhaps it was his good-natured strength of character and modest resolve, or perhaps it was because he had been born in 1890 and was a father figure to them both.

In 1954 the United States was fully engaged in the Cold War struggle against communism, a struggle that brought us both glory and shame. Remembering 1954 is to remember the shame. On December 2, the U.S. Senate voted 67–22 to censure forty-six-year-old Senator Joe McCarthy for contempt and abuse and ended the worst excesses of the anti-Communist movement that distorted our political debate, denigrated artistic expression, and debased our foreign policy. Fear of being accused of Communist sympathies made self-criticism rare and fear of being called an extremist made sustained opposition to the tyranny of Communism more difficult.

In 1954 consumers saw a transformation of the meaning of home. No technology changed the way we lived more than television. When I began school in 1948 few Americans had televisions. But in a single generation nearly all of America's over one hundred million households would spend more and more of their leisure time being amused, entertained, and sometimes informed by the new medium. Advertisers were given a powerfully different way to persuade us that we needed a second car, a larger house, more furniture and clothing, and every labor-saving household appliance we could afford. In 1954 materialism was king.

So was organized religion. American families were joining neighborhood churches or synagogues, listening to and making celebrities of Billy Graham, Bishop Sheen, and Norman Vincent Peale.

In 1954 science promised to revolutionize our lives, and for the first time, American children were being injected with the new Salk vaccine to kill the deadly poliomyelitis virus and end one of the great scares of my childhood. Ours would be the next-to-last generation to be vaccinated against smallpox. Even the test of a hydrogen bomb at Bikini Atoll that was hundreds of times more powerful than the atom bomb thrilled more than frightened us. The launch of Admiral Hyman Rickover's nuclear-powered submarine, the *Nautilus,* showed us how nuclear power would improve our lives.

If materialism governed our homes and the churches our spirit, engineers ruled over the difficulties and inconveniences of Mother Nature. There was nothing they could not do. You say a river is flooding your home or business? No problem, we'll design and build a dam that will generate electricity to boot. You say the slow pace of the two-lane highway cramps the style of your high-compression engine? No problem, we'll build a network of high-speed, high-volume highways from one end of America to the other.

But not everything was calm and peaceful in 1954. Out beyond the shores of my life, tidal waves were forming. On July 21 France accepted defeat in Indochina and signed a peace agreement in Geneva with Vietnamese guerrilla leaders that partitioned the country in two. The United States, which for four years had provided nearly eighty percent of the military support to the French, did not sign the agreement, nor did the government of South Vietnam.

A second tidal wave formed on May 17 when the U.S. Supreme Court ruled 9–0 against the school district of Topeka, Kansas, and overturned the fifty-eight-year-old "separate but equal" doctrine that allowed Topeka and every other school district in America to maintain schools that segregated black and white children. No longer would that division be allowed. "With all deliberate speed" the highest court of the land ordered us to change. The change would be traumatic, deadly, and good.

In 1954 neither the negotiations in Geneva nor *Brown v. Board of Education* had any impact on me. Had they, I would not have considered them as important as say the merger of Hudson Motor Car and Nash-Kelvinator, which meant the death of one of my favorite cars, the Hudson Hornet.

Much of this history I began to understand during a search I set out on thirty-four years after my father told me to leave his things alone. I was a candidate for the U.S. Senate and my father was dying of cancer. He told me his brother John had disappeared during the Second World War. He was officially recorded as dead, but his body had never been recovered. My father told me he was unsure of the circumstances and asked me to find out what had happened. I promised him I would try.

As I searched, I discovered many things I should have known before and many I wish I had known. I've learned that the most daunting of the barriers between us and the truth is this: the hard work of learning something new can bring about the need for personal change, compelling us to think differently, to believe differently, and to behave differently.

My effort to remember has taken me beyond learning about the circumstances of my uncle's death. I've also learned about his birth and life and explored the circumstances of my own. To understand those circumstances, I first need to tell a few stories my father never did.

3

MY GREAT-GRANDFATHER Thomas Kerry was born in 1830 in the village of Trieshon in Caythorpe Parish in Lincolnshire, England, a few miles south of London. His father was the town miller and his mother an ordained Methodist minister. Frances Reynolds was born in 1832 in the village of Stoke On Trent, Lincolnshire. Thomas and Frances were engaged in 1851, the year Thomas, two of his brothers, and a sister came to America. Frances sailed alone more than a year later. She and Thomas were married in Boston in 1853.

From there they went to Galena, Illinois, where a girl and two boys, Harry and my grandfather John, were born. It was here my great-grandfather added the extra "e" to our name. When the Civil War began in the spring of

1861, Ulysses S. Grant was working in his father's leather store in Galena. Grant, a West Point graduate and veteran of the Mexican War, was made a general by the governor. Thomas Kerrey volunteered and served under Grant for one year. After his discharge, Thomas and his family moved to Manistee, Michigan, a primitive new lumber mill town. Thomas found a lucrative position in a big mill. Frances raised the children and was active in church and the social life of the town. In 1863 Thomas answered the call of his adoptive country a second time. He raised a company of volunteer soldiers, was made their captain, left his family, and went to war. When he returned, he moved his family to an uncleared homestead in the Michigan woods south of Manistee and built a large timber house. Frances knew nothing about farm life. There were no neighbors other than wild animals, including an abundance of bears and wolves. Harry and John helped with the clearing and planting, and in a few years a splendid farm developed. Frances helped establish a school and throughout the rest of her life she cared for the sick, helped conduct funerals and weddings, and kept the school going. She had three more boys and a girl. Of their seven children only Harry did not manage to complete his education. In addition to farming, Thomas operated a lumber mill in the nearby village of Thompsonville until a spinning saw blade threw a board into his right shin, shattering the bone. His attempt at setting the bone himself failed and he never regained his health.

My grandfather John moved to Chattanooga, Ten-
nessee, where he opened a furniture store. He married
Annis Potts, a forty-one-year-old childless widow who bore
a son, John Marley, on September 24, 1911. Annis, a dia-
betic, was warned by her doctor not to have a second
child, but on November 23, 1913, she delivered my father
at home. They named the boy James and prayed for
Annis's recovery. But she bled uncontrollably, grew
weaker and weaker, and never left her bed. She held on
for more than two months, but according to the notes
of the attending physician, on a cold February night in
1914, my grandmother's lungs filled with fluid and she
suffocated. The diagnosis was toxemia of pregnancy, a
common and often deadly condition that claimed many
women before the discovery of antibiotics.

My grandfather was crushed by her death and particularly by her dying wish to be buried with her first husband
in Mississippi. He did not believe he could raise the boys
alone. Nor did he believe his marriage prospects were fa-
vorable. He refused the offer Annis's family made to take
the boys and would not even consider an orphanage. His
only hope was his sister, Frances.

Frances Potter was born on September 16, 1860, three
days after the birth of General John J. Pershing. She
was teased about being his secret sister, after Pershing became famous. She married Erastus Valentine Potter when
she was nineteen. She raised five children: Jessie, Percy,
Raymond, Sena, and Eva. Her husband Erastus died of

tuberculosis while staking a claim on farmland in Idaho on November 11, 1913, two weeks before my father was born.

Frances Sarah Potter, or Fannie as she was called, moved back to Michigan following the death of her husband. She was living with three grown daughters and her mother when John told her of his wife's death and asked if he could bring the boys north so she could help care for them. Fannie had just raised all her children and was reluctant, but in the end she agreed. So my grandfather sold his furniture store, packed the boys onto the train, and headed north. A year later he caught a chill and died, Fannie believed, of a broken heart.

In 1914 Fannie was fifty-four, a short white-haired woman with pink cheeks, blue eyes, an avid interest in books, and a determination to raise the boys right. She kept her waist-long hair tucked away in a sensible bun. She had an active mind and a strong belief in hard work. She had collected a small library and expected the children to read along with her. She kept up on the news and politics of the day, had strong opinions, and was an avowed Republican who loved Teddy Roosevelt and disliked Woodrow Wilson. She lived her beliefs and did not waste things, especially her feelings. To her, even birthday celebrations were excessive extravagances. Fannie was the person people in the family went to talk to when they had trouble.

My father loved Fannie and called her Mother. But he felt he was an outsider who never quite belonged in somebody else's family. Fannie had strict rules, such as when they should eat and when they had to study. She also had a sense of humor and loved to tease. Will Rogers was one of her favorite people. She had asthma, which became worse after she and the boys moved to Chicago in 1916, where her daughter, Jessie, taught school and could help Fannie support her nephews.

Chicago was a difficult place then. The streets were violent and Fannie worried over the safety of John and Jim. One of her daughters remembered that Fannie kept the boys in the apartment as long as she could, but when the heat and their energy conspired to overwhelm her, she would descend the stairs slowly, wheezing all the way. Outside she would let John run around freely. She tied Jim to a tree with a piece of cord that limited how far he could go. Then she sat on the porch and watched them both.

The four of them lived in a one-bedroom, third-floor apartment near the University of Chicago. The boys slept on a small porch. They went to Ray Elementary School just six blocks from their apartment, and Jackson High School, a bus ride away. John rebelled and regularly got into more trouble than his shyer younger brother, who lacked John's self-confidence and bravado. They were very close, and John acted as Jim's protector and guardian.

I try to imagine what life would have been like for these two boys in Chicago and how those early memories affected them as adults. It was a time of great change. Mass production of the automobile and the spread of the radio altered people's attitude toward the world around them. In *One of Ours*, Willa Cather's Pulitzer Prize–winning novel, a Nebraska farm boy leaves home for the war in France in 1917. The book tells how the land was farmed fence row to fence row in order to produce food for Europe and how farmers finally decided the time had come to replace their horses with tractors. Millions of horses were slaughtered during the Great War and replaced with hundreds of thousands of more efficient tractors. As a consequence, agriculture and the lives of farmers were radically altered. I once heard Warren Buffett say that if horses could vote, this never would have happened.

Change altered communications. Before the First World War, communication meant the telegraph. Radio was not yet broadcasting the events of the day, but by 1920 people in Chicago heard on their radios the news that Ohio's Senator Warren G. Harding had been elected president of the United States.

As an adolescent John became more difficult for Fannie and Jessie to handle. There were plenty of opportunities for him to get into trouble. Nightclubs and speakeasies were popping up everywhere, and sex magazines and explicit motion pictures were easily available. The temptations were endless. John was adventurous and independent. He stayed out late and too often ended the night with a fight. Fannie began to talk about his need for a man's discipline.

My father was better behaved. I once asked him what

was his happiest day as a boy, and he said it was the day he bought a new pair of boots with money he'd saved delivering the *Chicago Tribune*. Another of his prized possessions came from delivering papers. On his bike route he got to know a local merchant, an elderly Chinese grocer. They became such good friends that on John's tenth birthday the old man gave him a dictionary, which my father carried with him to college.

Both John and Jim liked going to the beach on weekends and to museums, particularly the Museum of Science and Industry. Both witnessed gunfights and beatings, and one crime in particular was seared into my father's memory. Richard Loeb, an eighteen-year-old University of Michigan graduate, and Nathan Leopold, a twenty-one-year-old University of Chicago law student, were sons of wealthy and respected Chicago Jewish families. In the summer of 1924 they committed what they called "the perfect crime": the kidnapping for ransom of a fourteen-year-old boy named Bobbie Franks. All three lived in the Hyde Park neighborhood near Jackson Park, where my father and his brother played. My father remembered every grisly detail of this case: how strongly anti-Semitic feelings ran in the community, and how his older brother had earned a sharp rebuke from Fannie when he repeated a slur he heard at school.

The murder was planned with brilliance, but the perfect crime failed because Leopold dropped his glasses beside the body. Less than a week after the murder, the two were arrested and confessed. Clarence Darrow led the defense and succeeded in getting life sentences instead of the death penalty demanded by the public. My father told me what Darrow said when he almost refused the case: "I was sixty-eight and tired of standing on the thin and lonely line that separates the good from the most destructive force in America: public opinion."

My father had fond memories of the summer pilgrimages north where cooler temperatures eased Fannie's asthma. Fannie's son, Percy, drove them all up in his car to a cabin on an island in Solon Springs, Wisconsin. Percy had a piano hauled up for his wife who played and sang for them all. Many nights Jim and John sat on the dock listening to the adults make music in the cabin while the loons made music on the lake.

They learned to swim, fished together on the dock, and explored along the railway tracks. Each morning they rowed a small boat a half mile to the mainland to collect the mail. Sometimes John impressed his little brother by swimming over and back as Jim rowed beside him.

In Chicago on the afternoon of September 11, 1926, my father suffered one of the worst events of his life. That afternoon John did not show up in front of the building for the walk home, as was their custom. Jim had to navigate the tough neighborhoods on his own and was greatly relieved when he finally reached the safety of the apartment. He ran up the stairs and flew into the room asking Fannie if John was home yet.

"No, he isn't home," she said. "I have sent your brother away for school. I think it's best."

Fannie believed that John was unmanageable because there was no man in the house. On the advice of a friend, she decided to send him to Wentworth Military Academy. Fannie had pulled John out of school and sent him by train to Missouri. It was the saddest day of Jim's childhood. John had always been there, and now he was gone.

John only stayed a year at the military academy. He returned to Chicago in the fall for his sophomore year at Parker High but he was still too much for Fannie. She persuaded her sister, May, who had married Will Mitchell, a prosperous grain merchant, in Duluth, Minnesota, to take him into their home. They lived in a luxuriously paneled house on a large lot in the best part of town. The Mitchells were well enough off to have servants wait on them at supper, an experience John never imagined.

The good times were about to end. The grain business was in trouble and would soon collapse. To make bad matters worse, Will Mitchell was diagnosed with incurable cancer the summer after John arrived and died shortly thereafter. Within months May had lost everything: her husband, her wealth, and her home. She moved her children into a small apartment down by the harbor and was fortunate to find work pumping gas and managing a service station.

John stayed in Duluth, moving into the home of one of his classmates. I imagine him standing on the shore of

Lake Superior early in the evening of June 5, 1930, the day before he would graduate from high school, watching the sun drop below the dark pines on the hills behind the city. Harbor business would normally be booming in the port of Duluth. But he was an experienced enough observer to see that the Depression had already slowed the loading and unloading of grain and iron ore barges that was going on below.

He thought about his prospects for the future. His year at the military academy had been wasted, but he had done well since coming to Duluth. His high school grades were good, especially in mathematics and science. He liked poetry and had written a few stanzas. He hadn't made a lot of friends, but was well enough liked and respected despite his temper.

He wanted to go to college, but having failed to earn a scholarship, he took the civil service examination and scored the highest in his group. But government jobs were just as scarce as jobs in the private sector. He worked through the summer in a Duluth dance club, but when it closed in the fall he was unemployed again. He knew he would be a financial burden on the Mitchells if he remained in Duluth.

In November 1930 John hit the road, looking for work. Like many others, he became a hobo, riding the rails and hanging out in the hobo camps. Or at least that is what the family guessed happened to him. Except for an occasional letter, they didn't hear from him for two and a half years.

When John set out on his own Jim was beginning his junior year at Parker High School. He was doing well and knew from his brother's experience that his only hope for college was to earn a scholarship. He succeeded. In the spring of 1932 he was offered full tuition, room, and board at both Loyola University of Chicago and Iowa State in Ames. He chose Iowa State because Fannie's son, Percy, lived just down the road in Des Moines.

John returned to Duluth in May 1933 because Mrs. Mitchell somehow persuaded the local Civilian Conservation Corps (CCC) to recommend him for a job. He joined thousands of others who exchanged their labor in Michigan's forests for a job, room, board, self-respect, and thirty dollars a month if they promised to send twenty-four dollars home. To get into this program—which Roosevelt signed into law twenty-seven days after his March 4 inauguration—you had to be male, a U.S. citizen, unemployed, between the ages of seventeen and twenty-three, free of venereal disease, and have "three serviceable teeth, top and bottom."

John's CCC work lasted a year. Afterward he moved to Evanston, Illinois, where Fannie's youngest daughter, Sena, and her husband, Cliff, lived. John and Cliff set up a home-based business manufacturing quality hairbrushes. Sold all over the country, the brushes in the end proved too expensive for Depression-era tastes and the business folded.

In 1936, John joined the army, which had a program that paid part of a man's tuition if he committed to active duty after four years of college. John enrolled at the University of Minnesota to study civil engineering. He worked in the cloakroom of the student union and at other odd jobs that came his way.

In 1936 Jim began his studies at Iowa State. In the spring he met a girl in church named Elinor Gonder, who was born and raised near Boone, Iowa, on a farm owned by her parents, Emmett and Josephine. The seminal event of Elinor's childhood occurred when she was twelve years old, and the principal came into her classroom and asked to speak to her. She was an exceptional student and could not imagine this interruption meant anything but bad news. At the railroad crossing in town, her father, who was nearly deaf, failed to hear the oncoming train as his car crossed the tracks. He was hit from the left, crushing his chest. He was still alive when the principal told Elinor the news, but before she arrived home he died.

Her mother could not run the farm alone so she moved her four girls and two boys to Des Moines, found a job working for a credit union, and married a man twenty years her senior. These changes did not slow Elinor down. She graduated at the top of her high school class and won a scholarship to Iowa State. She majored in home economics, but poetry and theater attracted her most. She read all the current books. Pearl Buck's *The Good Earth* made Elinor long to travel, and she dreamed of being alone in a foreign land.

She was a woman with considerable self-confidence. At five feet five inches tall and 135 pounds she had the build of a farm girl. Her large thighs and hips were life-long targets of her self-deprecating humor. Her teeth were crooked and she was nearsighted, which caused her to squint at the world. Her thick auburn hair had a natural curl, and her eyes were a radiant blue.

My father was over six feet tall and handsome with sandy brown hair combed straight back on his high forehead. A dashing photograph from his college days shows him in a sweater and white shoes leaning casually against the fender of a Ford. Another photograph taken about the same time also reveals how thin he was; he could not have weighed much more than 130 pounds. When my father saw my mother it was love at first sight. He knew this was the woman for him, but she was engaged to a boy from high school. When that boy died a year later, my father seized the opportunity and never let go.

They were not a perfect match. He had Fannie's emotional reserve; she was outgoing and expressive. A year after they met, she invited her family to the college to meet her new boyfriend. She and my father stood together on a hill facing the road on which her family would arrive. When the black Ford pulled up, my mother ran down the hill happy and excited. "We hugged, squealed, and jumped up and down with delight," she later said, "but when I turned around to look for your father, he had gone. My emotional outburst frightened him off. I never made that mistake again."

My mother finished college a year ahead of my father and found a position teaching home economics, drama, and English in a high school in Prescott, Iowa. Though she liked the job, it was a long way from Jim. She had more time for books and read Pearl Buck's latest, *A House Divided*, and James Farrell's *Judgment Day*, which she liked because it took place in Chicago.

My father was distracted by her absence and his grades suffered, but he managed to graduate in the spring of 1937. His first job was keeping track of time cards at Swift's packinghouse in Chicago. My mother joined him in Chicago, beginning a course in institutional management at the Wabash YMCA. By the fall she had decided the restaurant world was not for her and went back to teaching high school in Indianapolis.

They were married in Indianapolis in October 1938. John was sorry that he couldn't make it because of his studies and his job. All the carefully made wedding plans were upset when my dad and his relatives stopped to pick flowers on the drive down and arrived in Indianapolis after the clerk's office closed. My mother had to track the clerk down in a café to get the certificate. There were one hundred guests, mostly schoolteachers. They held their wedding supper in a restaurant and spent their honeymoon in a hotel on Saturday night. They both had to be back at their jobs on Monday.

In the spring they moved to Waterloo, Iowa, where they set up housekeeping in a two-room, second-story apartment, and my father tried without success to sell insurance. They were strapped financially but they were happy. Their first baby—a boy named Jim after my father—was born that summer. It was a difficult birth and my mother feared her son had been damaged by the doctor's clumsy use of the forceps. In her journal, my mother said she loved having children but not as much as my father did. She was willing to stop working when the babies started coming, but she never extinguished the fire that burned to do more.

4

JOHN FELL IN LOVE at college, too. Her name was Evangeline Mella, and when he first saw her she was sitting with her friends in the student union. John was clearing tables when he heard her laugh and turned to follow the ring of her voice. She had dark wavy hair and brown eyes. She looked like the actress Claudette Colbert, and when he saw her, his heart rose to his throat. He stood there in his white work pants and shirt and looked directly at her. She stopped talking and returned the look. Their eyes met with the intimacy of two people who had known each other a long time.

Days later he saw her again on campus and introduced himself. Her friends called her Vangie, she told him. She was younger than John, and the eldest daughter of five children. Her father was a doctor, an army career officer who had fought in the Great War. Her great-grandfather had helped runaway slaves through the Underground Railroad, and Dr. Mella had named her Evangeline after the character in *Uncle Tom's Cabin*. She had chosen the University of Minnesota because her father was the administrator of St. Paul's Veterans Hospital. Vangie stayed when he was promoted to a position in Washington, D.C.

Constantly together, she and John became an item. He was the love of her life, and she was the balm that calmed his anger. At Vangie's graduation in June 1939, she and John talked about marriage and a family. Under the terms of John's contract with the army, he had to go on active duty before he could finish the fifth year of his engineering degree. Beginning in June 1940, John would have to serve two years, then he could come back to college. They decided to postpone marriage until he had met his two-year obligation. Vangie enrolled in graduate school at the university in order to be with him during his fourth year at Minnesota and while he was in training in the army.

They had to know how precarious their situation was. One year had passed since the Munich conference where Britain, France, and Italy gave Germany license to occupy part of democratic Czechoslovakia. On September 1, 1939, Germany invaded Poland. Appeasement had dissolved into war. In November Finland fell and in April

1940 Germany attacked Denmark and Norway, and then swept across the Netherlands and broke through weak French defenses. By June, when John was leaving the university, German troops were in Paris and three hundred thousand British, French, and Belgian soldiers were being evacuated from Dunkirk.

John was put on orders to the Philippines. Just before he left, he and Vangie drove to Waterloo, Iowa, to visit my mother and father. They arrived ten days after my parents had their second baby, a son they named after John. By then my father had also enlisted in the army and had orders to report to Jefferson Barracks, Missouri, in November. It was the last time my father would see his brother alive.

From Waterloo John drove Vangie across the country to her parents' home in Washington, D.C., stayed a week, and embarked by train for San Francisco, where he would board a ship bound for Manila. After John's train pulled out, Vangie was the last to leave the empty, silent platform. Standing under a single incandescent bulb shining down from an iron pole painted emerald green, she could still hear the last of the laughter and the rustling of clothes as men and women embraced and said their tearful goodbyes. For the first time that day she noticed the cold and was glad she had worn her gray woolen coat and crescent-shaped hat. She pulled mittens from her pocket and slid them slowly over each hand, then her father took her arm and walked her back to his car.

Assigned to General Douglas MacArthur's headquarters in Manila, John found a casual attitude toward the defense of the islands. The Americans and their Filipino allies should have been better prepared for war. In July 1941 President Roosevelt had stiffened American opposition to Japan's aggression in China and Indochina by freezing all Japanese assets in the United States. At a September conference in Tokyo, the United States refused to lift the embargo, setting the stage for war.

On December 7 Japanese aircraft attacked the American naval base at Pearl Harbor and destroyed much of the American fleet. John and other officers on MacArthur's staff struggled to assess the meaning of the attack. They knew it meant war for them. Their world had changed and all their personal plans were put on hold. The battle was drawing nearer to Manila.

The next afternoon Japanese fighter bombers attacked undefended American aircraft on the ground at Clark Field, the U.S. command post in the Philippines. MacArthur's air commander had sought permission to fly his planes so they would be less vulnerable, but the general had refused. Two days later the Japanese landed troops on northern Luzon. On December 22, one hundred thousand Japanese went ashore at Lingayen Gulf. On Christmas Eve the American forces and their Filipino allies began to evacuate Manila for the Bataan Peninsula across the bay to the west. The Japanese occupied Manila on January 2.

General MacArthur had not prepared for a prolonged defense of Bataan. His troops did not have enough food, ammunition, or medical supplies to hold out for long. John and the other surviving defenders lasted four months against superior forces. But on April 9, John and his fellow soldiers surrendered to General Yamashita.

The next day the exhausted, dehydrated, and dysentery-ridden prisoners were forced to march up the peninsula. They did not know their destination or fate. The April heat and humidity were stifling. Drinking water was in short supply and food rations almost nonexistent. The Japanese soldiers were young and poorly trained. They had orders to kill all stragglers, which they did with exuberance and cruelty. Thousands of Americans and Filipinos lost their lives on the march.

After Bataan fell there was one last stronghold held by U.S. and Filipino forces: Corregidor, an island fortress that guarded Manila Bay off the southwestern tip of Bataan. General Jonathan Wainwright surrendered this garrison along with ten thousand American troops on May 6.

Vangie was still at the University of Minnesota when the Japanese invaded the Philippines. She followed the events in the news but heard nothing from John after December. When Bataan fell she still held out hope, but after Corregidor she feared the worst.

In June 1942 Vangie joined the Women's Auxiliary Army Corps. She wrote the War Department asking for information about John and received a curt reply: "The records show that Lieutenant Kerrey is on duty in the Philippine Islands." The War Department had been receiving reports of serious illnesses or casualties, the letter went on, and it "may be of some comfort to know that Lieutenant Kerrey has not been so reported."

She could only guess that John was among American prisoners on the Bataan death march. Vangie heard reports that the men who survived the march and ended up in Japanese captivity were victims of savage brutality. She also knew that some Americans were packed into "hell ships" bound for Japan, where they were sent by train to Manchuria to work in factories that produced war materiels.

In June John was officially classified as missing in action. His name did not appear on the list of prisoners. Vangie believed he had escaped and was alive. "If anybody could survive on his own," she told her sister Georgia, "it was John."

My mother and father were in St. Louis at Jefferson Barracks when the Japanese attacked Pearl Harbor and the Philippines. They learned what they could by reading every news account of Japanese advances and American retreats. When word reached them of the surrender of the Philippines, their best hope was that John had been taken prisoner.

In July my father, a captain in the Army Air Corps, got orders transferring him to Miami Beach. According to my mom's journal, Miami Beach became their long-delayed

honeymoon. Since landlords had lost the tourist trade because of blackouts and gas rationing, my parents could
rent a beautiful furnished house on a bay with two tiled
baths, four bedrooms, and a walled-in backyard, "all on an
Army lieutenant's pay." In her words, "they soaked in the
ocean, lay on lovely beaches, spent long, lazy days in the
sun, and continued to worry about John."

By June of 1943, Miami had started to get expensive,
and my father requested a transfer. He was ordered to an
air base in Lincoln, Nebraska. He went on ahead and in
July, my mother, eight months pregnant with her third
child, made the trip to Lincoln with her two boys. They
found a furnished second-floor apartment in the small
town of Bethany. Their third son was born on August 27 at
Bryan Memorial Hospital. Because the hospital was over-
crowded, the baby was delivered in the former home of
the hospital's namesake: William Jennings Bryan. I am
that third son.

During their time in Lincoln my parents joined
Bethany Christian Church where they were made to feel
welcome. A year later, when my father was ordered to the
University of Chicago to learn the Japanese language for
the expected invasion, he asked one of his new friends to
keep an eye out for a business opportunity. My mother
and father both wanted to come back to Lincoln after
the war.

The second battle of the Philippines began on October 20, 1944, when U.S. forces landed on the northwest

coast of the Bataan Peninsula. On January 9, 1945, the United States attacked Luzon by air and sixty-eight thousand Americans landed on Lingayen beaches. MacArthur returned to Manila on February 4. By then the war in Europe was in its final stages. The Germans counterattacked in the Ardennes forest of Belgium on December 16, 1944. President Roosevelt died on April 12, 1945, at sixty-three years of age. U.S. and Russian troops linked up on the Elbe River in Central Europe on April 25, and Hitler committed suicide on April 30. Victory in Europe was declared on May 8, 1945.

My father celebrated VE Day along with hundreds of thousands of others in Chicago that May 8. But he had mixed emotions, because his war was not over. He had no word of his brother except that John was not on any of the lists of released prisoners. And the country was preparing for the necessary invasion of Japan because the Japanese Army would not surrender unless they were ordered to by Japan's Emperor Hirohito.

My father, who expected to be part of the invasion of Japan, hoped the intensified air campaign led by General Curtis LeMay's B-29s would cause the Japanese emperor to surrender. Between March and June, five of Japan's largest industrial cities and later other smaller cities were targets of incendiary raids. The deadliness of these attacks can be seen in one statistic: in the March 9–10 bombing of Tokyo an estimated one hundred thousand people died.

But it would be a bomb of even more destructive power that ended the war. After a July 16 test near Alamogordo, New Mexico, the United States detonated atomic bombs over Hiroshima on August 6 and Nagasaki on August 9. On the tenth of August the Japanese emperor finally surrendered and Japan sued for peace. V-J Day was celebrated on August 14. Two weeks later U.S. forces landed in Japan and began an occupation with General MacArthur as supreme commander. My father went to Japan as part of an occupation rather than an invasion force.

He arrived in Yokohama on December 1, 1945, and he was assigned to General MacArthur's headquarters, where he tried without success to find out more details of John's disappearance. In February 1946 my father drove his jeep to Hiroshima. He stood at the center of the blast and looked at the circle of destruction around him. He walked half a mile before he could identify objects for what they were. He took a photograph of a glass bottle melted by the heat. A mile away he saw the charred frames of houses, their walls and roofs burned away. People continued to live on the fringes of this gray and flattened mass of rubble. They had begun to rebuild. As he returned to his jeep my father's jaw was set so hard that his chin jutted forward. He held his emotions in check until he saw the children, hundreds of children. These are the orphans, he was told, and my father wept with grief. He could not bear the thought of war destroying so many innocent families.

Soon afterward the army sent him confirmation of his brother's death in the Philippines. According to the regulations of the War Department, he was now a sole surviving brother and could request a transfer home. With demobilization already under way, he chose to leave the service for many reasons, among them his first daughter who had been born April 1, 1945. While my dad waited for the paperwork to go through, my mother's younger brother drove her and the kids to Nebraska and helped her find a place to live. The friend in Lincoln who had promised to watch for a business opportunity had kept his word. He paid one thousand dollars for a lumber and coal business that would be my father's for the asking.

5

LINCOLN WAS STILL A young city when our family arrived for good in 1946. In 1851—the year my dad's grandfather came to the United States—only thirty hardy souls lived in this treeless prairie. They called it Lancaster and they dreamed of making a fortune selling salt they had discovered nearby. But politics not salt made the founders wealthy when their town was chosen both for the state capitol, the state university, and the state penitentiary.

In 1946 when our family settled in Lincoln, parts of the city still had the look of a frontier town. My mother took a photograph of our family on a Sunday after church in early spring 1947 that reveals much about the place. My father stands behind his three boys. In front of us is a dirt street called Fairfax; behind us is our home. My mother's shadow falls across our images. Eight-year-old Jim, Jr., is already tall enough to reach a few inches below my father's left shoulder. Five-year-old John's confident head is chin high to his taller brother. I am three years old and my head doesn't yet reach John's shoulder. The left quarter of my face is hidden behind John's right arm, and I'm dressed in wool shorts and a matching jacket. Our baby sister, Jessie, is missing.

My brothers and father wear stylish fedoras; I am wearing a soft felt cap that is too small for my head. John's eyes are uncovered because his hat is back on his head. The sun is in my eyes because my tiny cap brim does not shade me. My brothers are dressed in identical suits with dark, military-style, four-button jackets and matching pants. They wear white shirts without ties and their collars are turned outside the jackets. My father wears a three-piece suit with a tie. His mouth is open and he appears to be talking to my mother. There is a small but noteworthy distance between my father and his children. His arms are at his sides. Jim, Jr., his hands in his pockets, is looking down and seems to be lost in thought. John stands as if defending us, his hands at his sides and a wide smile on his square face. I am watching my mother. My face appears to be asking, "Why are you doing this to me?"

Only a few trees are visible and they have a barren, scrubby look. Our white frame duplex is about twenty-five feet deep and forty feet long. Its pitched roof cuts the square footage of the second floor in half. Our front porch is five steps up from the concrete sidewalk, which is three steps up from the road. No car is in sight, and I would guess my father parked ours in back to avoid the muddy ruts. My parents' dream of a good place to live had come true. The postwar consumer and baby booms were just beginning. Their prospects had never been brighter.

Our neighborhood was in the northeast quarter of the city. We lived in a village called Bethany that had a block-long business district within walking distance. It contained everything we needed: a doctor's office, a drugstore, a grocery store with a butcher, a lumberyard, a barbershop, and a library. Between our house and the business district was Bethany Grade School. To the north of the shops stood the building that was the center of my parents' lives: Bethany Christian Church.

Every Sunday morning the whole family went to church for an hour of Bible study and another hour of worship. Our congregation practiced full-immersion baptism and shared the belief that Christ was God's son. We learned that human beings are sinners at birth. We believed that Christ's mission was to teach us the way to eternal salvation and that His love was the most powerful force for good. We were taught that Jesus Christ, the son of the living God, died for our sins and that forgiveness was ours only if we declared our belief in Christ. Our family was not enthusiastically religious, but we attended our church regularly and were deeply committed to its community.

The first time I entered the sanctuary of our church I was three years old, and what I remember most is fear. It was large and dark and forbidding. Our family always came in at the back and was met by members of the governing board. After greeting us, one of them would usher us down a side aisle. The sound of our heels hitting the red tiled floor echoed with the organ music. Two sections of dark-stained oak benches were separated by a center aisle reserved for the processional entrance of the minister and the choir, which heralded the beginning of services. Overhead the roof arched into a ceiling high enough to match my imagined estimate of God's actual, invisible size. On each of the sidewalls were six tall, clear, leaded glass windows, which were closed in winter and open in the summer. At the back above the balcony where we sat if we arrived late was a circular stained glass window eight feet in diameter depicting the Virgin Mary, the baby Jesus, and a cluster of attending angels.

Most fearsome to me was the altar in front where the organist played, the minister delivered his sermons from a raised podium, and churchgoers were baptized. An enormous wooden cross hung immediately above the baptismal font. Long after I no longer believed in Santa Claus and the Easter Bunny I still believed this was the cross actually used to crucify Christ.

I held tight to my mother's hand as we were guided to our seats and sat as close to her as possible until the choir entered. With the music came a warm feeling of safety.

My father refused to sit in either the first or the last three or four rows. He preferred a pew a half-dozen rows from the rear. He sat next to my mother, holding her hand or putting his arm around her if she was not cradling a new baby. As we kids grew up our status changed. When we were babies our mother carried us into services. Soon after we could walk we began our Christian instruction in the church basement. When we were deemed ready for baptism, a date would be set for the ceremony.

On my appointed day I got to church a half hour early and entered through the side door next to the minister's office. He gave me a white cotton robe and told me to undress and put it on. Alone in the small bathroom I took off my Sunday clothes and put the robe on over my underpants. I sat on a metal chair in the hallway leading to the baptismal font, waiting for that moment in the services when the minister came for me. While the congregation was singing, he led me down the hallway to the baptismal font, which was hidden on the altar behind a red velvet curtain. He went into the water. The curtain opened and he asked the congregation to stand and join him in welcoming me into the church. Then he motioned to me to come into the water. As I did he reached out, took me by the shoulders, and stood me in front of him. Then he placed his left hand behind my head, turned me so my side faced the congregation, and, offering one last prayer to God, leaned me back under the dark surface of the water and brought me up again. By magic I now belonged to the church. After services I was the center of attention at the potluck lunch served in the meeting hall on the second floor.

Our church service was predictable. At the beginning, the congregation stood and joined the choir in singing the processional hymn. Next came the minister's welcome, followed by a reading of scriptures, followed by another song during which we were allowed to remain seated; then we would stand for the Lord's Prayer and the passing of the offering trays. After the money was collected we sang the doxology. Next came the prayer announcing communion and another song during which six deacons walked down the center aisle to the front. At a small table the minister served them a communion consisting of Welch's grape juice and half-inch cubes of white bread. While the organ played, each deacon picked up a silver tray of small glasses of juice and another of bread. They moved row by row, passing each tray down the pews. Each person took a cube of bread and ate it and drank a cup of juice, taking care to put the tiny glass back onto the tray before passing it on. At the conclusion, the minister offered a final prayer and moved to the podium from which he gave the sermon.

For some time after I was baptized the sermons made no sense to me. Either I sat in perplexed wonder at my parents' ability to understand the droning baritone of our minister, or I offered one of them a chance to play tic-tac-toe in the margins of the church bulletin. The day I first began to understand the meaning of the preacher's sermon, it came as a shock. I was seven or eight years old and felt as if I had penetrated the veil of a secret adult ritual. Afterward I would listen and try to remember every word. Each sermon contained a simple lesson, which could be reduced to a single sentence. This sentence was posted on a sign at the entrance of the church.

Good sermons had quotations from books we all knew we should have read but hadn't. Good sermons had solid beginnings and perhaps funny stories. Good sermons told about poor souls who learned biblical lessons the hard way. Good sermons made sense and stayed with me all week.

After I lost my fear of the church sanctuary I came to love it. It provided my first experience with mystical forces. Sitting in church I felt the presence of God in the sunlight that poured through the leaded glass windows. I would bow my head and know that my prayers were heard. And if I sat quietly and listened closely to the silence, I could hear God's voice telling me what to do.

My heroes came from the stories I heard on Sunday. There were stories about fathers who had spared their children and about men who shared their wealth with strangers. I learned about men and women who had prayed, listened, waited, and then did what God told them to do. I learned that Mary and Joseph had risked ridicule and estrangement from their family and friends to be the mother and father of Christ, the son, who was sent to redeem with love. Christ said, "Whomsoever believeth in me shall not perish but shall have everlasting life." And so I believed.

I also learned heroic stories downtown at the Stuart Theater. Every Saturday morning long lines formed of kids waiting with the price of admission clutched in their hands: a quarter and the severed top of a wax-covered milk carton from the show's sponsor. The Stuart was originally built for live performances, and ornate plaster statues and carvings decorated the walls and ceilings. Pairs of ferocious-looking gargoyles flanked two full balconies with box seats on the sides. A rich purple velvet curtain drew back slowly as we waited eagerly in the dark for the show to begin.

The shows we hungered for were never-ending serials about Tarzan or Zorro or some obscure cowboy character. We remembered every detail of the previous week's episode as we waited breathlessly for our hero to continue his adventures. Each episode closed with the hero trapped and sinking rapidly in quicksand, surrounded by armed bandits or natives, or ensnared in some other life-threatening predicament. We would gasp when the words "continued next week" came on the screen.

The urge to live my life as these heroes did was mixed with the desire to be admired by my peers. I feared their disapproval almost as much as I did that of my father and my older brother, John. By my tenth year I learned how to make my friends laugh by misbehaving and playing practical jokes. I carried on so much in Bible study classes that

my teacher made me sit by myself and asked my classmates to pray for me. I wore this punishment as a badge of
honor. I alternated between being a boy clown and a boy
drawn to the great stories of the church and to the parallel dramas I saw on the Stuart Theater screen.

The other focus of our lives in Bethany was my father's
business: a lumber and coal yard three quarters of a mile
north of the church. What a wonderful place it was. I can
still close my eyes and smell the dry sawdust and freshly
cut lumber, hear the whirring whine of the saw, and feel
the warm boards waiting to be lifted from a pile of wood.
In my early years I seemed to always have a splinter
lodged in one of my fingers. Usually I could remove it
myself, but sometimes in the evening my mother took my
hand and gently, quietly nudged out the wooden dart
with one of her sewing needles.

I first met someone from a race other than my own
when Wardell Moore, a black truck driver who made
weekly coal deliveries in our neighborhood, let me ride
with him. He told me he had a son about my age and that
he was a good student in school. He taught me how to
jump down from the truck at each house and open the
door to the coal chute. After a while he even let me handle
the scoop shovel he used to push the black nuggets from
the front to the back of the truck bed.

Lincoln in the 1950s was about as safe and quiet a place
as you could find on earth. Except for the winters, which
were hard with freezing winds and punishing blizzards,

life was idyllic. Springtime brought floods and muddy roads and lilacs. Summers gave us fireflies, the buzzing chorus of cicadas, the smell of cut grass, and baseball games featuring our Class A team, the Lincoln Chiefs. On hot summer nights when the table fans no longer cooled us, my parents took us outside and spread blankets on the lawn. Sometimes we'd sleep outdoors, telling ghost stories to each other under the stars. When it was sweltering hot and the wind stood still, our father took us for car rides so we could catch the breeze with our hands.

My father loved the freedom our car gave us. Every summer we piled into it for a family trip. At first we traveled in a nine-passenger station wagon, but as we grew we needed two four-door sedans to carry our brood. Each trip was laid out for us on a map provided by the American Automobile Association. My father gathered the family around him and traced the route highlighted in red or yellow. "Follow the line; that's all we have to do," he would say. "No problem." While my father took care of transportation, my mother did all the rest. We ate what she cooked. We slept where she decided and wore the clothes she washed at Laundromats along the way. She organized games and encouraged us to sing songs like "Bill Grogan's Goat" and "I've Been Working on the Railroad" to "pass the time away."

We also found plenty of adventures in Lincoln. Close by our home was a small stream called Stephens Creek where we fished for crawfish and guppies and hid out in sandstone caves. My friends and I rode our bikes to the creek and spent the day exploring and telling stories. We smoked dried stalks of milkweed plants and imagined ourselves as leading men in action movies. We made up stories with ourselves as the heroes who rode in to save the day.

We biked everywhere. The edge of the universe lay at the ends of the dirt roads leading to those places where the wild and woolly frontier began. We were afraid to go farther until one of my friends invited us to his farm. There we got used to the smell of manure and learned how accomplished our farm friends were. They were not afraid of the cows, the horses, or the angry hogs. They knew how a windmill worked, could drive a tractor, and were entrusted with jobs we didn't think kids were capable of doing. I thought they were the bravest kids I knew.

Perhaps they thought we were brave when they spent the night in town. We were not afraid when we ventured out in our neighborhood, day or night. We could stay out until the streetlights came on and not cause our parents worry about foul play. And when we got into trouble and our parents came looking for us, we had plenty of places to hide.

My parents divided the worrying unequally. My mother kept track of all of us. She cooked our meals, cleaned our house, and sewed our clothes. Because of her I learned to play the piano and the trumpet, acquired a re-spect for the written word, and was given an example of heroic living I could never expect to equal. She was gentle and uncomplaining. In her entire life I knew her to cry only twice: once when she discovered she was pregnant for a seventh time and the other when she caused the untimely death of our cocker spaniel, Rusty, by shutting the garage door on his head.

In 1953 I saw my first television show. The morning of June 2, one of the last days of the school year, my father announced to us that we should come right home to watch the coronation of Queen Elizabeth together. He put the television set in the basement and ran a wire out the window to a makeshift antenna. When I saw the beautiful young queen and her dashing prince, I thought I was witnessing a fairy tale. It could not be real but my brother John assured me it was.

Television, forbidden during the supper meal, became a big part of our family life. Sunday nights we would gather to watch *Gunsmoke, Ed Sullivan,* and *Laugh-In.* We were even allowed to stay up to watch John Charles Daly host *What's My Line?* The struggles of Dorothy Kilgallen, Fred Allen, Arlene Francis, and Bennett Cerf to discover the hidden profession of their weekly guests entertained our entire family.

I carried their famous phrases into conversations with my friends. "Will the mystery guest sign in please?" Or from *To Tell The Truth,* "Would the real _____, please stand up?" I watched Garry Moore smoke one Winston cigarette after another on *I've Got a Secret* and longed to do the same. Popular fashion and culture were my guides to good taste. I listened to AM radio and memorized rock and roll lyrics. I knew every feature of the new model automobiles, dressed according to approved styles, and remained safely inside the circle of public approval.

When I was nine years old I got my first newspaper route. With this job came a liberating feeling of responsibility. I delivered the papers, billed my customers, and collected the money. People depended on me for their news. Every morning, seven days a week, fifty-two weeks a year, I brought seventy or eighty people a folded paper held fast with a red rubber band. On my bike I learned shortcuts and came to know the predawn sounds of a sleeping city, especially the lonesome sound of the trains miles away in the yards west of town. I learned to push on through the mud and rain and snow that often stood between my customers and me.

I had two fears. One was imaginary and the other was real. The imaginary fear came from watching the 1953 movie *Invaders from Mars*. In the movie the Martians lived underground, and unsuspecting victims were seized from below. A hole suddenly opened in the ground, some poor man or woman or kid fell in, and the hole then resealed itself. The Martians could make you disappear without a trace. In the early mornings before the sun rose and I was wrapping rubber bands around my newspapers, a cold chill of terrifying premonition would run down my spine. I was certain the Martians were going to get me.

The other fear was more realistic. Nebraska is a place of flooding rivers. For millions of years we have had floods every spring as the snow melted in the Rocky Mountains and the April showers fell. Engineers built dams and channeled the rivers to reduce their destructive power, but the water still rises in the spring. Once when I was six or seven years old I was in the car with my father when he got caught in a flood somewhere west of Lincoln. Without warning, the water surged and came across the road, blocking our path. He just managed to drive through to safety. I remember looking out the window and down on swirling dark water that seemed oblivious to my life and quite capable of sweeping me away to my death. To this day I am sometimes visited by a dream in which floodwaters threaten my life.

6

THOSE TWO FEARS ASIDE, my hometown seemed the safest place on earth. In my mind Lincoln contained the world's most important people. To me celebrities were the human beings who lived in my neighborhood and who managed through good fortune or tragedy to get their names printed in the newspaper. Outside my neighborhood was the great unknown and unknowable. World events happened somewhere other than my world, where everyone lived forever and no one ever died.

In the summer of 1951, my father asked me to drive with him to Chicago to see Fannie, who was in the hospital. It was my first car trip alone with my father and my first visit to a hospital. The excitement I felt ended when we went into the hospital room where the old woman lay.

She already looked dead. My father pushed me forward and made me give her a ceramic lion I had made in Cub Scouts. It was covered with fake brown fur and painted yellow. I don't remember anything she said, but I remember her very white hair and the blue veins in her hands.

Afterward we drove to the apartment building where he had grown up. We parked in front of the building and walked up to the third floor. Fannie's daughters, Jessie and Eva, invited us in. They had a bedroom where both women slept, a kitchen where Jessie had gone to make iced tea, and a tiny bathroom. The mahogany dining table and the living room furniture were in the same room along with two writing desks overflowing with papers and books. The last room was a screened porch with two wicker chairs and a low wicker table. "This is where your father used to sleep," Eva told me as I explored the place under her watchful eye.

Jessie and Eva were lean, straight-backed women with the same strong hands I had seen on my great-grandmother Frances in the photograph of her churning milk. Jessie suggested we sit in the living room to drink our iced teas and told Eva to turn on the oscillating fan as though running it were a special luxury. I listened to the three of them talk and noted a respect and deference in my father's voice I had not heard before. Though by blood they were cousins to him, these two were his older sisters; to me they would always be Aunt Jessie and Aunt Eva.

He told them that Fannie looked all right. I remember

he said, "She was having more trouble breathing than usual." Our iced teas finished, it was time to go. My dad wanted to make it to Peoria by nightfall so he could reach Lincoln in a single day's drive. Before we left Chicago we drove to the University of Chicago campus. My father stopped in front of Stagg field house. We walked in front of tall gray stone walls that made the building look like a medieval castle. My father showed me a plaque at the entrance that declared it was here on December 2, 1942, that Enrico Fermi and his team had achieved the first self-sustaining chain reaction and had initiated the controlled release of nuclear energy. My father thought I should be impressed that Fermi had done his work in a squash court under the west stands of the football field. But I didn't understand why this place was so important to him.

On the drive back to Lincoln my father told me I would not be working with my brother John that summer. At age ten John was already big enough to drive a twelve-penny nail through a board in two blows. I could barely hold a heavy hammer with one hand, let alone accomplish this superhuman feat. My father knew how big a disappointment this news was to me. I wanted to wear one of the canvas belts the men used to hold their hammers and a supply of nails. I wanted to join them as they hauled two-by-four studs to the foundation of a new house. I wanted to raise the skeleton frame and feel the itch of sawdust sticking to my sweating body.

My father said no. I was too small. As consolation he told me I could help out at the lumberyard and do odd jobs for the shop foreman. When summer came I filled the orders of builders who were putting up dream houses for young families in our growing neighborhood. I learned to mark plywood and lumber with a lead pencil and to hold the wood while the foreman sawed it. I cleaned up and prepared for our next order.

During a lunch break I took out one of the rolled-up paper tubes stored in an empty wooden nail barrel at one end of the table saw. I unrolled it, and as I did inhaled a whiff of ammonia. Inside were white lines on blue paper that I did not understand. I interrupted the foreman as he took a sandwich from his black metal lunch box and asked him about it. He told me it was the drawing for one of the houses my father was building. I was thrilled when he offered to teach me how to read the blueprint.

With one of the stubby wooden pencils that always seemed to be lying about, I began to draw sketches of my own on discarded pieces of lumber. My father, who seldom came into the lumberyard during the lunch hour, surprised us one day with a visit. I didn't see him at first because I was busy with one of my masterpieces. He saw what I was doing and asked what I had in mind. I told him I had picked out a tree in our backyard and wanted to build a house in it. He considered the details for a moment, took the drawing in his hand, and said, "No problem, we can do this." He went back to his office and I stood there wondering what would happen next.

Days later when I had finished supper and was heading out to join my friends, my father asked me to stick around. I followed him into his office. On the desk was a stack of rolled blueprints. My father took the rubber band off one and spread it out before me. The smell of ammonia and the bright blue paper distracted me from immediately realizing what the drawing was. I looked at him, confused, and without a word he pointed to the bottom of the plan where the title of the project was always printed. This one said, "Bob's Tree House." "This will be yours," he said. Had he presented me with a baseball autographed by Mickey Mantle, I would not have been as impressed and happy.

I didn't understand why he decided to reward me but whatever his reason, building this tree house ended my disappointment at not being able to work with my brother. I hauled lumber, held lightweight pieces in place, and even hammered a few nails in my slow and clumsy way. The house was twenty feet square, had a shingled roof, tongue-and-groove siding, and interior walls insulated with rolled asbestos. All four walls had windows, each with a hinged shutter that swung out. There was a door in the floor that swung up and could be fastened with an outside lock. This house was the best thing I had ever owned.

I spent many nights up in the tree, alone and with friends. Few things made me feel as secure as sitting inside my house during a heavy prairie storm. My father had insisted on installing a lightning rod, which seemed silly to me until a bolt hit close enough one afternoon to leave the smell of fire in its wake. Normally what I got from a storm was the sweetest, most intoxicating smell of freshness imaginable.

From this twenty-foot-high perch my friends and I saw and heard things we were not supposed to see and hear, most remarkably, our first look at a fully grown naked woman. Once a week—usually at 2 P.M. on the dot on Fridays—a neighbor lady who liked to sunbathe in the nude came out of her house wrapped only in a towel. My lucky friends and I would climb onto the roof of the tree house at least an hour early, lying and waiting for our world to get turned upside down one more time. We peered down over the edge of the roof breathless and confused about the feelings we were having. She would remove the towel and lay it on the ground. Then she would stand up for what seemed simultaneously the shortest and the longest period of time before lying facedown on the towel. It was as if she were offering herself as a gift to adolescence.

I entered the late summer with a dread of fall because at this age my asthma seemed to have gotten worse. I began to suffer major respiratory congestion and distress. From Labor Day until the first hard freeze, the symptoms progressed and raged on until the morning after the first heavy frost. Then, suddenly, they ended.

While others dreaded the approach of winter and farmers spoke with terror of early frosts, I waited in delighted anticipation for that glorious drop in temperature that would end the life of the annual weeds that tormented me. I wanted what others feared, and feared what they wanted.

The summer before seventh grade was particularly bad for my asthma. Pollen counts were up, the summer was hot and dry, and the excitement of going from Bethany Grade School to Lincoln Northeast High School put me in the danger zone. To say I was excited about going to the high school would be a misstatement. Fear is the more accurate word. The only human beings crueler to each other than seventh graders are older students. God help the kid who doesn't fit in.

At the time my brothers and I were sleeping in two bunk beds in the garage. My nighttime coughing attacks and the high-pitched shrieking I made when I breathed were keeping them awake. My mother had enough and called Elmer Hobbs, our family doctor. He said I was anemic and needed a blood transfusion. I was admitted to Bryan Memorial Hospital for a week. Alone in my bed after the time for sleep had come and gone, I listened to the whistling sound coming from inside my chest with each inhalation and exhalation of breath. An intravenous needle led from my little left arm to a tube through which blood passed into my anemic body. I was not frightened. I felt relieved and safe. I could sleep without worrying about keeping others awake, and anything was better than the trauma of walking down the halls of the high school.

Finally my father decided to do for me what Fannie had done for herself: he sent me north. Fannie's daughter Eva had bought a cabin on White Fish Lake near Gordon, Wisconsin. Because the air was cool and the vegetation different, my father thought the change would do me good. He was right. During four weeks with Eva I swam in the lake day and night. I explored the woods alone and picked blueberries for pancakes. I listened to Eva's stories about being a teenager at the dawn of the century, and I slept on a screened porch with the company of loons lamenting their loneliness and the sound of approaching thunderstorms marching like an army toward the roof of our cabin.

My asthma symptoms abated. I put on a few pounds and acquired the brown, wild look that makes adults love and fear twelve-year-old boys. And when my father came to drive me back to Nebraska for the start of seventh grade, he challenged me to swim across the lake to an island and back, a distance of about a mile. My older brother John had already done it, and that was motivation enough for me. I covered the distance easily and, with all the adrenaline pumping out of my happy heart, I could have swum it twice.

More than anything I wanted to match my brother John's performance. Without benefit of weight lifting or a bodybuilding diet, he became a six-foot-tall, 190-pound athlete. I grew slowly and could not gain weight no matter what I tried. When he was starting on the varsity football team in his sophomore year I was staring into the mirror at a body that was five feet two inches high and tipped our bathroom scale at eighty pounds with my shoes on.

He was a star and I wanted to be one. The girls loved his muscular body, square jaw, and sensuous lips. I dreamed of capturing their attention, but it was not to be. Not only did I remain small and skinny, but I was also cursed with remarkably slow legs, which would not carry me fast enough to compensate for my size. Worse, the arrival of my wheezing and breathlessness coincided with the beginning of football, the one sport I wanted to play more than any other.

I became self-conscious and shy about my body and tried many solutions. Charles Atlas's picture and his advertisements in *Boy's Life* magazine persuaded me to try his dynamic tension techniques. For hours I would press one hand against the other, shifting my arms up, down, in front, and behind me. With each repetition I dreamed of waking in the morning transformed into the anthropomorphic body of my brother. I noticed no change. I drank milk shakes and ate constantly, but could not turn myself into the man I wanted to be.

Most of my friends were having the same difficulties. Even those friends whose bodies grew fast enough to get them onto the football field or the basketball court appeared to have the same confidence deficit disorder I had. We compensated with rowdy behavior. We soaped windows on Halloween night. We acted up in class. I became a small hero when I was asked to leave my Boy Scout troop after many unsuccessful efforts to design my own merit badges. We started a club in the loft of a friend's garage, which was once a barn. We called ourselves the Angels but we became the Angles after we let our poorest speller write our name on our door.

In the winter the Angles gathered to ice-skate and took chances sliding on a sled tied with a rope to the bumper of a fast-moving car. In the spring we took to the streets, roller-skated, and hung out at a local drive-in restaurant, one of the first of its kind. On occasion we challenged boys at other high schools with attacks on their territory.

Fear of our parents and other adult leaders kept us from going too far with our misdeeds. The most important adult leader of my youth was a man named Harlan Johnson. He organized YMCA camp retreats, athletic activities for those who did not make the high school varsity squads, and unusual events that challenged us in unexpected ways.

During the summer before my sophomore year I spent a week that would affect me much later in life at the YMCA's model legislature. Forty-nine boys were given a chance to learn about Nebraska's legislative process. Each of us represented one of the districts in the Unicameral, the only single-house, nonpartisan legislative body in the country. We went to Nebraska's capitol, the tallest building in Lincoln and easily the most beautiful. There we were assigned desks in the actual chamber used by the real representatives of the people. The political issues we debated were contrived and irrelevant but not in my mind; at the time I thought that what we were doing was important.

My first personal experience with a political issue was when I went to meet a fellow Angle at his home. In a heavy accent his mother told me he had gone to take his driver's test and was on his way home with his father. When she invited me in I hesitated because my friend had made it clear he did not want us to meet his family. I knew the parents of all my friends except his, but he had used every excuse to keep us out of his home.

She wanted to talk and wasn't offended when I asked about her accent. She was from Latvia and showed me where it was on a map. She had come to America because of the Russians. "The Nazis and the Communists. They are the same to me. No difference; I hate them both." I had never met a Communist in Lincoln, but if my friend's mother hated them, so did I. We had been talking in their living room for nearly an hour when my friend walked in. He looked surprised and worried. I had violated his rule and he wanted me out of the house.

We left and drove off in his car. When I asked questions about what his mother had said, he would not tell me anything. He was ashamed of her heavy accent and his father's inability to speak any English at all. It didn't help that I thought he was brave to have been a part of this flight in the face of great danger. As we drove up the tree-lined street we quickly forgot the incident because this was our first ride in a car not driven by an adult. My friend's escape from Latvia had given him one enormous advantage over the rest of us: he was a year older and was driving a full year before we could. He would be much in demand.

One day that summer he drove several of us to an outdoor trampoline center. The trampolines were built so that the springy jumping surface was just above the ground. For twenty-five cents you could have fifteen minutes of acrobatic pleasure. The idea came into my head that I should attempt a maneuver I had tried on a swimming pool diving board: a one and a half somersault. I was confident I could do it. I came around in plenty of time to land flat on my stomach with my arms stretched forward to break the fall. Unfortunately I did not land on the trampoline. I landed on the sidewalk. The blow shattered my front teeth. I sat against the chain-link fence with my hands covering my mouth until my friends had used up their time on the trampolines. Then I went to my dentist who pulled what was left of the teeth.

7

ON JANUARY 21, 1958, nineteen-year-old Charlie Starkweather and fourteen-year-old Caril Ann Fugate
murdered eleven people during a two-day killing spree.
Three of their victims were at home in Lincoln. Fear flickered like lightning as word of the violence spread through
town. The radio broadcast a warning from school administrators and asked parents to pick up their children at
school. My mother took the risk seriously enough to
do just that. We all breathed a sigh of relief and went back
to our normal lives when the couple was arrested in
Wyoming.

In the 1950s we were told that the greatest danger to
our freedom was not Charlie Starkweather or Martians
or floods or trampolines. It was the threat of the Soviet

Union. The Soviets weren't the kind of danger that would cause a mother to pick her children up at school. We didn't fear a physical invasion, which would drive us from our homes. The conflict with the Soviet Union was more like gravity; it was simply a force that influenced much of what we did and thought.

Our presumption was that the Soviets were at war with us and were determined to conquer us however they could. We were told they were trying to take advantage of our open society by infiltrating our government, businesses, and even our churches. I never met a Communist when I was growing up, but in the rhetoric of the day that was because a Communist would never tell you he or she really was a Communist.

We heard that their centrally planned economy was producing tremendous gains in productivity and standards of living and that their schoolchildren were smarter, worked harder, and were likely to "bury us" unless our attitudes changed. It was traumatic for us when the Soviets launched *Sputnik*, the first artificial satellite to leave earth. And months later when a United States rocket blew up on the launching pad, we took it personally. It meant we were behind, that our scientists and engineers were inferior, that something was wrong with our schools, and that our students weren't as good as Soviet students in the subjects that mattered.

The Red Scare was a real experience in the fifties in Lincoln. The Reds were after our drinking water. They were after our children. President Eisenhower was speaking gospel when he used Joseph Alsop's phrase to justify U.S. aid to the French to fight Communism in Vietnam in 1954. Alsop said, "If you have a row of dominoes set up, you knock over the first one, and what will happen to the last one is the certainty that it will go over very quickly." The year I turned sixteen, Major Dale Buis and Master Sergeant Chester Ovnand became the first and second Americans to be killed in Vietnam.

My memories of most of the great moments of the Cold War are not vivid, but some were too big to miss entirely. I don't remember what happened during the 1948 Berlin airlift that overcame a Soviet blockade of Berlin from West Germany, but I remember hearing others talk excitedly about it. I don't remember the details of Alger Hiss being accused in 1948 by *Time* magazine senior editor Whittaker Chambers of being a Soviet spy, but I do remember something about secret messages hidden inside pumpkins. As I said before I remember the 1949 Communist victory in China, but only as something that happened to China to make it Red. The 1949 Soviet detonation of a nuclear weapon I remember; it was on a newsreel at the Stuart Theater. Senator Joe McCarthy's four years of anti-Communist efforts beginning in 1950 were a remote happening. I did not mark as significant either the death of Stalin in 1953 or the executions of Ethel and Julius Rosenberg that same year.

Some of my memories have come back only after

studying current events of the time. While I do not re-member the invasion of South Korea by the North and heard nothing about the terrible U.S. losses in the sum-mer of 1950 or the stunning success of Inchon, I do remember General MacArthur being recalled. And I remember talking about a *Life* magazine article the fol-lowing spring that told the story of wave after wave of Chi-nese soldiers attacking, seemingly without regard for the terrible losses being inflicted upon them. They had to be different than we were. They couldn't value life the same way we did. It seemed the only reasonable explanation for their behavior.

The same "us-versus-them" attitude carried over into the other great battle of the day: the struggle by black Americans for civil rights. My store of Cold War memo-ries is large compared to the battle for civil justice. *Brown v. Board of Education* overturned the legal principle of "separate but equal" and said in essence that segregation in our schools was a violation of the Fourteenth Amend-ment to the Constitution. It says a lot about my view of the world that I do not remember the day in 1954 this de-cision was announced by a unanimous Supreme Court. The key community represented in the *Brown* case was Topeka, Kansas, 125 miles southeast of Lincoln. And one of the key players was a Nebraska native, Herbert Brownell. Mr. Brownell was appointed Attorney General after he successfully managed President Eisenhower's 1952 cam-paign for president and promised Governor of California

Earl Warren the first slot on the U.S. Supreme Court if he agreed to support Ike.

In our nearly homogenous community, racism was a problem that infected the thinking of other people and not us. Not one black student attended Lincoln Northeast during my six years there. In fact, I didn't have a black classmate my entire thirteen years in the public schools. In part this was because the few blacks that lived in Lincoln were kept out of our neighborhood by discriminatory real estate practices. In part it was because black students were sent to a segregated grade school, though I was unaware of it at the time.

Today, when I read the defense used in 1954 by the Topeka School Board it seems likely I would have shared their sentiment. The Topeka board argued that because segregation in Topeka and elsewhere pervaded many other aspects of life, segregated schools simply prepared black children for the segregation they would face during adulthood. Segregated schools were not necessarily harmful to black children. Great African Americans such as Frederick Douglass, Booker T. Washington, and George Washington Carver had overcome more than just segregated schools. That was the mainstream logic of the time and nothing in my experience would have caused me to question it.

I simply did not know any minorities well enough to realize the kind of barriers they confronted. I had no experience with discrimination and no passion to end it. The only reasonable supposition is that I must have reached the same conclusion as the majority in Lincoln: there was no problem with things just as they were.

I did have one personal connection with problems facing people who were different. My eldest brother, Jim, was born slightly mentally retarded. He had been practically ripped from my mother's body by a young and inexperienced doctor who used forceps without regard for the damage that could be done to a baby's head. My mother thought this violence explained my brother's slowness. His physical development was as rapid as his intellect was slow. Jim grew faster and bigger than anyone in our family, and he didn't stop until he was six feet seven inches tall.

In the same year as *Brown v. Board of Education,* my parents were told Jim could no longer continue in public school. He was doing poorly in his classes, and the system simply judged that trying to help him was wasting taxpayers' dollars. So they sent him home and told him he would not be allowed to return.

The two choices my parents faced were to keep him at home or to find a private school. My mother found a program in Philadelphia that advertised itself as giving special care to children who could not do well in the public schools. They took the train to Philly to make certain the place was on the up and up. They liked what they saw and left Jim there.

This farewell must have been terribly painful for my brother and my parents in a way that I did not appreciate at the time. My father in particular would have been reminded of the ordeal of his older brother. For me my brother's departure wasn't an ordeal. I had other brothers and sisters to keep me company. Besides that, Jim's slowness embarrassed me. I didn't want people to know he was my brother. I was afraid I would be judged by others if they knew he was part of my family.

My brother was not away very long. At first my mom and dad attributed his unhappiness and complaints to his being homesick. "He'll be all right after he makes some new friends," they reasoned. But he didn't make new friends and he wasn't all right. After several months of letters from him describing the poor conditions, my parents decided to check things out for themselves. They found Jim with his head shaved, wearing a uniform that resembled prison pajamas, in a cold dormitory with bathrooms that did not work. On the spot my father decided to take him back to Lincoln.

My parents were as proud of Jim as they were of all their children. They hired a tutor and helped Jim find work. But his physical problems got worse when he began to have seizures diagnosed as epilepsy. Our doctor prescribed Dilantin, but he didn't know that long-term exposure to Dilantin produces alarming side effects, including loss of the blood supply to the mouth. Before this mistake was discovered, Jim's gums atrophied and he lost all his teeth.

People like Jim who are different but who want badly to be liked are vulnerable to abuse. One day in early June of 1960 between my junior and senior high school years, I ran downstairs to my room to change clothes. As I passed Jim's room I saw he had someone with him, a boy in my class who had been hanging around my brother for reasons I suspected were not good.

From my room I listened in on their conversation. I heard the boy ask my brother to lie down on the bed. I heard him say, "My, you sure are tall." Then I heard a rustling of clothes and the words, "My, you are big, too." I rushed into the room. Jim was lying down and the other boy's hands were on him. I told him to leave. Then I made him leave.

Afterward I was angry with myself because his punishment seemed incomplete. A week later I was given a chance to correct my mistake. Late in the afternoon I was driving my father's car when this same boy pulled his car alongside mine and extended his right hand in my direction with a single finger raised. This universally recognized insult gave me the excuse I needed.

He drove into the parking lot of a grocery store and went inside. I parked and waited for him inside the doorway. When he walked by me I hit him before he could raise his fists. I pushed him down and, with my knees on his shoulders, began to bang his head on the concrete. I was way ahead on points when I heard a woman shout, "Police! Call the police!" It seemed like a good time to stop what I was doing. When I looked up I saw one of my teachers. Now I was convinced it was a good time to make my exit.

We both got up. I was ready to leave but the boy was not through fighting. We were in the lawn and garden section of the store, and he grabbed a pair of pruning shears from a display rack. He began making lunging motions in my direction. I had seen some cowboy hero in a movie take a knife away from an attacking foe and I tried to do the same. But instead of twisting the pruning shears out of my opponent's hands I took the blades in my side. Both of us were shocked. My attacker pulled back; he did not pursue the advantage.

I decided the fight was over and ran out of the store unaware of the seriousness of my wound. In the car I realized I needed to visit the hospital. In the emergency room of Lincoln General a doctor stopped the bleeding, and as he was sewing up the incision told me the blades had come a half inch from penetrating my cardiac membrane. As soon as the wound was closed, a sheriff's deputy told me to follow him to his car for a ride to the jail.

There I was surprised to see my attacker sitting at a desk talking good-naturedly with one of the officers. He claimed to be a defenseless victim who had been harassed by me before and who was afraid I would hurt him. He had no idea why I had attacked him. I would not supply the missing piece. The county attorney charged me with assault with intent to do bodily harm and took out a peace bond against me. This meant that if I approached my classmate for any reason the official would file criminal charges. Then he called my mother and father to escort me home.

My father took the side of the law. My mother knew something was up, and she probably suspected what my classmate had done to my brother. She was angry with the county attorney for not listening to both sides of the matter. For me it was a lesson of some significance. My fighting had helped neither me nor my brother. I had embarrassed my family, and I got a brief but lasting look at the law. I did not like what I saw.

Though I wasn't constantly in trouble with the law, I thought the law was little more than a flashing red light in my rearview mirror. The law was there to keep me from doing things I wanted to do: drive fast or disrupt someone's peace at night. My difficulties seemed to grow when I got a car, escalating during the summer.

Saving me from a worse fate was my father's expectation that I would find work when school was out. One of my best jobs during my high school years was with Arnie Bartlett and Ray Watts, who built concrete foundations, slabs, and brick walls. Arnie and Ray were good-natured, a comic pair who could outwork all of the younger men they hired as helpers. They taught me to dig footings, form a slab with plywood, level sand, lay wire and iron bars, and move concrete as it came down the chute of the truck.

Most of the slabs were foundations for silos to store the grain of local farmers or grain elevator operators. We built corrugated steel structures in a dozen or so small towns within an hour's drive of Lincoln. Occasionally we got a job far enough away so we had to put up for the night in a local hotel. Those were the good nights when I shot pool, ate my meals with Arnie and Ray, and worked until the job was done. Though we were never more than an hour from Lincoln, it seemed as though we had gone to the other side of the universe, where I was free from my parents' authority.

8

L IKE SO MANY MEN my age, some of the most important
lessons I learned in school were outdoors on a playing
field surrounded by an oval running track. The Lincoln
Northeast High School track was north of the school's
three-story red brick building, and the field was of little
significance to anyone who never played high school football. For those who have, the sight of two white wooden
goalposts at opposite ends of a hundred-yard field of grass
surrounded by an oval quarter-mile track holds special
meaning.

It is a place where a man can recall an afternoon
or evening of his youth with absolute clarity. Thirty, forty,
fifty years later the memory will still be fresh. For this is
the place where a boy learns as much about the game of

life as he does about the game of football. This is the place where a boy learns that the confidence of a spectacular success is necessary to help him survive the deflation of a brutal failure, which can come on the very next play. It is a place where a boy learns that individual effort must be sustained through mind-numbing fatigue and that helping a team of players to succeed can be a more lasting glory than individual stardom.

I remember some forty-year-old moments as if they just happened. I once made an absolutely perfect block that made the coaches nod at each other in approval and fellow players nod at me with momentary respect. I once tackled a running back with enough force to reverse his forward motion. Practically an entire lifetime later I can hear sounds of that one block and that one tackle and recall the pride I felt afterward. I also remember missed blocks, missed tackles, and everything else in between, which is mostly where I performed.

As a player my contact with greatness was infrequent. In truth the only time I am certain I experienced greatness was as a witness to it. And greatest of all was the memory of playing an afternoon game of football against Omaha Central High School, whose star player was Gale Sayers, who went on to a hall of fame career with the Chicago Bears. We only lost by a touchdown. I played a good game on offense, but on defense I couldn't even touch the hem of Sayers's garment. I was playing right linebacker as he swung wide around his left side, eluded me with grace, and ran seventy and eighty yards for a touchdown.

The first time I suited up for practice was in August 1959, in a storage room next to the gym lockers. We were given plastic shoulder pads and heavy white cotton pants, with hard fiber pads for the thighs and softer pads for the knees. A plastic helmet with a canvas suspension was designed to limit the damage of crushing blows. A single half-inch curved metal bar fastened to either side of the helmet protected against larger objects, such as another player's helmet, but it was no protection against a fist, a forearm, or a kick. We wore black leather, high-top shoes with removable hard rubber cleats.

The only equipment we had to bring to this first practice were three articles of clothing: a jockstrap, a pair of sweat socks, and a T-shirt. Many players never took these items home to be washed until the season was over, and I will never forget the acrid smell of the locker room. It was almost as bad as my uncle Ronnie's turkey coops on my mother's family farm near Rippey, Iowa. The pungent smell in the locker room intensified as the season progressed.

A third of the 150 boys in my class tried out for the football team my sophomore year. On the first day each of us understood there were three possible outcomes: we would quit, we would be selected for the sophomore team, or best of all we would be good enough to make the varsity roster. The sophomore team was the coach's way to give a player a chance to stick around long enough to see if growth or experience would add something that would get him picked for the regular team during his junior year when there were only two options: varsity or no football.

When I left the locker room for the first time and ran to the practice field to face the coaches, I felt dread. My breathing was rapid and a tightness in my chest signaled something worse than physical pain. I dreaded the humiliation of performing poorly in front of others. My nightmare scenario was doing something so foolish, so pitiful that laughter would be my reward. But I also dreamed I would do something that elevated me to the status of legend. Both possibilities battled for my attention. As it turned out, neither became reality. I was assigned to the line coach where determination could make up for deficiencies in speed, size, and strength. And though I did not make the varsity roster I was a regular sophomore starter.

Our young bodies took a beating on the rock-hard bare field where thick grass grows only in the end zones. A few of the scars on my old body tell stories from those days. A pale white line between the third and fourth fingers of both hands came courtesy of the cleats of competitive upper classmen. My knees and elbows were almost always bloody thanks to regular trips to the ground. I have a mark below my lower lip due to having my teeth pushed through the soft flesh following a sharp blow to my mouth.

I will never forget the names of my coaches and how they looked. Our head varsity coach was Art Bauer, a dark-skinned man in his late thirties whose muscular legs made him look like he could still play the game. Max Hester was Coach Bauer's first assistant. The other was Hank Williamson, who doubled as head coach of the sophomore team. These three did something for me that strengthened my character as much as my parents did. They taught me why I had to fight on no matter how hopeless a situation seemed at the time.

When I was a sophomore my brother John was the starting senior fullback for the varsity squad, as he had been all three years. He was big and fast and was just what the coaches were looking for. I was small and slow and would have to grow some to be noticed. Because I did not make varsity my sophomore year, I did not get to play on the same team as my brother. My junior year I made the team and played enough to earn a letter.

Going into my senior year my goal was to make the starting team. I reasoned I had a fighting chance because in my junior year I played backup to the starting center who had graduated. Now, all I had to do was beat out the third-string kid and hope no one new showed up from the freshman ranks. My dream was to be announced with the starting roster at our first game against one of our crosstown rivals.

We began our practice in late August 1960 before school started. We had two weeks of a schedule known as two-a-days, meaning we practiced twice a day, once in the morning and once in the afternoon. It was cooler in the morning, and we could do wind sprints and other strenuous exercises without losing too much water. In the afternoons we were told to take salt tablets to prevent heat exhaustion or heat stroke.

The heat was nothing compared to my need to add weight and survive the asthma season. I had gained fifty pounds since my sophomore year, but still only weighed 155 at the beginning of practice. The previous year I had noticed that the boy who started at center had trouble snapping the ball accurately for punts, and I noticed how critical this relatively simple skill could be in a close game. I came to my last season having spent the summer working to master the punt-snap technique. Hundreds and hundreds of times I snapped the ball at a car tire hanging waist high from a rope on a clothesline pole fifteen yards behind me. I knew that throwing without shoulder pads was easier than with them, so I practiced throwing the ball farther and harder than would be needed in a game. As my accuracy improved my confidence soared.

Two-a-days began a few days after my seventeenth birthday. So did the asthma season. My determination to have my best year on the field collided with unusually high pollen counts. My body needed every calorie I could put into it just to deal with the attacks of asthma. The exertion of morning and afternoon practice burned pounds off me like ice melting in July. Whatever gains I had made that summer dripped away in the two weeks before our

TOP ROW: Henry, Horace, Mary (Mitchell), John Kerrey, George.
BOTTOM ROW: Frances (Potter), Thomas Kerrey,
Frances Reynolds Kerrey, Frank, c. 1890.
Courtesy of Bob Kerrey

Emmett and
Josephine
Gonder,
unknown date.
*Courtesy of
Bob Kerrey*

Frances Kerrey, unknown date.
Courtesy of Bob Kerrey

Annis Potts, unknown date.
Courtesy of Bob Kerrey

Frances Potter, c. 1920.
Courtesy of Bob Kerrey

John and Jim Kerrey, c. 1924.
Courtesy of Bob Kerrey

Elinor Gonder, 1932.
Courtesy of Bob Kerrey

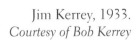

Jim Kerrey, 1933.
Courtesy of Bob Kerrey

Jim Kerrey, c. 1933.
Courtesy of Bob Kerrey

Jim Kerrey, unknown date.
Courtesy of Bob Kerrey

John Marley Kerrey, c. 1936.
Courtesy of Bob Kerrey

Jim and Elinor Kerrey, 1937.
Courtesy of Bob Kerrey

Bob Kerrey, 1944.
Courtesy of Bob Kerrey

Jim Kerrey, 1945.
Courtesy of the U.S. Army

Jim Kerrey with Bob, John, and Jim, Jr., 1947.
Courtesy of Townsend Studios—Lincoln, Nebraska

Fifth grade class, Bethany School—Bob Kerrey, bottom row, third from right, 1954. *Courtesy of Evans Photo Studio, Lincoln, Nebraska*

Jim Jr., John, Bob, Jessie, Bill, Sue, and Nancy Kerrey, 1958-59. *Courtesy of Bob Kerrey*

Bob Kerrey, 1960.
Courtesy of
Evans Photo Studio,
Lincoln, Nebraska

1960 Lincoln Northeast
Rockets—Bob Kerrey,
bottom row, third from right.
Courtesy of Evans Photo Studio,
Lincoln, Nebraska

Bob Kerrey, 1961.
Courtesy of Evans Photo Studio,
Lincoln, Nebraska

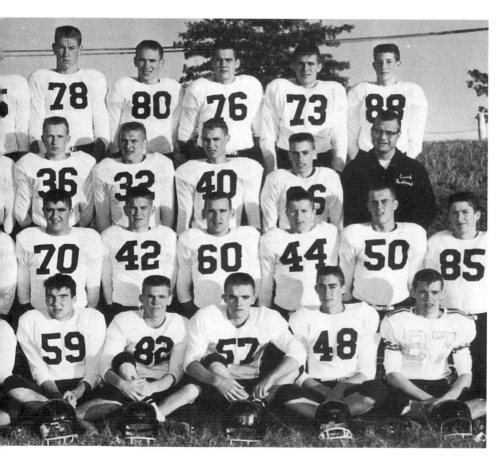

Bob Kerrey, President
of Phi Gamma Delta,
standing in front of frat
house, 1965.
© *University of*
Nebraska Photography

Bob Kerrey, 1968.
Courtesy of the U.S. Navy

Bob Kerrey with President Richard Nixon, Elinor and Jim Kerrey, 1970.
Courtesy of the Richard Nixon Library & Birthplace

Elinor and Jim Kerrey, 1975.
Courtesy of Bob Kerrey

first game. As that Saturday approached I no longer expected to start. On Friday the roster for Saturday's game was posted on the door of the locker room. I stopped to read the list. Not only had I failed to make the starting team, I had not even made the traveling roster. I would not suit up for the game. The news cut my heart. Tears welled up in my eyes, but I would not cry in front of my teammates. I went straight outside to my bike and headed home. Somewhere in the first few blocks I changed my mind. Rather than face my father—or worse, my brother—with this terrible failure, I decided to face the coach.

I knocked on Coach Bauer's door and asked if I could talk with him. No longer able to keep from crying I bowed my head while I spoke. "Coach, I can't keep trying. I have to quit." Coach Bauer asked me to sit down. He was reassuring. He told me this was just one game. I had worked too hard to quit. He urged me to give it one more try. I agreed.

At dinner that night my father asked about the next day's game. My brother John was sitting across from me. I made certain I did not look him in the eye. I answered that I would not be suiting up but would be on the sidelines. In a cheerful voice my father said, "No problem! You'll make it for one of the games." His optimism did not alter my dismal view of myself.

The next day the team looked terrible. We were favored to win but lost. And the starting center did poorly.

I started the next game and every other game that year. At season's end the bridge of my nose was permanently scarred from the attack of every noseguard I faced. This little scar would remind me how close I had once come to quitting and how much of a payoff there was for perseverance.

9

IN THE SPRING OF 1961 before high school graduation I decided to go to the University of Nebraska in Lincoln. I did not consider any other college. The university was the hometown school where my brother had gone before me and many of my friends were going. And the pride a Nebraskan feels for the university — even before our football team became famous — is something that cannot be understood by residents of states where the college scene is dominated by a venerable but private institution.

Most of my high school class of more than three hundred did not go on to college. They went right to work in factories where wages were still high enough to support their families. There were good jobs at Goodyear Tire and

Rubber, the Burlington Northern Railroad, Western Electric, Cushman Motors, Gooch's Mill, and other smaller manufacturing businesses. Every male knew that two years of military service was required by law, but only if there was a shortage of volunteers. The need for recruits was too small to present any real risk to us of being drafted. The Vietnam War was not much of an issue for the class of 1961.

I chose pharmacology because I loved chemistry and because a university counselor explained how I could complete my pharmacy training in four years by taking a heavy load and going to summer school. That convinced me. I was eager to finish school and get out into the world on my own.

In August before classes began I ventured outside the safety of my hometown for the first time. Three fellow Angles and I drove to New York City. We saw all the tourist attractions—the Statue of Liberty, the Empire State Building, and Ellis Island. We saw Mantle and Maris play at Yankee Stadium. And we went to Greenwich Village where we had our portraits sketched by a street artist and managed to get into the Bitter End for a performance by John Coltrane. We were four square young men from Lincoln, a universe away from the people we saw here. Driving out of New York we laughed at how different everyone in the city was—but knowing that we were the ones who did not belong.

I was beginning to sense that I could no longer remain

outside the flow of world events. Newly elected President Kennedy had said in his inaugural address on January 20, 1961, that Americans were willing to "pay any price and bear any burden" to win the battle against Communism. Two months before I graduated from high school in 1961, he authorized a CIA-supported invasion of Cuba at the Bay of Pigs. And the tensions were not confined to Cuba. In 1960 Soviet surface-to-air missiles had shot down an American U-2 spy plane and captured the pilot, Gary Powers. In August 1961, East Germany closed the border between East and West Berlin and constructed the Berlin Wall. Also in 1961 the Soviet Union detonated a thermonuclear device that was the largest ever exploded; its shock wave was felt around the world.

Around the world four hundred years of Western empires were coming to an end, in some cases peacefully and in some cases not. Colonies in Africa, Asia, and South America were becoming independent nations and some became Cold War battlegrounds. I would not have pretended to understand or care about the underlying nature or history of these conflicts. And as for emotional engagement, compared to the genuine sadness I felt when rock and roller Buddy Holly's plane flew into a snowstorm after a concert in Clear Lake, Iowa, on February 3, 1959, these other events barely registered with me.

When I entered college, I would have done poorly on any test that asked me questions about the origins of our country or about the great narratives of the men and women who built it. I would have done well on a test that asked about the periodic table and algebraic, geometric, and trigonometric problems. I did not understand the history of people, their lives, deaths, successes, failures, destructive ways, and creative abilities. I knew or cared little about the world outside of Lincoln.

I had one girlfriend who went to Alabama with the Freedom Riders in May 1961 just before we graduated. She told me how frightened she was by the police who stopped the bus she was riding in and by the hatred other white people showed toward her. I thought it was brave of her to go but had no interest in joining her.

For a story to reach me it would have to be in a movie theater. I went to most of the new movies that opened in Lincoln. In 1961 they included Jackie Gleason and Paul Newman in *The Hustler*, Stanley Kramer's *Judgment at Nuremberg*, and *A Raisin in the Sun* with Sidney Poitier. I saw Audrey Hepburn in *Breakfast at Tiffany's*, *The Guns of Navarone* with Gregory Peck and David Niven, Marilyn Monroe and Montgomery Clift in *The Misfits*, and Vincent Price in *The Pit and the Pendulum*.

I read what my mother recommended to me. Usually it was a Book of the Month Club selection, her source for books, or something she saw in *Reader's Digest*. In 1961 the only book I read that came out that year was Joseph Heller's *Catch-22*. Beyond that I had no contact with the world of culture. I knew a guy who became a painter, but in 1961 he was too strange for my company. I could not have told a Picasso from a Miró and did not know who Stella, Twombly, de Kooning, Johns, or Warhol were.

My pharmacy courses were mostly in the sciences — chemistry, math, physics, and pharmacology. I especially loved chemistry and its magical color changes, energy releases, and precipitations of newly created substances. In the dark labs smelling of strong acids and bases I learned to test for nitrates, sulfates, and phosphates and to tell which metals were present in various liquid and solid substances. I learned to measure precisely and to record the results meticulously in spiral notebooks that quickly gathered the stains of the laboratory reagents and dyes.

My only liberal arts courses were in elementary philosophy and elementary literature. I barely understood the difference between deductive and inductive logic. I was confused by the arguments, and did not know if I was a fatalist who believed in predestination or a determinist who believed I was the master of my own fate. In English I could not make sense of metaphors or muster excitement for the stories we were assigned to read. The only nonscientific course I remember well is economics, only because the lectures were broadcast from two television sets mounted from the ceiling in the front of a large room; they reliably put me to sleep.

In order to belong I joined a fraternity, Phi Gamma Delta, and lived by its written and unwritten rules. Some of my friends did not because they would not bend to the conformity that dominated every fraternity house. Those who did not fit in for physical, psychological, religious, or racial reasons — and a man could be blackballed for any of these — did not get in. I accepted the exclusionary conditions without hesitation; I was in and that was what counted most. The fraternity did give me a chance to lead. I was elected president of the house. Buoyed by this success, I ran for president of the student council and lost. I ran for vice president and won. In the spring of my junior year I was one of twelve men chosen to be members of the senior honors society.

The experience on the student council was blemished by a decision I made to take over a project organized by a graduating friend. The project was a student discount card that entitled students to lower prices from merchants who were eager enough for the business to pay to have their names on the cards. The cost of the cards was a few hundred dollars less than the revenue from the merchants. I got approval of the project from the council without disclosing that I was earning money, which I presumed, was obvious. The presumption led to a call for an investigation, which concluded I had done nothing wrong. But my integrity had been called into question because I had not been careful about the appearance of a conflict.

I decided not to approach the council with a problem created by the only failing grade I earned in college in a semester course in the Air Force Reserve Officers' Training Corps. The instructor judged me to be incorrigible and undisciplined during close-order drill and inspections. Because the university required all men to complete four semesters of ROTC in order to graduate, I needed to either get the rule changed or alter my behavior. I chose the first option, and led a grassroots campaign to persuade the university chancellor to change the policy. In my fourth year the university made the courses optional.

Before I could qualify for a pharmacist's license, I had to work for a year as an intern under the supervision of a licensed pharmacist. One of my best friends in the fraternity lived in Rushville, a town of twelve hundred in the heart of Nebraska's sand hills, three hundred miles north and west of Lincoln. His father was publisher of a weekly newspaper. They knew the local pharmacist who was looking for a low-cost employee. I took the job and lived with my friend's family.

Rushville is a dusty town, and if you approach from the east or west on U.S. Highway 20 when the grass is high and green it looks like a raft at sea. Driving northwest on a steady wind, you can be tricked into seeing the hills move like rolling waves. Looking north of Rushville a ridge of pine trees marks the beginning of a large Lakota Sioux reservation across the Niobrara River and the border into South Dakota. In all other directions hills of grass roll as far as the eye can see. At night when the sky is clear and the stars are bright, you can drive a car along the back roads without headlights. And if you lie on the ground and stare up at those stars, everything suddenly seems possible as if you are possessed by magic.

The writer Mari Sandoz grew up near Rushville. She wrote *Old Jules*, the story of her Swiss immigrant father, and *Cheyenne Autumn*, the story of Red Cloud, the last Sioux rebellion and pursuit by the U.S. Army. I read both that summer and had my view of the west transformed.

Sandoz describes the two great conflicts of the west. The first was the conflict between the settlers and the natives, whose attitudes toward the land were incompatible. The settler needed title to his property. The Native Americans were still hunter-gatherers and could not survive in a world where land was subdivided and sold to private owners. The second conflict was between the rancher who wanted grazing land and the farmer who brought the plow to break and turn the sod. Disease and force resolved the first conflict with the Native Americans in favor of the settler. Though there was violence between the rancher and farmer, it was drought that gave victory to the rancher.

The settlers who survived this country were not timid souls. They risked their lives in the pursuit of their dreams, and they never knew what lay ahead of them. Some knowledge guided their choices, but it was mostly the instinct for living free and unencumbered that drove them. Of course a prairie blizzard can change a snug little sod house into a frozen cell and make a person — often a young wife left alone while her husband made a long trip to the closest town—so lonely and dejected that death was preferable to life.

So I learned early that romantic dreams of the west are best left in the movie house. *Old Jules* typified the extremes of the western personality in a single man who was brave and determined with an explorer's spirit. And that same man hated the idea of his daughter becoming a writer. He called writers "the maggots of society" in part because he regarded any activity that did not produce something practical to be a drain on the energies of those who did the real work.

On my first weekend in Rushville, I went to a fundraiser at the American Legion Club sponsored by the Catholic Church. The party featured gambling, whiskey, and Rocky Mountain oysters, a delicacy made of thinly sliced beef or sheep testicles. That evening I met two sisters from Hays Springs, a town ten miles west on Highway 20. One was my age and the other two years younger. My second weekend they invited me to go swimming at Smith Lake. We stayed at the lake until the sun set and the stars came out. My imagination had not prepared me for this moment. Suddenly the world had become a much larger and more exciting place.

The world of voting in real elections was opened to me during college. In 1964 I reached twenty-one and cast my first vote in that year's election. My host family in Rushville heavily influenced the choices of political party and candidate. The father believed in limited government, which meant he usually lined up with Republican views rather than Democratic. I heard those views every Thursday night after he had finished printing and distributing his weekly paper.

On Thursdays he came home stained with ink and lead type. He engaged us in a lively discussion of history and politics. He was well read, strongly opinionated, and understood the lessons of history better than any person I had heard until then. He preferred freedom to government interference, advocated risk instead of guarantees of security, and preached the gospel of solving your own problems rather than complaining that life had treated you unfairly.

When I returned to classes in September 1963, I felt more aware of the importance of national politics thanks to these Thursday night discussions. But nothing that year affected me more than November 22, 1963, when Lee Harvey Oswald assassinated President John Kennedy. I was in the university library when I heard the news and quickly walked down R Street to my fraternity house to watch television. I stood in the card room of our house with other men who could not believe what they were seeing. I had not known such events were possible. They happened only in history books. Now the violence described in these books was visiting our lives.

Heavily influenced by my Rushville experience, I registered as a Republican. In November 1964 I cast my vote for Barry Goldwater, the man who was described as too extreme and bloodthirsty to be trusted with the nuclear button. My first vote was for a losing cause. Johnson's landslide victory included a Democratic win in Nebraska, a nearly unheard of event. I was told that if I voted for Barry Goldwater America would get deeper into the Vietnam War. Well, that is exactly what happened.

In the summer of 1964 as the presidential campaign was heading into its convention stage, I was taking a course in physics at Creighton University in Omaha. I had rented an apartment and found part-time work. President Johnson did not appear to be in any real trouble, but he was still concerned that Goldwater was scoring political points by accusing him of being weak on Communist aggression against South Vietnam. The president was looking for a chance to display his toughness. In the first week of August, two American destroyers were attacked in North Vietnam's Gulf of Tonkin, giving Johnson what he needed. He went to Congress and requested enactment of a resolution authorizing him to use whatever force was needed to respond to this aggression. On August 7, as my family was celebrating my mother's fiftieth birthday, both houses of Congress passed the authorization. With the passage of this resolution, life as I knew it was over. I did not know it at the time but within a year I would.

Black Elk, a famous Lakota Sioux medicine man, told the poet John Neihardt: "It is in the darkness of their eyes that men get lost." This darkness is a blind spot that prevents us from seeing that which we need to know most of all. The darkness makes it more difficult for us to tell right from wrong. We sleepwalk and respond to commands we do not challenge. We are guided by blind habit. When I left college in the spring of 1965, I was very much the sleepwalker. Looking back, the darkness in my eyes covered a very large territory.

10

My first job out of college was in Onawa, Iowa, a town of three thousand on the eastern side of the high-water bank of the Missouri River. I worked in one of the town's two pharmacies. Before I could take the licensing examination, I needed six more months of practical experience and six more credit hours acceptable to the university. My job took care of the first. A correspondence course and a class at Morningside College in Sioux City, an hour's drive north of Onawa, took care of the second.

My salary at the pharmacy was one thousand dollars a month, enough to buy my first brand-new car and rent an apartment. I lived upstairs in a two-story white frame house with an open porch on two sides of the first floor and a screened-in sleeping porch on the second. Down-stairs was a small nursing home that provided care for six.

On my first night I was awakened by a phone call from a man who worked downstairs. "There's something wrong with one of the patients. Can you come look at her?" I pulled on a pair of jeans and went down. A heavyset man about my age was waiting on the front porch. He took me back to a bedroom where an old woman lay on a bed. She had been dead a while. Her skin was cold to the touch, and her eyes were open and lifeless. She wore glasses and a Bible lay on the floor, apparently the last thing she read. A rosary was on the nightstand along with a bracelet and wedding ring. I thought I saw a look of surprise on her face. Though I had received no training in emergency ser-vices, the people of Onawa would have been surprised if the pharmacist had declined to be of assistance. So I con-firmed the death and the young man called the funeral home.

I finished a five-year pharmacy program in four years but was three credit hours short of what I needed for grad-uation. The closest college was in Sioux City, Iowa, a Mis-souri River town fifty miles northwest of Onawa.

In order to get to work when the store opened at 10 A.M., I enrolled in the only class at Morningside College that began at 8 A.M. The class was on the New Testament. My first week the professor talked about U.S. involvement in a war between North and South Vietnam. He said we were dropping lots of bombs hoping to gain a quick victory. He told us the operation was called Rolling Thunder. Though he had served in and supported our military, he thought President Johnson was wrong to escalate the war and that Congress was wrong to have passed the Gulf of Tonkin Resolution. He spoke to us in clear, passionate terms, but neither his clarity nor his passion awakened me to the possibility I might end up in Vietnam. I assumed I would have to serve but likewise assumed I could avoid this war.

Since President Johnson's landslide victory in 1964, the scene in Vietnam had changed considerably. In February 1965, in retaliation for an assault on U.S. advisers in South Vietnam, Johnson had ordered a bombing attack against North Vietnam that he said would continue in support of our ally, South Vietnam. In March, U.S. Marines landed near Da Nang. In April a North Vietnam MIG — the fighter plane supplied by the Soviet Union — shot down a U.S. plane. In May an antiwar "teach-in" that was broadcast to more than one hundred U.S. campuses did not keep Congress from voting on June 8 to authorize the use of ground troops in direct combat if the government of South Vietnam requested it.

By July, 125,000 U.S. troops were in Vietnam, and the president announced a doubling of the draft call. McGeorge Bundy, Special Assistant for National Security Affairs, expressed supreme confidence when he said, "The

Vietcong are going to collapse within weeks. Not months, but weeks." And as the draft calls went out the protests escalated.

In 1965 those protests were dwarfed by the civil rights demonstrations for passage of the Voting Rights Act. In February, Malcolm X was shot in Harlem. In March a voter registration march in Selma, Alabama, turned ugly as Alabama State police used tear gas, whips, nightsticks, and dogs to turn back demonstrators as they walked on the highway to Montgomery. On the street, discontent was running ahead of political will. In spite of the Voting Rights Act becoming law on August 6, five days later riots broke out in the Watts area of South Central Los Angeles. Over a period of six days, thirty-four people were killed, most of them black. A symbol of how fear and ignorance had driven white and black America apart was that the airing of *Amos and Andy* was suspended until after the Watts riots. Until then it had been a popular show for white audiences.

As President Johnson continued to increase the number of men sent to Vietnam, the gap widened between the number of volunteers and the number needed by our armed services. Thus the number of men who had to be conscripted increased, particularly for the army and the Marine Corps. Suddenly my draft status was becoming an issue. I had registered with my local selective service board when I turned eighteen. When I enrolled in college, I was given a student deferment. Now that I was no longer a college student, I was eligible for service pending a physical and mental examination. If a letter arrived telling me to report for a physical, military service would not be far behind.

I could have avoided being drafted by claiming a physical disability because of my asthma. By then my medical file had fifteen years of diagnoses and treatments. I cannot imagine I would have had much difficulty getting letters from my doctors saying I was unfit for the military. But I never considered this an option. If Coach Bauer found me fit enough for football, I was fit enough for the U.S. armed forces. My youthful competitive urge had not changed.

But the reading for my New Testament class was bringing about a change. A transformation of my spirit seemed to occur late one summer night in Onawa as I sat in a wicker rocking chair on the screened porch of my apartment reading a book by Rudolph Bultmann. A cool breeze blew and the hum of the cicadas and the smell of cut grass calmed me and helped focus my attention on the words in the book. A hundred-watt lightbulb lit the pages. We were assigned a chapter, but I read the book from cover to cover.

Bultmann argued that the myths used by the first-century writers of scriptures needed to be demythologized and remythologized to be understood today. He had examined original documents and believed the language of the scriptures had to be understood in the context of what was being said and done in the first century A.D. Bultmann had been a chaplain to German soldiers in the Great War like his contemporary, Paul Tillich. Tillich was also on our recommended reading list, and as I watched the sunrise turn the dark front lawn into a field of green and yellow, I decided to read him next. My stomach growled with hunger, but I felt another hunger that morning, a calling that would require a change in my life's course.

I phoned my father for his advice. I told him I was thinking about changing careers. Over the line I could hear his confusion. "What did you have in mind?" he wanted to know. "I was thinking about religion," I said. "I read a book last night that really moved me. It made me wonder if I was doing the right thing." He advised me to finish what I had started, sounding as if I had made him uncomfortable.

Over the Labor Day weekend I changed jobs. I found a position at a large pharmacy in Sioux City that paid five hundred dollars more a month than I was making in Onawa. I rented a house on the south bank of the Missouri River and continued my religious readings. And I read a book for pleasure that fall: Herman Wouk's *The Caine Mutiny*.

Just after Halloween I received a letter from the draft board directing me to report the following Saturday to an address in downtown Omaha. I drove the slow route across the Missouri and then south on Highway 75 along the river through a half-dozen small sleeping communities. The road winds through hilly country that has frustrated many a farmer trying with little success to get a row crop to hold in the eroding soil. I watched the sun rise fast and red through cottonwoods and scrub oak.

Downtown Omaha was empty on that cold morning. At the draft office, a dozen men stood outside smoking on the sidewalk. I parked and joined them. The office was not yet open, so I walked up the street to an old building with a clock tower on its east side. Notices pasted on the windows warned trespassers to keep away.

Ignoring the warnings I climbed the red marble stairs and passed through an arched portal into a dark, abandoned entrance. Sixty years of accumulated soot from car exhaust and the coal-fired engines of the Union Pacific locomotives had darkened the red sandstone and pink granite. The windows in the heavy doors were caked with dirt. I rubbed my leather-gloved fist on the glass until I made a circle large enough for me to look in. Light streamed down from above into a space that could have been a church. I saw human figures in the mosaic floor but could not distinguish more. From my construction days I knew that the men who had worked on the project must have felt more pride in this accomplishment than in anything else they had done in their lives.

A flyer pasted on the door told of a small group of preservationists who were trying to save the old building. There was a plan to demolish it and erect a Hilton hotel.

It was part of an effort to attract conventions and help re-
vitalize a deteriorating downtown. The plan went ahead.
In May the heavy equipment came and tore the old post
office down.

I arrived back at the draft office just as a man in an
army uniform was ordering us upstairs into a classroom.
We found chairs and were handed multiple-choice tests
and told to complete them in silence with our number
two Ticonderoga pencils. After the test we were told to
move our chairs aside and prepare for our physical exam.
Preparation meant to strip down to your underwear. One
by one a doctor examined our puny chests with a cold
stethoscope, prodded our abdomens, and directed us to
turn our heads and cough.

I was told I would be notified of my status and should
expect a draft notice very soon thereafter. Now I had a decision to make: wait for the army to draft me or volunteer
for one of the other services. I took the faster interstate
back to Sioux City. On the way I decided I would not wait
for the army. I would apply for the navy. Herman Wouk's
tale of the sea was the decisive factor.

The following week I asked my employer for a day off
to visit the navy recruiter in Omaha. He advised me to
apply for Officer Candidate School (OCS), but because
it would take some time to get an answer, he suggested
that I go back to college for long enough to restore my deferment and then join the Fleet Reserve. I called the dean
of the pharmacy college in Lincoln to explain the situa-

tion, and he invited me to return to do research. I asked if he could suggest a subject. He told me of a team investigating the effects of digitalis on the heart tissue of rabbits. It sounded good to me, and for the next four months a hundred or more rabbits laid down their lives so I could become an officer in the world's largest and most powerful navy. My acceptance notice arrived in the spring. In October 1966 I entered the Fleet Reserve of the United States Navy. I was now a seaman recruit.

The writer and scientist Loren Eiseley's story about a catfish is a perfect metaphor for how my choice now appears to me. Eiseley liked to explore the Platte River in all seasons, and one winter as he was walking along the banks between Lincoln and Omaha he came upon a smooth, clear piece of ice and was startled to see a live whiskered catfish staring back up at him. Apparently the fish remained in the shallows too long one night and the water changed form.

Eiseley chopped an ice block around the fish, hauled it back to his car, and put it in a bucket he had in his trunk. He drove home and put the bucket in his basement planning to transfer the fish to a tank and keep him there until the spring thaw. Then Eiseley would return the catfish to the Platte. Days later he went downstairs and discovered the catfish dead on the concrete floor. When the ice thawed the catfish gambled that one good jump would take him from the prison of the bucket to the freedom of the river. He lost his bet.

11

ONE AFTERNOON IN February 1967, the day I was to report for the flight to Newport, Rhode Island, where I would begin Officer Candidate School, I packed the clothes on the list supplied by the navy and said good-bye to my mother and father. A college friend who was driving me to Omaha for my flight east picked me up in his red Chevrolet Corvette and drove to a downtown Lincoln bar, where three or four other friends met us.

The place had shuffleboard and a pool table. We drank beer, played pool, and listened to the jukebox. Someone kept playing the closest thing to a modern martial tune, Nancy Sinatra's "These Boots Are Made for

Walkin'." As the clock approached my departure time we began to sing the lyrics.

> These boots are made for walkin' and that's just
> what they'll do,
> And one of these days these boots are gonna walk
> all over you.

When it was time to go the moment did not seem special. The air was not charged with suspense. We didn't shake hands or embrace; a few slaps on the back, and I was out the door. With a clear sky and warm temperatures we put the top down for the ride to Omaha. On the way my friend's car ran out of gas. A stranger in a station wagon saved me from being absent without leave on my first day of active duty.

I arrived in Providence, Rhode Island, in the early evening and rode a steel-gray navy bus to Newport with ten or fifteen others. We checked into the Viking Hotel and I went to bed without stopping in the bar where I suspected there would be a gathering of other candidates. I woke in the morning to find the bus out front. I could tell from the size of the waiting crowd that there would not be an empty seat for the short trip to the base.

We passed through the gates of the school and pulled to a stop in front of a building named Nimitz. I dismounted warily and was ordered by a stern-sounding officer into a formation of three columns. We were given our first "forward march" and in ragged fashion proceeded to one building where our heads were shaved, another where clothing and bedding were stacked in our outstretched arms, and a third where we were assigned a room and a roommate. By coincidence and good fortune my roommate was a classmate and fraternity brother of mine at the University of Nebraska.

Although the men in our class were from many backgrounds, professions, and places in the United States, our shaved heads and identical uniforms made us remarkably alike. That, of course, is the idea in the military. Reducing free will and choice, and increasing uniformity and standardization makes it easier to create a team that works and fights as one. In many ways medals go against the spirit of the military and are in conflict with the goal of serving a higher purpose.

The weather in Newport was cold and stormy. The winds blowing off Narragansett Bay were worse than any snowstorm on the plains. Freezing water blew through my heavy peacoat, wool shirt, and long underwear. I wished Herman Wouk had included an explicit warning of this hazard in his novel. After we marched half a mile in the freezing gale to lower the American flag for the night, the sight of Old Glory for me would forevermore produce the recollection of a chill.

Each day we trained from 5 A.M. until lights out at 10 P.M. In eighteen weeks we had to learn enough of the fundamental skills of being a reserve naval officer to earn the respect of the regular officers who had spent four years at the academy or in ROTC programs. We studied essential subjects like navigation, semaphore, and damage control, but other assignments seemed more like harassment. We had to get the floor of a bathroom — or *head* as it is known in the navy — clean enough to eat off or spit shine our dress shoes till they reflected our faces. We had to learn how to render a salute, where to pin the brass military insignia, the fundamentals of marching in formation, and much other military protocol.

My earlier problems with military discipline did not vanish. In my second month I wrote a letter directly to our commanding officer protesting a change of policy. When I had enlisted I was told that if I failed to pass officer's training, I would be sent out to the fleet as an enlisted man. Now I was being told I would be discharged, reclassified 1-A, and drafted by the army.

My letter to the commanding officer of the school was naïve and arrogant. I said I was "irritated" with this "casual reversal." I argued that "when I took my oath I pledged solemnly to give life if need be in service. But they're quite willing to break the contract for reasons that seem far more petty than those that prompted us to volunteer." The commanding officer did not answer my letter. He told my company commander, who hit the ceiling. He told me I had violated proper procedures by not discussing it with him first, and I lost liberty privileges for two weekends. Nevertheless, the policy was changed, and I was promoted to assistant company commander.

The key differences between life in the military and life as a civilian are that in the military one must follow orders, respect the chain of command, and understand the nature of command. The essence of being a civilian in the United States is learning how to do the opposite, such as making free and independent choices and answering simple questions. What am I going to do this morning? What clothes will I wear? Where do I want to live? Who do I want as my friends? It is certainly true that a long list of external factors reduces our freedoms, but not like they do in the military.

In the military freedom is surrendered the moment the oath of loyalty is administered. Harsh rules enforced by a range of penalties and less due process minimize freedom. The most significant difference between the military and civilian worlds, and the most important thing I learned in eighteen weeks of officer training, was what it means to be in command, or as it is described in the navy, to "have command" or "the con."

In *The Caine Mutiny*, the men knew they could not refuse to follow orders simply because they didn't like their captain. The fact that he was strange or obsessive about strawberries was not cause for their actions. They had to prove their captain was no longer capable of command—and the burden of proof was high and difficult to achieve—or they would be committing the crime of mutiny, the penalty for which can be death.

When a military man or woman assumes responsibility

for commanding others, rule number one is this: you can delegate your authority to others in your command to perform duties you assign them, but you cannot delegate the responsibility for what happens while you have command. In civilian life excuses and lawsuits follow failure, and the game often seems to be to blame everyone but the person in charge. Civilians often think the military way is extremely unfair and harsh. It doesn't seem right to mete out severe punishment to someone who only missed a small detail.

One of the smallest and best examples of this difference is a rule that every man or woman learns who has worn the uniform of the United States of America: Failure to get the word is no excuse. In civilian life the most common and effective excuse for failure is "no one told me." In civilian life the burden shifts and the culprit will point his finger at someone else who should have told him when and where to report and how much gear to bring. In the military the burden does not shift. If debarkation time is 0700 and you show up at 0715 rubbing sleep out of your eyes saying that you didn't get the word, you will be punished. Again, it seems harsh, but the military simply could not function as a fighting force if it went by civilian rules.

Most serious of all is the burden on a commanding officer if his ship or unit fails in its mission. Then — even if he has no direct hand in the failure — he is responsible. If his ship or unit succeeds he gets credit for the success. This is the military way, and it cannot be otherwise. The

downside of this standard is the tendency for career officers and enlisted men to avoid risk, knowing the seriousness of the penalty for failure. The upside is that everyone
learns to pay attention to the smallest detail, which could
be the very thing that brings the entire operation down.
That detail may result in either a medal of commendation
or a court-martial.

We also learned how the bureaucracy of the navy
functioned. It did not take long to figure out that the
organization with the most power over your life was the
Bureau of Personnel, BUPERS. BUPERS issued your orders, and your orders told you where and when to report
for duty if and when you became a naval officer. You
would be allowed to express your preferences for duty, but
the needs of the navy would always take precedence.

In March I listened to a presentation about a possibility I had not considered when I enlisted. I heard a naval
officer tell us why we should think about applying for
underwater demolition training or UDT School. He said
it was the toughest training in all the military services. Its
graduates were known as frogmen, and they had a brave
and distinguished legacy. Frogmen were created during
the Second World War when their skills at beach reconnaissance and explosives saved the lives of many who
made amphibious assaults. UDT School would teach
scuba, demolitions, and the techniques of clandestine operations. He warned us that fewer than twenty-five percent of those who began UDT School would finish, and

that we would need mental toughness more than physical strength to survive.

The most important test of OCS — especially for land-locked men like me — came in mid-April when we were given the chance to command a seagoing vessel. It was an eighty-five-foot, twin-screw, steel-hulled boat big enough to replicate what we would experience in the real navy. In navigation class we had studied the details of Narragansett Bay and knew the depths and channels as they appeared on the charts. We had studied the rules at sea, knew how to avoid colliding with approaching ships by calculating their speed and distance, and other essential skills. But all this was theory; in practice, I did not know if I could command my own ship.

When the moment arrived I wondered if I would forget everything I had been taught. On the bridge I ordered the crew to cast off the bow and stern lines in preparation for embarkation. I ordered power first to the starboard and then port screws to maneuver the boat away from the pier. Underway I slowly increased speed as we passed the few boats that were in the water this early in spring. It wasn't a pretty departure, and I took longer than a more experienced hand but I had succeeded.

I negotiated the channel and was soon heading out into open water. I could feel the bow of the ship as it cut through the waves and the power of the engines ready to take me where I directed them to go. The eastern horizon of the Atlantic was dark and foreboding. The ocean beckoned to be explored as if I were the first to be on her back. The rocking motion and the salty air were intoxicating. The anticipation of failure had been the same as I felt when I first went on the football practice field. However, unlike football, the sensation of command at sea was more exhilarating than I had imagined it would be when I read Wouk's *Caine*. When we pulled back into port and disembarked, I never felt more proud or confident in my life

Thus, it was a very difficult decision to choose to apply for underwater demolition training instead of accepting an assignment to the fleet as a junior officer. But UDT would still give me the chance to command smaller boats and to learn more rigorous skills. It seemed too exciting to pass up if I could get accepted. So, I applied, passed the physical, and was told by BUPERS I could report to the West Coast school in Coronado, California. It was a turning point with more dire consequences than I imagined.

My roommate from Nebraska had also decided to take the examination and had also been given the chance to sign up for UDT. We both said yes, but the navy had other ideas for him. Somehow Admiral Hyman Rickover, father of the nuclear submarine program, had discovered that my roommate had graduated with high honors from engineering school. That led to an interview in the admiral's Washington, D.C., office, which led him away from UDT into subs. I would be going to Coronado on my own.

In May as the glory of spring arrived in Newport and

just before I was awarded my ensign bars, I went to the Jazz Festival along with many soon-to-be junior naval officers. The music was fabulous and the crowd young and enthusiastic. I felt right at home. Wandering about in my naval uniform I was hoping to meet the love of my life. Then Joan Baez spoke of her opposition to the war in Vietnam. She urged the men in the audience to say no to the war and gave this advice to the women, "Say yes to the boys who say no."

The audience cheered wildly. Afterward I thought I saw a changed look on the faces of people I passed. I imagined I saw anger, disrespect, and disgust. But that night after the concert I was very happy to discover that the women at the bar in the Viking Hotel were not following Joan Baez's advice.

I could not fail to notice that popular sentiment was beginning to turn against the war. The civil rights leader and Nobel laureate Martin Luther King had spoken out in opposition. In March there had been protests after the United States rejected Ho Chi Minh's offer to begin peace talks if bombing was halted and all U.S. troops were withdrawn. Rather than pulling back, we had escalated our effort. The number of men being sent to Vietnam grew daily, and reports of enemy setbacks became more frequent. As the war grew, so did the protests. In April a demonstration in New York attracted over one hundred thousand people, the largest crowd to date.

But I wasn't going to New York; I was going to Nebraska where antiwar protests were unlikely and then on to Coronado where they were nonexistent. I was no longer the graduate pharmacist I had been a year earlier. I was now a United States naval officer and felt a sense of serving something large and good: our nation's defense, the protection of home, tradition, history, stories of bravery and glory. I felt a part of it all.

After ten days' leave I flew to San Diego and caught the ferry that was the fastest way across the bay to Coronado Island. The smell of salty air and the bright, warm sun greeted me like a long-lost friend. The ferry carried me south across the harbor's narrow neck. To the west was the Pacific Ocean and east was Coronado Bay. I recognized the silhouettes of ships I had memorized at OCS: aircraft carriers, cruisers, destroyers, destroyer escorts, transport ships, landing craft, and mine sweepers.

Coronado felt like Lincoln with an ocean, sand, palm trees, and sunshine 365 days a year. On the island were two navy installations: an air station and the amphibious base that would be my home for the next two years. I was assigned an apartment on the second floor of the officers' quarters. From my balcony I looked west across a strand of beach that ran from San Diego in the north to Imperial Beach and Tijuana, Mexico, in the south and separated Coronado Bay from the Pacific Ocean. I dumped my gear, ate a quick meal at the officers club, and returned to the balcony where I watched my first sunset over the ocean. I thought the navy had sent me to paradise.

The base was a collection of single-story office buildings for two commands: the boat command that operated the vessels used for amphibious assaults and the training command for UDT. To support these commands, there were maintenance shops, personnel offices, classrooms, a movie theater with a rounded roof, a small grocery store, and separate dining facilities for officers and enlisted men. Across the highway on the strand of beach were the long, low buildings where men were sent when they had finished training and joined UDT Eleven, Twelve, or Thirteen.

In the morning I reported for duty to the Naval Special Warfare Group, Pacific, where I learned that UDT class did not begin until the first week of September. Over the next fourteen weeks I crammed in a two-week class in amphibious tactics, a two-day pistol course that was supposed to produce expert marksmen but achieved far less in my case, and a two-day rifle course that yielded the same result. I ran on the beach and swam in the ocean every morning and in the evening explored the nightlife of San Diego. I found an ad for a four-year-old red Volkswagen bus that I bought for a few hundred dollars. With this I widened my circle of exploration east and north into the coastal mountains and across into the Sonoran Desert.

In *War and Peace*, Leo Tolstoy, who served with the Cossacks, observed that we human beings struggle with the idea of leisure time because it makes us feel guilty when we are doing "nothing." But, he said, there is one place where enforced idleness is institutionalized: the military. There, he said, you are expected to spend your time doing nothing. That certainly described my existence in the summer of 1967.

My hardest task in the morning after a run, a swim, and breakfast was reading the *San Diego Union*, trying to understand what was going on in the world. In June I read about the Six Day War in Israel, China's detonation of a hydrogen bomb, and race riots across the country that killed seventy-seven people in 125 cities. After this exertion I would drive to some place I wanted to see: Los Angeles, San Francisco, Tijuana, the mountains, the desert, or the ocean. Even when classes were being held I had large blocks of time for standing around and contemplating life or listening to others complain about some trivial inconvenience.

As the summer wound down I was given an unexpected gift: the approach of Labor Day without asthma symptoms. Apparently the absence of the prairie grasses was all I needed to breathe normally. My UDT classes began on the Friday afternoon after my twenty-fourth birthday. We were issued a pair of black leather combat boots, three pairs of green fatigue pants with matching shirts, one soft green hat, one hard fiber helmet liner, two pairs of khaki swimming trunks, one pair of coral booties, one snorkel, and one face mask. After we got our gear we were told to form columns of seven on the street between the UDT offices and the bay.

The senior officer in our class stood in front of a formation of about twenty-five columns, each headed by an officer with six enlisted men behind him. We waited at parade rest until a dark-skinned chief petty officer with what looked like coral poisoning on his legs walked out from behind the training offices. He wore the frogman uniform of khaki shorts with a blue and gold T-shirt. He swaggered over to the senior officer of our class and, rather than giving a smart salute, he lowered his head to the right and drew his right hand up lazily as if to say, You have not yet earned my full respect. Then he spat a stream of tobacco juice on the ground close to the officer's shoes.

"My name is Olivera," he said, "and you are the sorriest group of bananas I have ever seen." He then proceeded to give us a simple set of instructions. We could quit anytime we wanted, now or later. We simply had to go to the back of the training compound, rap our helmet on the door, and shout the two words, "I qweeet." He said he hoped and expected that more than half of us would say those magic words before we completed the course. He said our most important command was "Drop!" When we heard this command we were to drop to the ground and start doing push-ups. We could not stop or stand up until we heard the command, "Recover!" And when we recovered we were to shout, "Hoo Yah!" followed by the name of the person who had ordered us to drop.

Each seven-man column became a boat crew that was expected to carry or paddle a small inflatable rubber boat

(IBS) everywhere we went for the next eighteen weeks. Our training would begin on this same street at 6 A.M. Monday. Olivera told us to be there in formation with our boots spit-shined, our uniforms starched, our insignia sewn on our collars or shirtsleeves, and our names stenciled in black over our left shirt pockets. When our senior officer protested that this would be impossible because the laundry services were closed, Olivera took a step closer, spit on the ground, and said, "I expect you bananas to be standing tall at 0600 with everything done as I have asked. That means every one of you. If even one man is not ready, I'll march all of you into the bay. Dismissed."

Over the weekend we found a way to do what he told us. In my first weekend I learned that one of the sacrosanct boundaries I had learned in Newport—that it was taboo for officers and enlisted men to fraternize—was not sacrosanct in the teams. We still respected the chain of command. Enlisted men called us "sir," and we called them by their last names. Those in command were still held accountable, but in practice we worked as a team. We simply depended on each other too much for officers and enlisted men not to become friends.

Other boundaries remained. There was one between the rest of the navy and us. We called them the "black shoe Navy" and they called us "squids." There was a boundary between those officers and enlisted men who did not expect to make the navy a career and the "lifers" who did, and one between reserve officers and regular officers, the reserve officers being lower in the social hierarchy.

All boundaries disappeared as we scrambled to do what Olivera had ordered us to do. We organized ourselves into teams. We found self-employed contractors who were willing to do the weekend of washing, ironing, printing, and sewing that we needed. Most important, we made certain that no man failed. Had each of us gone off on our own we most certainly would not have gotten the job done. Working together we managed with time to spare.

On Monday our shirts were stenciled with our names, our insignia were sewn in their proper places, our pants were hemmed, our entire uniforms including our hats were starched, and our boots were spit-shined and gleaming. We arrived early and stood tall in the dark waiting for Olivera to appear. We felt proud and were ready to begin. Olivera appeared on schedule. He gave our senior officer another half-hearted salute and inspected our ranks with a quick glance left and right. Then he told our senior officer to bring the men to attention, ordered them to execute an about-face and a forward march. Following these orders would put us into the cold, black water. Our senior officer objected, "But, Olivera, we did everything you told us to do." Olivera answered, "Mister, it's time for a little suffering. To succeed in this program you must be willing to die before you can go to heaven." We began our day soaking wet.

Our class was separated into two sections of about 120 each: alpha and bravo. At the beginning there were about twelve boat crews of one officer and six enlisted men. The sections trained together for the first six weeks, were separated for eight, and brought back together for the final four. Our daily schedule began with calisthenics on an open field near the training offices. Then we marched on the double across the highway to the beach, each boat crew carrying its IBS on its heads. Lowering our boats, we ran two miles to the chain-link fence at the air station past the Hotel del Coronado and the two miles back. We wore combat boots, and whether high tide or low, we were expected to finish in thirty minutes.

Those who could not keep up were selected by the instructors for the "goon squad" and were subjected to physical abuse, like having to do push-ups in the surf zone or run the course a second time. Knowing that life was going to get a lot more difficult was an incentive for the trainees to perform at the expected level. It was also an incentive for trainees to quit, which they began to do in our first week.

After the run we negotiated an obstacle course on the beach side of the base. This course also took a terrible toll on trainees, especially those who had been in the goon squad during the run. It was common for trainees to be run repeatedly through the course until their bodies gave them little choice but to hang it up and quit. Those who survived were marched on the double back across the highway to the pool. In the pool we swam with face masks and snorkels but without fins. We were timed and daily increased our distance until we were circling the pool for a mile.

During the first four weeks each boat crew learned how to handle its IBS as a team. The officer served as coxswain except on long distances, when most of us rotated with our enlisted men, not only to give them a break but also to increase the performance of the crew. We learned how to hold the wooden paddles to minimize noise and reflection. We learned how to navigate through heavy surf. We learned how to secure our gear. In short order, the IBS became a physical extension of our bodies and part of everything we did.

Week five was called Hell Week because we trained nonstop, with little or no sleep. Most casualties—men who simply could not go on—occurred before or during that week. Instructors paid closest attention to those men struggling with the threshold requirements: doing ten pull-ups at the beginning of calisthenics, completing the four-mile run in thirty minutes, finishing the obstacle course, and completing the swim in the allotted time. Other failures that could result in extra running, swimming, or push-ups included falling asleep in class, forgetting to attach some required piece of equipment to the IBS, or failing to say "Hoo yah!" when recovering from push-ups. Those men who didn't make it were certainly traumatized by the defeat. But stress can also bring out the best and that was what the instructors were looking for.

I will never forget one enlisted man in our class named Thompson who rose to the challenge with great dignity. He must have been forty pounds overweight. He failed all the threshold tests. He couldn't do ten pull-ups and was kept at the bar by shouting instructors who heaped insult upon insult on him. He was always in the goon squad during the run and was ordered to do head-stands in the surf zone, run wind sprints in shallow water, and do push-ups until all his strength was gone. On the obstacle course he could not pull himself over a twenty-foot wooden wall and was once kept there until dark while two instructors screamed themselves hoarse trying to get him to quit. In the pool his large legs and torso made keeping up impossible. He got better in swimming when we were issued swim fins in our sixth week. Thompson went from being one of the slowest swimmers to one of the fastest, but he continued to suffer on runs and the obstacle course.

Hell Week was a series of competitions between boat crews. Points were awarded for first, second, and third places. According to a rumor that our instructors would neither confirm nor deny, the winner of the week's competition would be excused from the week's final event: an all night ten-mile ocean race in our boats down the coast to Tijuana and back.

My boat crew was ahead on points at the end of the week. Even if we lost the next-to-last event before we set off on the ten-mile IBS trip, our lead was big enough to win. That event was a quarter-mile foot race from the calisthenics field to our boats. Before the race we were told to lie down on our backs and rest a few minutes without going to sleep. Anyone caught sleeping was ordered to jump in the bay and make the trip to Tijuana soaking wet. The event was held in the darkness after sunset, and after six sleepless days it was impossible to stay awake. Soon all of us had visited the water. At the starting line we were told this was to be a Le Mans racing start: each boat crew would run down to the finish line to launch its boat. The boats were in a row in front of the training headquarters.

At the sound of the whistle the run began. When we neared our boat, we saw an oval shadow lying on the ground. While the other crews were heading for water, we stood and stared at a sad and deflated boat. Worse, the hand pump, which was supposed to be attached to the gunnels, was missing. A missing pump meant lost points, which in turn meant we could not possibly win the grand prize. Olivera asked me what I intended to do. I said I would find the pump, repair the damage, and join the others who were now long gone. He spat once on the ground and said, "No, I think you bananas should secure for the night. You won that right."

We whooped and laughed for joy like children who had received the most special gift we could ever have imagined. I saluted and said, "Thank you, Olivera." We showered and went to our barracks to sleep and dream the dreams of champions.

The first five weeks of training reduced our ranks by a third. During week six we were issued swim fins and began learning how to do a beach reconnaissance from the ocean. We still did calisthenics and a run to start the day, but the amount of abuse we took dropped sharply. At the same time our respect for and knowledge of the ocean rose dramatically. We learned it was unpredictable and more dangerous than it looked. A cold stream, the Japanese current, dropped water temperatures to the high fifties as early as October. Even in our wet suits an hour of exposure produced some very chilled young men. Often a man could not walk when he emerged from the icy water after a thousand-meter beach reconnaissance.

After week six I spent four weeks on scuba and four weeks on demolition. Scuba training in Coronado was a straightforward and deadly serious study of navy diving charts, the behavior of gases under pressure, and the mechanics of the device that regulates the flow of compressed air from a pair of ninety-cubic-foot tanks down a pair of rubber hoses into a mouthpiece. We divided our time between the classroom and the swimming pool, becoming familiar with the gear and our limits before we went to the ocean. Scuba would be more for recreation than for military operations, where we used swim fins, face masks, and snorkels.

On San Clemente Island, where goats, seals, and birds ruled, we learned how close death lurked. We were training to use plastic explosives, detonation cords, and fuse lighters to destroy both underwater and aboveground obstacles. We learned to tell a high- from a low-order explosion, how to calculate the size and shape of a charge needed to destroy various objects, and how to build our own explosives if government-issued materials were unavailable.

We were taught to organize our missions using the army's five-paragraph patrol order. This standard order helps the person in charge organize the operation and specify the mission's objective, describe in detail the terrain to be crossed, calculate the kind of gear needed, and determine the means of entry, the route to the objective, and the means of extraction and retreat. Communication call signs, fire support available, and other vital information are all part of a five-paragraph order.

One exercise entailed tying canvas satchels of plastic explosives to underwater concrete obstacles like those the Japanese had built in World War II. Our trainers thought these obstacles might be used again in some future conflict. A row of fifteen or twenty concrete pyramids topped with two protruding pipes was located just outside the surf zone. The obstacles were fifteen to twenty feet underwater, so the divers could see their target from the surface. Working in teams of two, the first swimmer in snorkel gear dove with the canvas bag of explosives, placed the strap of the bag over the pipes, and began fastening the bag to the concrete. When he could no longer hold his breath, he headed for the surface. The second swimmer started down when he saw his swim buddy coming up. After the bag was tied, an instructor dove down to inspect for mistakes. To complete this exercise satisfactorily, we had to tie off five obstacles.

During our first week on San Clemente, stormy seas churned the water and sand into a murky darkness. A swimmer at the surface could no longer see an obstacle on the bottom. To reduce the danger, the instructors' solution was to tie a plastic bottle to one end of a nylon line and the other end to the obstacle. A swim pair could find the obstacle by swimming out to the floating bottle and following the line down. The only problem was that the swimmer on the surface could not see the swimmer on the bottom.

We were two days behind schedule so our instructors had us working without a safety break at lunch. The safety break enables the instructors to check that all dive teams are accounted for. During the noon hour, dive teams only had time to grab a sandwich and run back to tie another obstacle. Just after lunch my swim partner and I were heading into the water when we heard a cry from the nearest swim pair, "There's someone floating on our line! It looks like Greco!" My partner, Baker, and I swam out to help. When we arrived Greco was floating just below the surface of the water with the nylon line wound around his right arm.

He had stayed at the bottom too long. Rising to the surface he probably had been rotating his arms, as is usual when ascending in water where visibility is poor. This caused the line to wrap round his right arm so that the line held him just short of the surface. He must have grabbed his swimming partner, McCoy, by the legs and pulled him down. He did not release him until both were unconscious. When death brought release, McCoy sank to the bottom. The plastic float gave Greco's body just enough buoyancy to keep it near the surface.

When Baker and I arrived, the other swim pair was frantically trying to untie Greco, thinking the line was still keeping him underwater. The opposite was the case. When we loosened the line, Greco's body sank like a rock and disappeared into darkness.

Baker, one of the strongest swimmers in the class, immediately dove for Greco. When he surfaced with the body he was gasping and sputtering with fear. "I swam right into his face. Look at his face. Look at it." Greco's face mask was still in place. His eyes were open and the glass was filled with green mucus.

We swam Greco's body to shore. One of the instructors tried to revive him with mouth to mouth but the exercise made him vomit and did nothing for Greco. He was long gone. He must have been on the line for at least half an hour. Then someone asked, "Where's McCoy?" An electronics technician who had recently been granted a substantial reenlistment bonus, McCoy was one of the smartest men in our class. Divers began searching for McCoy's body from a motorized Boston Whaler at the spot where Greco was found while we searched on shore. We hoped he had made the mistake of abandoning Greco. He would face a court-martial, but at least he would be alive. It was not to be. We heard a shout from the Whaler. "We've found him. We're bringing him up."

McCoy was dead. We gathered in a circle around the two bodies. The sky was gray and we shivered as the wind blew against our wet skin. The tragedy was a reminder of what could happen to any of us. The lead instructor then made the mistake of telling us to get back to work. I told him that we needed a break to absorb the deaths of our friends. The instructor yielded.

We returned to Coronado for the final four weeks of instruction. In this phase we learned advanced procedures for getting to our military destinations. One of these was exiting and entering a submerged moving submarine. Inside the sub we were told to climb up a steel ladder into a forward-locking chamber where we listened to the clanging of the hatch below being sealed, and a voice over a tinny-sounding loudspeaker told us what to do. We turned a valve to let the air escape, turned another to fill the chamber with water, and then turned the water valve off when it reached our chin. Twin ninety-cubic-foot scuba tanks were our source of air as the chamber filled. When the pressure of the water in the chamber equalized with the pressure outside, the hatch opened easily, allowing us to exit the submarine.

A more common method of dropping and picking up UDT swimmers was with a diesel-engine boat that had a top speed of twenty to twenty-five knots. An IBS would be lashed to the outside of the boat. The drop part was easiest. Swimmers would quickly enter the rubber boat single file and drop off the side with their fins, face mask, and snorkel. Pickup went in reverse. As the boat approached, the pickup man stood in the IBS holding out a ring-shaped hose to a line of swimmers. The swimmer would kick with his fins just before his arm hit the rubber ring, allowing the pickup man to pull him out of the water and into the IBS.

A considerable number of experiments were tried to improve the efficiency of drops and pickups. Efficiency and added risk were constantly at odds. A turboprop boat with a maximum speed of fifty knots delivered swimmers efficiently, but it could also knock a man unconscious. A metal cable attached to a helium-filled balloon, which was snagged by a fixed wing airplane, made for a terrific James Bond type of exit, but if the cable broke, the man picked up would exit life.

Rappelling is the most efficient and least risky means of descending from a helicopter onto land, or down the face of a building, or a steep natural incline. The rappel works by friction, in our case, the friction of a line against a metal link that slows the speed of fall.

In training we used two lines. A short line fastened around our thighs and waist formed a harness. The second and a longer line was the descent line. It was doubled for safety and anchored solidly at the point of departure.

An oval metal link was then snapped into the harness and attached to the descent line. A single turn of this line through the link was all that was needed to create the friction that became the difference between life and serious injury. To start the rappel we held the ascending part of the double line with our left hand and the descending part of the line with our right. We then looked over our left shoulder down to where we wanted to go. We could stop the rappel by bringing the descent line behind our backs. This was known as applying the brake. The brake could also be applied partially in order to slow the descent.

Safety took us first to the classroom, where an instructor demonstrated the physics of the rappel. Then we went into the obstacle course where we rappelled twenty feet into sawdust. Finally, we drove to a hydroelectric dam. There we anchored the double line to a steel handrail at the top of the 150-foot face. An instructor demonstrated the technique. He connected the line through the snap link, applied the brake with his right hand, and stepped over the handrail while facing the dam. Then he let go of the rail and jumped backward with his feet spread as wide as his shoulders. The line tightened and he came gracefully to a stop, his legs braced on the concrete partway down the dam. He repeated his descent several times, letting out more and more line each time. Finally he stood at the bottom, unhooked the line from the link, and told the first student to follow him.

A second instructor then helped the line of anxious trainees hook up and jump. When my turn came I was not the least bit afraid. I understood the science and had seen it work with my own eyes. I was quite surprised when I hooked up the line to the link, applied the brake, and stepped over the handrail that my mind could not persuade my left hand to let go. I don't know how long I would have stood motionless were it not for the instructor's sharp blow to my knuckles. Reflex did what thought could not.

Letting go is never easy. We like to hold on to known safety even when our minds are telling us to do otherwise. This was a powerful lesson; another thing learned in the navy I would apply all the days of my life.

By the end of training I was twenty pounds heavier and felt more physically capable than at any time in my life. I was ready for the teams. But during those eighteen weeks my future had changed even more than my body had. In November after we returned from San Clemente, President Johnson made a trip to San Diego, and even there he met war protesters. Some weeks before there had been a 150,000-person demonstration at the Pentagon, resulting in almost seven hundred arrests; it was so disturbing to the Johnson Administration, the director of selective service announced that students arrested in antiwar demonstrations would lose their draft deferments.

The protests did not stop President Johnson from ramping up the U.S. commitment in Vietnam. The increased demand for troops changed the course of events for those of us who completed UDT training after 1967. Before the escalation we expected to be assigned to one of three UDT teams in Coronado. But another option surfaced because of the war—direct recruitment into SEAL Team One.

In the early 1960s President Kennedy, because of his naval career in the Second World War, approved a navy unit equivalent to the Army's Special Forces. The unit would use the name SEAL, an acronym combining the three methods of their insertion into combat areas: sea, air, and land. The unit was formed of men from the underwater demolition teams and was kept largely secret until a 1967 *Reader's Digest* article appeared called "Warriors with Green Faces."

When our training was complete I was among twelve asked to volunteer for SEAL Team One. I would be given advanced training in the tactics of small units and would likely attend both Army Airborne and Ranger Schools before being assigned to a SEAL Team One platoon headed for Vietnam. Our instructors told us we could refuse the assignment. If we did, we would not be assigned to one of the UDT teams, but would be sent to a ship at sea, thus wasting all the training we had just endured.

On Monday morning the new "volunteers" gathered in a meeting room followed by a crowd of SEALs, all of us waiting for the arrival of the team's commanding officer, Captain Anderson. When he walked to the front we all came to attention. He told us to stand at ease and explained what SEAL Team One was and told us we had the right to refuse. All we had to do was stand to indicate that our answer was no. One man stood. It was Thompson, who had suffered more with good humor than any of us had in order to become a frogman. The instant he stood he was ushered from the room, and I never saw him again. His act was the bravest I had ever witnessed.

12

I HAD TWO WEEKS OF LIBERTY after graduating from training but did not make it home December 2 for my sister Jessie's wedding to Dean Rasmussen. By the time I got there, Nebraska was enjoying the coldest winter I had ever experienced. The marriage of my younger sister inspired me to spend several days and nights at my parents' lakeside cabin with a woman I had dated in college. We skated and sailed an iceboat until we were completely frozen and then sat by the fire talking about the possibility of a future together. The talks ended inconclusively.

In January I returned to Coronado and began my training for SEAL Team One with a six-week course on small arms and small unit tactics. After that I would take courses at the Army's Airborne and Ranger Schools at Fort

Benning, Georgia. I was in a new and different phase of my training. Before I had been taught how to blow things up. Now I was being taught how to kill. There was euphemism and other make-believe terminology to keep us from facing this truth, but occasionally that truth would appear in its full, unvarnished reality.

Vietnam was becoming a military and political quagmire. By the close of 1967, American casualties reached nearly a thousand a month. When the Communists launched the Tet Offensive on January 30, more than half a million American troops were on the ground in the country. The Tet battles, which lasted three weeks, resulted in forty thousand enemy deaths and were a decisive military victory for the South Vietnamese. But while the North and their Communist allies in the South failed on the battlefield, they succeeded with public opinion in the United States.

The aggressive ability of our enemy surprised many Americans who had supported the war. They were eloquently represented by Walter Cronkite, whose words "something is terribly wrong here" resonated throughout the United States. The constant assurances of our military and political leaders that we were winning the war did not square with the observations of those on the ground in Vietnam.

The Tet Offensive was still going on while I was in the SEAL team's six-week course. Our instructor was Chief Stone, a former sergeant in the army who had served in

Korea and joined the navy when he decided to return to military life. He was just what the navy thought their new special operations unit needed. To the navy he was a chief petty officer, but he looked and acted like he was still training soldiers in an infantry platoon. He organized the class by the book, teaching us such things as which foot to fire on when we advanced, how to execute small unit fire and maneuver, how to set an ambush with claymore mines, and how to avoid aiming an assault rifle high at night. We learned to assemble, disassemble, and fire the AR-15 or M-16 assault rifles and the M-60 automatic rifle. We practiced the M-79 grenade launcher, the light anti-tank weapon or LAW, and the hand-thrown fragmentation grenade.

We learned to distinguish between the smaller .556 caliber rounds fired by the M-16 from the larger .762 NATO round fired by the M-60. We learned the difference between deadly "aimed fire" and firing a rifle for the effect of the noise. We were shown how to use nonstandard weapons like the carbine, the shotgun, the silenced 9-mm pistol, and the AK-47, a Soviet and Chinese assault rifle with a wooden stock that was popular with U.S. soldiers in Vietnam. We learned how to call in artillery and how to use Willy Peter rounds to mark the target. We learned basic first aid and began developing a list of standard operating procedures for Vietnam.

We practiced these procedures while patrolling and maneuvering in both day and night situations. Usually we operated in seven-man groups, learned to recognize hand signals so we could remain silent and eventually to read the person in front and behind us without intentional signals. We learned how to secure and inspect small buildings and why injured men could jeopardize the lives of an entire seven-man squad, since it took two men to carry one out, leaving too few to return fire during a withdrawal. We learned how and when to call in medevac helicopters and gunships, though we were told not to expect them always to be available. We practiced sitting for long periods of time without falling asleep and were warned to avoid amphetamines, since they often produced hallucinations. We learned how time and silence enabled us to notice what we had previously missed.

We learned more of the orienteering we had been taught in UDT. Orienteering is the technique of reading a topographical map, which uses grid lines to illustrate the varying elevations of the terrain. Each grid line represents a different elevation above sea level. A topographical map can be very confusing at first. But soon the curving lines begin to resemble hills, valleys, plateaus, gradual slopes, steep ravines, and other land formations. Navigating through unknown terrain becomes easier and you are less likely to get lost.

Under the right circumstances getting lost can be a good experience. Knowing that you are lost makes you humble and forces you to discover things about yourself. Out in the field it is the rare person who doesn't at least momentarily ask, "Where am I?" Sometimes the answer comes quickly. Sometimes not. Sometimes you are certain you know where you are only to discover miles and hours later that you were wrong. And sometimes you misread a land feature and get in trouble as a result.

That happened to me in an orienteering exercise during underwater demolition training. We were on a night compass course in the open hills and orchards that in 1967 were part of the San Diego landscape. The boat crews were competing. At about 3 A.M. our crew was ahead after three of the four legs. We knew the end of the leg was clearly marked by the trucks that would take us back to Coronado. We could not go wrong.

My crew and I avoided detection by reading our map under a plastic poncho with a red flashlight. Seven heads tried to interpret the curving lines that separated us from our goal. The most prominent feature on the map was a five-thousand-meter lake. We simply had to choose whether to walk down the left or the right side of the lake. The shorter distance was down the left side, but there the grid lines were stacked tight, right to the water's edge, meaning that the land was very steep, perhaps a sheer cliff. The right side of the lake was a much longer distance but the spacing of the grid lines was wide, indicating a level, easy walk. Most of the crew favored the safe bet, but I was convinced we would find a path on the left side that would take us quickly to the trucks.

Unfortunately we went with my instincts. Not only did

the cliff go right to the water's edge but the water was deep and cold. The best we could do was to make our way slowly along the face of the cliff. Every so often I would reassure my men with the words "there must be a path just a little ways farther; there must be a path." The sun was up and all the other crews were waiting for us in the trucks when we finally finished. And for years after, whenever I saw or talked to one of my crew, the phrase "there must be a path" was a guaranteed laugh line.

SEAL team orienteering was more realistic. We were training for military operations in terrain that resembled what we expected when we deployed. The place was east of the San Gabriel Mountains near the southern shore of the Salton Sea. The town closest to our camp was Niland, a community that existed to serve the needs of farmers in the Imperial Valley to the south. The irrigation canals were large enough to carry the river patrol boats that we would use in Vietnam.

At the end of the six weeks Lieutenant Arch Woodard, our senior officer, led us in the preparation of a critique of Chief Stone's course. We wrote a detailed description of improvements we thought were needed and put the report in a plastic folder along with an introductory letter to Chief Stone. We were granted a meeting. Chief Stone learned the reason for the meeting as we passed our report across his desk. In a single continuous motion and without breaking eye contact with us he threw our pages into a trash basket. Then he said in a friendly, respectful tone free of condescension, "That was an excellent report, Mr. Woodard. Was there anything else?" With that our meeting was over.

Our training was just beginning. In March I began Airborne and Ranger Schools at Fort Benning, Georgia. While I was there Minnesota Senator Eugene McCarthy, running against President Johnson as an antiwar candidate for the Democratic nomination for president, got forty-two percent of the vote in the New Hampshire primary. This surprise victory set the stage for president Johnson's remarkable and unexpected televised address on March 31. He announced that he would not be a candidate for a second full term in office. He promised to begin more serious negotiations with North Vietnam to end the war as quickly as possible. Though we did not know it at the time, this decision ended any hope that South Vietnam would survive as an independent country.

I was relieved that the war would be ending before I was ready to go. I thought that the reason for our involvement — the freedom and self-determination of the South Vietnamese — could not have been so important after all if we were willing to negotiate it away to North Vietnam. For this had to be the outcome of any negotiated settlement. Following their successful war with France, the Communists had yielded to Russian and Chinese pressure in Geneva to allow for the creation of two countries divided at the seventeenth parallel. They had begun a second war against South Vietnam in order to extend their political control over the entire Indochinese peninsula. In my mind the question of who would win this war was resolved on March 31, 1968. It was now only a question of time.

If President Johnson had faced the voters of Georgia in 1968 he probably would not have been forced out of the race. There are few places where the uniform of our military is more respected or where military personnel are made to feel so welcome. I came to know and love the red clay and pine tree–covered hills of Georgia better than any place I had ever been.

The objective of Airborne School is to train young men to do a very unnatural thing: to jump out the door of a perfectly good airplane. We would earn our jump wings after we successfully completed five static line jumps from a C-118 twin-engine aircraft using a T-10 parachute. The jumps were all in daylight, though we joked that it seemed like night, since so many of us closed our eyes as we stood in the door and jumped.

The basic physics of the parachute are simple: a fabric canopy fills with air and slows the descent of a falling object enough so that the object is not badly damaged when gravity brings it down to earth. Unlike most of today's civilian parachutists, we did not pull a rip cord to open the chute. That was accomplished by a static line attached to the parachute and connected by a snap link to another line that was anchored fore and aft to the bulkhead of the plane. When the plane approached the drop zone, a yellow light told the jump master to prepare his "stick" of jumpers by giving them two commands: "Stand up!" and "Hook up!" Then the door was opened and one by one we shuffled forward and waited for the jump master's command to jump.

We were supposed to jump out with both feet together in front of us, our hands to our sides, holding either end of our reserve parachute, and our heads tucked down. This position kept the body from tumbling when hit by the on-rushing air. We were supposed to count, "One thousand, two thousand, three thousand," before looking up to see if our canopy had opened properly. If it had not, we were trained in emergency procedures that would deploy our reserve chute.

There was one contingency plan. When the main chute became entangled in the plane's tail, the runway was foamed and the plane would land. Just before we boarded for our first jump we were advised that the best position for survival in this situation was a tight tuck. Presumably, the function of the foam was to prevent spectators from witnessing the jumper's body being crushed on the runway's surface.

If the chute opened normally, as was the case nine times out of ten, then you had a minute or two to enjoy the ride. With a T-10 parachute the risk of getting hurt during the landing was quite high. Even if the wind was calm, the rapid descent could lead to trouble if you did not execute a proper parachute landing fall: feet tightly together, head tucked, and a safe roll in the direction of the fall. If the wind was blowing, the risk of injury rose; the only way to control the T-10's direction was to grab the two canvas risers that connected the harness to the canopy in the direction you wanted to go, and pull them to your chest. The maneuver — difficult to hold for very long — produced uncertain results.

As earth approached, we looked for smoke rising from flares that showed where we were supposed to land and the direction of the wind. Some of us tried steering our chutes by pulling two risers to slip toward the smoke. But this technique did not work with wind velocities over ten to fifteen knots, and with the metal helmets given jump school students in 1967, the chances of a serious head injury increased with the speed of the wind at ground level.

I managed to complete five successful jumps and received my wings in a closing ceremony that contained a brief but memorable military speech. The school's commanding officer said in a mock-serious tone that we were no longer the "sorry legs" that we had been before we earned our wings. "What are you?" he shouted. "Airborne!" we answered in one voice. "What are you?" he challenged again. "Airborne!"

The pride the group felt at that moment was palpable. I felt it, too. But not everything I saw at Airborne School made me feel proud. Airborne was supposed to be an elite program that accepted only the most highly qualified soldiers. My class contained a large number of poorly motivated, poorly trained soldiers, most of whom were also poor and black. Many of them did not complete the course and were sent, I suspected, to combat units in Vietnam. Afterward I would always believe that Vietnam was a poor man's war, no matter what was said to the contrary.

Twenty-four years later I returned to Georgia, as a candidate for the Democratic nomination for president. I spoke to students at Spelman College about what I had seen here in 1968. On stage with me was a small group of men and women who were supporting my candidacy, though it was clear that I could not possibly win. One of them was a black man about my age who introduced himself as one of my drill sergeants during Airborne School. He told me the large number of black soldiers I had seen were part of a program initiated by Secretary of Defense McNamara. The program authorized the army to lower its standards in order to meet its induction targets. This plan symbolized the tragic paradox of Lyndon Johnson's presidency. While fighting a war for civil rights and against poverty at home, he was sending minorities and the sons of poor families to die in Vietnam. On April 4, the week we were given our jump wings, Martin Luther King was shot and killed in Memphis. His death set off another round of violence in most of America's largest cities.

I had a long weekend between the end of my Airborne training and the beginning of Ranger School. I rented a car and drove to Fort Lauderdale to meet my father who had flown south on business. There were still a few hours of sunlight left when I pulled out of Columbus, Georgia, and headed for Fort Lauderdale. Driving through the star-filled night I listened to music and religious broadcasts on my AM radio and was comforted by the sight and smell of the red clay and pine trees that sped by my windows.

I arrived an hour before the sun rose over the motel where my father was staying. He would be awake soon, and I was trying to hold on to my resolve to talk with him about his war and the one I was training to fight. On the way down I decided to push past my father's defenses and my fear to tell him that I was worried I would not perform well in combat. Although I acted the part of the tough-guy SEAL, I knew this mask would not get me through the ordeal of Vietnam.

I checked into the motel, changed clothes, and went for a run on the beach. I watched the sunrise on the Atlantic turn the dark sky to pink and blue. When I got back to my room I called my father. We met for breakfast and the instant I saw him the courage I needed to talk to him in a different way disappeared. He asked me how things were going. I told him they were fine, just fine. I asked him how business was going, and his answer was the same as mine. He told me how proud he was of me and wanted to know how jump school had gone. When a business associate of his joined us, my father beamed as he told the man what I was doing.

In his book *Man's Search for Meaning*, the psychiatrist and Holocaust survivor Viktor Frankl made an observation that reminded me of this trip to Fort Lauderdale when I read it a few years ago. "Live as if you were living for the second time and had acted as wrongly the first time as you are about to act now," Dr. Frankl advised. I would like to have a chance to live that weekend a second time and have another chance to really talk with my father.

I drove back to Fort Benning on Sunday night. On the way I tried to understand why I was unable to have an intimate conversation with him. The most satisfactory answer was circular: because he is my dad and that is the way things are supposed to be. I should expect nothing else. Besides, the way things were looking, the war would be over long before I would have to go.

Army Ranger School was a tremendous confidence builder. I learned more about my limits and myself than I had in UDT or Airborne School combined. We spent three weeks at Benning, three weeks in the mountains around Dahlonega, Georgia, and three weeks in the swamps near Eglin Air Force Base on Florida's gulf coast. I learned to lead as many as four hundred men across unfamiliar terrain in unpredictable circumstances. I learned to plan with a life-or-death sense of urgency that overrode concerns about hunger, sleep, or weather. By the end of the course I was confident I could survive almost any condition on earth.

My orders gave me five days to get back to Coronado, and I decided to hitchhike across Alabama and Mississippi to Louisiana, spend a few days in New Orleans, and then fly to San Diego. On the road I saw poverty I had not imagined existed in America. The way so many people lived shocked me. Only the Lakota Sioux on the Pine Ridge Reservation endured conditions this bad. I stopped in towns and talked with white and black men about their lives. The black men were wary of my questioning and seemed relieved when I went on my way. The whites gave me their negative views of the federal government and Lyndon Johnson. In Mississippi I was picked up by a county sheriff who told me it was against the law to hitch-hike. He drove me to his office and threatened to put me in jail. I sat across the desk from him while he played with his .38-caliber revolver. He smiled and said he would do me the favor of letting me go after a lecture about the need for outsiders to obey the law in the South.

Within days of my return to Coronado, Robert Kennedy was killed in Los Angeles. The image of him lying helpless on the floor of a hotel kitchen with his mouth open and his head in a growing pool of blood was all over the news. I grieved over Bobby Kennedy's death more than I had for his brother. I liked him because I thought he would end the war before it was time for me to go. My reasons were personal and not geopolitical. I had neither a deep-seated moral opposition to the war nor a reasoned alternative to fighting the Vietcong and the

North Vietnamese. I just preferred to miss this one if possible, and to do so without my having to refuse to go. As long as the war continued, it was my duty to serve, and I would serve enthusiastically.

I revealed my political confusion in a letter to my parents that summer. I told them I was glad Ronald Reagan had lost out in Miami but was sad that my choice, Nelson Rockefeller, had lost, too. I said I preferred the Democratic candidate, Eugene McCarthy, but would go with Nixon if Hubert Humphrey won the nomination. Nixon's secret plan to end the war was more appealing to me than Humphrey's vague promise to change things.

In the summer of 1968 I became administrative officer of SEAL Team One, a job most of us thought the worst imaginable because it was all paperwork. I also felt bad that many of the men I had trained with were already in Vietnam. Organizing an efficient flow of documents was not my idea of what a glamorous, swashbuckling SEAL officer should be doing. It was more like being president of a fraternity. To my parents I described the job as that of a child king. It was all responsibility with no real authority.

My job was to process the paper that documented the movements and lives of every man on the team and every piece of equipment assigned to us. Four enlisted men did most of the work, but I was responsible to the commanding officer if anything got lost or misplaced, and I took the assignment seriously.

While running this office, I learned that SEAL team deployments to Vietnam were unusual in two ways. Our orders were temporary duty (or TDY), which meant we stayed only six months. Platoons were operationally attached to the team's commanding officer in Coronado. Administratively, a platoon would be assigned to a navy command in Vietnam, but that command could not issue orders to conduct operations. They could offer suggestions, but the command to operate had to come from back in the States. I processed the reports that were filed after every combat operation, and as a result was often asked by our commanding officer to write recommendations for medals. Neither of these responsibilities made me more confident in the war effort.

The duty that eroded my confidence most was my visits to teammates who had been wounded in Vietnam. Most of them went to Balboa Naval Hospital, and I was surprised to see how changed they were. When I asked two of them who had been injured at the same time what had happened, they did not answer directly. Both had become deeply skeptical about the war and their contribution to winning it. Their attitude and the stories told by men I processed through my office lessened my disappointment at not being assigned to a platoon. The situation they described was beginning to sound hopeless. No one seemed optimistic that the war could be won, and few could give a compelling explanation of why we were continuing. Most advised me to do the best I could to get home alive. I still hoped that Nixon would win the election and implement his secret plan to end the war before I had to go.

Shortly after Labor Day I was assigned to a platoon to be led by Lieutenant Tim Wettack from Coffeyville, Kansas. Tim was also making his maiden tour to Vietnam. We were assigned twelve enlisted men, put in a rotation, and scheduled to leave in January 1969. Tim and I organized a series of training operations to get us as comfortable as possible working together. We practiced the three patrolling configurations used by SEAL platoons: all fourteen men led by the senior officer, seven men led either by one of the officers or one of the senior enlisted men, and two- or three-man groups. Our training emphasized the value of allowing men to make independent judgments without waiting for specific orders. To achieve this unity we needed time together.

We took our platoon to the SEAL camp near the Salton Sea and to the Chocolate Mountains. We went to Vallejo, California, a few miles north of San Francisco, to train with the PBRs, the navy's river patrol boats. And we spent a week at Eglin Air Force Base, operating as an aggressor force against the Army's Ranger trainees.

In Vallejo about a hundred army soldiers who were heading to Vietnam to join the Ninth Division were training with the riverboats. Their commanding officer challenged us to penetrate his nighttime perimeter. That night the clouds hid the stars, and under cover of darkness we not only penetrated their perimeter, we captured an army corporal asleep at his post. We bound his wrists behind his back and put duct tape over his mouth and eyes. We put an inflatable life preserver on him and swam him across a canal where we marched to our camp. On the way the only SEALs who spoke pretended to be speaking Vietnamese. We removed the tape from the corporal's mouth and in broken English ordered him to confess that he was a spy and to give us the name of his officer and the purpose of their mission. It did not take long before he told us everything. Then we made him get down on his knees and talk to his fellow soldiers over our radio. As he gave his name, rank, and serial number he broke down and cried. He wailed that he had held out as long as he could and begged the others to surrender so he could live. I felt terrible for him. We radioed his superior officer, gave him our approximate location, and said we would pop a red flare so he could find his missing soldier, who at this point was untied and kneeling on the ground. When we hit the flare the report sounded to our prisoner like a gunshot. He fell to the ground unconscious, thinking we had shot him. That night I learned how effective and destructive terror could be, and I learned that the road to cruelty can be very easy to find.

At Eglin we went into the field for days at a time, searching out and ambushing Ranger patrols. One night we were cooking dinner in the woods and the smell of our food carried to the poorly fed soldiers. Three of them followed their noses to our camp and begged for some of our rations. Their faces were haunting. Their eyes were vacant, and they said they would do anything we asked if only we would feed them. These men were no longer in control of themselves. I hoped I never got that bad.

Early on election night it looked as though my hope for a Nixon victory might be disappointed after Humphrey won New York and Pennsylvania, and the numbers were close in Ohio and Illinois. But Nixon rallied and Nebraska gave the new president his biggest plurality. I voted for him because I took him at his word. Soon my hope for peace began to fade. In a letter home on November 26, I wrote:

> As expected the Johnson "peace talks" aren't
> progressing too well. From all indications it looks
> like they'll break the record for most days spent
> negotiating a settlement. We speculate quite a bit as
> to when the cease-fire will occur, and you have to
> give pretty good odds to find any money betting on
> a 1969 date. I occasionally find myself thinking that
> it would be better if nothing happens in Paris until
> we've made our deployment, so that we will not
> have wasted all of this time training.

My last leave began on December 20. Our whole family went on vacation to the Bahamas. I filled several sea bags with diving tanks, regulators, fins, masks, and snorkels so I could teach my brothers and sisters to dive. I invited a woman along whom I had dated off and on in high school and college. We had a great Christmas. I would never have another like it.

My father drove me to the Lincoln airport for the flight to San Diego. It was hot inside his four-door Buick in spite of a winter storm that had hit the town during the night. My dad started the car early to let the engine and heater run before we left the house. My mother said good-bye at the side door we always used for our comings and goings. As we backed out of the snowy driveway, I saw her standing in the kitchen window. Later my sister told me my mother cried when I was gone. She would have to cry twice. My flight was canceled, and I did not leave for good until the next day. Both days my father and I talked about everything but the war. The closest he got to saying he was worried was to tell me to be careful. I offered no easy way for him to broach the subject.

The Sunday before I left for Vietnam, Joe Namath led the New York Jets to a victory over Earl Morrall and the Baltimore Colts. No one had bet on that outcome, but we celebrated the victory anyway at the Down Winds, a favorite bar at the North Island Air Station. The evening ended in a fight between a group of pilots and us. One of them told us he would be flying with us to Vietnam.

Monday morning was hot and clear. We loaded our gear into a twin-engine prop plane that was slow but reliable. The noise of the engines filled my ears like wet cotton balls, and at first we could not hear each other speak.

Our seats were modified canvas slings, but the best accommodations were on top of the six-foot wooden Con-ex boxes that we used to transport our gear. Through the sides of these containers I smelled the D-40 lubricant we had sprayed on our weapons. It seemed as dark inside the plane as it was light outside. I looked out one of the small windows at the bright pink buildings and remembered our boisterous farewell party the previous night.

I was pleased to be going over with Tim Wettack because I did not have to worry about his risking our lives unnecessarily. Like me, he had no desire to be a hero. Our definition of success was the same: do the job and bring everyone home alive. At twenty-five, I was the third or fourth oldest man in the group. A slight foreboding welled up in my stomach. I had been late for the group photograph because I had to stop at the flight center to sign documents. Someone had joked that I was headed for a bad ending because I would be missing from the picture. I told them I wasn't superstitious, but it did give me one more thing to worry about. We would be in Vietnam in twenty-four hours. Our training was over and I was ready for my part in the war.

13

OUR DESTINATION WAS Cam Ranh Bay, a coastal city on the South China Sea, 120 miles northeast of Saigon. On approach in darkness we saw stars reflecting on the water, and white floodlight beams along the airstrip reached up to greet us. Behind these flickered dull, yellow lamps in the Vietnamese houses and shops. Farther back, the black and brooding land seemed annoyed by our arrival. It did not feel welcoming. Our plane rolled to a stop and the door opened. It was near midnight local time.

We climbed down to the longest concrete runway I had ever seen. Gary Parrott—senior officer of the platoon we were replacing—waited for us with a Vietnamese navy officer and frogman who would be our liaison with the

Army of the Republic of Vietnam (ARVN) and our interpreter. As we unloaded our gear into a pair of five-ton trucks, the hot humid air carried the comforting fumes of aromatic fuel mixed with an unfamiliar and wild scent. I felt this was an outpost surrounded by life that did not know or care about my training or purpose. We rode in open trucks to the naval base on sandy roads leading toward the ocean. I was on full alert to imaginary dangers lurking in the shadows on either side of us. Ambush seemed a real possibility. Wettack and I ordered our men to stand at the ready with their rifles locked and loaded. Parrott, smiling and relaxed, allowed us to make this harmless mistake.

Gary Parrott seemed like a natural SEAL to me. I felt toward him what Joe DiMaggio's teammates must have felt when they first saw him play his rookie year. He was of average height and weight and not at all imposing physically. If you did not know him and were asked to guess his line of work, accounting might spring to mind, until you looked at his eyes or followed him around for a few days. When I saw Parrott's blue eyes I understood why some writers used the word *sharp* to describe this part of the human body. Whether a gift of birth or a trait he developed fly-fishing and hunting as a young man in Michigan, he could see things others missed. He was a man who looked and listened more than he talked.

He fell in love with the people of Vietnam and their land because it was still relatively undeveloped even after thirty years of war. Gary had the gene that made explorers willing to risk it all to go where no man had been before. He preferred the outdoors and knew how to travel light. He was a great storyteller and one of the most sociable men I ever knew, but he seemed to prefer his own company.

He once told me how he loved bow-hunting deer because of the long wait for a quarry. Sitting in a tree from predawn to darkness without getting a single shot was not cause for complaint. To Gary it made the entire effort worthwhile. As a boy he had learned fly-fishing with James Jesus Angleton, who became famous searching for moles in the CIA. To understand how good Parrott's company could be, Angleton willed his beloved fly rod to him when he died. And to understand how far Gary would go to be alone, know that while he was a student at OCS he secretly lived in the abandoned and cavernous top floor of one of the school's administrative buildings.

Gary had scoped out Cam Ranh Bay before we arrived and told us what he had learned. It was a natural harbor that had been used by the Japanese during the Second World War. In 1965 the United States began converting it to one of our largest military installations. That it was also one of our safest made it a favorite stop for dignitaries, including President Johnson's in 1967.

As the navy's role in the war increased, the coastal patrol headquarters—code-named Market Time—was moved up from Saigon to the eastern side of the base, where there was a harbor and some world-class beaches. The navy installation included a communications station, a support facility, and joint service ammunition depot for coastal surveillance, river patrol, mobile riverine forces, as well as the Seventh Fleet's gunfire support destroyers and landing ships. A naval air facility was home base for the coastal surveillance aircraft.

Market Time's task, to patrol the entire coast of Vietnam, was a colossal undertaking. The distance from the demilitarized zone in the north to the Ca Mau Peninsula in the south was fifteen hundred miles. Market Time — or Task Force 115 as it was also known — was a joint navy and coast guard mission. The navy used a boat called a PCF (patrol craft fast) or swift boat along with coastal minesweepers. The Coast Guard used a WPB (a cutter). Farther out, the navy and the coast guard had high-speed gunboats, radar picket escort ships, and oceangoing minesweepers.

The swift boat, our platoon's principal means of transportation, was a fifty-foot-long, thirteen-foot-wide, quarter-inch aluminum alloy craft powered by two 480-horsepower GM diesel engines. With a maximum speed of thirty-two knots, the boat could make a 180-degree turn in seventy-five yards at twenty knots. Twin .50-caliber Browning machine guns were positioned at the boat's centerline in a gun tub mounted on top of the pilothouse. On the fantail was an eighty-one-millimeter trigger-fired mortar with a .50-caliber semiautomatic Browning fixed on top. The crew's weapons included M-60 machine guns, M-79 grenade launchers, M-16 rifles, 12-gauge shotguns, .38- and .45-caliber pistols, hand grenades, and occasionally C-4 explosives.

The swift boat was commissioned in 1965 when the war effort was ramped up to provide the navy with a boat for counterinsurgency warfare. They modified an all-metal crew boat used to service oil rigs in the Gulf of Mexico, and forty days later, the first two boats arrived in Vietnam.

The platoon we were replacing had not used the swift boats because they had been operating in the Mekong Delta, as were most inexperienced, first-tour platoons. They used PBRs or river patrol boats and were part of the Game Warden operation. They had accumulated six months' worth of intelligence on their area of operation, which was useless to us in Cam Ranh. Thus we were starting from scratch without the benefit of reliable intelligence and had essentially the entire coast of Vietnam as our area of operation. Since our mission was to set ambushes, abduct enemy personnel, and gather intelligence we hardly knew where to begin.

The day after we arrived at the naval base we reported to the offices of Captain Roy Hoffman, the commander of Task Force 115 which was composed of the swift boats and their support personnel. Hoffman was a tough, experienced officer who had volunteered for the navy during

World War II. He was discharged in the general down-sizing that took place in 1948, and was recalled during the Korean conflict in 1950.

In Vietnam Captain Hoffman faced an enemy who did not have a navy. The enemy's coastal activity was mostly limited to moving small amounts of materiel and people. Our navy became so frustrated with the limited amount of combat that in late 1968 they combined the coastal command, Market Time, with the Mekong Delta command, Game Warden. The combined operation would be called Operation Sea Lord. This new command focused more and more attention on the rivers and canals of the Mekong Delta. As our efforts shifted, our tactics became more aggressive.

A December 1968 report filed by the commander of U.S. Naval Forces, Vietnam, to the commander in chief, U.S. Pacific Fleet, tells a lot about what was going on. During the entire month Market Time accounted for 49,264 "detections" and 20,656 "inspections." Destroyed were 669 junks or sampans and 736 structures; 1,119 "persons" were "detained," of whom 26 were "Vietcong suspects." There were 23 "hostile fire incidents" resulting in 68 "enemy casualties" by body count and 51 other "estimated casualties." Three U.S. Navy personnel were killed during the month.

In ordinary language this report says that swift boat crews physically inspected forty percent of the vessels they saw and destroyed about one out of thirty vessels they inspected, had one hostile fire incident for every one thousand inspections, and killed about three enemies per hostile fire incident. The ratio of enemy to U.S. dead was more than 20 to 1. For the Americans and South Vietnamese, each of those inspections, destroyed junks, sampans, and structures, and persons detained was a source of frustration. For the enemy each was a potential opportunity for recruitment.

Captain Hoffman briefed us on the success of Market Time and his plans to move farther up the Mekong River. He would provide us with swift boats for almost anything we wanted to do, but he had a limited number of helicopter gunships, and most of those were committed to covering the operations of his crews. He recommended we make contact with naval intelligence and with the army to gather a list of potential targets.

I left his office more confused than when I walked in. To say that I barely had a clue about what I would be doing in Vietnam understates the case. I was well trained in all the techniques of armed conflict, but I lacked a clear understanding of our enemy other than that they were opponents of our ally, the government of South Vietnam. No doubt Captain Hoffman was just as confused. As I said earlier, SEAL team platoons were not under the operational control of the commands they were assigned to in Vietnam. The commanding officer of SEAL Team One in Coronado retained operational authority over our patrol.

Everyone's experience in Vietnam was different, and it is impossible to generalize from my own. The war changed from year to year. Men who went to Vietnam in the early 1960s were participants in a war that was being conducted on a very small scale, mostly by South Vietnamese defending against North Vietnam's proxy, the National Liberation Front. By 1965 American soldiers and their South Vietnamese allies were fighting a large-scale classic conventional campaign against the North Vietnamese army. In 1969 the nature of the war was wildly different depending on where you were. In the central or northern provinces there were clearly defined battles between mostly American forces and the North Vietnamese. In the Mekong Delta, we were still more likely to face irregular forces with fewer weapons than we were organized North Vietnamese soldiers.

After 1969 the most important factor affecting a soldier's experience in Vietnam was the deterioration of troop morale. Drug use and racial tension became more common, and soldiers were more likely to believe that the South Vietnamese could not and would not win the war. Men who served in the Mekong Delta saw a different war than those in the central and northern provinces. The coastal areas were different from the interior. The major cities were more likely to seem peaceful than the countryside, though every place seemed peaceful just before fighting began. The last variable was the unit you served with. In 1969 an army soldier with the Ninth Division saw a different war than one with the First Air Cavalry. A marine with the First Division would not have recognized the war fought by navy SEALs. Pilots faced a different set of risks, as did navy Seabees or army engineers or for that matter any of the so-called support personnel who often found themselves at greater risk than a combat grunt.

After Wettack and I left Captain Hoffman's briefing, we faced the problem of deciding where to conduct our operations. Naval intelligence informed us that Vietcong soldiers carrying satchel charges—plastic explosives with small scrap metal pieces wrapped inside a canvas bag—had conducted an attack the night before we arrived. They hit a South Vietnamese perimeter near Phan Rang twenty miles to our south. One of the sappers was discovered crouching under a guard tower and shot, point blank, with an M-60. He had received medical attention because the South Vietnamese hoped to learn something from him.

They asked us to join in the interrogation, so Parrott, Wettack, and I drove down in a jeep. As we did, I realized how groundless my nighttime fears had been during our trip from the plane to our quarters. In daylight, the only obstacles to our safe passage were Americans moving in the other direction, headed for the beach carrying food, drink, chairs, and surfboards.

We found the Vietcong sapper in a field hospital; he lay dying on a canvas cot, wearing black silk shorts. Calluses covered his feet, and his short olive body was strong and lean. His thick black hair was cut short, and his eyes showed no fear. A liter bottle containing a solution of five percent dextrose hung from a pole, and a plastic tube carried the liquid through a needle into his veins. He wasn't receiving blood; his wounds had been cleaned and the bleeding stopped. The bullets had torn three holes in his chest and stomach.

He refused to answer any of our questions. Toward the end his eyes went blank, his mouth opened, and he labored mightily for breath. As I stood above him I tried to guess who he was. He was a few years older than I was. Perhaps he had joined the Vietcong after a family member had been killed. Unlike me he did not have a six-month tour of duty. His orders were to fight until the war ended or he was killed. His war was ending.

We learned from the ARVN officer who had interrogated him before we arrived that the dead man was one of six Vietcong who broke through the barbed-wire perimeter. All the rest had been killed, but not before they killed four South Vietnamese and wounded four. According to the ARVN officer, these men were part of a larger force operating in the mountains along the coast that was infrequently patrolled by ARVN soldiers. This area would be a perfect place for us to conduct patrols.

The next day we met with the army's Fifth Special Forces in Nha Trang twenty miles north of Cam Ranh. Nha Trang was a small port town with around one hundred thousand inhabitants. With a market for farmers and small businessmen of the central highlands, Nha Trang, like most major cities in Vietnam, became a center for U.S. military advisers, businessmen, and journalists. Although it lacked the glamour of Vung Tau or Saigon, it had one street with American bars, local prostitutes, and any other legal or illegal temptations.

The city had its share of enemy sympathizers and had suffered attacks from sappers who had killed civilians trying to get on with their lives. Getting on with your life was threatening behavior for both sides in this war. I was impressed by how normal civilian life managed to be despite the threats, violence, and perversions caused by the necessities of combat.

The Special Forces compound was a rectangle of nondescript army buildings. There we were told the coast offered little in the way of acceptable targets. Most of their work was conducted in the highlands, where we did not have authority to go. They identified some targets, including an island 130 miles to the north. Parrott suggested splitting the platoon in half. He would go north with Wettack and six enlisted men, and I would go south to the area where the sappers had hit the night we arrived in country.

Accompanying Wettack was the senior petty officer in our platoon and two of the most remarkable men I knew in the teams: Richard Solano and Richard Gore. Solano and Gore had become close friends in training; they were practically joined at the hip. When you thought of one you thought of the other. It was hard to say Solano without saying Gore. Both were fresh-faced young men in their early twenties, above-average athletes, and enthusiastic about everything they chose to do. They could turn a room full of men in foul moods into a bunch of dizzy optimists. Something about seeing these two made the day seem better, and we all preferred their company. Wettack had chosen well when he put them in his squad.

Mike Ambrose and Gerhard Klann, who had both done a previous tour to Vietnam, were my most experienced men. Gene Peterson was the quietest and probably our most reliable. Doc Schrier was our corpsman, and at thirty the oldest member of the platoon. Rick Knepper was our youngest and strongest. Bill Tucker was inarguably the best looking and the favorite of every female who encountered our group. A Vietnamese frogman was essential to our squad because he spoke the language and understood the people of Vietnam.

The coastal mountains south of Phan Rang were a natural hideout for Vietcong and their North Vietnamese army advisers. We did not know how large their forces were, but we had reason to believe they were large enough for us to be careful not to engage without the certainty that we could prevail. With my senior men's agreement I decided to set an ambush on a trail believed to be traveled by the enemy. This was my first operation, and I was excited by the prospect of finally getting some action. My plan called for us to leave our base an hour after sunset. A swift boat would carry us to the beach below the mountains. The long slope of the beach would allow the boat to stay outside of the surf line and still let us walk through waist-deep water. We would patrol inland, set up the ambush, and spend the night awaiting traffic. If none came we could leave our position an hour before sunrise, signal the swift boat to pick us up, and return to base.

Our platoon had been on many training exercises where we sat all night long in a mock ambush. Most of what we did that night I had done before, but one element was new: sitting with a loaded M-16 across my crossed legs knowing that I might have to give the order to fire. My first kill-or-be-killed situation might occur soon. I thought of the sapper and wondered if my rifle could do that kind of damage. I knew it could and I knew the enemy's AK-47s could do the same to me. The night was uneventful. No one came down the trail. The only excitement occurred when the swift boat's captain made the mistake of driving the boat through the surf to make our extraction easier. He made it more difficult, and the boat grounded on the beach. As the sun rose, seven well-trained SEALs strained to turn the boat and push it back out to sea.

14

M Y MEMORIES OF South Vietnam are almost entirely of the Mekong Delta where the villages and small towns and the many farms reminded me of Nebraska. The headwaters of the Mekong are in the Tibetan Himalayas, and the river drops over twenty thousand feet on a journey of nearly three thousand miles across China, Laos, Thailand, Cambodia, and Vietnam before its four mouths fan out like giant arteries to form the richest natural river delta in the world. In that delta you can see the fertile soil that creates wealth in the form of rice harvested and sold at market. To produce as much food as the South Vietnamese did without modern technology during wartime was an impressive accomplishment.

In the delta, away from the larger cities and American bases, the people tried to go about their business, raise their families, and survive the war. They tended to give their sympathy to whomever they feared the most. Either way they could lose. They risked having us destroy their villages if they cooperated with the Vietcong and having the Vietcong destroy their villages if they cooperated with us.

The war was corrupting everything. Journalists were willing to do anything to get a scoop, and businessmen and government officials were trying to make a buck. Military and political leaders struggled to look as good as possible, and alcohol, prostitution, and drugs prevailed. I knew no American who talked about winning the war or who seemed to believe we could. Though we were in a strong position militarily, it did not feel as if victory was right around the corner.

Much has been said and written about what the United States might have done to win in Vietnam. One view is that we simply had to apply more force to destroy the war-making abilities of North Vietnam. The proponents of this argument say: "We were fighting this war with one hand tied behind our backs. If you are going to fight a war, then you must be prepared to go all out to win it. In Vietnam, we simply weren't." According to this school, we proved this point when we drove Iraq out of Kuwait in 1991.

But this argument underestimates the determination of the North Vietnamese to pay the price necessary to win, unlike the Iraqis who surrendered to television crews. In Vietnam we applied considerable force in our effort to defeat the North Vietnamese and their ally, the National Liberation Front. In the end they defeated our B-52s with entrenching tools because we lost the battle for public opinion not only in the United States but also in South Vietnam's countryside.

I see three reasons for why we lost that battle. We became too closely allied with the former colonial power and, in too many minds, became just another western nation propping up a puppet regime in order to gain access to Vietnam's natural resources. "Throw the bums out!" is, as we know in our own political system, a very powerful battle cry. We did a terrible job of making it clear that the choice was freedom versus Communism. The word "freedom" not only had lost its appeal to people who just wanted the terror to end but also was discredited by our political and military tactics. Our military tactics on the ground — especially where I was in the delta — were appallingly counterproductive. In too many cases we applied too much force, not too little.

For Ho Chi Minh the cause was "freedom and independence." The words are chiseled into his mausoleum in Hanoi. As long as he lived, he was prepared to fight to the death for that cause. He and his compatriots demonstrated their willingness to go the distance with vision, bravery, and ruthlessness. To the North Vietnamese, "freedom and independence" meant freedom and independence from foreign control of Vietnam. In the south—which had the same battle cry—freedom and independence meant political freedom and independence from the north.

Freedom and independence were powerful words, especially when they had been sustained by Vietnamese freedom fighters for such a long time against such great odds. By the time the north chose to start the second Indochina war they had both tradition and great mythical heroes to rally the troops. They could even talk of the days when they fought alongside the Americans to free themselves from Japanese domination.

For the South Vietnamese and the American military who supported them, our "freedom and independence" campaign began as part of a greater global struggle for freedom, a cause that could hardly be expected to motivate farmers in the Mekong Delta. What did motivate many South Vietnamese was freedom for themselves and independence from northern domination. There were many more men and women in South Vietnam who were willing to die for the cause of freedom than public opinion in the United States cared to acknowledge.

South Vietnam's government was vulnerable to accusation of corruption because corruption is only visible in a government that is open and free. North Vietnam had plenty of corruption, but it was not visible to the press. In the modern world if you cannot put it on television, it does not exist. And there were plenty of stories about South Vietnamese corruption to put on television, stories about coups and countercoups, religious minorities demonstrating for more political rights, money that was being siphoned off to accounts outside Vietnam, sex scandals, involvement with the CIA, and military units that failed to put up a good fight. All these and more were fair game in South Vietnam. The fact that we neither read, heard, nor saw stories about corruption in North Vietnam led us to assume incorrectly that nothing of the kind was going on there because their hearts were pure and good. There were no protests in Hanoi because the government did not allow freedom of expression, freedom of religion, or freedom of assembly.

Making matters worse was this terrible truth: a free and open government was a lot more vulnerable to the subversive activities of the National Liberation Front, which had the overthrow of South Vietnam's government as its open objective. The government of South Vietnam was in a lose-lose situation. If it responded with violence and terror when the Vietcong used violence and terror to establish control in the countryside, it would face public criticism and likely increase the number of Vietnamese who opposed the government; if it did nothing it lost territory.

My simple view of the war is that it could not be won because we focused too much on stopping Communism and too little on building a free and independent nation. We thought we could win a military war without winning a political one and were bitterly wrong. We underestimated the determination of our opponents, and we trivialized the willingness of our allies to pay the price necessary to succeed. For all these reasons, we had by 1969 lost our way and were merely looking for an honorable exit. We would discover there wasn't one.

Soldiers must learn to fight well and honorably without necessarily believing in the cause for which they put themselves into terrifying danger. Henry Abbott served with the Twentieth Regiment of Massachusetts Volunteers during the American Civil War and distinguished himself with brave and heroic conduct. He was killed standing up, directing his men during the Battle of the Wilderness in May 1864. Abbott was one of the pro-slavery Northerners known as Copperheads. He did not believe in the Northern cause and yet he volunteered, fought bravely, and was killed in the line of duty. This did not make him a mercenary. It made him an exemplary soldier.

Wettack and I tried to do our duty as we had been trained to do it. When Tim returned from Qui Nhon he reported that he had set up an unsuccessful ambush near a trail in bitter cold water and waited in vain for action. He and Gary Parrott thought it would be best if we found a position somewhere in the Mekong Delta rather than staying in Cam Ranh. After some discussion, we decided to split the platoon into two squads. My squad would go to Vung Tau to talk with the Market Time forces there and then confer with other SEAL platoons in the delta. But our main goal was to see whether we could find a stable area of operation. Tim would take his squad to the Ca Mau Peninsula where earlier SEAL platoons were located, since Parrott thought they would have access to much more reliable intelligence.

Vung Tau was another paradise location. It was on the tip of a half-moon bay that opened into the mouth of the Mekong River. The beaches were long and beautiful. Helicopter pilots and other American military came there for rest and relaxation, which meant the town was full of bars and prostitutes. We spent a few days talking to army and navy intelligence officers, American and Vietnamese, but could not find a suitable home for the entire platoon. We took a swift boat up to a barge near Vinh Long that supported the PBRs on the Co Chien River. We patrolled and set unsuccessful night ambushes for five days straight before moving to another barge at Ben Tre, where another SEAL platoon operated. I celebrated my first Buddhist New Year on the barge.

Then we went to Cat Lo, a town on the northern edge of Vung Tau Bay, and headquarters for one of the Market Time divisions. The officer in charge had not been informed of our arrival and was too busy with his own patrols to be very interested in ours. He agreed to provide us with boats for operations into an area of Thanh Phu province reportedly controlled by the Vietcong, but he was not willing to back us up with air or naval gunfire support.

Mike Ambrose, who had become my friend in UDT training and was my most trusted enlisted man, advised against going into the area. Mike was from Iowa and had made one tour immediately after Ranger School with an officer who was also a good friend of mine. Mike was quick and nimble on patrol and ran point on most of our operations. His experience made him valuable to me because I could trust him to make good independent judgments.

Mike was against our going into Thanh Phu because our Vietnamese scout was on leave. In the delta, an operation without an interpreter was more risky, and the lack of air support, though not unusual, was dangerous. Mike had also grown very negative about Vietnam. He thought we were wasting our energy because it was only a matter of time before we walked away from the war. This skepticism made survival his most important consideration when he gave me planning advice. So when we were told by the government of Vietnam's district chief that a high-level meeting would be taking place in a village called Thanh Phong in Thanh Phu province, Mike still thought we should pass on the operation. That the district chief said the entire village was Vietcong and that there would be no civilians present did nothing to change Mike's mind.

The district chief was an official of the South Vietnamese government and when he said there were no civilians in this village he made a statement that illustrates the tragedy of guerrilla wars. The government of South Vietnam was fighting against an enemy that included South as well as North Vietnamese. The tactics of the enemy against their own government included a range of activities from terror to simply passing on information about troop movements of the South Vietnamese and United States military forces.

So, when the district chief said the entire village was Vietcong, he meant that the men and women of this village had joined the forces of opposition to the government. The men and some of the women were probably part of the enemy's irregular forces that had lethal, though limited, capability. The chief knew there were innocent noncombatants in the village, but he warned us to take great care because the area was considered especially dangerous at night.

In the end I decided to do the operation. As an extra precaution I arranged to fly the terrain in daylight in a single-engine plane to identify the houses where the meeting would take place. That surveillance flight confirmed that there were no women and children in the area. I located the village on a map and then briefed the rest of the squad on the mission. Several hours after sundown we took a swift boat from Cat Lo up the canal to the village. The boat touched its bow on the shore and we scrambled on to the dry land. We waited in silence to make certain we had not been detected. Sweat ran in rivers down my back. Our plan was to move perpendicular to the canal for five hundred meters and then turn right another five hundred meters where we would find the meeting place.

Even without our Vietnamese scout the terrain was easy to navigate and we moved quickly. Along the canals the buffalo grass was high and lush providing dense cover for us and our enemy. Beyond this cover the land opened into rectangular rice fields, which lay fallow and dry. We walked along the top of the earthen dikes that surrounded the fields. Before the war villagers in places like Thanh Phong lived just above subsistence level by growing rice and fishing in the rivers and selling a little of their harvest in good years.

The people lived in thatch houses with bamboo walls and woven grass ceilings. The floors of these homes were usually covered with grass mats though sometimes even this luxury was outside their reach. During the war the people dug bunkers underneath the houses where they would go if there were attacks from the air. They used grass and smaller bamboo mats for mattresses and whatever fabric was available, often silk, to cover themselves at night. The entire family slept in a single bed.

The village and the area around it was described by the South Vietnamese government and by U.S. military as a Free Fire Zone. In essence this meant it was controlled by the enemy at night. In daylight, South Vietnamese forces might enter the area seeking intelligence about the movement of enemy forces, but they rarely went in at night. Thus, we expected to have the advantage of surprise on our side. It was about midnight when I told my point man to head out. The only noises we could hear were a few dogs barking in the distance. The night was quiet and calm.

My point man led the way. He came to a house he said he believed was occupied by sentries. We had been trained that in such situations it would be too risky to move forward knowing that they would warn the men in the village unless we killed them or aborted the mission. I did not have to give an order to begin the killing but I could have stopped it and I didn't.

In truth, I remember very little of what happened in a clear and reliable way. The pulse of my own blood was pounding in my ears. I no longer believed we had the element of surprise on our side, but I was still determined to proceed to the main village. At the village we approached the house where the meeting was to take place. Once again, we had been trained to approach a potentially hostile environment and the patrol required no orders from me. One man entered the building while six others remained outside to provide security from all angles of approach. We waited, spread out with one man on point, and from my position I did not see any security. Our point man came out of the house and whispered excitedly that the men were not there. No meeting was taking place and all the men were gone. He said their sleeping places had been recently abandoned. He went into two other houses and reported the same thing. When he came out of the second one he had a look of real fear on his face.

The women and children in each of the three houses woke, gathered outside, and began to talk loudly in high singsong voices. We knew we were in trouble. The absence of men told us we had been compromised. We were certain there were armed cadre in the village now on full alert. We had two choices: withdraw or continue to search houses in the dark. Before we could make the decision, someone shot at us from the direction of the women and children, trapping them in a cross fire. We returned a tremendous barrage of fire and began to withdraw, continuing to fire. I saw women and children in front of us being hit and cut to pieces. I heard their cries and other voices in the darkness as we made our retreat to the canal. We radioed the swift boat and moved quickly but carefully toward the canal. The possibility of being pursued or of being caught in an ambush ourselves seemed very real to me.

We came to the canal and hid in the buffalo grass in a semicircle facing outward for security. We heard the deepthroated boat engines approach and signaled our location with a small, red, handheld light. When the bow of the boat touched shore, we pulled ourselves on board. I could feel the screws turning in reverse and the boat swing out and away from land. In less than an hour, we were back at our base in Cat Lo.

I did not speak of my doubts on the way back to our base camp. Our actions were not considered out of the ordinary for guerrilla warfare where the number of civilian casualties is quite high. We cleaned our faces and our weapons before going to sleep for the few hours remaining in the night. At first light we packed our gear and drove to the port in Vung Tau, where we caught a ride on a destroyer that was heading north to Cam Ranh. Standing on the fantail of the destroyer watching the silvery wake recede behind us, I felt a sickness in my heart for what we had done.

The young, innocent man who went to Vietnam died that night. After that night, I no longer had illusions or objectivity about the war. I had become someone I did not recognize. I had been in Vietnam for five weeks and this was my first live firefight. It had not ended in the heroic way I had expected.

BACK AT CAM RANH I told myself that this war was not clean and that victory does not go to the warrior who languishes long in the backwaters of self-doubt and self-incrimination. We remained in Cam Ranh for a week waiting for Wettack to order us down to join him and the other squad. One night after dinner a messenger told me a radio transmission had been sent to me from the Fifth Special Forces in Nha Trang. It said a Vietcong sapper who had been working with a team of explosive specialists let his love of family get the better of him. He swam off an island near Nha Trang and turned himself in to the U.S. Army. He said he wanted to join a program called *chieu hoi*, which translates roughly into "open arms," meaning he would be allowed to go home if he gave us useful information. He became a *hoi chanh* and was not only willing to provide information, but volunteered to lead Americans to the other sappers on the island in exchange for his freedom.

The army colonel in command of the Special Forces told me it was a mission he would have loved to do but couldn't because he was shorthanded. If I could bring my men to Nha Trang immediately, he believed there would be time to conduct a successful operation. The sappers, operating on an island close to the harbor, had killed many civilians in Nha Trang. If we could kill or capture them, we would save a lot of lives.

I told Mike Ambrose about the message and ordered him to get the men ready for a possible mission. We boarded the swift boat and headed north. When we arrived in Nha Trang an army sergeant took us to the sapper. After a brief interrogation, I decided to do the operation. The plan was to go in quietly with the *hoi chanh* as our guide and capture the other sappers. Some of the senior officers argued unsuccessfully that we should not try to take prisoners; we should just kill them as they slept and leave.

With our *hoi chanh* we boarded the swift and headed east a mile beyond the island. The engines were idled long enough for us to drop two small rubber boats, which we paddled as quietly as possible to the seaward side of the island. It was one of the darkest nights we had in Vietnam making it ideal for this operation. I had every detail of what we would do in my mind. I was completely calm. We would land, hide our boats, hand climb a cliff to where our targets were sleeping, awaken them with force, bind and gag them with tape, and call for a helicopter to remove them to Nha Trang.

The landing and the climb up the cliff went well. We moved slowly through the rocky terrain. I kept the *hoi chanh* directly in front of me within arm's reach. He knew the terrain and quickly led us to his former comrades. The sappers were sleeping in two groups. We found the first group with no difficulty. I left four of my men close by them while I continued on to find the second. Once I reached them I would flash a small red light as a signal for the capture.

The second sleeping group was not where the defector told us they would be. He feared they were on the move. We saw them coming toward us. I dropped into a hurdler's position with my right leg extended in front of me. I had just fired a short burst when the crack of an explosion ripped the air. I was thrown backward and my rifle torn from my hands. I knew immediately I had been seriously wounded. I smelled burning flesh in the air. The pain was most intense in my right leg. In the darkness I reached my hands down toward my foot to assess the damage. The shape of it was gone. The foot was detached from the calf.

Gunfire rocked the night. We were under attack at close range. I had time only to tie a tourniquet around the leg above my knee. We were not yet out of trouble. Small-arms fire was coming in our direction. With difficulty I pulled myself upright so I could direct my men. They had begun to circle to get the enemy in cross fire. After they did the fighting did not last more than an hour. Then came silence. My corpsman had taken shrapnel in his eye and could not help me, but there wasn't much to be done. I broke a glass styrette of morphine and injected the drug into my thigh. Immediately I could taste it in my mouth. Gerhard Klann, our automatic weapons man, sat behind me and propped me up in his arms. He gave me an unfiltered Camel cigarette and I smoked while my radioman called for a medevac helicopter. All was quiet except for the city noise of Nha Trang.

The pilot would not land on the island. He lowered a sling and my men wrapped me inside it. As I rose from the rocks a finger on my left hand caught on a tree limb and broke. Thanks to the morphine I felt nothing. As the darkness of the island disappeared beneath me, the eastern sky began to show signs of morning; the ocean horizon was visible. Once I was in the chopper, medics cut my clothes away and added more morphine to my bloodstream. We landed, and before the chopper blades had gone silent, I heard the sounds of men running. I was carried on a stretcher into a building I presumed was a hospital. As I faded into unconsciousness I had one thought: my war was over.

I awoke in a hospital in Cam Ranh Bay. Ambrose and two other men from the squad stood over me. They told me I was being shipped back to the States through Japan. We joked about how I had been injured because I missed the group photo back in Coronado. We joked about how messed up our tour had been. I told them I was sorry things had not worked out as well as we had hoped, and I wished them good luck with the new officer who would be shipped over to replace me. The conversation was beginning to wear on us as I drifted in and out of consciousness. So we said our good-byes and parted company.

15

Two of the letters in my mother's collection were sent days after my injury. Both were written on American National Red Cross stationery. The first is dated March 15 and the second March 18. Neither is in my handwriting.

Dear Folks:

I suppose that by now you have received the singing telegram that your son was hit. I do not know exactly what condition or prognosis I am in but there is no immediate danger. I had a chunk blown away from my right foot. I will be having plastic surgery in Japan. I am in good spirits but part of my foot is in a bad way right now. After they work on me for a while in Japan, I will be medevaced to a hospital near home. I would be writing this letter myself but my hands are bandaged. Later I shall write myself. Try not to worry as I am in good hands and I will be seeing you in a couple of weeks and am in good spirits. I do have a lot of exciting material for war stories and I will keep you all in stitches when I return. I will be able to walk again after they do some more surgery but now it really looks like hell, but will be OK.

The second reads

Dear Folks:

I made it to Yokosuka, Japan, Sunday night. They have a real good staff here and I'm being well taken care of. I have a lot of confidence in Dr. Bingham, the head orthopedic surgeon. He's going to take a look at my foot tomorrow morning. They'll probably send me from here to Great Lakes although I don't know when. I sort of have this Dr. Bingham labeled as the man I'd like to have operate on me, so I may spend more time here than ordinary.

I really hated to leave the platoon after having trained with them for so long. It's my only single regret about the incident. Perhaps I'm still dazed but I don't feel any bitterness about the war or anyone or any group of people. It looks like everything is going to turn out all right. I'll write again and keep you posted about my progress. Give all my regards to the rest of the family. I'll be seeing all of you shortly.

Both letters were full of lies. My injury was worse. I didn't have any war stories worth telling. My fifty-plus days in Vietnam seemed to me to be at best a waste of time. I didn't hate to be leaving the platoon, and I was happy to be going home even in the condition I was in. I had convinced myself that my injury was retribution, punishment, rather than a combat wound from heroic duty. My spirit was in darkness. Like Jonah, the whale had swallowed me; unlike him, I believed I would spend eternity inside the belly of the beast.

I fell asleep in a nearly empty hospital ward on the base in Cam Ranh. When I opened my eyes, I was in a rectangular room with five other patients. It was night and I guessed I must have slept through the entire flight. There were six beds in the room and all were occupied. Only one other patient was awake and he was making a low, weak moaning sound full of sadness and pain. When I turned my head to the right I could see him. He was crying.

His left leg had been amputated above the knee. The sheet was pulled back from the stump so that I looked directly into the bloody bandage wrapped around his wound. While staring at him I fell asleep. When I woke again the bandage was gone and I was looking at a cross section of his upper thigh. It looked like a piece of meat in a butcher shop. The femur had been neatly sawed, and to me it looked like the white eye of the Cyclops in a monster's face. I could not take my eyes off it, but once again I fell asleep. When I awoke, in the morning the man had been moved, his bed neatly made as though he had never been there at all.

In the clear light of day I saw I was in a single-story wood frame building that seemed more like a temporary clinic than a hospital. Looking out my window I saw a postcard-perfect green mountain in the distance. When my nurse appeared he confirmed that I was in Japan. He told me I would stay here for two or three days and then be shipped back to the States. He asked if I would like to call my family in Nebraska. I told him yes and later that morning he returned with a wheelchair. A five-foot-long piece of plywood extended from the seat and supported my right leg when he lifted me into the chair. He pushed me down the hallway to a phone. He dialed my parents' number. My father answered.

"Hello, Dad. It's me. I'm in Japan."

"Yes, we know. How are you?"

"I'm fine, just fine. The foot doesn't look too good, but there's a good chance they'll save it. Other than that I feel lucky to be alive. How is everyone there?"

"Fine. They are just fine. When are you coming home?"

"In a few days. I don't know which hospital yet. Maybe Denver or Chicago. I hope you can come."

"No problem. We'll be there. Do you know where you are now? I was in Yokohama in '46. Are you near Yokohama?"

"I don't know, Dad. I don't know where I am. Is Mom there?"

My mother and I had much the same conversation. I told her I was fine and that I would be home soon. I told her I loved her. She said she loved me, too. I said good-bye. She said good-bye. When the nurse lifted me back into bed I asked him about the man I had heard in the night. He told me he had died of a pulmonary embolism, a blood clot in the lungs. Early that afternoon I was loaded into a helicopter and taken to a larger hospital. There I was taken to an operating room. They told me they were going to do surgical debridement, which meant I would be injected with a general anesthetic, so they could scrub the wounds on my leg to reduce the chances of serious infection. I wasn't fully conscious again until the next morning. When I awoke I was in a room with only one other patient, a curious-looking man wearing a fluorescent purple robe and a shower cap. He was being treated for a scalp condition. He and I did not talk much.

When the doctor came around in the middle of the afternoon, he was not optimistic about saving any of the foot. "It's mostly blown away," he said. "So little is left it's not fair to call it a foot. But we leave the final cut to the surgeons in the States. Now we are only trying to remove as much of the debris as possible and keep the infections at bay. You'll have one more surgical debriding before you leave."

Then he asked me which hospital I would like to be sent to in the States. I asked what was available on the East Coast and chose Philadelphia because it was the farthest from home and the people I knew. I wanted to recover alone. I wanted as few visitors as possible. I did not want to have to answer questions about what I had done in the war.

After he left, I focused my attention on my damaged leg. I had no control over the nerves and muscles that seemed to writhe like snakes under the white plaster cast. One wave of contractions followed another, reminding me of my childhood coughing. Once the first cough came I could not stop the second, and soon an agonizing and exhausting crescendo of coughs ensued until my ears rang from the noise. I remembered the voice of my older brother, John, calling out to me in the dark garage from his bunk bed below, "Are you all right? Is everything OK?"

I missed that comforting voice and the childhood that seemed more permanently amputated from my life than my foot. I would certainly walk again, perhaps even run again. But I grieved more for my lost innocence, which could never be reattached to my spirit.

With my mind fully concentrated on my leg a miracle happened: the pain lifted. One instant the pain was with me; the next it was gone. It vanished. Disappeared. And in its place there was something that felt like much more than the absence of pain. What I felt was perfect clarity, perfect awareness. It was as if I had been blind and now could see.

I could see backward into my life with perfect recall of everything I had done beginning with my first conscious memory: I was two years old exploring a shed behind our house and hearing the frightened voice of my mother calling out to me. I saw how hard I had worked to do things that would please my parents and my friends. I saw how this had sometimes caused me to do things I should not have done. I saw and laughed at how foolishly I had behaved trying to be what I imagined others wanted me to be. A hero. A star. The strong one. The problem solver. The lifesaver.

I was free of pain and more peaceful and calm than I had ever been before or have been since. My life unfolded before my eyes like a motion picture run backward. I could see myself doing things I thought others would like and admire. I saw myself going along to get along, how I hid characteristics I believed were socially unacceptable. This willingness to conform and this need to be liked had become a habit so ingrained I had forgotten independent action was possible. The longer I acted out of concern for the opinions of others the more I became afraid of doing something that would displease them.

In the present I could also see things I would have

missed before. When I looked at inanimate objects, I saw into the depths of their beginnings. I saw the page of a book that once lived in a forest and the cowhide on a chair that was once a living animal. I saw the words of a magazine lying on a table and was certain I could hear the voices and know the lives of the writers of the stories inside. Even the man in the purple robe whom I had previously found uninteresting became a story worth hearing. He thought I needed help and buzzed the nurses. When they came to see what was the matter, I no longer saw people who were taking care of me; I saw men and women with lives, histories, problems, and value beyond satisfying my medical needs.

It was as if all time had been compressed into a single fraction of a moment, a kaleidoscope of possibilities I had not considered before. Somehow the whole of life had been opened to me. I saw that my own death was more than an inevitability to be feared but a necessary part of life to be embraced. I saw that the fear of losing something I valued—my property, popularity, my life—was what had enslaved me. Freedom would come when I could lose the fear of losing everything but my eternal soul. I laughed out loud from the happiness I felt at being able to see these things.

As the minutes wore on I became afraid that this new awareness would not last for long. The pain was going to return. This was going to become a memory I would want to remember. I needed to write down everything I saw and felt. Because my hands were bandaged, I tried without success to persuade someone, anyone, to record my thoughts. The more I worried about time running out the sooner came the moment when the pain began to return like a train far off in the distance. Closer and closer, louder and louder it became until I was back where I had been before.

The pain was with me again and I was left to wonder what had happened, wondering if there was any way for me to go back to that place where I had known such happiness, such peace, and such joy. Two days later I was on a plane with other wounded men being shipped to various places in the States. As the plane left Japan I watched the sun set over the islands. I saw the round distinct boundary of this ball of gas melt and flatten against the earth's horizon. It became a fiery, molten lake and then it disappeared. Daylight was gone and I slept.

When I awoke, the plane was still in darkness but we were motionless on the tarmac of a military base in Alaska having our plane refueled. The man who had been sleeping above me remained silent when I called him, and he was no longer dripping blood on my blanket. When the nurse came by I asked if he had died. She would not answer my question. "Get some rest," she said, and since she controlled the morphine dripping from the intravenous bag into my arm, she knew how to help me take her advice. I didn't know the man; he had been wounded and was flying home. Now he was gone.

When we landed at Fort Dix, New Jersey, I knew how Alice felt after she fell down the rabbit's hole. I had taken a drink from the bottle that made people smaller and had shrunk so I could get through the doors of this new life. Six young enlisted men in white uniforms carried us on stretchers to a gray U.S. Navy bus much like the one I rode from Providence to Newport a lifetime ago. The sun's brightness and warmth startled me. I squinted to see what was around me: more of the familiar military buildings with men coming and going, unloading the plane.

As soon as the driver had signed the form taking responsibility for us, we were on our way to the naval hospital in Philadelphia. My stretcher was suspended from slings attached to vertical chrome poles, which stood directly over the right rear wheels. Every pothole or bump in the road sent a shock wave up the poles through the slings to my body. The wave crested as it hit the white plaster cast on my right leg. As it did, my body would flinch in reflex. I cursed the driver, the road, and myself.

I was thankful when we finally pulled up to the semicircular entrance of the hospital, a circa-1930s building with two twelve-story towers and several long wings. We were lifted onto hospital gurneys, covered with cool sheets, and lined up for processing. A female nurse went from man to man, asking our names and checking our answers against the charts attached to us. A male attendant gave each of us a cardboard box. Inside we found a baloney sandwich on white bread, an apple, a hard-boiled egg, and a cookie. All four of my items went uneaten.

A dark-haired female nurse pushed my gurney down a long hallway with pale green walls and a brown linoleum floor toward an elevator. I watched the fluorescent light fixtures pass overhead. The elevator door opened and closed behind us. We were alone for one exciting moment until the elevator stopped and the door opened onto other floors, each time admitting another wounded man or two. All wore blue cotton robes over blue cotton pajamas. Some walked and some were pushed in wheelchairs.

As I observed the other patients, I remember thinking how remarkable it was that flying metal could produce such a wide variety of wounds on these male bodies without killing them. I was amazed at how a well-packed metal canister could destroy parts of a human being and still not end life. The mortars, box mines, howitzers, grenades, and bullets had exploded close enough to bring an untimely end to every man I passed that day. But they had lived on to face life in misshapen bodies. Their scar tissue would always tell a silent story to those initiated into the ways of damaged flesh.

Turning my head to the right I was startled to see a man in a wheelchair. He did not make a sound. He leaned toward me with the weight of his body resting on the elbow of his remaining arm. His right arm was missing above the elbow, as were both of his legs. I looked directly into his face except there was no face. In the place of eyes, nose, and lips was a sunken cavity smooth and free of scars. I thought of the boy in Dalton Trumbo's *Johnny Got His Gun* and wondered how he could have survived.

The English poet Wilford Owen survived some of the worst fighting of the First World War only to be killed a few days before the Armistice. He had seen how terrible flying steel can be and wrote about the moment it makes contact with the flesh of man:

> "O Jesus Christ! I'm hit," he said; and died
> Whether he vainly cursed, or prayed indeed,
> The Bullets chirped—In vain! Vain! Vain!
> Machine-guns chuckled—Tut-tut! Tut-tut!
> And the Big Gun guffawed.

But the man I was looking at had not died or at least his body had not. Somehow and for some reason he had lived. The door opened on the twelfth floor and I was rolled into quarters for sick and wounded navy and Marine Corps officers. This would be my new home.

16

MOST OF THE MEN ON THE twelfth floor were Marines injured in the war. All of them were in the acute stage of their treatment. The hospital must have been a difficult organization to manage because you never knew how many customers would be coming your way from month to month. The pace of the war was the biggest variable, and I often wondered if there were ways to predict how many amputees, paraplegics, and other wounded would be produced when men go to war.

Most of the men had been injured very early in their tours. This timing is quite common and is either the result of fateful coincidence, which is certainly possible in war, or of frightful inexperience, which is a more likely explanation. Gary Parrott and I once got into a discussion about this fact and the unfairness of the medal system. I suggested a fairer way to give medals was to eliminate all but one, the Purple Heart, since this is the only one we can be certain the wounded deserve. Gary had a better idea. "Why not give a Purple Heart to everybody who goes into combat and then if they mess up and get injured, take it away from them."

At Philadelphia they took beds away from the patients instead. When I arrived, there was only one bed open on the floor and I was given it. They had taken it away from someone else. That's the way the place ran. Every bed was always in use so that every new arrival had to be preceded by a departure. Someone had to be discharged whenever a new man arrived. This simple physical law governed our hospital.

One way administrators accommodated the large number of customers was simply to add beds. This policy affected enlisted men more than it did officers. When we officers were well enough to go to the prosthetic clinic or when an event was scheduled on the hospital lawn, we had to pass by the enlisted men's wards. Not only were there ten or more beds in each room, but enlisted men also were expected to swab the decks and clean their own spaces.

We officers, on the other hand, lived in the lap of luxury. Two men shared a room and two rooms shared a bathroom. There was a solarium on the floor where we could gather to play cards, smoke, and watch television.

Orderlies kept everything clean and waxed. And we had a much better nurse-to-patient ratio.

I was assigned a bed in a room directly across from the nurse's station. The nurse who wheeled me in called for a male orderly to help lift me onto my bed. They asked if I needed anything, told me a doctor would be by shortly, and left. Turning my head to the right I met the eyes of my roommate, who had watched the entire unloading in silence.

His name was Jim Crotty and when he said his last name—with an elongated vowel that made me think of *crawdaddy*—I knew that Philadelphia was his home. He lay stiffly on top of his sheets, then pulled himself up with a trapeze that hung above him and said hello with a confident sincerity that made me like him immediately. He was not wearing a pajama top and his chest was covered with bright red eight-by-three-inch rectangles. His feet were bare and undamaged, but his ankles were wrapped in white gauze bandages that disappeared up his shortened pant legs and reappeared again above his waist stopping about midstomach.

The first question most men will ask when they meet another man who has been injured in the war is, What happened to you? Maybe this is a sign of a special bond between men who have suffered similar fates. Or maybe it isn't special at all and comes from the same robotic mindset that makes a passenger in a taxicab ask the driver, "Where are you from?" My wound was obviously caused by an explosion and required little explanation, but Jim Crotty's was not self-evident. He had been burned badly, that much was clear, but I had never seen burns cover so much of the body of a living person.

He had been training to become a Marine helicopter pilot when his chopper lost its tail rotor. He tried to land but when he came in hard, his fuel tank exploded. His crew chief was killed instantly, but he and his instructor managed to get free with minor injuries. Later as a nurse examined him, he watched large areas of the skin on his legs slough away as she tried to clean what he had thought were superficial wounds. He had third-degree burns that went from the tops of his shoes to just above his navel.

Third-degree burns destroy the skin. Only transplants can restore its vital protective function. The bright red rectangles on Jim's upper body were where skin had been cut, peeled away, and grafted to some part of his lower body. It was a long and painful process during which his grafts struggled with limited success to adapt to their new locations.

Circumferential burns pose a special problem because the patient always suffers the full weight of his body pressing down on the damaged and fragile surface no matter which way he lies. For a long time Jim had lived in a rotating contraption so the nurses could turn him easily and regularly. Recently he had been transferred to a normal bed. It had been months since he had stood upright, and it would be months more before his doctors would risk putting him in a vertical position because they were afraid it would result in the loss of some of the grafted areas.

As a result of lying down so long, Jim's body was flat and stiff as a board. For exercise he pulled himself up on his trapeze, which also kept him from getting bedsores and provided relief from the stress of being immobile. Once a day he was lifted onto a gurney and taken to another floor, where he was lowered into a whirlpool. Because his gauze bandages were stuck so tightly to dried blood, immersing him in water was the only way the nurses could change his dressings. The pain of this process caused him to thrash uncontrollably in the water, which darkened with his blood as though he were being attacked by piranhas.

Pain was Jim's constant companion. His doctor made certain he did not have to ask for relief. Dilaudid, the most powerful synthetic narcotic, was injected into his bloodstream every three hours around the clock. His regime was enlightened compared to the miserly way narcotics are typically administered to patients out of fear they will become addicts. Jim Crotty had most certainly become an addict who was physiologically dependent upon Dilaudid to control pain. However, he was not taking narcotics because he suffered from a need to substitute the temporary pleasure of the needle for the more difficult but longer lasting pleasures of life.

What surprised me was that even when he was under the influence of the narcotic, he was completely conscious. His speech was not slurred and his thoughts were expressed in clear and understandable sentences. If I had met him on the street, I could not have guessed that he was addicted to Dilaudid.

Jim came from Philadelphia and he taught me to eat scrapple, steak and onion sandwiches, and what seemed like a lifetime supply of Hostess Ho Hos and Ding Dongs brought by his mother and father. He taught me to write odes and poems to unique hospital objects like stump socks, those woolen garments worn over an amputee's limb in order to cushion the hard socket of the prosthesis. Jim had a lyrical gift and upon request would sing songs he had composed in a mock Joan Baez falsetto. I remember a couple of verses from his "Ode to a Stump Sock":

Wrapped in plastic clean and white
The stump sock waited in the night
On a shelf with all his friends;

He longed to have his eyes first sight
Of that special stump on which he might
Spend the life a stump sock spends.

Jim told me that we shared our bathroom with a man who was dying of brain cancer and another who had made his third unsuccessful suicide attempt. The cancer victim was already blind and bedridden, and his cries in the night would increase as his pain grew more intense and death came closer. The would-be suicide's name was Jackson Roark, a navy meteorologist from Boonville, Missouri. Jack was an alcoholic — a condition more common in the navy in 1969 than it is today — who became so depressed when he drank that on three occasions he had returned to his room and cut his throat. On the third try he came close to success. The loss of blood killed a large part of his brain, leaving him paralyzed on one side, unable to speak, and incapable of any but the most simple gestures.

Jim was not only up-to-date on the men in the next room, he knew everything happening on the floor and much of what was going on in the entire hospital because he didn't sleep at night. He lay awake blowing smoke rings and gossiping with nurses who were glad to have some company. He gathered stories like an attentive shopper.

He was in the middle of one of his stories when my doctor, a thirty-something orthopedic surgeon with coal black hair and a very noticeable limp, came into our room. He examined my medical records and the two blackened toes that protruded from the cast on my right leg.

"I'm afraid you have gangrene," he said. "I need to get you down to the casting room to see what's underneath." He said it would be painful and ordered an injection of Demerol, my favorite narcotic. I told him I would prefer to stay fully awake for this one, since he would probably be making the final decision about my foot. If he wanted to amputate, I wanted to have a say in the matter.

The casting room smelled of plaster dust and rubbing alcohol and had the look and feel of a high school industrial arts classroom. My doctor was talking with a man who held a power saw in his right hand. He hit the switch and brought the blade down toward my leg, and I was certain he was going to slip and cut through the cast to the flesh on the other side. But he cut only through the plaster from hip to toe, pried the cast apart with his hands, made another cut, and removed the entire casing like he was opening a lobster for dinner.

While the doctor pulled the dried bandages away, I had to be held down by a male nurse. With my leg exposed I saw the damage for the first time. In spite of the warnings of the doctors in Japan not to get my hopes up about saving the leg, I had done just that. One look at the mass of angry, swollen red tissue and my hopes crashed. It no longer resembled a leg. Bones stuck out at disorderly angles from flesh spread wide and flat across the blood-stained sheet. My ankle and heel were completely gone. The blackened toes were attached to my only remaining metacarpals, which were no longer attached to anything at all.

"We'll need to operate soon," the doctor said. "The infection is spreading. I'll come see you in your room."

Back in my room I asked for Demerol. As the nurse

prepared to stick a needle into my upper arm, I noted she was giving me a fifty-milligram dose and was thankful to the doctor for his generosity. The needle drove into my muscle and the taste of the drug entered my mouth. The pain didn't disappear; it seemed to move outside of my body where I could see it like a distant light. Crotty asked what was up, and I told him I thought I was headed for surgery because there was no chance of saving the leg. Minutes later the surgeon came by to tell me I was scheduled for the operating room in two hours. He asked if I was ready. "I'm up for it, Doc," I answered with false and groggy bravery.

Before the attendants from the operating room came to take me away I was visited by a group of patients in wheelchairs and on crutches. One of them, Jim Harwood, a swift boat commander whose left leg had been amputated below the knee, sat in a chair by Crotty's bed. He took his prosthesis off and got to the point quickly. He urged me clearly and passionately not to let them cut off any more than was absolutely necessary. "They'll play it safe in surgery. Don't let them do it. You'll need every inch you can get."

I thanked Harwood for his advice and closed my eyes to give it some thought. When I opened them the nurse was back with another needle, a preoperative tranquilizer and muscle relaxant. It was time to go.

17

I FADED IN AND OUT OF consciousness while I waited in the line of five or six gurneys outside the swinging doors of the operating room. When my turn came I was wheeled into the cold, bright space from which someone had just been wheeled out. Around me moved human figures covered in pale green surgical uniforms. Voices buzzed in my ears. I was lifted onto the table and an IV needle was inserted into a vein on the inside of my right arm near the elbow. My doctor placed his hand on my shoulder and asked how I was. "Fine," I replied, "just fine. And, Doc? You won't cut off more than you need, will you?" A mask went over my face and I was gone before he could answer.

When I opened my eyes I was in the recovery room. My mother and father were there, sitting in chairs against the wall. They were holding hands. My mother's eyes were red and puffy. "Mom? Dad? Is that you?" I called. They came to my bedside and looked down upon me. "How are you feeling?" my father asked me. "Fine," I answered. "Just fine." My mother held my hand and put a wet washcloth to my lips. Two other men were alone and still asleep in their beds. As my head cleared, I remembered where I was and what had just been done to me. I remembered my question to the surgeon, but could not lift my head high enough to see how much he had taken. "Do you need something, son?" my father asked. I addressed the answer to my mother. "Mom, I need to know how much is left. Tell me how much is left." She looked down at me, held my hand, and said, "There's a lot left, Bob. There is a lot left." She was not talking about my leg. From that moment I did not doubt that my body and spirit would heal.

My parents stayed a few days and when they left for Lincoln, I was relieved to be alone again. The hospital was a refuge I wanted for myself. I needed to separate myself from the past. Among my fellow patients I felt safe. I did not have to hide my deformities because we were all disfigured. We were a brotherhood of cripples, bound together by our deformities and by the indignities we endured. It is hard to remain self-centered seated on top of a stainless steel bedpan.

One day, when I was perched atop a pan, the woman

friend who had come to the Bahamas with my family and me walked into the room unannounced. She had been traveling abroad and had written me regularly from places like Cairo, Rome, and Athens. Her arrival at this moment embarrassed me and I asked her to leave. When I was finished with the bedpan and had called for the nurse, she came back into the room.

I couldn't bring myself to tell her how much I loved her for being brave and caring enough to come to my bedside. I said I was planning a trip back to Nebraska as soon as I could and hoped I could see her then. I told her I should be fitted with a prosthesis soon and would be able to run and swim and dance, and do all the things I had done prior to the injury. When she left, I was even more relieved than I had been with my mom and dad.

It takes a brave man to let someone they love see them as they are. It takes a brave man to allow himself to be loved. And it takes a brave man to ask for help. All three of these are blood relatives, and my reluctance about each was a child of the same fear. In time I would learn how big the payoff was from trusting the love of a woman who was not turned off by the way I looked. In time I would also learn that I should quit trying to go back to the way I had been. I would have to face the truth that there were things I could never do again in order that I might do things I never dreamed possible before.

In the beginning of my recovery, overcoming physical weakness was my most obsessive wish. One of the big moments on this road was the first day I was able to make my own way into the bathroom to urinate standing up. It is one of the great joys of male life. After lowering myself into the wheelchair and waiting for the dizziness to subside, I rolled to the doorway of the bathroom we shared with our neighbors, stood on one leg, and peed into the bowl. The only thing better would have been to be standing outdoors. The excitement of controlling my own stream was tempered somewhat by the sight of myself in the mirror. When I turned to wash my hands, I was surprised at how skinny and unhealthy I looked. I had already traveled a long way from the tanned and strong SEAL team look I had worked so hard to achieve.

All my training had produced a look I thought people admired. I had created an image for myself of being tough, self-reliant, physically strong, and imposing. Now, looking into the mirror, I saw a weak, pale, and scrawny man. This was not a face that would intimidate the bad guys and save the damsel in distress. It was the face of a man who would have to be saved by someone else. At first I neither recognized nor liked this scrawny, pathetic looking face. And I was reluctant to admit that I would have to ask others for help with even the simplest of tasks. Asking for help was not optional; it was essential in order to recover. What surprised me was learning that asking for help made me stronger than I had been before. But old habits die hard and for many years this new understanding did not govern me, though I was able to do something

I had not done very well before: feel sympathy for others. And I found that sympathy for others opened doors to a kind of learning I had not imagined was possible before.

I was drawn to the lives of new friends and to their stories. Lew Puller was the son of the most highly decorated officer in the history of the Marine Corps. Lew's wounds were terrible. On patrol with the First Marine Division near Hue City, he hit a trip wire stretched across the path by North Vietnamese soldiers. The wire pulled a fuse that detonated a 105-millimeter howitzer. The explosion threw him into the air and severed both legs just below his hips. His hands were mauled by the blast of metal, and his lower abdomen was pierced. The heat of the rapidly burning explosive cauterized his wounds and allowed just enough blood to remain in his system for him to live. The speedy arrival of a medevac helicopter saved him.

When Lew awoke, he learned what he had lost. The more conscious he became, the less he wanted to live. By the time he arrived at Philadelphia in October, he would neither eat nor make any effort to hold on to life. Not until his wife, Toddy, who was pregnant when he went overseas, brought his new son to see him, did Lew's desire to survive awaken. His boy gave him reason enough.

Shortly after I arrived, Lew's father came to see him. The stir his presence caused confused me. He was a general, but it was not his rank that impressed us. He was much more than just a general. This was Chesty Puller.

He had earned five Navy Crosses fighting in Haiti in the 1920s, in the banana wars in Nicaragua in the 1930s, in the Pacific in the Second World War, and in Korea. When I saw him, I understood how he got his nickname. He was all chest. A short man with a face that launched a thousand battles, his jaw was square, his lips full, and his eyes sized up everything and everyone he saw. He asked my name and the story of how I was injured. When I got to the end of the firefight, his face drew so close to me I could feel his hot breath when he asked: "Well? Did you kill them? Did you kill them, son?" Here was a true warrior. Next to him I felt like an imposter.

Next to him we were all imposters. It was a heavy burden to be Chesty's son, especially if you were not physically equipped to follow in your father's footsteps. The son had poor vision and lacked the athletic ability a combat leader needed. He was taller than his father but much thinner, and had the serious look of an intellectual. When he graduated from college he was classified 4-F by his draft board, unfit for military service. He persuaded the board to reverse their decision and convinced the Marine Corps to give him a try. He dedicated himself to becoming an infantry officer who would make his father proud. When Lew shipped out to Vietnam he dreamt he would someday sit on the porch of the family home in Saluda, Virginia, drinking whiskey with his father and talking about their wars.

Two years later I went home with him to Saluda. By

then he was in law school at William and Mary. His father had died a broken man from the pain of seeing his son so monstrously shattered. His mother was full of old school Southern charm with the steely will that enables one to survive tragedy through denial. She was dignified, aloof, and fully committed to the role of military wife. She served Lew, Toddy, and me iced tea. We sat on the porch and talked for an hour. It was not the conversation Lew had hoped to have.

In the hospital we listened and paid attention to each other. We were just wounded men with lots of stories to tell, and Crotty told us the best ones. He talked about the night a despondent patient climbed to the roof in hopeless and suicidal resignation because a nurse had not responded to his advances. He told us about the screams of our neighbor—who was dying of cancer—when his roommate crawled from his bed and with one pull removed his catheter.

The victim's roommate was Jack Roark, a challenging mystery. When his neurosurgeon told Crotty and me that so much of his brain was destroyed he would never be able to talk, we decided to try to reach him. Actually, we didn't reach him; a nurse did, and without even trying. She was blond and beautiful, with high Nordic cheekbones. She broke the heart of every man on the floor. Her body was stunning and her smooth pale skin turned my blood hot, but I could not gather courage to advance beyond mild flirtation.

One afternoon, while Roark was sitting in his wheel-chair by the nurses' workstation, my dream nurse came upon him as she went from room to room taking meal orders from the patients. The last person she asked was Roark. Believing there was no risk, she sat on the arms of his wheelchair, resting her magnificent thighs against him. She laughed and asked what he wanted for breakfast, lunch, and dinner. He responded, but not with words. When she heard the splashing sound and saw the yellow stains on her white stockings, she shrieked and retreated. In the small silence that followed, Roark pointed a bony finger at her and spoke his first words: "Lollipop. Nurse Lollipop." Roark had a poet's economy with words. Any man with such a gift could not be a hopeless case.

After he had been cleaned up we beckoned him into our room. Slowly he wheeled himself to the foot of our beds by pushing his good right foot against the floor. The scar from his surgery angled six inches up toward the top of his head. Roark had the thin, angular look of a man whose drinking had destroyed his stomach's capacity to absorb food. He had a heavy beard, which he infrequently shaved, and the hair on his head was beginning to grow back. His teeth were gapped and pointed. He looked like one of Faulkner's Snopeses.

Both Jim and I spoke to him but got no response. We asked questions he didn't answer. His eyes darted back and forth from one of us to the other. We could see he wanted to talk but could not form the words. Silence rose up in the spaces between the three of us. Failing in our first attempt at conversation, we resumed talking as though he was not in the room. Jim lit a cigarette and began to blow the elaborate smoke rings that he practiced all night long. The rings triggered a response from somewhere deep inside Jack's remaining gray matter. Holding up two fingers of his bony right hand and blowing the word out his nose like a horn, he said loud enough to be heard down the hall, "Cigarette!"

Jim gave him a cigarette and a light. Jack inhaled hungrily, burning a good half inch with his first drag. He exhaled and sat looking at Jim as a dog would look at his master at feeding time. So Jim gave him another cigarette. We resumed our questioning. What did you do before the hospital? Where were you stationed? Are you in the navy or the corps? Jack had a cigarette going in each hand.

When he was finished smoking he said, in a nasal voice that reminded me of Willie Nelson on helium, "Where and what and how as far as the weather business?" He spoke every word distinctly as if to savor the sound of each. Then he looked at us as though he had spoken for hours and had given us every detail of his life since his first childhood memory. Jack had confirmed his existence as a forecaster of weather and confirmed he knew his days of predicting rain were over.

Later on, after Jack had learned to propel himself by leaning forward and pushing the small front wheels of his chair, he composed a short phrase that perfectly summarized the condition of all the other patients on the floor. Six of us were playing cards and smoking in the solarium. Among the six we could count less than half the normal supply of arms and legs. Like some giant snail Jack rounded the corner, surveyed the scene, bummed a smoke, and sat contentedly, rocking his head side to side like one of those toy dogs you sometimes see in the rear window of a car. Then, holding up a bony finger, he proclaimed: "Absence! Artillery!" We stopped our talking and turned to him. I thought this man was a genius.

18

PART OF THE INTELLIGENCE of the human body is how quickly it forgets pain. It cannot be recalled no matter how hard you try or how much you pretend. It would be blasphemy to call healing, another characteristic of the human body, intelligence. Healing is miraculous. Certainly medical science and its practitioners contribute a lot to healing, but the body with no outside help does the most important work.

I have been witness to and beneficiary of this miracle. My wound was dirty. Metal, wood, dirt, and stone were driven deep into flesh and bone. The surgeons were reluctant to close the wound until they were certain the infection had abated. The disadvantage of this strategy was that it left a lot of scar tissue on the limb. The benefit was

I did not need to go back into surgery to have the wound reopened, which would shorten the limb. Among the amputees this was known as whittling you down. So I did not object to the stump being left wide open and cleaned by the nurses twice a day. Later, when infection was no longer a risk, a patch of skin from my right thigh would be peeled off and put over the end of the leg. If this graft took a prosthesis would be fitted.

During the early days and weeks after our amputations those of us with dirty wounds endured twice-a-day cleanings. None of us looked forward to these, and I have forgotten all but one. A nurse, standing at the end of my bed looking down at the stump of my right leg, began the first of the day's cleanings. I dreaded these because peeling the dried and sticking bandage was not just painful but gave me time to think about how painful it was going to be. It was the thinking that worked me into a sweat.

After all the dressings this nurse had changed and all the abuse she had taken in the process, she would have been within her rights as a normal woman to have become hardened to the repeated wailings of her patients. But she hadn't. We were not routine for her. In my case she tried to lessen my discomfort by beginning with the least difficult wound, directly on the tibia below the kneecap where there was an inch-deep gouge into which she had tucked a long strand of iodoform gauze. Finished with that she turned her attention to the end of my stump. Now the fun began.

She used hydrogen peroxide to remove the wrapping. Then she took cotton swabs and more peroxide to clean the bright red oval where my calf used to be. She used a heavy steel floor lamp to illuminate the shadows where I presume bacteria liked to hide. On this day as she began her work, she lifted the lamp by its neck to slide it a few inches closer to my bed. As she did this the base fell off and the shade end of the lamp came down violently on the exposed stump. The blow made me retreat against and up the wall. My nurse was horrified and apologetic and offered to request Demerol to make up for the accident. Because I knew the pain would subside quickly, I figured I had come out ahead on the exchange.

I was thoroughly enjoying my Demerol buzz when a man came into our room and introduced himself as a surgeon whose specialty was hands. From across the great canyon that stood between his nonsedated state of consciousness and mine, I heard him say, "I want to have a look at your right hand." He unwrapped the bandages and spoke again. "Can you open your fingers?"

"No," I told him, "I can't.

Since Japan the hand had been given little attention. I thought of it as belonging to someone else. It was clenched into a grotesque, tight fist. The bone on the heel of the hand, the fifth metacarpal, had been broken in several places. The bone was at least half an inch shorter now, and the pinky finger had turned at a right angle across the back of my hand. Both tendons on that finger had been cut making voluntary movement impossible. But the cut tendons were not the main problem. I couldn't open my hand because the joints were frozen in place from inactivity and from small metal fragments scattered through the flesh.

"We've got to get this working again," he told me, and with the hurried manner of a man with a long list of patients he left to order physical therapy for me. Weeks later he came back to examine the hand again. He was unhappy with my lack of progress. "Still can't extend the fingers?" he asked as he took my hand in his. Then, without warning, he took my index finger in his hands and with a pop snapped it open. Before I had time to protest he did the same with the middle and the ring fingers. "Now, keep them open," he said and left without a word.

On his next visit he was pleased with the results, but told me I would need surgery to fix the pinky finger and to slip one of the tendons from my ring finger over to the pinky. He scheduled the operation for the next Friday, the weekend I had been invited to dinner with some Philadelphia relatives of my father. So I asked for a local anesthetic because the recovery time would be shorter and because I wanted to stay awake to watch.

When Friday morning came I was wheeled downstairs to the hallway outside the operating rooms. I was surprised to see how many others were waiting on their gurneys for the next available table. I counted a train of ten other patients resting end to end. When my turn finally came, the anesthetist applied a block administered through a needle into my armpit. He asked me to tell him when I felt an electric current in each of my fingers. When I did he pushed in some juice. He repeated the process until all five were dead to the world.

It was as if the arm were no longer attached. No feeling remained and all control was gone. It was quite amazing. The surgeon began to scrub and prepare my left hand.

"Oh, Doc," I said, "I believe you have the wrong one."

"Really," he responded and rechecked the X ray in the light box. He turned the film over and proceeded. "Oops," he said. My least favorite word as a patient.

The surgeon began by rebreaking the hand with a hammer and a chisel. The arm bounced around like a frozen fish each time he struck it. Then he turned the pinky finger back and drilled pins into the bone to set it in place. He sutured up the hand and drilled a pin through the end of the pinky finger. After the cast was put on the arm he stretched a rubber band from this pin to a wire harness built into the cast. The tension kept the pinky from turning back to its earlier deformed position. Fifty years earlier a man with my injury would probably have lost the use of his hand. I was in high spirits when I returned to my room and ready to spend the weekend with my father's cousin.

Her name was Dr. Harriet Mitchell Arey. She was a pediatrician at Philadelphia Children's Hospital. Her mother was sister to Fannie, the woman who raised my father and his brother. Harriet was born in Duluth, Minnesota, in the home to which Fannie had sent John in 1928 after his year at Wentworth Military Academy. She was a little girl when John came, and she remembered him as handsome, funny, kind, and serious.

Harriet had heard about my injury from my father who had told Fannie's daughters, Jessie and Eva. When she invited me to her home, I was reluctant at first but ended up glad I went. In our short time together we became close enough to talk about the war. And the feeling of family in her home made me want to make a trip back to Nebraska.

I made arrangements for a three-day weekend in early June and got crutches rigged with a metal cradle on the right side on which I rested my cast. I flew to O'Hare in Chicago where I connected to Lincoln. As I hobbled the long distance between gates, I grew very tired, but what bothered me most were the stares at my empty pant leg. With each swing of my good foot, I imagined what people were thinking and seethed with rage at imaginary insults. My father picked me up at the Lincoln airport. We talked about my future plans on the drive home. The only thing I had in mind was a half-baked idea about attending business school and perhaps returning to pharmacy in some way.

The car windows were rolled down and the smell of early summer lilacs filled the air. When the car stopped in our driveway, I lurched through the breezeway into the house and thought of the many times I had run through this space with boundless energy. This time I was exhausted and collapsed wearily into a chair. I asked my mom to bring me a stool so I could elevate my leg to keep the stump from swelling. My dad took my suitcase down to my old bedroom. My two youngest sisters were still at home, and the five of us sat together uncomfortably and talked about their school and what was going on in town. Mom cooked a big welcome home dinner for the whole family, which gathered with much laughter around our dining table. She served wine — the first time my mother ever allowed alcoholic beverages at her table. The wine helped loosen our conversation, and for two hours we told stories from our past, laughed, and forgot what had brought us together.

That night I went to sleep in my old room downstairs. I was happy to be home, but when I tried to go to sleep I saw the people in Thanh Phong for the first time since I had come back. I heard their voices crying out to me. When I tried to put them out of my mind all I could see behind my closed eyes was a solid wall of blood. When I finally fell asleep my dreams were frightening. Something about being home had brought back these memories.

The following night the woman who had come to see me in Philadelphia invited me to her home for dinner with her family. I would not let their kindness penetrate the fortress of resistance I had built around me. When dinner was over, she drove me home. I wanted her to hold me and say that everything would be all right. Instead we kissed briefly, and I went back to my old room for a repeat performance of bad dreams and memories.

On Saturday night a friend picked me up and we drove to a bar in downtown Lincoln across from the Cornhusker Hotel, where friends from high school and college were drinking and shooting pool. I could not play pool but I could drink beer, and my friends made certain my glass was never empty. I needed help getting back to the car.

On Sunday I stayed home from church to avoid the questions, but I also no longer felt I belonged. Something had changed. The strong line that had been my connection to God had broken. Not even a thread connected me to the way I had been before. When the family got back from church we went to lunch, and both my mom and dad drove me to the airport. My father checked my bag through to Philadelphia. Both of them walked me to the gate. I was grateful for their love, but even more grateful to be leaving.

Soon after I returned I was fitted for my first prosthesis. The day I went to the clinic I was shocked by how difficult it was to adjust to it. The limb, made of wood, was larger and heavier than I had imagined and needed a cumbersome waist belt to hold it in place. I had dreamed of slipping it on and running and dancing. But I found I could not put my full weight on the leg without sharp pain, and could not wear it for more than an hour before swelling would make it difficult to take off and impossible to put back on.

The prosthetist in the clinic saw my disappointment. "Don't worry, son, it will get easier, a lot easier. You have got to learn early not to let this thing push you around." Every time I went to his clinic he offered the right mix of encouragement and advice. He wanted me to get well. He wanted me to do well.

Over the years I learned that for an amputee it is the prosthetist who is the most important, beginning with his advice to the surgeon about the size, shape, and other details of the limb. In my case I had extensive fragile scarring, which was broken down by the jarring friction of the prosthesis's hard socket. Broken skin does not heal well inside the dark, tight, hot, and moist environment of a prosthesis socket. Skin heals best in fresh, dry air, and with regular antiseptic cleanings. So sometimes I had to remove the leg for twenty-four to forty-eight hours and from time to time my prosthetist would advise me to have surgical revisions done to reduce the size of the remaining scar tissue. I had my last surgical revision nine years after I was discharged from Philadelphia.

In late May I left the hospital to go to the first annual Martin Luther King track meet at Villanova. I wanted to watch a Nebraskan, Charlie Green, run the hundred-yard dash. Bob Carlos, Charlie's competition for world's fastest human, was also entered. I went hoping to see a classic duel and it happened. Charlie won the race in near record time. After the race, I was taunted by a group of long-haired men who blocked the exit and knocked me to the ground as I pushed past them to leave. It was a reminder that life outside the hospital was more difficult than life inside.

Hospital life was protected and safe. Early in the summer John Zier, a Marine, asked me to go with him on his first trip home to Rye, New York, to visit his family. He had stepped on a box mine that tore one leg off above the knee and severely damaged the other. Now John was debating with his doctors about what to do with his other leg. His surgeon wanted to amputate it but John said no. He was determined to nurse it back to health.

John was a big man with wide shoulders and a naturally muscular body. He and his twin brother, Bobby, had gone to high school in Rye and earned football scholarships at George Washington University in Washington, D.C. They were starting offensive and defensive tackles for three years until they were kicked off the team for fighting. John met his wife, Linde, at GW. She was an art history major whose gentle ways were in sharp contrast to her husband. After the brothers graduated, they joined the Marine Corps, where their size and aggressive behavior were more prized.

John told stories of so many fights I began to categorize them. There were fights in bars, fights for revenge or the honor of his wife, fights begun by John and fights started by Bobby, fights before he went to Vietnam and fights while he was in country. There was even a small category of fights he lost, but there was no category for fights he didn't enjoy. Fighting was a hobby like golf.

He was a gifted storyteller with a high-pitched voice that would squeak just a little when he got wound up in some old memory. There was the fight at a party after a fellow student took the unfortunate liberty of biting Linde on her ass. There was another after Bobby had been thrown out of a bar. He and John returned to the scene and drove everyone behind a barricade of chairs they built in self-defense. From behind this wall came a shower of beer bottles, one of which hit Bobby and knocked him out. That was the fight that got them kicked off the football team. There was the fight to avenge a friend who had been beaten so badly he was hospitalized. John visited him and kneeled close so the friend could whisper the name of the bully in John's ear. Afterward, when the unsuspecting target opened his door, John hit him in the face with the flat side of a trash can lid he had picked up en route. And there was the fight with a man much smaller than either Bobby or John who put each of them on the floor with one blow to the head. "I think he must have been a professional boxer. He had a great right hand," John explained.

In Vietnam his fighting had a more useful purpose. Once John was checking his perimeter and discovered two men missing. Their breach of security put the entire company at risk, so John was understandably upset. The normal procedure would have been to court-martial them both. Instead John searched for them, found them watching a movie, warned them to prepare for a thrashing, and proceeded to do just that.

John Zier was neither a bully nor a braggart. He just wove his tales in from time to time as casually as he would an account of going to the grocery store for milk. He could tell about his mistakes as readily as his successes. Once John was leading a combat patrol that included some men who had just arrived in Vietnam. His compass man got them lost. In frustration John moved up the column so he was right behind the point man who was twenty or thirty meters in front. He saw the point man stop suddenly and motion with a closed fist to bring the column to a halt and drop down on the trail. John sent the same closed fist signal down the line and every man went down into firing position. John crawled up to talk with his point man.

"I saw figures, sir, moving across the trail up ahead about fifty meters."

"Where are they now?"

"Right after we stopped they hit the deck. I think they are still up there on the ground."

"What else did you see?"

His point man hesitated before answering. "They were carrying weapons, sir. I think they are Americans. I think they are ours."

Zier was livid at this news. He had cleared the area of operations. Only his company was meant to be out there. He whispered violently to the point man: "I'm going back to the radio to find out who the hell is out here where they're not supposed to be."

Again his point man hesitated. "Sir, I wouldn't do that. When I said they were ours, I meant our company. I think we've gone in a circle and cut off the rear of our column."

Zier's response impressed me more than all his fights. He laughed, signaled for his men to get up, and proceeded on. As he passed by the confused-looking Marines, he asked whom they were with.

"We're with some Lieutenant by the name of Zier."

"Oh," John hollered back. "I know him. He's a good man. You're in good hands."

On our trip to John's home Linde drove and I rode shotgun with John stretched out sideways in the backseat, telling stories full of drama and excitement. But when we reached the outskirts of Rye his mood changed and he became silent. At his house I saw the same scene I had played out in Lincoln. His mother and father came excitedly to the car. John needed to use a wheelchair to get into the house, and his dad helped him up the stairs. At dinner we talked but kept the subjects remote and light. On the mantel was a photograph of John and his brother. They were wearing their dress blue Marine uniforms. They had just become officers and looked as good as men could possibly look. Silently they gazed down upon us from inside their glass frame. They reminded us of what we used to be.

I loved retreating to the comfort of the hospital or to the houses of one of the married patients. I often visited Lew and Toddy's house on the naval base. Toddy cooked and kept us well supplied with beer. Lew and I and others drank and talked and listened to music. Lew loved Credence Clearwater Revival and had memorized the lyrics of "Fortunate Son." He would ask Toddy to cue the tape and turn up the volume. It became Lew's song.

By summer I learned the navy had recommended me for the congressional Medal of Honor for my actions on the night I was wounded. My men had recommended me for the Silver Star and it had been upgraded. The news stunned and embarrassed me. I did not believe the action deserved the highest honor.

In the fall I went back to San Diego to visit my friends in SEAL team. After my injury, another officer had replaced me and he had performed well. The platoon had returned from Vietnam with me as the only casualty. I loved these men, but we were now separated by our experiences. A gulf lay between us that we could not bridge. For us, subjects like loss and moral failure were taboo.

I did manage to talk to them of my reservations about accepting the Medal of Honor. Chief Petty Officer Barry Enoch, a man I respected for his fighting skill, told me I had no choice. "You must accept this award for everyone who should have been recognized but was not. You must wear it for others." On the flight back to Philadelphia I decided he was probably right. I did not like the idea of being known as a hero but disliked the idea of disappointing my teammates even more.

19

As soon as I was able to walk without crutches, I was ready to go home. The navy notified me I would be discharged and retired with a medical disability effective December 1, 1969. The hospital needed my bed a few days early, which was fine with me. I shipped all my belongings to Nebraska and planned on going home with only the clothes on my back.

Before leaving I called on Harriet Mitchell Arey to thank her for bringing me into her home and making me feel that I belonged. She told me I was welcome anytime and said I reminded her of my uncle John. "He didn't make it. I'm glad you did."

She was glad that I had come home alive. That's all she meant, no more and no less. I heard a lot more in her words. I heard her say I should make the most of this second chance; I should begin this second life with gratitude. I left Philadelphia determined to try.

Two memorable events happened the weekend I was released. The moratorium, the largest of the antiwar protests, took place in Washington, D.C., and Seymour Hersh's account of My Lai, where American soldiers massacred Vietnamese civilians, was published. I went home thinking my country was turning against me or I against it. Either way I wanted to escape. Hatred was in the air in the America of 1969. Though many sought to avoid it, the antiwar movement had become antimilitary. The hospital that had sheltered me was now releasing me. It was time to face the music.

My blue dress uniform fit poorly. A tailor in Newport, Rhode Island, had made it during Officer Candidate School. I had never worn it before and would never wear it again. It now hung loose on a body that had become considerably smaller during the previous eight months. I weighed less than 140 pounds, including my new wooden leg. A dark blue, wool peacoat hid my shrunken body but could not hide my puny face and scrawny neck.

I said farewell to the nurses on the floor and to my fellow patients, most of whom would be my friends all my life. An administrative officer escorted me down the elevators and the front steps where I met an off-duty nurse who had agreed to drive me to Fort Dix, New Jersey, where I could catch a ride on a military flight to Offutt

Air Force Base just south of Omaha. From there I would hitchhike the last fifty miles to Lincoln.

An icy wind found its way through the gap in my shirt collar and crawled down my back. I shivered and pulled the collar of my coat up around my ears. My new wooden leg was fastened to my right thigh with a leather strap. A wide scar across the shinbone of the stump of my right leg had broken open and bled as I walked. To lessen the pain from the scar tissue I shifted my weight to my left leg while I watched my breath spin like cotton candy in the wind and then disappear. I squeezed a rubber ball in my pocket to exercise my right hand to keep the fingers from becoming stiff and contracted.

Looking southwest across Packer Avenue I saw Veterans Stadium where Army and Navy would soon be playing their annual football game. A year ago I would have cared, but I had lost interest in the sport somewhere along the line. Farther south along Broad Street was the Navy Yard, where Lew and Toddy Puller were just beginning their day.

A bus drove up to the emergency entrance to my right. Corpsmen ran out with gurneys to unload the Marines from the bus. The left arm of one man fell limp and loose as they lifted him. He was in no condition for a box lunch. I wished them all well.

As I stood there bearing most of my weight on my left leg, I questioned my decision to take a military flight and then hitchhike home. A commercial flight with my father waiting to meet me would have been much easier. But I couldn't bear the thought of sitting with civilians or the idea of the long walk through O'Hare to change planes. And I wanted to be the master of this homecoming; I wanted to do this one alone.

I got lucky at Fort Dix and caught a space-available seat as soon as I got there. In two hours I was onboard heading west. The earth turned east below us, and I watched the sky change from blue to black. An air force officer on the plane offered to drive me as far as the interstate and said he would even be glad to take me all the way to Lincoln. I accepted the first half of his offer.

Standing in darkness on the shoulder of the highway I let a few cars and trucks pass before I stuck out my right thumb. The very first driver decided to stop after he had gone a good distance past me. My walk was more of a hop-step like Jingle Jones, the limping character played by Andy Devine in the television series *Wild Bill Hickok*. I almost yelled out, "Hey, Wild Bill, wait for me!"

There were four young men in the car, two in front and two in back. As I squeezed into the back my prosthesis began to pinch the skin behind my knee. I tried to shift my weight to ease the pain, but nothing worked. Gritting my teeth, I introduced myself. One of them told me they were students on their way home from the moratorium. The driver said he stopped because of my uniform. "We're not against the soldiers," he said, "just the war."

My views on the war had taken a U-turn while I was in

the hospital. The day I flipped from silent doubt to vocal opposition I was watching President Nixon on television. One line in his speech detonated a bomb inside me. "I've seen the ugly face of war. I know what you are going through," he said, and went on to give a rational explanation of the progress being made under Vietnamization, his plan to turn the war over to the Vietnamese. He appealed to America for unity. He got no support from me. "Bullshit," I said out loud. "You have no idea how ugly it is."

Bitter anger and resentment colored my view of all politicians and most political issues, especially the question of what to do in Vietnam. Men were dying and killing on both sides and in large numbers with little chance the outcome would be different as a consequence. Ending the war sooner rather than later seemed the only obvious and humane answer.

The students dropped me off in front of my parents' home. I thanked them for the lift and was grateful beyond words to be able to straighten my leg and end the pain of the prosthesis. As I walked the length of our driveway, my stump was swollen tight in its socket. The cold trickle of blood told me that my scar had broken down. My mother and father were standing in the doorway waiting for me. I ate a sandwich with them and told them I needed sleep. What I needed was to get my leg off and inspect the damage. In my small bedroom downstairs I dropped my trousers and removed the prosthesis. The sock covering the stump was bloody, and I felt great relief as I pulled it free of the hard socket. I took off my uniform, folding it neatly on a table, lay down on clean sheets, and went to sleep.

I was wakened at 2 A.M. by the same bloody nightmares I had during my last visit home. In the dream I saw the faces of the people I had killed and many more besides. They walked past me in an unending line. Their faces and bodies were mangled and rotting from their wounds. As they drew close every one of them asked the same question, "Why? Why did you do this to me?" I could not answer and I could not move. I was permanently mute and immobile. All I could do was listen to the cries and the identical, repeated question. Awake, I was too terrified to close my eyes again for fear I would fall asleep and the dream would return.

In the morning my father was eager to talk to me about my future. It was time to get to work on the plans I had made before I went into the navy. He had a friend who was willing to help me get into Stanford Business School in Palo Alto, California. I had doubts but did not speak of them while my mother served us a breakfast of eggs, bacon, toast, and juice. She sat down to join us. I looked into her eyes and tried to communicate what I was feeling. I believe she understood, but not a word passed between us.

My father's persistence and my lack of an alternative led me to apply to Stanford for the fall 1970 quarter. Meanwhile, I began looking for a pharmacy job and a place to live. I enrolled at the University of Nebraska to get used to studying again and signed up for a class in beginning accounting and one in political science on revolution. My brother Bill who was finishing college, agreed to share his apartment with me. I put away my navy uniforms and rejoined civilian life wishing to become anonymous.

The debate on the war was in full bloom. In Nebraska the opposition was centered at the university, and I attended several events where the speakers condemned both our involvement and President Nixon. At one, Don Walton, a reporter for the *Lincoln Star,* saw me and asked if he could call me to talk about the war. I said yes. During the interview he asked if I would go to Vietnam again knowing what I now knew. My answer was no, asking him in return if he would cross the street knowing he would get hit by a car. The headline of the morning paper read something like "Returning Veteran: I would not go again." Seeing the words made me wish I had kept my mouth shut.

Thanks to a man named Oliver Waite, I landed a job at Bryan Memorial Hospital, where I had been born. Dr. Waite managed the hospital's pharmacy and practiced dentistry in a private clinic. He had fought with the Marine Corps in two wars—against the Japanese in the Pacific and against the Communists in Korea—and he gave me the job because I had served. Perhaps for the same reason he hired two Cuban pharmacists driven from their homes by Castro.

Ollie knew what it was like to come home from a war and to feel bitterness toward your country. He told me how angry he had been when President Truman recalled men who had already served in World War II to fight in Korea rather than declaring war and using the draft. Ollie's experience with politicians had been far worse than mine, and the company of his remembered misery was comforting.

Standing for hours at a pharmacy counter was more difficult and painful than I had expected. I had to lean against a stool to make it through an eight-hour day and took so many aspirin that by the close of business my ears were ringing. Even without my physical problems, which I knew would heal in time, I had lost my enthusiasm for counting pills.

In my accounting class I met two women who helped me figure out where to go next. They invited me to their church and gave me the chance to join their circle of young friends. During their discussions of the Bible I brought in quotes from authors I was reading in political science: Hannah Arendt, Albert Camus, Bernard Fall, Jean Lacouture, and Tom Dooley. The women and the reading kindled a desire to pursue something other than business.

All through this time the nightmares continued, and I found no one I could trust enough to talk about them. The minister at Bethany Christian Church was a kind and considerate man who tried to help, but I would not let him in. When I went to church with the women from my accounting class, I began to feel close to something I needed: loving kindness and forgiveness. But I kept trying to substitute intellectual discussions of Camus and Arendt for healing. These served more as distractions than as serious self-examination. I simply did not know what to do.

I did know what to do about physical rehabilitation and began rebuilding my body with vigor and determination. Because my scar tissue continued to break down even under the stress of walking, running was out of the question. So I swam. Six days a week I went to the downtown YMCA and swam laps in a twenty-yard four-lane indoor pool. I did fifty laps up and back each morning. My leg was not waterproof, so I left it at the side of the pool. I wore a rubber band around the fingers of my right hand to hold them together. But once I was in the water I felt normal again. Slowly, surely, my strength returned.

Something else returned during the swimming hour. An hour in the silence of the water and the rhythm of the overhand crawl was like an hour of submerged meditation. I left the pool each day with an inner peace that stayed with me while I dressed, walked to a downtown restaurant, and had breakfast. I drank coffee and watched people hurrying to work. During these moments I started trying to understand what I had done in Vietnam and to consider what I should do now.

I had been assigned Camus's *The Rebel* in my political science class. It opens with a vividly authentic terrorist assassination. Camus, who fought with the French underground, apparently had learned to use a knife. At least he seemed to understand the techniques. Then I read another book by Camus entitled *The Fall,* which tells the story of a man who was walking along the Seine in Paris at night when he heard something fall into the water. It could have been a body. He hesitated but did not stop, convincing himself that the sound was something other than a person in trouble. He tried to forget but the memory haunted him more and more. In the end he faced the truth: he had allowed someone to drown because he did not want to risk saving him.

At the beginning of the book I thought the title referred to the man who fell in the water. In the end it was clear that the one who fell was the man who did not save him. He believed he was a brave man, capable and willing to risk his life for another. He believed he would choose to do the right thing. But when the moment came, he was a coward. The fall was his fall from grace.

The Fall reminded me of the doctrine of original sin, which I had learned in church as a boy. According to this teaching, we are all sinners at birth. Our fall — the legacy of Adam and Eve's sins in the Garden of Eden — occurs at birth. We are born into sin and can only be forgiven by accepting Christ. That is what I had been taught, and I had believed it when my sins were still quite small. After the war forgiveness did not seem as likely. My minister at Bethany Christian Church told me I could be forgiven. He said it didn't matter what I had done. He said God's capacity to forgive is absolute. All I had to do was ask and God would forgive me. So I asked. And waited for the change.

The change I wanted — to go back to the way I was as a child lying under the summer stars and dreaming, playing in a field near the red sandstone caves carved by the floodwaters of Dead Man's Creek, splayed out on the concrete by the pool at the country club where I caddied, oblivious to everything except the sight of a dark, cool wet mark where my face lay and the sounds of people splashing in the water — I could not make happen. I had suffered physical and spiritual loss, and I would just have to learn to live with it.

Second chances to correct mistakes are the stuff of movies, not life. I knew from the answer given to me in the Japanese hospital during the fifteen minutes I was in the eye of the storm that I had spent my life preparing for easy decisions and that when the difficult one came I wasn't ready. Physical stamina and intellectual strength were not enough.

Forgiveness came in small doses and at unexpected moments. I felt it during the movie *The Deer Hunter.* I was moved by the scene at a wedding when the bride and groom are sharing a ceremonial glass of red wine. According to tradition, if any wine spills it is an omen of bad luck to come. The camera draws close to the bride as her innocent mouth touches the wine. A drop falls from her lips and stains her white dress. No one sees it. She is unaware of the accident and betrays no sign of foreboding. Her new husband is sent to Vietnam and is horribly wounded. The lesson was the same: once the stain appears there is no turning back; there can be no second chance.

Grief at the loss of my innocence and the death of innocents followed me day and night. There were dark times when this grief would rise in my chest like hot water. I would become short of breath and feel that death was a better option than living. But I rejected that course of action. I could give meaning to the lives of the people I saw in my dreams only by choosing life. When the water of self-pity began to rise this was the rope I used to pull myself out.

During my physical recovery I had learned about the power of the only thing in life in which I completely believe: human kindness. Kindness — unselfish and un-afraid — could lift my spirit most of all. My feelings of unworthiness dissolved the moment the new friends extended kindness to me. And better, worries about my loss ended when I learned that giving kindness was more liberating than receiving it.

Sister Prejean, a Catholic nun who ministers to death row inmates and to the families of their victims, once said, "Human beings are a lot more than the worst thing they have done in their lives." She spoke the truth. We are not as bad as our memories tell us we are.

In April a letter came from the navy informing me that President Nixon would present the congressional

Medal of Honor to me and twelve other men at the White House in May. I was still deeply skeptical of these honors and did not feel like a hero. I was still not sure I should accept and again considered refusing in protest. I was beginning to see the danger of believing that our greatest heroes live and die on battlefields. And I thought the medals were meant to make Americans feel better about the war.

When I was administrative officer of SEAL Team One, I dealt with the procedure for granting medals, and I knew that many men got nothing for bravery far greater than mine. There were five prerequisites for receiving a medal: Step one was the action itself. Step two was a living witness who had seen it. Step three was a living witness who could write (many a brave man's actions went unsung because the witness did not have a gift for words). Step four was a literate living witness who liked the brave man in question. No matter what the witness saw or how profound his gift for words, there would be no medal if he hated the brave man's guts. Step five was surviving the bureaucratic process. Even a brave man whom everyone liked could go without reward if his papers got lost in the bureaucratic shuffle.

All my doubts seemed small measured against the pride my parents felt. They wanted me to succeed and believed the award meant I had. For that reason, I decided to go to Washington and to bring all my brothers and sisters.

But the ceremony at the White House was scheduled

only days after the invasion of Cambodia and the killings at Kent State. My skepticism resurfaced as I wondered whether the award ceremony was an attempt to use us for political cover. On the plane heading east I talked to my father about my suspicion. I could tell he was worried I might do something rash.

We landed at National Airport in the early afternoon and were met by a naval attaché who escorted us to two black cars waiting to drive us to the Shoreham Hotel. None of us had been to the nation's capital before. The monuments and famous buildings dazzled me. This city was the place where history had been made, where the great debates had taken place, and great laws had been passed.

We checked into our hotel and were driven to the Mall to see the Lincoln Memorial and the Washington Monument. We explored the Capitol and got our picture taken on the Senate steps with Nebraska Senator Roman Hruska. We went to Arlington Cemetery and watched the ceremony at the Tomb of the Unknown Soldier. At day's end we saw the sun set on the Iwo Jima Memorial.

Our naval attaché took us to dinner at Trader Vic's. His quiet, respectful manner changed after he had downed three Suffering Bastards. Drunk, he was a loud and irritating bore. For two long hours he interrupted my mother and father when they tried to speak, complained about the navy, ordered the waiters to bring our food faster, and bragged about his underappreciated skills.

At the Shoreham I told my brother Bill to take revenge by pulling out all the stops on room service. Apparently I thought our escort officer was paying the bills. I said good night to my family and went to my room to inspect the day's damage to my leg and repair it as best that I could. The pounding had taken a toll on me physically, but not mentally. I was wide awake, so I went back downstairs to the bar and ordered a drink.

As I looked around the place, I wished I could share some of the pride my parents felt. I envied the moral clarity of their generation. I remembered the songs my parents listened to when I was a boy and imagined those tunes being played in the Shoreham thirty years earlier. I imagined the bar echoing with the music and the laughter of ghosts having a good time as they fought the good fight of the Second World War.

The next morning I awoke to discover that my stump had swollen so badly I almost could not put on my prosthesis. The fit was tight and painful. I took three aspirin and shoved a handful of tablets into the jacket of my tan navy uniform, which I would wear that day for the last time. Before I went downstairs I checked myself in the mirror and did not like the grim, unhappy face looking back at me. When I came off the elevator, everyone was waiting in the lobby — except my younger brother. He had taken up my challenge to order as much room service as possible and was working his way through a second tray when my father told him we were going to be late if he didn't finish.

We loaded into the two black cars and headed for the White House. Our route took us through Rock Creek Park and along the Potomac River. It was a glorious morning. The sky was clear and the sun bright, the air rich with the smell of flowers. We turned east and passed between the Lincoln Memorial and the Washington Monument. My heart was pounding with a pulse of dread and pride: dread of the ceremony, pride in my family. On the way, my father and I talked briefly. He was still worried I might do something foolish at the ceremony. He knew my dislike of medals and my distaste for President Nixon. The two might become an explosive mixture. He advised me to think about the future; my anger, he said, would subside in time.

A small group of sleepy-looking antiwar protestors were gathered on either side of the entrance as we drove through the White House gates. A Marine color guard stood at attention and saluted. The marble steps ahead looked insurmountable. I could not put my full weight on my right leg without producing a sharp pain. Each step increased the amount of sweat forming on my face, chest, and back. As I followed our naval attaché up the stairs to the second floor and turned right down the hallway, I smiled, thinking that perhaps my perspiration would produce a moment of genuine bonding with the often sweaty president.

The twelve families were arranged in a half circle facing an audience of the press, friends, military leaders, and a few members of Congress. A military band played. After a few bars of "Hail to the Chief," President Nixon came in and walked to a podium set up in front of us facing the audience, leaving him no choice but to turn his back on us.

The president's remarks were brief. We were heroes, he said, heroes in a heroic cause, the heroic cause of freedom. After he spoke, he moved around the half circle with a military aide beside him and placed the light blue ribbon and medal around each of our necks. My family was third or fourth in line. My mother wore a white short-sleeved dress with large gold buttons matching her metallic gold shoes. She wore a scarf around her neck and a corsage given to her by the navy. Her watch and wedding ring were her only jewelry. At fifty-six she looked young and happy, though her glasses gave her a serious look. Her bare hands, crossed in front of her, held the program that told the stories of the twelve men. The women of every family but ours were wearing gloves. My mother had insisted to my sisters that they would need gloves, but they convinced her they were unnecessary. She said she felt ashamed at this mistake, but it did not show in her face.

I let the president give me the medal. In truth I was badly confused. The war seemed like such a terrible mistake: politically, morally, and militarily. The suffering that was being inflicted on the people of Indochina did not seem worth the potential gain. Still I was moved by the ceremony and by the bravery of the other men who were there that day. There was something heroic about American men who were willing to travel to that strange country and fight for the freedom of people they did not know or understand. Nixon's words were not wrong. As much as I wanted the war to end quickly, and as strong as my belief that fighting on was futile, I could not deny how impressed I was by what these other men had done.

My dislike of President Nixon was more personal than political. I had believed him during the campaign of 1968 when he said he had a plan to end the war. I trusted him and it turned out he had lied. My trust betrayed I did not believe his plan for "peace with honor" would produce honor for any of the unfortunate Americans and Vietnamese who would fight on until an agreement could be reached. Perhaps there would be honor for the president or for Henry Kissinger, but not for very many others.

After the ceremony there was a reception for all of us, our families, and guests. The first thing I did was to take three more aspirin and drink a bottle of Coke. The president came by to shake all our hands again. I spoke with our hostess, Julie Nixon Eisenhower, and tried to be as charming as possible. She showed no interest in my charm. My ears were ringing and my body sweating from the aspirin. I wanted only to get back to the Shoreham to take off my leg. We were scheduled to fly out in the late afternoon and would be back in Lincoln that night. I had been in the nation's capital for a day and already I was eager to go home.

There was no parade in Lincoln to celebrate my

honor, which was just fine with me. I was pleased to be back in the shadow of anonymity. But the silence at other homes was not so easy for other young men who were changed by what they had seen and done, and needed the moral comfort of being welcomed and thanked by their communities. I had been to the White House, received the Medal of Honor, and enjoyed enough glory to salve some of my wounds. I measured the lack of response by the fact that the only letter I received was from a politician congratulating me on my award and thanking me for my service. His name was Jim Exon, and he had just won a primary election for governor. When politicians do not rush to have their pictures taken with Medal of Honor recipients, it is a sign that those who did not receive the medal were treated much worse.

Which is not to say I was treated badly. Just the opposite was true. My old friends, my family, and new friends welcomed me home. I was only harassed once at the track meet in Philadelphia. Other than that I was loved and cared for beyond anything I had a right to expect.

At work Ollie Waite and I spoke only a few words about the ceremony. I told him I was deeply moved by the Iwo Jima Memorial. He said he had never seen it. I told him I thought I did not deserve the medal. He said no one ever does. By then Stanford had accepted me, so I knew that when the semester ended my time at Bryan would as well. I thanked Ollie for giving me the job, but could not find words to do it adequately.

20

I CANNOT GIVE MEANING to remembering my life without remembering my father and his brother. From the moment of my father's death I began to think about the circumstances of his birth in a way I had not done before. Until then I had never thought of my father as an orphan. It had never occurred to me that he might have felt some responsibility for the death of his mother. I never asked what the Great War meant to his brother and to him. Indeed, I hardly thought about the Great War until my father asked me to find out what had happened to his brother. As I searched, I began to see a continuous thread from Versailles to the Philippines to Vietnam.

Just as the Cold War struggle between the Soviet Union

and the United States has been the defining political reality for my generation, I assumed the Depression and
World War II were what defined my father's. As I look
back at his life now it appears to me that the defining
events of his life happened when he was a small boy.
They were the Great War, the premature Armistice, and
the failure of the diplomats in Versailles to establish the
foundation for a lasting peace in the shambles of vanished
empires. And just as I was completely unaware of the reality of the Cold War in 1948, the fifth year of my life, I
know my father was unaware of the significance of the
war, which ended in the fifth year of his.

Paul Fussell argues in *The Great War and Modern
Memory* that World War I changed our way of thinking
about the world around us. The Great War was a cata-
clysmic event that shattered the widely held view that hu-
mankind was making steady progress toward perfection.
It divided modern European history in two. At President
Lyndon Johnson's library in Austin, Texas, the curator
once described the circumstances of Johnson's birth on
August 27, 1908, in words that sum up how I feel about
the Great War. "Times were so different when Johnson
was born that it seems like those days were 'before' and we
are living in 'after.'" It was the same for my uncle and my
father. The Great War left a great no-man's-land between
"then" and "now."

When my father and his brother were young, the men
who were returning home from the war had experienced

a trauma worse than any I had experienced in my life. Their entire generation had been laid on the altar for sacrifice. No one in my generation felt the way Wilfred Owen did when he wrote "The Parable of the Old Man and the Young":

> So Abram rose, and clave the wood, and went,
> And took the fire with him, and a knife.
> And as they sojourned both of them together,
> Isaac the first-born spake and said, My Father,
> Behold the preparations, fire and iron,
> But where the lamb for this burnt offering?
> Then Abram bound the youth with belts and straps,
> And builded parapets and trenches there,
> And stretched forth the knife to slay his son.
> When lo! An angel called him out of heaven,
> Saying, Lay not thy hand upon the lad,
> Neither do anything to him. Behold,
> A ram, caught in a thicket by its horns;
> Offer the Ram of Pride instead of him.
> But the old man would not so, but slew his son,
> And half the seed of Europe, one by one.

I doubt my father thought of this when he made his request of me. He just wanted me to know what happened on October 17, 1944, the day he believed his brother had died. I began to search for the answer in the summer of 1995 after my first term in the Senate and reelection to my second.

My search began at my youngest sister's farm where I could look through family records and letters she had gathered over the years. I was particularly interested in my mother's file of letters and her journal and in Vangie's letters to my parents. One letter described where John had been during the war and said that the Japanese had taken him prisoner. Another letter said that he had escaped and was alive. A third said he had disappeared again. And a fourth reported his death. There was a letter from General Douglas MacArthur that also said he had died.

Vangie's sister, Georgia, gave me a typewritten letter from John to Vangie, sent from the Philippines. The letter excited my imagination. It was erudite and witty, romantic and serious. It mentioned his family in Nebraska, which connected me to him. The date, November 17, did not indicate the year. Had it been written in 1941 before the Japanese attacked or afterward when John was operating with the guerrillas against the Japanese? The argument for a later date was that the envelope addressed Vangie as "Lt. Mella" and, in military style, did not have a postmark, suggesting it was mailed after the United States and Japan were at war.

An entire paragraph spoke of time they spent together at the Shoreham Hotel in Washington, D.C. He ended the letter with a plea to her: "Don't forget to remember, darling," and signed it "Wolf." Oh, how I loved that name. It suggested so much about John's nature and character. This was a man whose blood I was proud to share.

It was Georgia who told me that before he shipped out to the Philippines, John had driven alone with Vangie from Minneapolis to D.C., a fact that had scandalized her father. He became so angry he wouldn't speak to John, especially after Vangie secretly met him at the Shoreham Hotel.

I found two firsthand accounts of the guerrilla activity during the Japanese occupation of the Philippines. Both of the authors were still living but recalled very little about John. They did remember what happened to them from April 1942 until October 1944, when they served with a few hundred Americans allied with several thousand Filipinos in clandestine operations, spying on the Japanese and reporting what they learned to General MacArthur in Australia.

I read documents from the National Archives that contained the debriefings of the three men who were with John on October 17, 1944. Their account of the circumstances that led to John's death confirmed the one told to me by the American who commanded U.S. operations on that part of Luzon: John died because he made a single decision to follow his own instincts. Two years and ten months after the Japanese had attacked and invaded the Philippines, after he had fought in the defense of Bataan and had been surrendered, after he had survived by his wits as a guerrilla, he made one mistake and it cost him his life.

Vangie had not given up hope after Pearl Harbor. After John was surrendered on April 9, 1942, and disappeared, she joined the army and worked in army intelligence. She was certain he would survive. Late in the war Vangie worked in the Office of Strategic Services and then for the Central Intelligence Agency, which was created in 1947, where she remained until her death from cancer in 1975. She became a highly skilled and admired liaison with clandestine U.S. agents working in Eastern Europe against the Soviet Union.

On a night in the summer of 1995, I went to the Shoreham in order to imagine John and Vangie there in the spring of 1941. At the hotel, limousines and taxicabs were unloading guests for a banquet. The lobby was filled with conventioneers who had come to Washington to lobby Congress. I went to the bar, ordered a beer, and took it outside away from the sounds of laughter and the buzzing rumble of conversation. In the darkness I could hear cars racing along Rock Creek Park below. I sat by the pool where John and Vangie had swum. I closed my eyes and could hear John and Vangie talking and laughing in the pool.

I thought about John's last letter. He wrote it on October 4, 1944, to his aunt Sena, Fannie's daughter. He asked her to save ration stamps for apples because he expected to be home soon and would want some pie when he got there. He mentioned that he and four other men had arrived at headquarters. This particular event was later described to me in a letter from his commanding officer:

They came with some of our guerrillas from the
area around the town of Tarlac. We were all in
good spirits, anticipating the arrival of an American
submarine. John seemed to be in excellent physical
shape, too.

On October 14 John wrote a postscript to his letter:
"What does everybody look like now? Can you send some
pictures?"

Three days later on October 17 John and the four men
left the command post for Baler Bay where they faced a
fateful choice: a three-hour walk northwest through the
mountains or a much shorter boat trip around the cape in
an outrigger called a *banca*. They decided to go by boat,
but when the motor sputtered out, everyone but John and
one of the Filipinos began to walk. John managed to get
the engine going again and they set off. But they never arrived at Dibut Bay, the rendezvous point with the sub.

John's commanding officer wrote me with the most
likely explanation:

For some reason they couldn't round the point and
bring the banca into the bay. The winds were
strong and the water outside the bay was pretty
rough at the time. Whether they capsized or were
being swept out to sea, I don't know. However, the
Filipino was able to swim to shore but John did not
make it. I talked to the Filipino after he came

ashore, but he was so upset and agitated that it was difficult to understand for sure what had happened. The others were taken out on the sub, and I'm sure gave statements concerning all their activities, including John's and the circumstances surrounding his death.

John had swum this same distance many times when he and my father spent summers with Fannie in Wisconsin. In a letter home to Vangie before the Japanese attack he said he was swimming regularly. Even in heavy seas it didn't seem likely he would give out halfway to shore. Suspicions were raised in the debriefing documents that John had been killed by the Japanese or by the Filipino who was with him. I do not know for certain what happened. However, this much is inarguable. John died on October 17, 1944. He would have lived if he had walked the trail with the other men and been taken to Australia. Three days after John's death, General MacArthur returned to the islands, as he had promised, to begin the second battle of the Philippines, the bloodiest clash of the war in the Pacific.

John almost made it home. He came within half a mile of being reunited with Vangie and his brother. He died because he made a bad decision. Somewhere in the murky sea beating the shores of the Philippines the water swallowed him. The story of my uncle came to an end.

21

I HAD A DREAM IN WHICH I met Uncle John. I awaken in a hotel room. The clock says three in the morning, and a ceiling fan turns slowly above me. The surf pounds on a distant beach. The light of a full moon transforms my white sheet into a pool of glistening mercury. My body looks dark against the bed's surface. I put on a pair of shorts and head for the beach. The moon lights everything within my view. I walk the sand, my senses at full alert. A premonition hangs in the air.

The air feels cool on my legs, chest, and back. My muscles are strong from exercise and rest. I am wearing my prosthesis but feel as if I could keep walking a great distance. Instead, I stop and turn to face the ocean. The place is Luzon and I am looking east into Baler Bay where my uncle drowned.

Rising steeply behind me are the remains of a volcano, its gray soil covered with lush vegetation. Fifty meters of sand separate the trees from the water's edge. I sit on the slope and feel as if I am in the bleachers watching a performance. My heels dig easily into the sand and I half squat in a resting position. Before me is the shimmering surface of the Philippine Sea.

Vietnam lies eight hundred miles west. The rhythm of the waves and the line of the moon's reflection create a mood of introspection and peace. Old memories are brought to life by the smell of the dark salty water. I remember moving through the surf with the inflatable rubber boats I used in the navy. I knew these waves could rise suddenly with the wind and understood how a storm could have ended my uncle's life.

The sound of the ocean, the smell of it, the taste of it, and the sight of it capture me completely. I am dizzy with the sensation of the night. In this reverie I do not see the swimmer in the water until he reaches the outer edge of the surf. He is coming directly toward me. He raises his head to see where he is going. I know from the many times I have swum into shore at night that he cannot see much beyond the general shape of the land. I can tell he is tired and weak. I think he may need help and move toward him. Premonition returns and my chest is gripped by fear. Fear becomes dread. I rise and move toward this man who now struggles to stand in the surging water.

We face each other on dry land. He is exhausted and disoriented by the water. Minutes elapse before he gets his bearings. Fear is in his eyes. As he sizes me up, fear changes quickly to anger. He is in his early thirties. He has the look of a natural athlete, about my height, but carries at least twenty more pounds. His hair is thinning and the square face and full lips make him handsome. I am impressed by how quickly he recovers from the ordeal of the swim.

He motions me to follow him up the beach and I do. We walk a path that rises up and away from the ocean before it turns to run parallel to the beach. We continue in silence for several miles. I ask him how much he knows about my life and his brother's. He does not answer. I ask him what happened to him after he escaped from the Japanese. No response. I tell him that I am sorry, and that I know he died because of a bad choice. When I tell him I have read his letters to Vangie, he turns to face me and a terrible sadness darkens his face. We continue until we reach a clearing that commands a view of the bay. At the edge of the clearing he finds a hiding place I would have missed. Inside there is a rough bench that I guess was used by men who watched enemy movements during the war. He motions to me to take a seat and he sits down beside me. No words pass between us. We sit and watch the bay.

I fall asleep and when I wake the moon is gone and so is my uncle. I am no longer on the beach; I am lying in the bed of my apartment, a mile from the Senate, my place of work. It is a half hour before sunrise, and I dress to go for a run to the Lincoln Memorial.

AUTHOR'S NOTE

ONE NIGHT OF MY LIFE as a combatant in the Vietnam War has been previously examined in great detail by the press and the public. I agreed to talk publicly about that night in part because I was trying to write about it for this book. I did not anticipate the intensity of the press interest and the public exposure that occurred to each of the six men I led that night. As a consequence, we gathered for the first time since the war to talk about our individual memories of what happened. The discussion that followed altered what I did and didn't remember. Thus, the story told in this book—though the most important details remain the same—is different than the one I first told, and even today I would not swear that my memory is 100% accurate. It is merely the best I can remember today.

ACKNOWLEDGMENTS

I WOULD LIKE TO THANK Flip Brophy, who was patient when all appeared lost; Barbara Feinman, who nagged me in the beginning; Greg Weiner, who made me feel it was important to write this book; Jim Silberman, who helped me write it well; and my wife, Sarah, who helped me proofread it when I was tired of reading it myself.